In the Buddha's Words

Tamed, he is supreme among those who tame;
At peace, he is the sage among those who bring peace;
Freed, he is the chief of those who set free;
Delivered, he is the best of those who deliver.

—*Aṅguttara Nikāya* 4:23

In the Buddha's Words

An Anthology of Discourses from the Pāli Canon

Edited and introduced by

Bhikkhu Bodhi

WISDOM PUBLICATIONS • BOSTON

Wisdom Publications, Inc.
199 Elm Street
Somerville MA 02144 USA
www.wisdompubs.org

Library of Congress Cataloging-in-Publication Data
Tipiṭaka. Suttapiṭaka. English. Selections.
In the Buddha's words : an anthology of discourses from the Pali canon / edited and introduced
by Bhikkhu Bodhi. — 1st ed.
p. cm.
Includes bibliographical references and indexes.
ISBN 0-86171-491-1 (pbk. : alk. paper)
I. Bodhi, Bhikkhu. II. Title.
BQ1192.E53B63 2005
294.3'823--dc22 2005018336

ISBN 978-0-86171-491-9
eBook ISBN 978-0-86171-996-9

13 12 11
9 8 7 6

The publisher thanks AltaMira Press for kindly granting permission to include in this anthology selections from *Numerical Discourses of the Buddha: An Anthology of Suttas from the Aṅguttara Nikāya*, translated and edited by Nyanaponika Thera and Bhikkhu Bodhi.

Cover and interior design by Gopa&Ted2, Inc. Set in DPalatino 10/13.75 pt.

Frontispiece: Standing Buddha Shakyamuni. Pakistan, Gandhara, second century A.D. Height 250cm. Courtesy of the Miho Museum, Japan. www.miho.jp

Wisdom Publications' books are printed on acid-free paper and meet the guidelines for permanence and durability set by the Council of Library Resources.

Printed in the United States of America.

MIX Paper FSC FSC® C011935

This book was produced with environmental mindfulness. We have elected to print this title on 30% PCW recycled paper. As a result, we have saved the following resources: 81 trees, 36 million BTUs of energy, 8,281 lbs. of greenhouse gases, 37,052 gallons of water, and 2,349 lbs. of solid waste. For more information, please visit our website, www.wisdompubs.org. This paper is also FSC® certified. For more information, please visit www.fscus.org.

Contents

Publisher's Acknowledgment

For their help in sponsoring the printing of this book, the publisher gratefully acknowledges the generous help of the Hershey Family Foundation and the kind contribution made in loving memory of Gan Chin Hong by his family.

Foreword

THE DALAI LAMA

More than two thousand five hundred years have passed since our kind teacher, Buddha Śākyamuni, taught in India. He offered advice to all who wished to heed it, inviting them to listen, reflect, and critically examine what he had to say. He addressed different individuals and groups of people over a period of more than forty years.

After the Buddha's passing, a record of what he said was maintained as an oral tradition. Those who heard the teachings would periodically meet with others for communal recitations of what they had heard and memorized. In due course, these recitations from memory were written down, laying the basis for all subsequent Buddhist literature. The Pāli Canon is one of the earliest of these written records and the only complete early version that has survived intact. Within the Pāli Canon, the texts known as the Nikāyas have the special value of being a single cohesive collection of the Buddha's teachings in his own words. These teachings cover a wide range of topics; they deal not only with renunciation and liberation, but also with the proper relations between husbands and wives, the management of the household, and the way countries should be governed. They explain the path of spiritual development—from generosity and ethics, through mind training and the realization of wisdom, all the way up to the attainment of liberation.

The teachings from the Nikāyas collected here provide fascinating insights into how the Buddha's teachings were studied, preserved, and understood in the early days of Buddhism's development. Modern readers will find them especially valuable for reinvigorating and clarifying their understanding of many fundamental Buddhist doctrines. Clearly the Buddha's essential message of compassion, ethical responsibility, mental tranquillity, and discernment is as relevant today as it was more than twenty-five hundred years ago.

Although Buddhism spread and took root in many parts of Asia, evolving into diverse traditions according to the place and occasion, distance and differences of language limited exchange between Buddhists in the past. One of the results of modern improvements in transport and communication that I most appreciate is the vastly expanded opportunities those interested in Buddhism now have to acquaint themselves with the full range of Buddhist teaching and practice. What I find especially encouraging about this book is that it shows so clearly how much fundamentally all schools of Buddhism have in common. I congratulate Bhikkhu Bodhi for this careful work of compilation and translation. I offer my prayers that readers may find advice here—and the inspiration to put it into practice—that will enable them to develop inner peace, which I believe is essential for the creation of a happier and more peaceful world.

Venerable Tenzin Gyatso, the Fourteenth Dalai Lama
May 10, 2005

Preface

The Buddha's discourses preserved in the Pāli Canon are called *suttas*, the Pāli equivalent of the Sanskrit word *sūtras*. Although the Pāli Canon belongs to a particular Buddhist school—the Theravāda, or School of the Elders—the suttas are by no means exclusively Theravāda Buddhist texts. They stem from the earliest period of Buddhist literary history, a period lasting roughly a hundred years after the Buddha's death, before the original Buddhist community divided into different schools. The Pāli suttas have counterparts from other early Buddhist schools now extinct, texts sometimes strikingly similar to the Pāli version, differing mainly in settings and arrangements but not in points of doctrine. The suttas, along with their counterparts, thus constitute the most ancient records of the Buddha's teachings available to us; they are the closest we can come to what the historical Buddha Gotama himself actually taught. The teachings found in them have served as the fountainhead, the primal source, for all the evolving streams of Buddhist doctrine and practice through the centuries. For this reason, they constitute the common heritage of the entire Buddhist tradition, and Buddhists of all schools who wish to understand the taproot of Buddhism should make a close and careful study of them a priority.

In the Pāli Canon the Buddha's discourses are preserved in collections called *Nikāyas*. Over the past twenty years, fresh translations of the four major Nikāyas have appeared in print, issued in attractive and affordable editions. Wisdom Publications pioneered this development in 1987 when it published Maurice Walshe's translation of the Dīgha Nikāya, *The Long Discourses of the Buddha*. Wisdom followed this precedent by bringing out, in 1995, my revised and edited version of Bhikkhu Ñāṇamoli's handwritten translation of the Majjhima Nikāya, *The Middle Length Discourses of the Buddha*, followed in 2000 by my new translation of the complete Saṃyutta Nikāya, *The Connected Discourses of the Buddha*. In 1999, under the imprint of The Sacred Literature Trust Series, AltaMira Press published an anthology of suttas from the Aṅguttara Nikāya, translated by the late Nyanaponika Thera and myself, titled *Numerical Discourses of the Buddha.* I am currently working on a new translation of the entire Aṅguttara Nikāya, intended for Wisdom Publication's Teachings of the Buddha series.

Many who have read these larger works have told me, to my satisfaction, that the translations brought the suttas to life for them. Yet others who earnestly sought to enter the deep ocean of the Nikāyas told me something else. They said that while the language of the translations made them far more accessible than earlier translations, they were still grappling for a standpoint from which to see the suttas' overall structure, a framework within which they all fit together. The Nikāyas themselves do not offer much help in this respect, for their arrangement—with the notable exception of the Saṃyutta Nikāya, which does have a thematic structure—appears almost haphazard.

In an ongoing series of lectures I began giving at Bodhi Monastery in New Jersey in January 2003, I devised a scheme of my own to organize the contents of the Majjhima Nikāya. This scheme unfolds the Buddha's message progressively, from the simple to the difficult, from the elementary to the profound. Upon reflection, I saw that this scheme could be applied not only to the Majjhima Nikāya, but to the four Nikāyas as a whole. The present book organizes suttas selected from all four Nikāyas within this thematic and progressive framework.

This book is intended for two types of readers. The first are those not yet acquainted with the Buddha's discourses who feel the need for a systematic introduction. For such readers, any of the Nikāyas is bound to appear opaque. All four of them, viewed at once, may seem like a jungle—entangling and bewildering, full of unknown beasts—or like the great ocean—vast, tumultuous, and forbidding. I hope that this book will serve as a map to help them wend their way through the jungle of the suttas or as a sturdy ship to carry them across the ocean of the Dhamma.

The second type of readers for whom this book is meant are those, already acquainted with the suttas, who still cannot see how they fit together into an intelligible whole. For such readers, individual suttas may be comprehensible in themselves, but the texts in their totality appear like pieces of a jigsaw puzzle scattered across a table. Once one understands the scheme in this book, one should come away with a clear idea of the architecture of the teaching. Then, with a little reflection, one should be able to determine the place any sutta occupies in the edifice of the Dhamma, whether or not it has been included in this anthology.

This anthology, or any other anthology of suttas, is no substitute for the Nikāyas themselves. My hope is twofold, corresponding to the two types of readers for whom this volume is designed: (1) that newcomers to Early Buddhist literature find this volume whets their appetite for more and encourages them to take the plunge into the full Nikāyas; and (2) that experienced readers of the Nikāyas finish the book with a better understanding of material with which they are already familiar.

If this anthology is meant to make any other point, it is to convey the sheer breadth and range of the Buddha's wisdom. While Early Buddhism is sometimes depicted as a discipline of world renunciation intended primarily for ascetics and contemplatives, the ancient discourses of the Pāli Canon clearly show us how the Buddha's wisdom and compassion reached into the very depths of mundane life, providing ordinary people with guidelines for proper conduct and right understanding. Far from being a creed for a monastic élite, ancient Buddhism involved the close collaboration of householders and monastics in the twin tasks of maintaining the Buddha's teachings and assisting one another in their efforts to walk the path to the extinction of suffering. To fulfill these tasks meaningfully, the Dhamma had to provide them with deep and inexhaustible guidance, inspiration, joy, and consolation. It could never have done this if it had not directly addressed their earnest efforts to combine social and family obligations with an aspiration to realize the highest.

Almost all the passages included in this book have been selected from the above-mentioned publications of the four Nikāyas. Almost all have undergone revisions, usually slight but sometimes major, to accord with my own evolving understanding of the texts and the Pāli language. I have newly translated a small number of suttas from the Aṅguttara Nikāya not included in the above-mentioned anthology. I have also included a handful of suttas from the Udāna and Itivuttaka, two small books belonging to the fifth Nikāya, the Khuddaka Nikāya, the Minor or Miscellaneous Collection. I have based these on John D. Ireland's translation, published by the Buddhist Publication Society in Sri Lanka, but again I have freely modified them to fit my own preferred diction and terminology. I have given preference to suttas in prose over those in verse, as being more direct and explicit. When a sutta concludes with verses, if these merely restate the preceding prose, in the interest of space I have omitted them.

Each chapter begins with an introduction in which I explain the salient concepts relevant to the theme of the chapter and try to show how the texts I have chosen exemplify that theme. To clarify points arising from both the introductions and the texts, I have included endnotes. These often draw upon the classical commentaries to the Nikāyas ascribed to the great South Indian commentator Ācariya Buddhaghosa, who worked in Sri Lanka in the fifth century C.E. For the sake of concision, I have not included as many notes in this book as I have in my other translations of the Nikāyas. These notes are also not as technical as those in the full translations.

References to the sources follow each selection. References to texts from the Dīgha Nikāya and Majjhima Nikāya cite the number and name of the sutta (in Pāli); passages from these two collections retain the paragraph numbers used in *The Long Discourses of the Buddha* and *The Middle Length Discourses of the Buddha*, so readers who wish to locate these passages within the full translations can easily do so. References to texts from the Saṃyutta Nikāya cite *saṃyutta* and sutta number; texts from the Aṅguttara Nikāya cite *nipāta* and sutta number (the Ones and the Twos also cite chapters within the *nipāta* followed by the sutta number). References to texts from the Udāna cite *nipāta* and sutta number; texts from the Itivuttaka cite simply the sutta number. All references are followed by the volume and page number in the Pali Text Society's standard edition of these works.

I am grateful to Timothy McNeill and David Kittelstrom of Wisdom Publications for urging me to persist with this project in the face of long periods of indifferent health. Sāmaṇera Anālayo and Bhikkhu Nyanasobhano read and commented on my introductions, and John Kelly reviewed proofs of the entire book. All three made useful suggestions, for which I am grateful. John Kelly also prepared the table of sources that appears at the back of the book. Finally, I am grateful to my students of Pāli and Dhamma studies at Bodhi Monastery for their enthusiastic interest in the teachings of the Nikāyas, which inspired me to compile this anthology. I am especially thankful to the monastery's extraordinary founder, Ven. Master Jen-Chun, for welcoming a monk of another Buddhist tradition to his monastery and for his interest in bridging the Northern and Southern transmissions of the Early Buddhist teachings.

Bhikkhu Bodhi

List of Abbreviations

AN	Aṅguttara Nikāya
Be	Burmese-script Chaṭṭha Saṅgāyana ed.
Ce	Sinhala-script ed.
DN	Dīgha Nikāya
Ee	Roman-script ed. (PTS)
It	Itivuttaka
MN	Majjhima Nikāya
Mp	Manorathapūraṇī (Aṅguttara Nikāya Commentary)
Ppn	Path of Purification (Visuddhimagga translation)
Ps	Papañcasūdanī (Majjhima Nikāya Commentary)
Ps-pṭ	Papañcasūdanī-purāṇa-ṭīkā (Majjhima Nikāya Subcommentary)
Skt	Sanskrit
SN	Saṃyutta Nikāya
Spk	Sāratthappakāsinī (Saṃyutta Nikāya Commentary)
Spk-pṭ	Sāratthappakāsinī-purāṇa-ṭīkā (Saṃyutta Nikāya Subcommentary)
Sv	Sumaṅgalavilāsinī (Dīgha Nikāya Commentary)
Ud	Udāna
Vibh	Vibhaṅga
Vin	Vinaya
Vism	Visuddhimagga

All page references to Pāli texts are to the page numbers of the Pali Text Society's editions.

Key to the Pronunciation of Pāli

The Pāli Alphabet

Vowels: a, ā, i, ī, u, ū, e, o

Consonants:

Gutterals	k, kh, g, gh, ṅ
Palatals	c, ch, j, jh, ñ
Cerebrals	ṭ, ṭh, ḍ, ḍh, ṇ
Dentals	t, th, d, dh, n
Labials	p, ph, b, bh, m
Other	y, r, ḷ, l, v, s, h, ṃ

Pronunciation

a as in "cut"	u as in "put"
ā as in "father"	ū as in "rule"
i as in "king"	e as in "way"
ī as in "keen"	o as in "home"

Of the vowels, *e* and *o* are long before a single consonant and short before a double consonant. Among the consonants, *g* is always pronounced as in "good," *c* as in "church," *ñ* as in "onion." The cerebrals (or retroflexes) are spoken with the tongue on the roof of the mouth; the dentals with the tongue on the upper teeth. The aspirates—*kh, gh, ch, jh, ṭh, ḍh, th, dh, ph, bh*—are single consonants pronounced with slightly more force than the nonaspirates, e.g., *th* as in "Thomas" (not as in "thin"); *ph* as in "putter" (not as in "phone"). Double consonants are always enunciated separately, e.g., *dd* as in "mad dog," *gg* as in "big gun." The pure nasal (*niggahīta*) *ṃ* is pronounced like the *ng* in "song." An *o* and an *e* always carry a stress; otherwise the stress falls on a long vowel—*ā, ī, ū,*—or on a double consonant, or on *ṃ.*

Detailed List of Contents

VII. The Path to Liberation

VIII. Mastering the Mind

IX. Shining the Light of Wisdom

General Introduction

Uncovering the Structure of the Teaching

Though his teaching is highly systematic, there is no single text that can be ascribed to the Buddha in which he defines the architecture of the Dhamma, the scaffolding upon which he has framed his specific expressions of the doctrine. In the course of his long ministry, the Buddha taught in different ways as determined by occasion and circumstances. Sometimes he would enunciate invariable principles that stand at the heart of the teaching. Sometimes he would adapt the teaching to accord with the proclivities and aptitudes of the people who came to him for guidance. Sometimes he would adjust his exposition to fit a situation that required a particular response. But throughout the collections of texts that have come down to us as authorized "Word of the Buddha," we do not find a single *sutta*, a single discourse, in which the Buddha has drawn together all the elements of his teaching and assigned them to their appropriate place within some comprehensive system.

While in a literate culture in which systematic thought is highly prized the lack of such a text with a unifying function might be viewed as a defect, in an entirely oral culture—as was the culture in which the Buddha lived and moved—the lack of a descriptive key to the Dhamma would hardly be considered significant. Within this culture neither teacher nor student aimed at conceptual completeness. The teacher did not intend to present a complete system of ideas; his pupils did not aspire to learn a complete system of ideas. The aim that united them in the process of learning—the process of transmission—was that of practical training, self-transformation, the realization of truth, and unshakable liberation of the mind. This does not mean, however, that the teaching was always expediently adapted to the situation at hand. At times the Buddha would present more panoramic views of the Dhamma that united many components of the path in a graded or wide-ranging structure. But though there are several discourses that exhibit a broad scope, they still do not embrace all elements of the Dhamma in one overarching scheme.

The purpose of the present book is to develop and exemplify such a scheme. I here attempt to provide a comprehensive picture of the Buddha's teaching that incorporates a wide variety of suttas into an organic structure. This structure, I hope, will bring to light the intentional pattern underlying the Buddha's formulation of the Dhamma and thus provide the reader with guidelines for understanding Early Buddhism as a whole. I have selected the suttas almost entirely from the four major collections or Nikāyas of the Pāli Canon, though I have also included a few texts from the Udāna and Itivuttaka, two small books of the fifth collection, the Khuddaka Nikāya. Each chapter opens with its own introduction, in which I explain the basic concepts of Early Buddhism that the texts exemplify and show how the texts give expression to these ideas.

I will briefly supply background information about the Nikāyas later in this introduction. First, however, I want to outline the scheme that I have devised to organize the suttas. Although my particular use of this scheme may be original, it is not sheer innovation but is based upon a threefold distinction that the Pāli commentaries make among the types of benefits to which the practice of the Dhamma leads: (1) welfare and happiness visible in this present life; (2) welfare and happiness pertaining to future lives; and (3) the ultimate good, Nibbāna (Skt: *nirvāṇa*).

Three preliminary chapters are designed to lead up to those that embody this threefold scheme. Chapter I is a survey of the human condition as it is apart from the appearance of a Buddha in the world. Perhaps this was the way human life appeared to the Bodhisatta—the future Buddha—as he dwelled in the Tusita heaven gazing down upon the earth, awaiting the appropriate occasion to descend and take his final birth. We behold a world in which human beings are driven helplessly toward old age and death; in which they are spun around by circumstances so that they are oppressed by bodily pain, cast down by failure and misfortune, made anxious and fearful by change and deterioration. It is a world in which people aspire to live in harmony, but in which their untamed emotions repeatedly compel them, against their better judgment, to lock horns in conflicts that escalate into violence and wholesale devastation. Finally, taking the broadest view of all, it is a world in which sentient beings are propelled forward, by their own ignorance and craving, from one life to the next, wandering blindly through the cycle of rebirths called *saṃsāra*.

Chapter II gives an account of the Buddha's descent into this world. He comes as the "one person" who appears out of compassion for the world, whose arising in the world is "the manifestation of great light." We follow the story of his conception and birth, of his renunciation and quest for enlightenment, of his realization of the Dhamma, and of his decision to teach. The chapter ends with his first discourse to the five monks, his first disciples, in the Deer Park near Bārāṇasī.

Chapter III is intended to sketch the special features of the Buddha's teaching, and by implication, the attitude with which a prospective student should approach the teaching. The texts tell us that the Dhamma is not a secret or esoteric teaching but one which "shines when taught openly." It does not demand blind faith in authoritarian scriptures, in divine revelations, or infallible dogmas, but invites investigation and appeals to personal experience as the ultimate criterion for determining its validity. The teaching is concerned with the arising and cessation of suffering, which can be observed in one's own experience. It does not set up even the Buddha as an unimpeachable authority but invites us to examine him to determine whether he fully deserves our trust and confidence. Finally, it offers a step-by-step procedure whereby we can put the teaching to the test, and by doing so realize the ultimate truth for ourselves.

With chapter IV, we come to texts dealing with the first of the three types of benefit the Buddha's teaching is intended to bring. This is called "the welfare and happiness visible in this present life" (*diṭṭha-dhamma-hitasukha*), the happiness that comes from following ethical norms in one's family relationships, livelihood, and communal activities. Although Early Buddhism is often depicted as a radical discipline of renunciation directed to a transcendental goal, the Nikāyas reveal the Buddha to have been a compassionate and pragmatic teacher who was intent on promoting a social order in which people can live together peacefully and harmoniously in accordance with ethical guidelines. This aspect of Early Buddhism is evident in the Buddha's teachings on the duties of children to their parents, on the mutual obligations of husbands and wives, on right livelihood, on the duties of the ruler toward his subjects, and on the principles of communal harmony and respect.

The second type of benefit to which the Buddha's teaching leads is the subject of chapter V, called the welfare and happiness pertaining to the future life (*samparāyika-hitasukha*). This is the happiness achieved by obtaining a fortunate rebirth and success in future lives through one's accumulation of merit. The term "merit" (*puñña*) refers to wholesome kamma (Skt: *karma*) considered in terms of its capacity to produce favorable results within the round of rebirths. I begin this chapter with a selection of texts on the teaching of kamma and rebirth. This leads us to general texts on the idea of merit, followed by selections on the three principal "bases of merit" recognized in the Buddha's discourses: giving (*dāna*), moral discipline (*sīla*), and meditation (*bhāvanā*). Since meditation figures prominently in the third type of benefit, the kind of meditation emphasized here, as a basis for merit, is that productive of the most abundant mundane fruits, the four "divine abodes" (*brahmavihāra*), particularly the development of loving-kindness.

Chapter VI is transitional, intended to prepare the way for the chapters to follow. While demonstrating that the practice of his teaching does indeed conduce to happiness and good fortune within the bounds of mundane life, in order to lead people beyond these bounds, the Buddha exposes the danger and inadequacy in all conditioned existence. He shows the defects in sensual pleasures, the shortcomings of material success, the inevitability of death, and the impermanence of all conditioned realms of being. To arouse in his disciples an aspiration for the ultimate good, Nibbāna, the Buddha again and again underscores the perils of saṃsāra. Thus this chapter comes to a climax with two dramatic texts that dwell on the misery of bondage to the round of repeated birth and death.

The following four chapters are devoted to the third benefit that the Buddha's teaching is intended to bring: the ultimate good (*paramattha*), the attainment of Nibbāna. The first of these, chapter VII, gives a general overview of the path to liberation, which is treated analytically through definitions of the factors of the Noble Eightfold Path and dynamically through an account of the training of the monk. A long sutta on the graduated path surveys the monastic training from the monk's initial entry upon the life of renunciation to his attainment of arahantship, the final goal.

Chapter VIII focuses upon the taming of the mind, the major emphasis in the monastic training. I here present texts that discuss the obstacles to mental development, the means of overcoming these obstacles, different methods of meditation, and the states to be attained when the obstacles are overcome and the disciple gains mastery over the mind. In this chapter I introduce the distinction between *samatha* and *vipassanā*, serenity and insight, the one leading to *samādhi* or concentration, the other to *paññā* or wisdom. However, I include texts that treat insight only in terms of the methods used to generate it, not in terms of its actual contents.

Chapter IX, titled "Shining the Light of Wisdom," deals with the content of insight. For Early Buddhism, and indeed for almost all schools of Buddhism, insight or wisdom is the principal instrument of liberation. Thus in this chapter I focus on the Buddha's teachings about such topics pivotal to the development of wisdom as right view, the five aggregates, the six sense bases, the eighteen elements, dependent origination, and the Four Noble Truths. This chapter ends with a selection of texts on Nibbāna, the ultimate goal of wisdom.

The final goal is not achieved abruptly but by passing through a series of stages that transforms an individual from a worldling into an arahant, a liberated one. Thus chapter X, "The Planes of Realization," offers a selection of texts on the main stages along the way. I first present the series of stages as a progressive sequence; then I return to the starting point and examine three major milestones within this progression: stream-entry, the stage of nonreturner, and arahantship. I conclude with a selection of suttas on the Buddha, the foremost among the arahants, here spoken of under the epithet he used most often when referring to himself, the Tathāgata.

The Origins of the Nikāyas

The texts I have drawn upon to fill out my scheme are, as I said above, all selected from the Nikāyas, the main sutta collections of the Pāli Canon. Some words are needed to explain the origin and nature of these sources.

The Buddha did not write down any of his teachings, nor were his teachings recorded in writing by his disciples. Indian culture at the time the Buddha lived was still predominantly preliterate.[1] The Buddha wandered from town to town in the Ganges plain, instructing his monks and nuns, giving sermons to the householders who flocked to hear him speak, answering the questions of curious inquirers, and engaging in discussions with people from all classes of society. The records of his teachings that we have do not come from his own pen or from transcriptions made by those who heard the teaching from him, but from monastic councils held after his *parinibbāna*—his passing away into Nibbāna—for the purpose of preserving his teaching.

It is unlikely that the teachings that derive from these councils reproduce the Buddha's words verbatim. The Buddha must have spoken spontaneously and elaborated upon his themes in countless ways in response to the varied needs of those who sought his guidance. Preserving by oral transmission such a vast and diverse range of material would have bordered on the impossible. To mold the teachings into a format suitable for preservation, the monks responsible for the texts would have had to collate and edit them to make them better fit for listening, retention, recitation, memorization, and repetition—the five major elements in oral transmission. This process, which may have already been started during the Buddha's lifetime, would have led to a fair degree of simplification and standardization of the material to be preserved.

During the Buddha's life, the discourses were classified into nine categories according to literary genre: *sutta* (prose discourses), *geyya* (mixed prose and verse), *veyyākaraṇa* (answers to questions), *gāthā* (verse), *udāna* (inspired utterances), *itivuttaka* (memorable sayings), *jātaka* (stories of past births), *abbhutadhamma* (marvelous qualities), and *vedalla* (catechism).[2] At some point after his passing, this older system of classification was superceded by a new scheme that ordered the texts into larger collections called Nikāyas in the Theravāda Buddhist tradition, Āgamas in the North Indian Buddhist schools.[3] Exactly when the Nikāya-Āgama scheme became ascendant is not known with certainty, but once it appeared it almost completely replaced the older system.

The Cullavagga, one of the books of the Pāli Vinaya Piṭaka, gives an account of how the authorized texts were compiled at the first Buddhist council, held three months after the Buddha's parinibbāna. According to this report, shortly after the Buddha's death the Elder Mahākassapa, the de facto head of the Saṅgha, selected five hundred monks, all *arahants* or liberated ones, to meet and compile an authoritative version of the teachings. The council took place during the rains retreat at Rājagaha (modern Rajgir), the capital of Magadha, then the dominant state of Middle India.[4] Mahākassapa first requested the Venerable Upāli, the foremost specialist on disciplinary matters, to recite the Vinaya. On the basis of this recitation, the Vinaya Piṭaka, the Compilation on Discipline, was compiled. Mahākassapa then asked the Venerable Ānanda to recite "the Dhamma," that is, the discourses, and on the basis of this recitation, the Sutta Piṭaka, the Compilation of Discourses, was compiled.

The Cullavagga states that when Ānanda recited the Sutta Piṭaka, the Nikāyas had the same contents as they do now, with the suttas arranged in the same sequence as they now appear in the Pāli Canon. This narrative doubtlessly records past history through the lens of a later period. The Āgamas of the Buddhist schools other than the Theravāda correspond to the four main Nikāyas, but they classify suttas differently and arrange their contents in a different order from the Pāli Nikāyas. This suggests that if the Nikāya-Āgama arrangement did arise at the first council, the council had not yet assigned suttas to their definitive places within this scheme. Alternatively, it is possible that this scheme arose at a later time. It could have arisen at some point after the first council but before the Saṅgha split into different schools. If it arose during the age of sectarian divisions, it might have been introduced by one school and then been borrowed by others, so that the different schools would assign their texts to different places within the scheme.

While the Cullavagga's account of the first council may include legendary material mixed with historical fact, there seems no reason to doubt Ānanda's role in the preservation of the discourses. As the Buddha's personal attendant, Ānanda had learned the discourses from him and the other great disciples, kept them in mind, and taught them to others. During the Buddha's life he was praised for his retentive capacities and was appointed "foremost of those who have learned much" (*etadaggaṃ bahussutānaṃ*).[5] Few monks might have had memories that could equal Ānanda's, but already during the Buddha's lifetime individual monks must already have begun to specialize in particular texts. The standardization and simplification of the material would have facilitated memorization. Once the texts became classified into the Nikāyas or Āgamas, the challenges of preserving and transmitting the textual heritage were solved by organizing the textual specialists into companies dedicated to specific collections. Different companies within the Saṅgha could thus focus on memorizing and interpreting different collections and the community as a whole could avoid placing excessive demands on the memories of individual monks. It is in this way that the teachings would continue to be transmitted for the next three or four hundred years, until they were finally committed to writing.[6]

In the centuries following the Buddha's death, the Saṅgha became divided over disciplinary and doctrinal issues until by the third century after the parinibbāna there were at least eighteen schools of Sectarian Buddhism. Each sect probably had its own collection of texts regarded more or less as canonical, though it is possible that several closely affiliated sects shared the same collection of authorized texts. While the different Buddhist schools may have organized their collections differently and though their suttas show differences of detail, the individual suttas are often remarkably similar, sometimes almost identical, and the doctrines and practices they delineate are essentially the same.[7] The doctrinal differences between the schools did not arise from the suttas themselves but from the interpretations the textual specialists imposed upon them. Such differences hardened after the rival schools formalized their philosophical principles in treatises and commentaries expressive of their distinctive standpoints on doctrinal issues. So far as we can determine, the refined philosophical systems had only minimal impact on the original texts themselves, which the schools seemed disinclined to manipulate to suit their doctrinal agendas. Instead, by means of their commentaries, they endeavored to interpret the suttas in such a way as to draw out ideas that supported their own views. It is not unusual for such interpretations to appear defensive and contrived, apologetic against the words of the original texts themselves.

The Pāli Canon

Sadly, the canonical collections belonging to most of the early mainstream Indian Buddhist schools were lost when Indian Buddhism was devastated by the Muslims that invaded northern India in the eleventh and twelfth centuries. These invasions effectively sounded the death knell for Buddhism in the land of its birth. Only one complete collection of texts belonging to one of the early Indian Buddhist schools managed to survive intact. This is the collection preserved in the language that we know as Pāli. This collection belonged to the ancient Theravāda school, which had been transplanted to Sri Lanka in the third century B.C.E. and thus managed to escape the havoc wrought upon Buddhism in the motherland. About the same time, the Theravāda also spread to southeast Asia and in later centuries became dominant throughout the region.

The Pāli Canon is the collection of texts the Theravāda regards as Word of the Buddha (*buddhavacana*). The fact that the texts of this collection have survived as a single canon does not mean that they can all be dated from the same period; nor does it mean that the texts forming its most archaic nucleus are necessarily more ancient than their counterparts from the other Buddhist schools, many of which have survived in Chinese or Tibetan translation as parts of entire canons or, in a few cases, as isolated texts in another Indian language. Nevertheless, the Pāli Canon has a special importance for us, and that is so for at least three reasons.

First, it is a complete collection all belonging to a single school. Even though we can detect clear signs of historical development between different portions of the canon, this alignment with a single school gives the texts a certain degree of uniformity. Among the texts stemming from the same period, we can even speak of a homogeneity of contents, a single flavor underlying the manifold expressions of the doctrine. This homogeneity is most evident in the four Nikāyas and the older parts of the fifth Nikāya and gives us reason to believe that with these texts—allowing for the qualification expressed above, that they have counterparts in other extinct Buddhist schools—we have reached the most ancient stratum of Buddhist literature discoverable.

Second, the entire collection has been preserved in a Middle Indo-Aryan language, one closely related to the language (or, more likely, the various regional dialects) that the Buddha himself spoke. We call this language Pāli, but the name for the language actually arose through a misunderstanding. The word *pāli* properly means "text," that is, the canonical text as distinct from the commentaries. The commentators refer to the language in which the texts are preserved as *pālibhāsā,* "the language of the texts." At some point, the term was misunderstood to mean "the Pāli language," and once the misconception arose, it took root and has been with us ever since. Scholars regard this language as a hybrid showing features of several Prakrit dialects used around the third century B.C.E., subjected to a partial process of Sanskritization.[8] While the language is not identical with any the Buddha himself would have spoken, it belongs to the same broad linguistic family as those he might have used and originates from the same conceptual matrix. This language thus reflects the thought-world that the Buddha inherited from the wider Indian culture into which he was born, so that its words capture the subtle nuances of that thought-world without the intrusion of alien influences inevitable in even the best and most scrupulous translations. This contrasts with Chinese, Tibetan, or English translations of the texts, which reverberate with the connotations of the words chosen from the target languages.

The *third* reason the Pāli Canon has special importance is that this collection is authoritative for a contemporary Buddhist school. Unlike the textual collections of the extinct schools of Early Buddhism, which are purely of academic interest, this collection still brims with life. It inspires the faith of millions of Buddhists from the villages and monasteries of Sri Lanka, Myanmar, and Southeast Asia to the cities and meditation centers of Europe and the Americas. It shapes their understanding, guides them in the face of difficult ethical choices, informs their meditative practices, and offers them the keys to liberating insight.

The Pāli Canon is commonly known as the Tipiṭaka, the "Three Baskets" or "Three Compilations." This threefold classification was not unique to the Theravāda school but was in common use among the Indian Buddhist schools as a way to categorize the Buddhist canonical texts. Even today the scriptures preserved in Chinese translation are known as the Chinese Tripiṭaka. The three compilations of the Pāli Canon are:

1. The *Vinaya Piṭaka*, the Compilation of Discipline, which contains the rules laid down for the guidance of the monks and nuns and the regulations prescribed for the harmonious functioning of the monastic order.
2. The *Sutta Piṭaka*, the Compilation of Discourses, which contains the *suttas*, the discourses of the Buddha and those of his chief disciples as well as inspirational works in verse, verse narratives, and certain works of a commentarial nature.

3. The *Abhidhamma Piṭaka*, the Compilation of Philosophy, a collection of seven treatises which subject the Buddha's teachings to rigorous philosophical systematization.

The Abhidhamma Piṭaka is obviously the product of a later phase in the evolution of Buddhist thought than the other two Piṭakas. The Pāli version represents the Theravāda school's attempt to systematize the older teachings. Other early schools apparently had their own Abhidhamma systems. The Sarvāstivāda system is the only one whose canonical texts have survived intact in their entirety. Its canonical collection, like the Pāli version, also consists of seven texts. These were originally composed in Sanskrit but are preserved in full only in Chinese translation. The system they define differs significantly from that of its Theravāda counterpart in both formulation and philosophy.

The Sutta Piṭaka, which contains the records of the Buddha's discourses and discussions, consists of five collections called Nikāyas. In the age of the commentators they were also known as Āgamas, like their counterparts in northern Buddhism. The four major Nikāyas are:

1. The *Dīgha Nikāya*: the Collection of Long Discourses, thirty-four suttas arranged into three *vaggas*, or books.
2. The *Majjhima Nikāya*: the Collection of Middle Length Discourses, 152 suttas arranged into three vaggas.
3. The *Saṃyutta Nikāya*: the Collection of Connected Discourses, close to three thousand short suttas grouped into fifty-six chapters, called *saṃyuttas*, which are in turn collected into five vaggas.
4. The *Aṅguttara Nikāya*: the Collection of Numerical Discourses (or, perhaps, "Incremental Discourses"), approximately 2,400 short suttas arranged into eleven chapters, called *nipātas*.

The Dīgha Nikāya and Majjhima Nikāya, at first glance, seem to be established principally on the basis of length: the longer discourses go into the Dīgha, the middle-length discourses into the Majjhima. Careful tabulations of their contents, however, suggest that another factor might underlie the distinction between these two collections. The suttas of the Dīgha Nikāya are largely aimed at a popular audience and seem intended to attract potential converts to the teaching by demonstrating the superiority of the Buddha and his doctrine. The suttas of the Majjhima Nikāya are largely directed inward toward the Buddhist community and seem designed to acquaint newly ordained monks with the doctrines and practices of Buddhism.[9] It remains an open question whether these pragmatic purposes are the determining criteria behind these two Nikāyas or whether the primary criterion is length, with these pragmatic purposes following as incidental consequences of their respective differences in length.

The Saṃyutta Nikāya is organized by way of subject matter. Each subject is the "yoke" (*saṃyoga*) that connects the discourses into a *saṃyutta* or chapter. Hence the title of the collection, the "connected (*saṃyutta*) discourses." The first book, the Book with Verses, is unique in being compiled on the basis of literary genre. It contains suttas in mixed prose and verse, arranged in eleven chapters by way of subject. The other four books each contain long chapters dealing with the principal doctrines of Early Buddhism. Books II, III, and IV each open with a long chapter devoted to a theme of major importance, respectively, dependent origination (chapter 12: *Nidānasaṃyutta*); the five aggregates (chapter 22: *Khandhasaṃyutta*); and the six internal and external sense bases (chapter 35: *Saḷāyatanasaṃyutta*). Part V deals with the principal groups of training factors that, in the post-canonical period, come to be called the thirty-seven aids to enlightenment (*bodhipakkhiyā dhammā*). These include the Noble Eightfold Path (chapter 45: *Maggasaṃyutta*), the seven factors of enlightenment (chapter 46: *Bojjhaṅgasaṃyutta*), and the four establishments of mindfulness (chapter 47: *Satipaṭṭhānasaṃyutta*). From its contents, we might infer that the Saṃyutta Nikāya was intended to serve the needs of two groups within the monastic order. One consisted of the doctrinal specialists, those monks and nuns who sought to explore the deep implications of the Dhamma and to elucidate them for their companions in the religious life. The other consisted of those devoted to the meditative development of insight.

The Aṅguttara Nikāya is arranged according to a numerical scheme derived from a peculiar feature of the Buddha's pedagogic method. To facilitate easy comprehension and memorization, the Buddha often formulated his discourses by way of numerical sets, a format that helped to ensure that the ideas he conveyed would be easily retained in mind. The Aṅguttara Nikāya assembles these numerical discourses into a single massive work of eleven *nipātas* or chapters, each representing the number of terms upon which the constituent suttas have been framed. Thus there is the Chapter of the Ones (*ekakanipāta*), the Chapter of the Twos (*dukanipāta*), the Chapter of the Threes (*tikanipāta*), and so forth, up to and ending with the Chapter of the Elevens (*ekādasanipāta*). Since the various groups of path factors have been included in the Saṃyutta, the Aṅguttara can focus on those aspects of the training that have not been incorporated in the repetitive sets. The Aṅguttara includes a notable proportion of suttas addressed to lay followers dealing with the ethical and spiritual concerns of life within the world, including family relationships (husbands and wives, children and parents) and the proper ways to acquire, save, and utilize wealth. Other suttas deal with the practical training of monks. The numerical arrangement of this collection makes it particularly convenient for formal instruction, and thus it could easily be drawn upon by elder monks when teaching their pupils and by preachers when giving sermons to the laity.

Besides the four major Nikāyas, the Pāli Sutta Piṭaka includes a fifth Nikāya, called the Khuddaka Nikāya. This name means the Minor Collection. Perhaps it originally consisted merely of a number of minor works that could not be included in the four major Nikāyas. But as more and more works were composed over the centuries and added to it, its dimensions swelled until it became the most voluminous of the five Nikāyas. At the heart of the Khuddaka, however, is a small constellation of short works composed either entirely in verse (namely, the Dhammapada, the Theragāthā, and the Therīgāthā) or in mixed prose and verse (the Suttanipāta, the Udāna, and the Itivuttaka) whose style and contents suggest that they are of great antiquity. Other texts of the Khuddaka Nikāya—such as the Paṭisambhidāmagga and the two Niddesas—represent the standpoint of the Theravāda school and thus must have been composed during the period of Sectarian Buddhism, when the early schools had taken their separate paths of doctrinal development.

The four Nikāyas of the Pāli Canon have counterparts in the Āgamas of the Chinese Tripiṭaka, though these are from different early schools. Corresponding to each respectively there is a Dirghāgama, probably stemming from the Dharmaguptaka school, originally translated from a Prakrit; a Madhyamāgama and Samyuktāgama, both stemming from the Sarvāstivāda school and translated from Sanskrit; and an Ekottarāgama, corresponding to the Aṅguttara Nikāya, generally thought to have belonged to a branch of the Mahāsāṅghika school and to have been translated from a dialect of Middle Indo-Aryan or a mixed dialect of Prakrit with Sanskrit elements. The Chinese Tripiṭaka also contains translations of individual sūtras from the four collections, perhaps from still other unidentified schools, and translations of individual books from the Minor Collection, including two translations of a Dhammapada (one said to be very close to the Pāli version) and parts of the Suttanipāta, which, as a unified work, does not exist in Chinese translation.[10]

A Note on Style

Readers of the Pāli suttas are often annoyed by the repetitiveness of the texts. It is difficult to tell how much of this stems from the Buddha himself, who as an itinerant preacher must have used repetition to reinforce his points, and how much is due to the compilers. It is obvious, however, that a high proportion of the repetitiveness derives from the process of oral transmission.

To avoid excessive repetitiveness in the translation I have had to make ample use of elisions. In this respect I follow the printed editions of the Pāli texts, which are also highly abridged, but a translation intended for a contemporary reader requires still more compression if it is to avoid risking the reader's wrath. On the other hand, I have been keen to see that nothing essential to the original text, including the flavor, has been lost due to the abridgment. The ideals of considerateness to the reader and fidelity to the text sometimes make contrary demands on a translator.

The treatment of repetition patterns in which the same utterance is made regarding a set of items is a perpetual problem in translating Pāli suttas. When translating a sutta about the five aggregates, for example, one is tempted to forgo the enumeration of the individual aggregates and instead turn the sutta into a general statement about the aggregates as a class. To my mind, such an approach risks turning translation into paraphrase and thereby losing too much of the original. My general policy has been to translate the full utterance in relation to the first and last members of the set and merely to enumerate the intermediate members separated by ellipsis points. Thus, in a sutta about the five aggregates, I render the statement in full only for form and consciousness, and in between have "feeling ... perception ... volitional formations ...," implying thereby that the full statement likewise applies to them.

This approach has required the frequent use of ellipsis points, a practice that also invites criticism. When faced with repetitive passages in the narrative framework, I have sometimes condensed them rather than use ellipsis points to show where text is being elided. However, with texts of doctrinal exposition I adhere to the practice described in the preceding paragraph. I think the translator has the responsibility, when translating passages of doctrinal significance, to show exactly where text is being elided, and for this ellipsis points remain the best tool at hand.

I. The Human Condition

Introduction

Like other religious teachings, the Buddha's teaching originates as a response to the strains at the heart of the human condition. What distinguishes his teaching from other religious approaches to the human condition is the directness, thoroughness, and uncompromising realism with which he looks at these strains. The Buddha does not offer us palliatives that leave the underlying maladies untouched beneath the surface; rather, he traces our existential illness down to its most fundamental causes, so persistent and destructive, and shows us how these can be totally uprooted. However, while the Dhamma will eventually lead to the wisdom that eradicates the causes of suffering, it does not begin there but with observations about the hard facts of everyday experience. Here too its directness, thoroughness, and tough realism are evident. The teaching begins by calling upon us to develop a faculty called *yoniso manasikāra,* careful attention. The Buddha asks us to stop drifting thoughtlessly through our lives and instead to pay careful attention to simple truths that are everywhere available to us, clamoring for the sustained consideration they deserve.

One of the most obvious and inescapable of these truths is also among the most difficult for us to fully acknowledge, namely, that we are bound to grow old, fall ill, and die. It is commonly assumed that the Buddha beckons us to recognize the reality of old age and death in order to motivate us to enter the path of renunciation leading to Nibbāna, complete liberation from the round of birth and death. However, while this may be his ultimate intention, it is not the first response he seeks to evoke in us when we turn to him for guidance. The initial response the Buddha intends to arouse in us is an ethical one. By calling our attention to our bondage to old age and death, he seeks to inspire in us a firm resolution to turn away from unwholesome ways of living and to embrace instead wholesome alternatives.

Again, the Buddha grounds his initial ethical appeal not only upon a compassionate feeling for other beings, but also upon our instinctive concern for our own long-term welfare and happiness. He tries to make us see that to act in accordance with ethical guidelines will enable us to secure our own well-being both now and in the long-term future. His argument hinges on the important premise that actions have consequences. If we are to alter our accustomed ways, we must be convinced of the validity of this principle. Specifically, to change from a self-stultifying way of life to one that is truly fruitful and inwardly rewarding, we must realize that our actions have consequences for ourselves, consequences that can rebound upon us both in this life and in subsequent lives.

The three suttas that constitute the first section of this chapter establish this point eloquently, each in its own way. **Text I,1(1)** enunciates the inevitable law that all beings who have taken birth must undergo aging and death. Although at first glance the discourse seems to be stating a mere fact of nature, by citing as examples members of the upper strata of society (wealthy rulers, brahmins, and householders) and liberated arahants, it insinuates a subtle moral message into its words. **Text I,1(2)** brings out this message more explicitly with its impressive simile of the mountain, which drives home the point that when "aging and death are rolling in" on us, our task in life is to live righteously and do wholesome and meritorious deeds. The sutta on the "divine messengers"—**Text I,1(3)**—establishes the corollary to this: when we fail to recognize the "divine messengers" in our midst, when we miss the hidden warning signals of old age, illness, and death, we become negligent and behave recklessly, creating unwholesome kamma with the potential to yield dreadful consequences.

The realization that we are bound to grow old and die breaks the spell of infatuation cast over us by sensual pleasures, wealth, and power. It dispels the mist of confusion and motivates us to take fresh stock of our purposes in life. We may not be ready to give up family and possessions for a life of homeless wandering and solitary meditation, but this is not an option the Buddha generally expects of his householder disciples. Rather, as we saw above, the first lesson he draws from the fact that our lives end in old age and death is an ethical one interwoven with the twin principles of kamma and rebirth. The law of kamma stipulates that our unwholesome and wholesome actions have consequences extending far beyond this present life: unwholesome actions lead to rebirth in states of misery and bring future pain and suffering; wholesome actions lead to a pleasant rebirth and bring future well-being and happiness. Since we have to grow old and die, we should be constantly aware that any present prosperity we might enjoy is merely temporary. We can enjoy it only as long as we are young and healthy; and when we die, our newly acquired kamma will gain the opportunity to ripen and bring forth its own results. We must then reap the due fruits of our deeds. With an eye to our long-term future welfare, we should scrupulously avoid evil deeds that result in suffering and diligently engage in wholesome deeds that generate happiness here and in future lives.

In the second section, we explore three aspects of human life that I have collected under the heading "The Tribulations of Unreflective Living." These types of suffering differ from those connected with old age and death in an important respect. Old age and death are bound up with bodily existence and are thus unavoidable, common to both ordinary people and liberated arahants—a point made in the first text of this chapter. In contrast, the three texts included in this section all distinguish between the ordinary person, called "the uninstructed worldling" (*assutavā puthujjana*), and the wise follower of the Buddha, called the "instructed noble disciple" (*sutavā ariyasāvaka*).

The first of these distinctions, drawn in **Text I,2(1)**, revolves around the response to painful feelings. Both the worldling and the noble disciple experience painful bodily feelings, but they respond to these feelings differently. The worldling reacts to them with aversion and therefore, on top of the painful bodily feeling, also experiences a painful mental feeling: sorrow, resentment, or distress. The noble disciple, when afflicted with bodily pain, endures such feeling patiently, without sorrow, resentment, or distress. It is commonly assumed that physical and mental pain are inseparably linked, but the Buddha makes a clear demarcation between the two. He holds that while bodily existence is inevitably bound up with physical pain, such pain need not trigger the emotional reactions of misery, fear, resentment, and distress with which we habitually respond to it. Through mental training we can develop the mindfulness and clear comprehension necessary to endure physical pain courageously, with patience and equanimity. Through insight we can develop sufficient wisdom to overcome our dread of painful feelings and our need to seek relief in distracting binges of sensual self-indulgence.

Another aspect of human life that brings to the fore the differences between the worldling and the noble disciple is the changing vicissitudes of fortune. The Buddhist texts neatly reduce these to four pairs of opposites, known as the eight worldly conditions (*aṭṭha lokadhammā*): gain and loss, fame and disrepute, praise and blame, pleasure and pain. **Text I,2(2)** shows how the worldling and the noble disciple differ in their responses to these changes. While the worldling is elated by success in achieving gain, fame, praise, and pleasure, and dejected when confronted with their undesired opposites, the noble disciple remains unperturbed. By applying the understanding of impermanence to both favorable and unfavorable conditions, the noble disciple can abide in equanimity, not attached to favorable conditions, not repelled by unfavorable ones. Such a disciple gives up likes and dislikes, sorrow and distress, and ultimately wins the highest blessing of all: complete freedom from suffering.

Text I,2(3) examines the plight of the worldling at a still more fundamental level. Because they misconceive things, worldlings are agitated by change, especially when that change affects their own bodies and minds. The Buddha classifies the constituents of body and mind into five categories known as "the five aggregates subject to clinging" (*pañc'upādānakkhandhā*): form, feeling, perception, volitional formations, and consciousness (for details, see pp. 305–07). These five aggregates are the building blocks that we typically use to construct our sense of personal identity; they are the things that we cling to as being "mine," "I," and "my self." Whatever we identify with, whatever we take to be a self or the possessions of a self, can all be classified among these five aggregates. The five aggregates are thus the ultimate grounds of "identification" and "appropriation," the two basic activities by which we establish a sense of selfhood. Since we invest our notions of selfhood and personal identity with an intense emotional concern, when the objects to which they are fastened—the five aggregates—undergo change, we naturally experience anxiety and distress. In our perception, it is not mere impersonal phenomena that are undergoing change, but our very identities, our cherished selves, and this is what we fear most of all. However, as the present text shows, a noble disciple has clearly seen with wisdom the delusive nature of all notions of permanent selfhood and thus no longer identifies with the five aggregates. Therefore the noble disciple can confront their change without anxious concern, unperturbed in the face of their alteration, decay, and destruction.

Agitation and turmoil afflict human life not only at the personal and private level, but also in our social interactions. From the most ancient times, our world has always been one of violent confrontations and conflict. The names, places, and instruments of destruction may change, but the forces behind them, the motivations, the expressions of greed and hate, remain fairly constant. The Nikāyas testify that the Buddha was intensely aware of this dimension of the human condition. Although his teaching, with its stress on ethical self-discipline and mental self-cultivation, aims primarily at personal enlightenment and liberation, the Buddha also sought to offer people a refuge from the violence and injustice that rack human lives in such cruel ways. This is apparent in his emphasis on loving-kindness and compassion; on harmlessness in action and gentleness in speech; and on the peaceful resolution of disputes.

The third section of this chapter includes four short texts dealing with the underlying roots of violent conflict and injustice. We can see from these texts that the Buddha does not clamor for changes merely in the outer structures of society. He demonstrates that these dark phenomena are external projections of the unwholesome proclivities of the human mind and thus points to the need for inner change as a parallel condition for establishing peace and social justice. Each of the four texts included in this section traces conflict, violence, political oppression, and economic injustice back to their causes; each in its own way locates these causes within the mind.

Text I,3(1) explains conflicts between laypeople as arising from attachment to sensual pleasures, conflicts between ascetics as arising from attachment to views. **Text I,3(2)**, a dialogue between the Buddha and Sakka, the pre-Buddhistic Indian ruler of the devas, traces hatred and enmity to envy and niggardliness; from there the Buddha traces them back to fundamental distortions that affect the way our perception and cognition process the information provided by the senses. **Text I,3(3)** offers another version of the famous chain of causation, which proceeds from feeling to craving, and from craving via other conditions to "the taking up of clubs and weapons" and other types of violent behavior. **Text I,3(4)** depicts how the three roots of evil—greed, hatred, and delusion—have terrible repercussions on a whole society, issuing in violence, the lust for power, and the unjust infliction of suffering. All four texts imply that any significant and lasting transformations of society require significant changes in the moral fiber of individual human beings; for as long as greed, hatred, and delusion run rampant as determinants of conduct, the consequences are bound to be consistently detrimental.

The Buddha's teaching addresses a fourth aspect of the human condition which, unlike the three we have so far examined, is not immediately perceptible to us. This is our bondage to the round of rebirths. From the selection of texts included in the final section in this chapter, we see that the Buddha teaches our individual lifespan to be merely a single phase within a series of rebirths that has been proceeding without any discernible beginning in time. This series of rebirths is called *saṃsāra*, a Pāli word which suggests the idea of directionless wandering. No matter how far back in time we may seek a beginning to the universe, we never find an initial moment of creation. No matter how far back we may trace any given individual sequence of lives, we can never arrive at a first point. According to **Texts I,4(1)** and **I,4(2)**, even if we were to trace the sequence of our mothers and fathers across world systems, we would only come upon still more mothers and fathers stretching back into the far horizons.

Moreover, the process is not only beginningless but is also potentially endless. As long as ignorance and craving remain intact, the process will continue indefinitely into the future with no end in sight. For the Buddha and Early Buddhism, this is above all the defining crisis at the heart of the human condition: we are bound to a chain of rebirths, and bound to it by nothing other than our own ignorance and craving. The pointless wandering on in saṃsāra occurs against a cosmic background of inconceivably vast dimensions. The period of time that it takes for a world system to evolve, reach its phase of maximum expansion, contract, and then disintegrate is called a *kappa* (Skt: *kalpa*), an eon. **Text I,4(3)** offers a vivid simile to suggest the eon's duration; **Text I,4(4)**, another vivid simile to illustrate the incalculable number of the eons through which we have wandered.

As beings wander and roam from life to life, shrouded in darkness, they fall again and again into the chasm of birth, aging, sickness, and death. But because their craving propels them forward in a relentless quest for gratification, they seldom pause long enough to step back and attend carefully to their existential plight. As **Text I,4(5)** states, they instead just keep revolving around the "five aggregates" in the way a dog on a leash might run around a post or pillar. Since their ignorance prevents them from recognizing the vicious nature of their condition, they cannot discern even the tracks of a path to deliverance. Most beings live immersed in the enjoyment of sensual pleasures. Others, driven by the need for power, status, and esteem, pass their lives in vain attempts to fill an unquenchable thirst. Many, fearful of annihilation at death, construct belief systems that ascribe to their individual selves, their souls, the prospect of eternal life. A few yearn for a path to liberation but do not know where to find one. It was precisely to offer such a path that the Buddha has appeared in our midst.

I. The Human Condition

1. Old Age, Illness, and Death

(1) Aging and Death

At Sāvatthī, King Pasenadi of Kosala said to the Blessed One: "Venerable sir, is anyone who is born free from aging and death?"[1]

"Great king, no one who is born is free from aging and death. Even those affluent khattiyas—rich, with great wealth and property, with abundant gold and silver, abundant treasures and commodities, abundant wealth and grain—because they have been born, are not free from aging and death. Even those affluent brahmins ... affluent householders—rich ... with abundant wealth and grain—because they have been born, are not free from aging and death. Even those monks who are arahants, whose taints are destroyed, who have lived the holy life, done what had to be done, laid down the burden, reached their own goal, utterly destroyed the fetters of existence, and are completely liberated through final knowledge: even for them this body is subject to breaking up, subject to being laid down.[2]

"The beautiful chariots of kings wear out,
This body too undergoes decay.
But the Dhamma of the good does not decay:
So the good proclaim along with the good."

(SN 3:3; I 71 <163–64>)

(2) The Simile of the Mountain

At Sāvatthī, in the middle of the day, King Pasenadi of Kosala approached the Blessed One, paid homage to him, and sat down to one side. The Blessed One then asked him: "Now where are you coming from, great king, in the middle of the day?"

"Just now, venerable sir, I have been engaged in those affairs of kingship typical for kings, who are intoxicated with the intoxication of sovereignty, who are obsessed by greed for sensual pleasures, who have attained stable control in their country, and who rule having conquered a great sphere of territory on earth."

"What do you think, great king? Suppose a man would come to you from the east, one who is trustworthy and reliable, and would tell you: 'For sure, great king, you should know this: I am coming from the east, and there I saw a great mountain high as the clouds coming this way, crushing all living beings. Do whatever you think should be done, great king.' Then a second man would come to you from the west … a third man from the north … and a fourth man from the south, one who is trustworthy and reliable, and would tell you: 'For sure, great king, you should know this: I am coming from the south, and there I saw a great mountain high as the clouds coming this way, crushing all living beings. Do whatever you think should be done, great king.' If, great king, such a great peril should arise, such a terrible destruction of human life, the human state being so difficult to obtain, what should be done?"

"If, venerable sir, such a great peril should arise, such a terrible destruction of human life, the human state being so difficult to obtain, what else should be done but to live by the Dhamma, to live righteously, and to do wholesome and meritorious deeds?"

"I inform you, great king, I announce to you, great king: aging and death are rolling in on you. When aging and death are rolling in on you, great king, what should be done?"

"As aging and death are rolling in on me, venerable sir, what else should be done but to live by the Dhamma, to live righteously, and to do wholesome and meritorious deeds?

"Venerable sir, kings intoxicated with the intoxication of sovereignty, obsessed by greed for sensual pleasures, who have attained stable control in their country and rule over a great sphere of territory, conquer by means of elephant battles, cavalry battles, chariot battles, and infantry battles; but there is no hope of victory by such battles, no chance of success, when aging and death are rolling in. In this royal court, venerable sir, there are counselors who, when the enemies arrive, are capable of dividing them by subterfuge; but there is no hope of victory by subterfuge, no chance of success, when aging and death are rolling in. In this royal court, venerable sir, there exists abundant bullion and gold stored in vaults and lofts, and with such wealth we are capable of mollifying the enemies when they come; but there is no hope of victory by wealth, no chance of success, when aging and death are rolling in. As aging and death are rolling in on me, venerable sir, what else should I do but live by the Dhamma, live righteously, and do wholesome and meritorious deeds?"

"So it is, great king! So it is, great king! As aging and death are rolling in on you, what else should you do but live by the Dhamma, live righteously, and do wholesome and meritorious deeds?"

This is what the Blessed One said. Having said this, the Fortunate One, the Teacher, further said this:

"Just as mountains of solid rock,
Massive, reaching to the sky,
Might draw together from all sides,
Crushing all in the four quarters—
So aging and death come
Rolling over living beings—

"Khattiyas, brahmins, vessas, suddas,
Outcasts and scavengers:
They spare none along the way
But come crushing everything.

"There's no hope there for victory
By elephant troops, chariots, and infantry.
One can't defeat them by subterfuge,
Or buy them off by means of wealth.

"Therefore a person of wisdom here,
Out of regard for his own good,
Steadfast, should settle faith
In the Buddha, Dhamma, and Saṅgha.

"When one conducts oneself by Dhamma
With body, speech, and mind,
They praise one here in the present life,
And after death one rejoices in heaven."

(SN 3:25; I 100–102 <224–29>)

(3) The Divine Messengers

"There are, monks, three divine messengers.[3] What three?

"There is a person of bad conduct in body, speech, and mind. On the dissolution of the body, after death, he is reborn in the plane of misery, in a bad destination, in a lower world, in hell. There the warders of hell seize him by both arms and take him before Yama, the Lord of Death,[4] saying: 'This man, your majesty, had no respect for father and mother, nor for ascetics and brahmins, nor did he honor the elders of the family. May your majesty inflict due punishment on him!'

"Then, monks, King Yama questions that man, examines him, and addresses him concerning the first divine messenger: 'Didn't you ever see, my good man, the first divine messenger appearing among humankind?'

"And he replies: 'No, Lord, I did not see him.'

"Then King Yama says to him: 'But, my good man, didn't you ever see a woman or a man, eighty, ninety, or a hundred years old, frail, bent like a roof bracket, crooked, leaning on a stick, shakily going along, ailing, youth and vigor gone, with broken teeth, with gray and scanty hair or bald, wrinkled, with blotched limbs?'

"And the man replies: 'Yes, Lord, I have seen this.'

"Then King Yama says to him: 'My good man, didn't it ever occur to you, an intelligent and mature person, "I too am subject to old age and cannot escape it. Let me now do noble deeds by body, speech, and mind"?'

"'No, Lord, I could not do it. I was negligent.'

"Then King Yama says: 'Through negligence, my good man, you have failed to do noble deeds by body, speech, and mind. Well, you will be treated as befits your negligence. That evil action of yours was not done by mother or father, brothers, sisters, friends or companions, nor by relatives, devas, ascetics, or brahmins. But you alone have done that evil deed, and you will have to experience the fruit.'

"When, monks, King Yama has questioned, examined, and addressed him thus concerning the first divine messenger, he again questions, examines, and addresses the man about the second one, saying: 'Didn't you ever see, my good man, the second divine messenger appearing among humankind?'

"'No, Lord, I did not see him.'

"'But, my good man, didn't you ever see a woman or a man who was sick and in pain, seriously ill, lying in his own filth, having to be lifted up by some and put to bed by others?'

"'Yes, Lord, I have seen this.'

"'My good man, didn't it ever occur to you, an intelligent and mature person, "I too am subject to illness and cannot escape it. Let me now do noble deeds by body, speech, and mind"?'

"'No, Lord, I could not do it. I was negligent.'

"'Through negligence, my good man, you have failed to do noble deeds by body, speech, and mind. Well, you will be treated as befits your negligence. That evil action of yours was not done by mother or father, brothers, sisters, friends or companions, nor by relatives, devas, ascetics, or brahmins. But you alone have done that evil deed, and you will have to experience the fruit.'

"When, monks, King Yama has questioned, examined, and addressed him thus concerning the second divine messenger, he again questions, examines, and addresses the man about the third one, saying: 'Didn't you ever see, my good man, the third divine messenger appearing among humankind?'

"'No, Lord, I did not see him.'

"'But, my good man, didn't you ever see a woman or a man one, two, or three days dead, the corpse swollen, discolored, and festering?'

"'Yes, Lord, I have seen this.'

"'Then, my good man, didn't it ever occur to you, an intelligent and mature person, "I too am subject to death and cannot escape it. Let me now do noble deeds by body, speech, and mind"?'

"'No, Lord, I could not do it. I was negligent.'

"'Through negligence, my good man, you have failed to do noble deeds by body, speech, and mind. Well, you will be treated as befits your negligence. That evil action of yours was not done by mother or father, brothers, sisters, friends or companions, nor by relatives, devas, ascetics, or brahmins. But you alone have done that evil deed, and you will have to experience the fruit.'"

(from AN 3:35; I 138–40)

2. The Tribulations of Unreflective Living

(1) The Dart of Painful Feeling

"Monks, when the uninstructed worldling experiences a painful feeling, he sorrows, grieves, and laments; he weeps beating his breast and becomes distraught. He feels two feelings—a bodily one and a mental one. Suppose they were to strike a man with a dart, and then strike him immediately afterward with a second dart, so that the man would feel a feeling caused by two darts. So too, when the uninstructed worldling experiences a painful feeling, he feels two feelings—a bodily one and a mental one.

"While experiencing that same painful feeling, he harbors aversion toward it. When he harbors aversion toward painful feeling, the underlying tendency to aversion toward painful feeling lies behind this.[5] While experiencing painful feeling, he seeks delight in sensual pleasure. For what reason? Because the uninstructed worldling does not know of any escape from painful feeling other than sensual pleasure.[6] When he seeks delight in sensual pleasure, the underlying tendency to lust for pleasant feeling lies behind this. He does not understand as it really is the origin and the passing away, the gratification, the danger, and the escape in the case of these feelings.[7] When he does not understand these things, the underlying tendency to ignorance in regard to neither-painful-nor-pleasant feeling lies behind this.

"If he feels a pleasant feeling, he feels it attached. If he feels a painful feeling, he feels it attached. If he feels a neither-painful-nor-pleasant feeling, he feels it attached. This, monks, is called an uninstructed worldling who is attached to birth, aging, and death; who is attached to sorrow, lamentation, pain, dejection, and despair; who is attached to suffering, I say.

"Monks, when the instructed noble disciple experiences a painful feeling, he does not sorrow, grieve, or lament; he does not weep beating his breast and become distraught.[8] He feels one feeling—a bodily one, not a mental one. Suppose they were to strike a man with a dart, but they would not strike him immediately afterward with a second dart, so that the man would feel a feeling caused by one dart only. So too, when the instructed noble disciple experiences a painful feeling, he feels one feeling—a bodily one, and not a mental one.

"While experiencing that same painful feeling, he harbors no aversion toward it. Since he harbors no aversion toward painful feeling, the underlying tendency to aversion toward painful feeling does not lie behind this. While experiencing painful feeling, he does not seek delight in sensual pleasure. For what reason? Because the instructed noble disciple knows of an escape from painful feeling other than sensual pleasure. Since he does not seek delight in sensual pleasure, the underlying tendency to lust for pleasant feeling does not lie behind this. He understands as it really is the origin and the passing away, the gratification, the danger, and the escape in the case of these feelings. Since he understands these things, the underlying tendency to ignorance in regard to neither-painful-nor-pleasant feeling does not lie behind this.

"If he feels a pleasant feeling, he feels it detached. If he feels a painful feeling, he feels it detached. If he feels a neither-painful-nor-pleasant feeling, he feels it detached. This, monks, is called a noble disciple who is detached from birth, aging, and death; who is detached from sorrow, lamentation, pain, dejection, and despair; who is detached from suffering, I say.

"This, monks, is the distinction, the disparity, the difference between the instructed noble disciple and the uninstructed worldling."

(SN 36:6; IV 207–10)

(2) The Vicissitudes of Life

"These eight worldly conditions, monks, keep the world turning around, and the world turns around these eight worldly conditions. What eight? Gain and loss, fame and disrepute, praise and blame, pleasure and pain.

"These eight worldly conditions, monks, are encountered by an uninstructed worldling, and they are also encountered by an instructed noble disciple. What now is the distinction, the disparity, the difference between an instructed noble disciple and an uninstructed worldling?"

"Venerable sir, our knowledge of these things has its roots in the Blessed One; it has the Blessed One as guide and resort. It would be good, venerable sir, if the Blessed One would clarify the meaning of that statement. Having heard it from him, the monks will bear it in mind."

"Listen then, monks, and attend carefully. I shall speak."

"Yes, venerable sir," the monks replied. The Blessed One then spoke thus:

"When an uninstructed worldling, monks, comes upon gain, he does not reflect on it thus: 'This gain that has come to me is impermanent, bound up with suffering, subject to change.' He does not know it as it really is. And when he comes upon loss, fame and disrepute, praise and blame, he does not reflect on them thus: 'All these are impermanent, bound up with suffering, subject to change.' He does not know them as they really are. With such a person, gain and loss, fame and disrepute, praise and blame, pleasure and pain keep his mind engrossed. When gain comes he is elated and when he meets with loss he is dejected. When fame comes he is elated and when he meets with disrepute he is dejected. When praise comes he is elated and when he meets with blame he is dejected. When he experiences pleasure he is elated and when he experiences pain he is dejected. Being thus involved in likes and dislikes, he will not be freed from birth, aging, and death, from sorrow, lamentation, pain, dejection, and despair; he will not be freed from suffering, I say.

"But, monks, when an instructed noble disciple comes upon gain, he reflects on it thus: 'This gain that has come to me is impermanent, bound up with suffering, subject to change.' And so he will reflect when loss and so forth come upon him. He understands all these things as they really are, and they do not engross his mind. Thus he will not be elated by gain and dejected by loss; elated by fame and dejected by disrepute; elated by praise and dejected by blame; elated by pleasure and dejected by pain. Having thus given up likes and dislikes, he will be freed from birth, aging, and death, from sorrow, lamentation, pain, dejection, and despair; he will be freed from suffering, I say.

"This, monks, is the distinction, the disparity, the difference between an instructed noble disciple and an uninstructed worldling."

(AN 8:6; IV 157–59)

(3) Anxiety Due to Change

"Monks, I will teach you agitation through clinging and non-agitation through nonclinging.[9] Listen and attend carefully. I shall speak."

"Yes, venerable sir," those monks replied. The Blessed One said this:

"And how, monks, is there agitation through clinging? Here, monks, the uninstructed worldling, who is not a seer of the noble ones and is unskilled and undisciplined in their Dhamma, who is not a seer of superior persons and is unskilled and undisciplined in their Dhamma, regards form as self, or self as possessing form, or form as in self, or self as in form.[10] That form of his changes and alters. With the change and alteration of form, his consciousness becomes preoccupied with the change of form. Agitation and a constellation of mental states born of preoccupation with the change of form remain obsessing his mind. Because his mind is obsessed, he is frightened, distressed, and anxious, and through clinging he becomes agitated.

"He regards feeling as self ... perception as self ... volitional formations as self ... consciousness as self, or self as possessing consciousness, or consciousness as in self, or self as in consciousness. That consciousness of his changes and alters. With the change and alteration of consciousness, his consciousness becomes preoccupied with the change of consciousness. Agitation and a constellation of mental states born of preoccupation with the change of consciousness remain obsessing his mind. Because his mind is obsessed, he is frightened, distressed, and anxious, and through clinging he becomes agitated.

"It is in such a way, monks, that there is agitation through clinging.

"And how, monks, is there non-agitation through nonclinging? Here, monks, the instructed noble disciple, who is a seer of the noble ones and is skilled and disciplined in their Dhamma, who is a seer of superior persons and is skilled and disciplined in their Dhamma, does not regard form as self, or self as possessing form, or form as in self, or self as in form.[11] That form of his changes and alters. Despite the change and alteration of form, his consciousness does not become preoccupied with the change of form. No agitation and constellation of mental states born of preoccupation with the change of form remain obsessing his mind. Because his mind is not obsessed, he is not frightened, distressed, or anxious, and through nonclinging he does not become agitated.

"He does not regard feeling as self ... perception as self ... volitional formations as self ... consciousness as self, or self as possessing consciousness, or consciousness as in self, or self as in consciousness. That consciousness of his changes and alters. Despite the change and alteration of consciousness, his consciousness does not become preoccupied with the change of consciousness. No agitation and constellation of mental states born of preoccupation with the change of consciousness remain obsessing his mind. Because his mind is not obsessed, he is not frightened, distressed, or anxious, and through nonclinging he does not become agitated.

"It is in such a way, monks, that there is non-agitation through nonclinging."

(SN 22:7; III 15–18)

3. A World in Turmoil

(1) The Origin of Conflict

The brahmin Ārāmadaṇḍa approached the Venerable Mahākaccāna,[12] exchanged friendly greetings with him, and asked him: "Why is it, Master Kaccāna, that khattiyas fight with khattiyas, brahmins with brahmins, and householders with householders?"

"It is, brahmin, because of attachment to sensual pleasures, adherence to sensual pleasures, fixation on sensual pleasures, addiction to sensual pleasures, obsession with sensual pleasures, holding firmly to sensual pleasures that khattiyas fight with khattiyas, brahmins with brahmins, and householders with householders."

"Why is it, Master Kaccāna, that ascetics fight with ascetics?"

"It is, brahmin, because of attachment to views, adherence to views, fixation on views, addiction to views, obsession with views, holding firmly to views that ascetics fight with ascetics."

(AN 2: iv, 6, abridged; I 66)

(2) Why Do Beings Live in Hate?

2.1. Sakka, ruler of the devas,[13] asked the Blessed One: "Beings wish to live without hate, harming, hostility, or enmity; they wish to live in peace. Yet they live in hate, harming one another, hostile, and as enemies. By what fetters are they bound, sir, that they live in such a way?"

[The Blessed One said:] "Ruler of the devas, it is the bonds of envy and niggardliness that bind beings so that, although they wish to live without hate, hostility, or enmity, and to live in peace, yet they live in hate, harming one another, hostile, and as enemies."

This was the Blessed One's reply, and Sakka, delighted, exclaimed: "So it is, Blessed One! So it is, Fortunate One! Through the Blessed One's answer I have overcome my doubt and gotten rid of uncertainty."

2.2. Then Sakka, having expressed his appreciation, asked another question: "But, sir, what gives rise to envy and niggardliness, what is their origin, how are they born, how do they arise? When what is present do they arise, and when what is absent do they not arise?"

"Envy and niggardliness, ruler of the devas, arise from liking and disliking; this is their origin, this is how they are born, how they arise. When these are present, they arise, when these are absent, they do not arise."

"But, sir, what gives rise to liking and disliking...?"—"They arise, ruler of the devas, from desire...."—"And what gives rise to desire...?"—"It arises, ruler of the devas, from thinking. When the mind thinks about something, desire arises; when the mind thinks of nothing, desire does not arise."

"But, sir, what gives rise to thinking...?"

"Thinking, ruler of the devas, arises from elaborated perceptions and notions.[14] When elaborated perceptions and notions are present, thinking arises. When elaborated perceptions and notions are absent, thinking does not arise."

(from DN 21: *Sakkapañha Sutta;* II 276–77)

(3) The Dark Chain of Causation

9. "Thus, Ānanda, in dependence upon feeling there is craving; in dependence upon craving there is pursuit; in dependence upon pursuit there is gain; in dependence upon gain there is decision-making; in dependence upon decision-making there is desire and lust; in dependence upon desire and lust there is attachment; in dependence upon attachment there is possessiveness; in dependence upon possessiveness there is niggardliness; in dependence upon niggardliness there is defensiveness; and because of defensiveness, various evil unwholesome things originate—the taking up of clubs and weapons, conflicts, quarrels, and disputes, insults, slander, and falsehood."[15]

(from DN 15: *Mahānidāna Sutta;* II 58)

(4) The Roots of Violence and Oppression

"Greed, hatred, and delusion of every kind are unwholesome.[16] Whatever action a greedy, hating, and deluded person heaps up—by deeds, words, or thoughts—that too is unwholesome. Whatever suffering such a person, overpowered by greed, hatred, and delusion, his thoughts controlled by them, inflicts under false pretexts upon another—by killing, imprisonment, confiscation of property, false accusations, or expulsion—being prompted in this by the thought, 'I have power and I want power,' all this is unwholesome too."

(from AN 3:69; I 201–2)

4. Without Discoverable Beginning

(1) Grass and Sticks

The Blessed One said this: "Monks, this saṃsāra is without discoverable beginning.[17] A first point is not discerned of beings roaming and wandering on hindered by ignorance and fettered by craving. Suppose, monks, a man would cut up whatever grass, sticks, branches, and foliage there are in this Jambudīpa[18] and collect them together into a single heap. Having done so, he would put them down, saying for each one: 'This is my mother, this my mother's mother.' The sequence of that man's mothers and grandmothers would not come to an end, yet the grass, sticks, branches, and foliage in this Jambudīpa would be used up and exhausted. For what reason? Because, monks, this saṃsāra is without discoverable beginning. A first point is not discerned of beings roaming and wandering on hindered by ignorance and fettered by craving. For such a long time, monks, you have experienced suffering, anguish, and disaster, and swelled the cemetery. It is enough to become disenchanted with all formations, enough to become dispassionate toward them, enough to be liberated from them."

(SN 15:1; II 178)

(2) Balls of Clay

"Monks, this saṃsāra is without discoverable beginning. A first point is not discerned of beings roaming and wandering on hindered by ignorance and fettered by craving. Suppose, monks, a man would reduce this great earth to balls of clay the size of jujube kernels and put them down, saying [for each one]: 'This is my father, this my father's father.' The sequence of that man's fathers and grandfathers would not come to an end, yet this great earth would be used up and exhausted. For what reason? Because, monks, this saṃsāra is without discoverable beginning. A first point is not discerned of beings roaming and wandering on hindered by ignorance and fettered by craving. For such a long time, monks, you have experienced suffering, anguish, and disaster, and swelled the cemetery. It is enough to become disenchanted with all formations, enough to become dispassionate toward them, enough to be liberated from them."

(SN 15:2; II 179)

(3) The Mountain

A certain monk approached the Blessed One, paid homage to him, sat down to one side, and said to him: "Venerable sir, how long is an eon?"[19]

"An eon is long, monk. It is not easy to count it and say it is so many years, or so many hundreds of years, or so many thousands of years, or so many hundreds of thousands of years."

"Then is it possible to give a simile, venerable sir?"

"It is possible, monk," the Blessed One said. "Suppose, monk, there was a great stone mountain a *yojana* long, a *yojana* wide, and a *yojana* high, without holes or crevices, one solid mass of rock.[20] At the end of every hundred years a man would stroke it once with a piece of fine cloth. That great stone mountain might by this effort be worn away and eliminated but the eon would still not have come to an end. So long is an eon, monk. And of eons of such length, we have wandered through so many eons, so many hundreds of eons, so many thousands of eons, so many hundreds of thousands of eons. For what reason? Because, monk, this saṃsāra is without discoverable beginning.... It is enough to be liberated from them."

(SN 15:5; II 181–82)

(4) The River Ganges

At Rājagaha, in the Bamboo Grove, the Squirrel Sanctuary, a certain brahmin approached the Blessed One and exchanged greetings with him. When they had concluded their greetings and cordial talk, he sat down to one side and asked him: "Master Gotama, how many eons have elapsed and gone by?"

"Brahmin, many eons have elapsed and gone by. It is not easy to count them and say they are so many eons, or so many hundreds of eons, or so many thousands of eons, or so many hundreds of thousands of eons."

"But is it possible to give a simile, Master Gotama?"

"It is possible, brahmin," the Blessed One said. "Imagine, brahmin, the grains of sand between the point where the river Ganges originates and the point where it enters the great ocean: it is not easy to count these and say there are so many grains of sand, or so many hundreds of grains, or so many thousands of grains, or so many hundreds of thousands of grains. Brahmin, the eons that have elapsed and gone by are even more numerous than that. It is not easy to count them and say that they are so many eons, or so many hundreds of eons, or so many thousands of eons, or so many hundreds of thousands of eons. For what reason? Because, brahmin, this saṃsāra is without discoverable beginning.... It is enough to be liberated from them."

(SN 15:8; II 183–84)

(5) Dog on a Leash

"Monks, this saṃsāra is without discoverable beginning. A first point is not discerned of beings roaming and wandering on hindered by ignorance and fettered by craving.

"There comes a time, monks, when the great ocean dries up and evaporates and no longer exists, but still, I say, there is no making an end of suffering for those beings roaming and wandering on hindered by ignorance and fettered by craving.

"There comes a time, monks, when Sineru, the king of mountains, burns up and perishes and no longer exists, but still, I say, there is no making an end of suffering for those beings roaming and wandering on hindered by ignorance and fettered by craving.

"There comes a time, monks, when the great earth burns up and perishes and no longer exists, but still, I say, there is no making an end of suffering for those beings roaming and wandering on hindered by ignorance and fettered by craving.

"Suppose, monks, a dog tied up on a leash was bound to a strong post or pillar: it would just keep on running and revolving around that same post or pillar. So too, the uninstructed worldling regards form as self … feeling as self … perception as self … volitional formations as self … consciousness as self…. He just keeps running and revolving around form, around feeling, around perception, around volitional formations, around consciousness. As he keeps on running and revolving around them, he is not freed from form, not freed from feeling, not freed from perception, not freed from volitional formations, not freed from consciousness. He is not freed from birth, aging, and death; not freed from sorrow, lamentation, pain, dejection, and despair; not freed from suffering, I say."

(SN 22:99; II 149–50)

II. The Bringer of Light

Introduction

The picture of the human condition that emerges from the Nikāyas, as sketched in the preceding chapter, is the background against which the manifestation of the Buddha in the world acquires a heightened and deepened significance. Unless we view the Buddha against this multi-dimensional background, extending from the most personal and individual exigencies of the present to the vast, impersonal rhythms of cosmic time, any interpretation we may arrive at about his role is bound to be incomplete. Far from capturing the viewpoint of the compilers of the Nikāyas, our interpretation will be influenced as much by our own presuppositions as by theirs, perhaps even more so. Depending on our biases and predispositions, we may choose to regard the Buddha as a liberal ethical reformer of a degenerate Brahmanism, as a great secular humanist, as a radical empiricist, as an existential psychologist, as the proponent of a sweeping agnosticism, or as the precursor of any other intellectual fashion that meets our fancy. The Buddha who stares back at us from the texts will be too much a reflection of ourselves, too little an image of the Enlightened One.

Perhaps in interpreting a body of ancient religious literature we can never fully avoid inserting ourselves and our own values into the subject we are interpreting. However, though we may never achieve perfect transparency, we can limit the impact of personal bias upon the process of interpretation by giving the words of the texts due respect. When we pay this act of homage to the Nikāyas, when we take seriously their own account of the background to the Buddha's manifestation in the world, we will see that they ascribe to his mission nothing short of a cosmic scope. Against the background of a universe with no conceivable bounds in time, a universe within which living beings enveloped in the darkness of ignorance wander along bound to the suffering of old age, sickness, and death, the Buddha arrives as the "torchbearer of humankind" (*ukkādhāro manussānaṃ*) bringing the light of wisdom.[1] In the words of **Text II,1**, his arising in the world is "the manifestation of great vision, of great light, of great radiance." Having discovered for himself the perfect peace of liberation, he kindles for us the light of knowledge, which reveals both the truths that we must see for ourselves and the path of practice that culminates in this liberating vision.

According to Buddhist tradition, the Buddha Gotama is not merely one unique individual who puts in an unprecedented appearance on the stage of human history and then bows out forever. He is, rather, the fulfillment of a primordial archetype, the most recent member of a cosmic "dynasty" of Buddhas constituted by numberless Perfectly Enlightened Ones of the past and sustained by Perfectly Enlightened Ones continuing indefinitely onward into the future. Early Buddhism, even in the archaic root texts of the Nikāyas, already recognizes a plurality of Buddhas who all conform to certain fixed patterns of behavior, the broad outlines of which are described in the opening sections of the Mahāpadāna Sutta (Dīgha Nikāya 14, not represented in the present anthology). The word "Tathāgata," which the texts use as an epithet for a Buddha, points to this fulfillment of a primordial archetype. The word means both "the one who has come thus" (*tathā āgata*), that is, who has come into our midst in the same way that the Buddhas of the past have come; and "the one who has gone thus" (*tathā gata*), that is, who has gone to the ultimate peace, Nibbāna, in the same way that the Buddhas of the past have gone.

Though the Nikāyas stipulate that in any given world system, at any given time, only one Perfectly Enlightened Buddha can arise, the arising of Buddhas is intrinsic to the cosmic process. Like a meteor against the blackness of the night sky, from time to time a Buddha will appear against the backdrop of boundless space and time, lighting up the spiritual firmament of the world, shedding the brilliance of his wisdom upon those capable of seeing the truths that he illuminates. The being who is to become a Buddha is called, in Pāli, a *bodhisatta,* a word better known in the Sanskrit form, *bodhisattva*. According to common Buddhist tradition, a bodhisatta is one who undertakes a long course of spiritual development consciously motivated by the aspiration to attain future Buddhahood.[2] Inspired and sustained by great compassion for living beings mired in the suffering of birth and death, a bodhisatta fulfills, over many eons of cosmic time, the difficult course needed to fully master the requisites for supreme enlightenment. When all these requisites are complete, he attains Buddhahood in order to establish the

Dhamma in the world. A Buddha discovers the long-lost path to liberation, the "ancient path" traveled by the Buddhas of the past that culminates in the boundless freedom of Nibbāna. Having found the path and traveled it to its end, he then teaches it in all its fullness to humanity so that many others can enter the way to final liberation.

This, however, does not exhaust the function of a Buddha. A Buddha understands and teaches not only the path leading to the supreme state of ultimate liberation, the perfect bliss of Nibbāna, but also the paths leading to the various types of wholesome mundane happiness to which human beings aspire. A Buddha proclaims both a path of mundane enhancement that enables sentient beings to plant wholesome roots productive of happiness, peace, and security in the worldly dimensions of their lives, and a path of world-transcendence to guide sentient beings to Nibbāna. His role is thus much wider than an exclusive focus on the transcendent aspects of his teaching might suggest. He is not merely a mentor of ascetics and contemplatives, not merely a teacher of meditation techniques and philosophical insights, but a guide to the Dhamma in its full range and depth: one who reveals, proclaims, and establishes all the principles integral to correct understanding and wholesome conduct, whether mundane or transcendental. **Text II,1** highlights this wide-ranging altruistic dimension of a Buddha's career when it praises the Buddha as the one person who arises in the world "for the welfare of the multitude, for the happiness of the multitude, out of compassion for the world, for the good, welfare, and happiness of devas and humans."

The Nikāyas offer two perspectives on the Buddha as a person, and to do justice to the texts it is important to hold these two perspectives in balance, without letting one cancel out the other. A correct view of the Buddha can only arise from the merging of these two perspectives, just as the correct view of an object can arise only when the perspectives presented by our two eyes are merged in the brain into a single image. One perspective, the one highlighted most often in modernist presentations of Buddhism, shows the Buddha as a human being who, like other human beings, had to struggle with the common frailties of human nature to arrive at the state of an Enlightened One. After his enlightenment at the age of thirty-five, he walked among us for forty-five years as a wise and compassionate human teacher, sharing his realization with others and ensuring that his teachings would remain in the world long after his death. This is the side of the Buddha's nature that figures most prominently in the Nikāyas. Since it corresponds closely with contemporary agnostic attitudes toward the ideals of religious faith, it has an immediate appeal to those nurtured by modern modes of thought.

The other aspect of the Buddha's person is likely to seem strange to us, but it looms large in Buddhist tradition and serves as the bedrock for popular Buddhist devotion. Though secondary in the Nikāyas, it occasionally surfaces so conspicuously that it cannot be ignored, despite the efforts of Buddhist modernists to downplay its significance or rationalize its intrusions. From this perspective, the Buddha is seen as one who had already made preparations for his supreme attainment over countless past lives and was destined from birth to fulfill the mission of a world teacher. **Text II,2** is an example of how the Buddha is viewed from this perspective. Here, it is said, the future Buddha descends fully conscious from the Tusita heaven into his mother's womb; his conception and birth are accompanied by wonders; deities worship the newborn infant; and as soon as he is born he walks seven steps and announces his future destiny. Obviously, for the compilers of such a sutta as this, the Buddha was already destined to attain Buddhahood even prior to his conception and thus his struggle for enlightenment was a battle whose outcome was already predetermined. The final paragraph of the sutta, however, ironically hearkens back to the realistic picture of the Buddha. What the Buddha himself considers to be truly wondrous are not the miracles accompanying his conception and birth, but his mindfulness and clear comprehension in the midst of feelings, thoughts, and perceptions.

The three texts in section 3 are biographical accounts consistent with this naturalistic point of view. They offer us a portrait of the Buddha stark in its realism, bare in its naturalism, striking in its ability to convey deep psychological insights with minimal descriptive technique. In **Text II,3(1)** we read about his renunciation, his training under two famous meditation teachers, his disillusionment with their teachings, his solitary struggle, and his triumphant realization of the Deathless. **Text II,3(2)** fills in the gaps of the above narrative with a detailed account of the bodhisatta's practice of self-mortification, strangely missing from the previous discourse. This text also gives us the classic description of the enlightenment experience as involving the attainment of the four *jhānas*, states of deep meditation, followed by the three *vijjās* or higher types of knowledge: the knowledge of the recollection of past lives, the knowledge of the passing away and rebirth of beings, and the knowledge of the destruction of the taints. While this text may convey the impression that the last knowledge broke upon the Buddha's mind as a sudden and spontaneous intuition, **Text II,3(3)** corrects this impression with an account of the Bodhisatta on the eve of his enlightenment reflecting deeply upon the suffering of old age and death. He then methodically traces this suffering back to its conditions by a process that involves, at each step, "careful attention" (*yoniso manasikāra*) leading to "a breakthrough by wisdom" (*paññāya abhisamaya*). This process of investigation culminates in the discovery of dependent origination, which thereby becomes the philosophical cornerstone of his teaching.

It is important to emphasize that, as presented here and elsewhere in the Nikāyas (see below, pp. 353-59), dependent origination does not signify a joyous celebration of the interconnectedness of all things but a precise articulation of the conditional pattern in dependence upon which suffering arises and ceases. In the same text, the Buddha declares that he discovered the path to enlightenment only when he found the way to bring dependent origination to an end. It was thus the realization of the *cessation* of dependent origination, and not merely the discovery of its origination aspect, that precipitated the Buddha's enlightenment. The simile of the ancient city, introduced later in the discourse, illustrates the point that the Buddha's enlightenment was not a unique event but the rediscovery of the same "ancient path" that had been followed by the Buddhas of the past.

Text II,4 resumes the narrative of **Text II,3(1)**, which I had divided by splicing in the two alternative versions of the bodhisatta's quest for the path to enlightenment. We now rejoin the Buddha immediately after his enlightenment as he ponders the weighty question whether to attempt to share his realization with the world. Just at this point, in the midst of a text that has so far appeared so convincingly naturalistic, a deity named Brahmā Sahampati descends from the heavens to plead with the Buddha to wander forth and teach the Dhamma for the benefit of those "with little dust in their eyes." Should this scene be interpreted literally or as a symbolic enactment of an internal drama taking place in the Buddha's mind? It is hard to give a definitive answer to this question; perhaps the scene could be understood as occurring at both levels at once. In any event, Brahmā's appearance at this point marks a shift from the realism that colors the earlier part of the sutta back toward the mythical-symbolic mode. The transition again underscores the cosmic significance of the Buddha's enlightenment and his future mission as a teacher.

Brahmā's appeal eventually prevails and the Buddha agrees to teach. He chooses as the first recipients of his teaching the five ascetics who had attended on him during his years of ascetic practices. The narrative culminates in a brief statement that the Buddha instructed them in such a way that they all attained the deathless Nibbāna for themselves. However, it gives no indication of the specific teaching that the Buddha imparted to them when he first met them after his enlightenment. That teaching is the First Discourse itself, known as "The Setting in Motion of the Wheel of the Dhamma."

This sutta is included here as **Text II,5**. When the sutta opens, the Buddha announces to the five ascetics that he has discovered "the middle way," which he identifies with the Noble Eightfold Path. In the light of the preceding biographical account, we can understand why the Buddha should begin his discourse in this way. The five ascetics had initially refused to acknowledge the Buddha's claim to enlightenment and spurned him as one who had betrayed the higher calling to revert to a life of luxury. Thus he first had to assure them that, far from reverting to a life of self-indulgence, he had discovered a new approach to the timeless quest for enlightenment. This new approach, he told them, remains faithful to the renunciation of sensual pleasures yet eschews tormenting the body as pointless and unproductive. He then explained to them the true path to liberation, the Noble Eightfold Path, which avoids the two extremes and thereby gives rise to the light of wisdom and culminates in the destruction of all bondage, Nibbāna.

Once he has cleared up their misunderstanding, the Buddha then proclaims the truths he had realized on the night of his enlightenment. These are the Four Noble Truths. Not only does he enunciate each truth and briefly define its meaning, but he describes each truth from three perspectives. These constitute the three "turnings of the wheel of the Dhamma" referred to later in the discourse. With respect to each truth, the first turning is the wisdom that illuminates the particular nature of that noble truth. The second turning is the understanding that each noble truth imposes a particular task to be accomplished. Thus the first noble truth, the truth of suffering, *is to be* fully understood; the second truth, the truth of suffering's origin or craving, *is to be* abandoned; the third truth, the truth of the cessation of suffering, *is to be* realized; and the fourth truth, the truth of the path, *is to be* developed. The third turning is the understanding that the four functions regarding the Four Noble Truths have been completed: the truth of suffering *has been* fully understood; craving *has been* abandoned; the cessation of suffering *has been* realized; and the path *has been* fully developed. It was only when he understood the Four Noble Truths in these three turnings and twelve modes, he says, that he could claim that he had attained unsurpassed perfect enlightenment.

The Dhammacakkappavattana Sutta illustrates once again the blending of the two stylistic modes I referred to earlier. The discourse proceeds almost entirely in the realistic-naturalistic mode until we approach the end. When the Buddha completes his sermon, the cosmic significance of the event is illuminated by a passage showing how the deities in each successive celestial realm applaud the discourse and shout the good news up to the deities in the next higher realm. At the same time, the entire world system quakes and shakes, and a great light surpassing the radiance of the gods appears in the world. Then, at the very end, we return from this glorious scene back to the prosaic human realm, to behold the Buddha briefly congratulating the ascetic Koṇḍañña for gaining "the dust-free, stainless vision of the Dhamma." In one split-second, the Lamp of the Doctrine has passed from master to disciple, to begin its journey throughout India and across the world.

II. The Bringer of Light

1. One Person

"Monks, there is one person who arises in the world for the welfare of the multitude, for the happiness of the multitude, out of compassion for the world, for the good, welfare, and happiness of devas and humans. Who is that one person? It is the Tathāgata, the Arahant, the Perfectly Enlightened One. This is that one person.

"Monks, there is one person arising in the world who is unique, without a peer, without counterpart, incomparable, unequalled, matchless, unrivalled, the best of humans. Who is that one person? It is the Tathāgata, the Arahant, the Perfectly Enlightened One. This is that one person.

"Monks, the manifestation of one person is the manifestation of great vision, of great light, of great radiance; it is the manifestation of the six things unsurpassed; the realization of the four analytical knowledges; the penetration of the various elements, of the diversity of elements; it is the realization of the fruit of knowledge and liberation; the realization of the fruits of stream-entry, once-returning, nonreturning, and arahantship.[3] Who is that one person? It is the Tathāgata, the Arahant, the Perfectly Enlightened One. This is that one person."

(AN 1: xiii, 1, 5, 6; I 22–23)

2. The Buddha's Conception and Birth

1. Thus have I heard. On one occasion the Blessed One was living at Sāvatthī in Jeta's Grove, Anāthapiṇḍika's Park.

2. Now a number of monks were sitting in the assembly hall, where they had met together on returning from their almsround, after their meal, when this discussion arose among them: "It is wonderful, friends, it is marvelous, how mighty and powerful is the Tathāgata! For he is able to know about the Buddhas of the past—who attained

final Nibbāna, cut [the tangle of] proliferation, broke the cycle, ended the round, and surmounted all suffering—that for those Blessed Ones their birth was thus, their names were thus, their clans were thus, their moral discipline was thus, their qualities [of concentration] were thus, their wisdom was thus, their meditative dwellings were thus, their liberation was thus."

When this was said, the Venerable Ānanda told the monks: "Friends, Tathāgatas are wonderful and have wonderful qualities. Tathāgatas are marvelous and have marvelous qualities."[4]

However, their discussion was interrupted; for the Blessed One rose from meditation when it was evening, went to the assembly hall, and sat down on a seat made ready. Then he addressed the monks thus: "Monks, for what discussion are you sitting together here now? And what was your discussion that was interrupted?"

"Here, venerable sir, we were sitting in the assembly hall, where we had met together on returning from our almsround, after our meal, when this discussion arose among us: 'It is wonderful, friends, it is marvelous ... their liberation was thus.' When this was said, venerable sir, the Venerable Ānanda said to us: 'Friends, Tathāgatas are wonderful and have wonderful qualities. Tathāgatas are marvelous and have marvelous qualities.' This was our discussion, venerable sir, that was interrupted when the Blessed One arrived."

Then the Blessed One addressed the Venerable Ānanda: "That being so, Ānanda, explain more fully the Tathāgata's wonderful and marvelous qualities."

3. "I heard and learned this, venerable sir, from the Blessed One's own lips: 'Mindful and clearly comprehending, Ānanda, the Bodhisatta appeared in the Tusita heaven.'[5] That mindful and clearly comprehending the Bodhisatta appeared in the Tusita heaven—this I remember as a wonderful and marvelous quality of the Blessed One.

4. "I heard and learned this from the Blessed One's own lips: 'Mindful and clearly comprehending the Bodhisatta remained in the Tusita heaven.' This too I remember as a wonderful and marvelous quality of the Blessed One.

5. "I heard and learned this from the Blessed One's own lips: 'For the whole of his lifespan the Bodhisatta remained in the Tusita heaven.' This too I remember as a wonderful and marvelous quality of the Blessed One.

6. "I heard and learned this from the Blessed One's own lips: 'Mindful and clearly comprehending the Bodhisatta passed away from the Tusita heaven and descended into his mother's womb.' This too I remember as a wonderful and marvelous quality of the Blessed One.

7. "I heard and learned this from the Blessed One's own lips: 'When the Bodhisatta passed away from the Tusita heaven and descended into his mother's womb, an immeasurable great radiance surpassing the divine majesty of the devas appeared in the world with its devas, Māra, and Brahmā, in this population with its ascetics and brahmins, with its devas and human beings. And even in those abysmal world intervals of vacancy, gloom, and utter darkness, where the moon and the sun, mighty and powerful as they are, cannot make their light prevail, there too an immeasurable great radiance surpassing the divine majesty of the devas appeared.[6] And the beings reborn there perceived each other by that light: "So indeed, there are also other beings reborn here." And this ten-thousand-fold world system shook, quaked, and trembled, and again an immeasurable great radiance surpassing the divine majesty of the devas appeared in the world.' This too I remember as a wonderful and marvelous quality of the Blessed One.

8. "I heard and learned this from the Blessed One's own lips: 'When the Bodhisatta had descended into his mother's womb, four young devas came to guard him at the four quarters so that no humans or nonhumans or anyone at all could harm the Bodhisatta or his mother."[7] This too I remember as a wonderful and marvelous quality of the Blessed One.

9. "I heard and learned this from the Blessed One's own lips: 'When the Bodhisatta had descended into his mother's womb, she became intrinsically virtuous, refraining from killing living beings, from taking what is not given, from sexual misconduct, from false speech, and from wines, liquors, and intoxicants, the basis of negligence.' This too I remember as a wonderful and marvelous quality of the Blessed One....

14. "I heard and learned this from the Blessed One's own lips: 'Other women give birth after carrying the child in the womb for nine or ten months, but not so the Bodhisatta's mother. The Bodhisatta's mother gave birth to him after carrying him in her womb for exactly ten months.' This too I remember as a wonderful and marvelous quality of the Blessed One.

15. "I heard and learned this from the Blessed One's own lips: 'Other women give birth seated or lying down, but not so the Bodhisatta's mother. The Bodhisatta's mother gave birth to him standing up.' This too I remember as a wonderful and marvelous quality of the Blessed One.

16. "I heard and learned this from the Blessed One's own lips: 'When the Bodhisatta came forth from his mother's womb, first devas received him, then human beings.' This too I remember as a wonderful and marvelous quality of the Blessed One.

17. "I heard and learned this from the Blessed One's own lips: 'When the Bodhisatta came forth from his mother's womb, he did not touch the earth. The four young devas received him and set him before his mother saying: "Rejoice, O queen, a son of great power has been born to you."' This too I remember as a wonderful and marvelous quality of the Blessed One.

18. "I heard and learned this from the Blessed One's own lips: 'When the Bodhisatta came forth from his mother's womb, he came forth unsullied, unsmeared by water, humors, blood, or any kind of impurity, clean and unsullied. Suppose there were a gem placed on fine cloth, then the gem would not smear the cloth or the cloth the gem. Why is that? Because of the purity of both. So too when the Bodhisatta came forth ... he came forth clean and unsullied.' This too I remember as a wonderful and marvelous quality of the Blessed One.

19. "I heard and learned this from the Blessed One's own lips: 'When the Bodhisatta came forth from his mother's womb, two jets of water appeared to pour from the sky, one cool and one warm, for bathing the Bodhisatta and his mother.' This too I remember as a wonderful and marvelous quality of the Blessed One.

20. "I heard and learned this from the Blessed One's own lips: 'As soon as the Bodhisatta was born, he stood firmly with his feet on the ground; then he took seven steps facing north, and with a white parasol held over him, he surveyed each quarter and uttered the words of the leader of the herd: "I am the highest in the world; I am the best in the world; I am the foremost in the world. This is my last birth; now there is no renewed existence for me."'[8] This too I remember as a wonderful and marvelous quality of the Blessed One.

21. "I heard and learned this from the Blessed One's own lips: 'When the Bodhisatta came forth from his mother's womb, an immeasurable

great radiance surpassing the divine majesty of the devas appeared in the world with its devas, Māra, and Brahmā, in this population with its ascetics and brahmins, with its devas and human beings. And even in those abysmal world intervals of vacancy, gloom, and utter darkness, where the moon and the sun, mighty and powerful as they are, cannot make their light prevail—there too an immeasurable great radiance surpassing the divine majesty of the devas appeared in the world. And the beings reborn there perceived each other by that light: "So indeed, there are also other beings reborn here." And this ten-thousand-fold world system shook, quaked, and trembled, and there too an immeasurable great radiance surpassing the divine majesty of the devas appeared in the world.' That when the Bodhisatta came forth from his mother's womb, an immeasurable great radiance surpassing the divine majesty of the devas appeared in the world ... this too I remember as a wonderful and marvelous quality of the Blessed One."

22. "That being so, Ānanda, remember this too as a wonderful and marvelous quality of the Tathāgata: Here, Ānanda, for the Tathāgata feelings are known as they arise, as they are present, as they disappear; perceptions are known as they arise, as they are present, as they disappear; thoughts are known as they arise, as they are present, as they disappear.[9] Remember this too, Ānanda, as a wonderful and marvelous quality of the Tathāgata."

23. "Venerable sir, since for the Blessed One feelings are known as they arise, as they are present, as they disappear; perceptions are known as they arise, as they are present, as they disappear; thoughts are known as they arise, as they are present, as they disappear—this too I remember as a wonderful and marvelous quality of the Blessed One."

That is what the Venerable Ānanda said. The Teacher approved. The monks were satisfied and delighted in the Venerable Ānanda's words.

(MN 123: *Acchariya-abbhūta Sutta*, abridged; III 118–20; 122–24)

3. The Quest for Enlightenment

(1) Seeking the Supreme State of Sublime Peace

5. "Monks, there are these two kinds of search: the noble search and the ignoble search. And what is the ignoble search? Here someone being himself subject to birth seeks what is also subject to birth; being

himself subject to aging, he seeks what is also subject to aging; being himself subject to sickness, he seeks what is also subject to sickness; being himself subject to death, he seeks what is also subject to death; being himself subject to sorrow, he seeks what is also subject to sorrow; being himself subject to defilement, he seeks what is also subject to defilement.

6–11. "And what may be said to be subject to birth, aging, sickness, and death; to sorrow and defilement? Wife and children, men and women slaves, goats and sheep, fowl and pigs, elephants, cattle, horses, and mares, gold and silver: these acquisitions are subject to birth, aging, sickness, and death; to sorrow and defilement; and one who is tied to these things, infatuated with them, and utterly absorbed in them, being himself subject to birth … to sorrow and defilement, seeks what it also subject to birth … to sorrow and defilement.[10]

12. "And what is the noble search? Here someone being himself subject to birth, having understood the danger in what is subject to birth, seeks the unborn supreme security from bondage, Nibbāna; being himself subject to aging, having understood the danger in what is subject to aging, he seeks the unaging supreme security from bondage, Nibbāna; being himself subject to sickness, having understood the danger in what is subject to sickness, he seeks the unailing supreme security from bondage, Nibbāna; being himself subject to death, having understood the danger in what is subject to death, he seeks the deathless supreme security from bondage, Nibbāna; being himself subject to sorrow, having understood the danger in what is subject to sorrow, he seeks the sorrowless supreme security from bondage, Nibbāna; being himself subject to defilement, having understood the danger in what is subject to defilement, he seeks the undefiled supreme security from bondage, Nibbāna. This is the noble search.

13. "Monks, before my enlightenment, while I was still only an unenlightened bodhisatta, I too, being myself subject to birth, sought what was also subject to birth; being myself subject to aging, sickness, death, sorrow, and defilement, I sought what was also subject to aging, sickness, death, sorrow, and defilement. Then I considered thus: 'Why, being myself subject to birth, do I seek what is also subject to birth? Why, being myself subject to aging, sickness, death, sorrow, and defilement, do I seek what is also subject to aging, sickness, death, sorrow, and defilement? Suppose that, being myself subject to birth, having

understood the danger in what is subject to birth, I seek the unborn supreme security from bondage, Nibbāna. Suppose that, being myself subject to aging, sickness, death, sorrow, and defilement, having understood the danger in what is subject to aging, sickness, death, sorrow, and defilement, I seek the unaging, unailing, deathless, sorrowless, and undefiled supreme security from bondage, Nibbāna.'

14. "Later, while still young, a black-haired young man endowed with the blessing of youth, in the prime of life, though my mother and father wished otherwise and wept with tearful faces, I shaved off my hair and beard, put on the ochre robe, and went forth from the home life into homelessness.

15. "Having gone forth, monks, in search of what is wholesome, seeking the supreme state of sublime peace, I went to Āḷāra Kālāma and said to him: 'Friend Kālāma, I want to lead the spiritual life in this Dhamma and Discipline.' Āḷāra Kālāma replied: 'The venerable one may stay here. This Dhamma is such that a wise man can soon enter upon and dwell in it, realizing for himself through direct knowledge his own teacher's doctrine.' I soon quickly learned that Dhamma. As far as mere lip-reciting and rehearsal of his teaching went, I could speak with knowledge and assurance, and I claimed, 'I know and see'—and there were others who did likewise.

"I considered: 'It is not through mere faith alone that Āḷāra Kālāma declares: "By realizing it for myself with direct knowledge, I enter upon and dwell in this Dhamma." Certainly Āḷāra Kālāma dwells knowing and seeing this Dhamma.' Then I went to Āḷāra Kālāma and asked him: 'Friend Kālāma, in what way do you declare that by realizing it for yourself with direct knowledge you enter upon and dwell in this Dhamma?' In reply he declared the base of nothingness.[11]

"I considered: 'Not only Āḷāra Kālāma has faith, energy, mindfulness, concentration, and wisdom. I too have faith, energy, mindfulness, concentration, and wisdom. Suppose I endeavor to realize the Dhamma that Āḷāra Kālāma declares he enters upon and dwells in by realizing it for himself with direct knowledge?'

"I soon quickly entered upon and dwelled in that Dhamma by realizing it for myself with direct knowledge. Then I went to Āḷāra Kālāma and asked him: 'Friend Kālāma, is it in this way that you declare that you enter upon and dwell in this Dhamma by realizing it for yourself with direct knowledge?'—'That is the way, friend.'—'It is in this way, friend, that I also enter upon and dwell in this Dhamma by realizing it for myself with direct knowledge.'—'It is a gain for us, friend, it is a great gain for us that we have such a venerable one for our fellow monk. So the Dhamma that I declare I enter upon and dwell in by realizing it for myself with direct knowledge is the Dhamma that you enter upon and dwell in by realizing it for yourself with direct knowledge. And the Dhamma that you enter upon and dwell in by realizing it for yourself with direct knowledge is the Dhamma that I declare I enter upon and dwell in by realizing it for myself with direct knowledge. So you know the Dhamma that I know and I know the Dhamma that you know. As I am, so are you; as you are, so am I. Come, friend, let us now lead this community together.'

"Thus Āḷāra Kālāma, my teacher, placed me, his pupil, on an equal footing with himself and awarded me the highest honor. But it occurred to me: 'This Dhamma does not lead to disenchantment, to dispassion, to cessation, to peace, to direct knowledge, to enlightenment, to Nibbāna, but only to rebirth in the base of nothingness.'[12] Not being satisfied with that Dhamma, disappointed with it, I left.

16. "Still in search, monks, of what is wholesome, seeking the supreme state of sublime peace, I went to Uddaka Rāmaputta and said to him: 'Friend, I want to lead the spiritual life in this Dhamma and Discipline.' Uddaka Rāmaputta replied: 'The venerable one may stay here. This Dhamma is such that a wise man can soon enter upon and dwell in it, himself realizing through direct knowledge his own teacher's doctrine.' I soon quickly learned that Dhamma. As far as mere lip-reciting and rehearsal of his teaching went, I could speak with knowledge and assurance, and I claimed, 'I know and see'—and there were others who did likewise.

"I considered: 'It was not through mere faith alone that Rāma declared: "By realizing it for myself with direct knowledge, I enter upon and dwell in this Dhamma." Certainly Rāma dwelled knowing and seeing this Dhamma.' Then I went to Uddaka Rāmaputta and asked him: 'Friend, in what way did Rāma declare that by realizing it for himself with direct knowledge he entered upon and dwelled in this Dhamma?' In reply Uddaka Rāmaputta declared the base of neither-perception-nor-nonperception.[13]

"I considered: 'Not only Rāma had faith, energy, mindfulness, concentration, and wisdom. I too have faith, energy, mindfulness, concentration, and wisdom. Suppose I endeavor to realize the Dhamma that Rāma declared he entered upon and dwelled in by realizing it for himself with direct knowledge.'

"I soon quickly entered upon and dwelled in that Dhamma by realizing it for myself with direct knowledge. Then I went to Uddaka Rāmaputta and asked him: 'Friend, was it in this way that Rāma declared that he entered upon and dwelled in this Dhamma by realizing it for himself with direct knowledge?'—'That is the way, friend.'—'It is in this way, friend, that I also enter upon and dwell in this Dhamma by realizing it for myself with direct knowledge.'—'It is a gain for us, friend, it is a great gain for us that we have such a venerable one for our fellow monk. So the Dhamma that Rāma declared he entered upon and dwelled in by realizing it for himself with direct knowledge is the Dhamma that you enter upon and dwell in by realizing it for yourself with direct knowledge. And the Dhamma that you enter upon and dwell in by realizing it for yourself with direct knowledge is the Dhamma that Rāma declared he entered upon and dwelled in by realizing it for himself with direct knowledge. So you know the Dhamma that Rāma knew and Rāma knew the Dhamma that you know. As Rāma was, so are you; as you are, so was Rāma. Come, friend, now lead this community.'

"Thus Uddaka Rāmaputta, my fellow monk, placed me in the position of a teacher and accorded me the highest honor. But it occurred to me: 'This Dhamma does not lead to disenchantment, to dispassion, to cessation, to peace, to direct knowledge, to enlightenment, to Nibbāna, but only to rebirth in the base of neither-perception-nor-nonperception.' Not being satisfied with that Dhamma, disappointed with it, I left.

17. "Still in search, monks, of what is wholesome, seeking the supreme state of sublime peace, I wandered by stages through the Magadhan country until eventually I arrived at Uruvelā near Senānigama. There I saw an agreeable piece of ground, a delightful grove with a clear-flowing river with pleasant, smooth banks and nearby a village for alms resort. I considered: 'This is an agreeable piece of ground, this is a delightful grove with a clear-flowing river with pleasant, smooth banks and nearby a village for alms resort. This will serve for the striving of a clansman intent on striving.' And I sat down there thinking: 'This will serve for striving.'[14]

18. "Then, monks, being myself subject to birth, having understood the danger in what is subject to birth, seeking the unborn supreme security from bondage, Nibbāna, I attained the unborn supreme security from bondage, Nibbāna; being myself subject to aging, having understood the danger in what is subject to aging, seeking the unaging supreme security from bondage, Nibbāna, I attained the unaging supreme security from bondage, Nibbāna; being myself subject to sickness, having understood the danger in what is subject to sickness, seeking the unailing supreme security from bondage, Nibbāna, I attained the unailing supreme security from bondage, Nibbāna; being myself subject to death, having understood the danger in what is subject to death, seeking the deathless supreme security from bondage, Nibbāna, I attained the deathless supreme security from bondage, Nibbāna; being myself subject to sorrow, having understood the danger in what is subject to sorrow, seeking the sorrowless supreme security from bondage, Nibbāna, I attained the sorrowless supreme security from bondage, Nibbāna; being myself subject to defilement, having understood the danger in what is subject to defilement, seeking the undefiled supreme security from bondage, Nibbāna, I attained the undefiled supreme security from bondage, Nibbāna. The knowledge and vision arose in me: 'My liberation is unshakable. This is my last birth. Now there is no more renewed existence.'"

(from MN 26: *Ariyapariyesana Sutta*; I 160–67)

(2) The Realization of the Three True Knowledges

11. [Saccaka asked the Blessed One:][15] "Has there never arisen in Master Gotama a feeling so pleasant that it could invade his mind and remain? Has there never arisen in Master Gotama a feeling so painful that it could invade his mind and remain?"

12. "Why not, Aggivessana? Here, Aggivessana, before my enlightenment, while I was still only an unenlightened bodhisatta, I thought: 'Household life is crowded and dusty; life gone forth is wide open. It is not easy, while living in a home, to lead the holy life utterly perfect and pure as a polished shell. Suppose I shave off my hair and beard, put on the ochre robe, and go forth from the home life into homelessness.'

13–16. "Later, while still young, a black-haired young man endowed with the blessing of youth, in the prime of life ... [as in Text II,3(1) §§14–17] ... And I sat down there thinking: 'This will serve for striving.'

17. "Now these three similes occurred to me spontaneously, never heard before. Suppose there were a wet sappy piece of wood lying in water, and a man came with an upper fire-stick, thinking: 'I shall light a fire, I shall produce heat.' What do you think, Aggivessana? Could the man light a fire and produce heat by taking the upper fire-stick and rubbing it against the wet sappy piece of wood lying in the water?"

"No, Master Gotama. Why not? Because it is a wet sappy piece of wood, and it is lying in water. Eventually the man would reap only weariness and disappointment."

"So too, Aggivessana, as to those ascetics and brahmins who still do not live bodily withdrawn from sensual pleasures, and whose sensual desire, affection, infatuation, thirst, and fever for sensual pleasures has not been fully abandoned and suppressed internally, even if those good ascetics and brahmins feel painful, racking, piercing feelings due to exertion, they are incapable of knowledge and vision and supreme enlightenment; and even if those good ascetics and brahmins do not feel painful, racking, piercing feelings due to exertion, they are incapable of knowledge and vision and supreme enlightenment. This was the first simile that occurred to me spontaneously, never heard before.

18. "Again, Aggivessana, a second simile occurred to me spontaneously, never heard before. Suppose there were a wet sappy piece of wood lying on dry land far from water, and a man came with an upper fire-stick, thinking: 'I shall light a fire, I shall produce heat.' What do you think, Aggivessana? Could the man light a fire and produce heat by taking the upper fire-stick and rubbing it against the wet sappy piece of wood lying on dry land far from water?"

"No, Master Gotama. Why not? Because it is a wet sappy piece of wood, even though it is lying on dry land far from water. Eventually the man would reap only weariness and disappointment."

"So too, Aggivessana, as to those ascetics and brahmins who live bodily withdrawn from sensual pleasures, but whose sensual desire, affection, infatuation, thirst, and fever for sensual pleasures has not been fully abandoned and suppressed internally, even if those good ascetics and brahmins feel painful, racking, piercing feelings due to exertion, they are incapable of knowledge and vision and supreme enlightenment; and even if those good ascetics and brahmins do not feel painful, racking, piercing feelings due to exertion, they are incapable of knowledge and vision and supreme enlightenment. This was the second simile that occurred to me spontaneously, never heard before.

19. "Again, Aggivessana, a third simile occurred to me spontaneously, never heard before. Suppose there were a dry sapless piece of wood lying on dry land far from water, and a man came with an upper fire-stick, thinking: 'I shall light a fire, I shall produce heat.' What do you think, Aggivessana? Could the man light a fire and produce heat by rubbing it against the dry sapless piece of wood lying on dry land far from water?"

"Yes, Master Gotama. Why so? Because it is a dry sapless piece of wood, and it is lying on dry land far from water."

"So too, Aggivessana, as to those ascetics and brahmins who live bodily withdrawn from sensual pleasures, and whose sensual desire, affection, infatuation, thirst, and fever for sensual pleasures has been fully abandoned and suppressed internally, even if those good ascetics and brahmins feel painful, racking, piercing feelings due to exertion, they are capable of knowledge and vision and supreme enlightenment; and even if those good ascetics and brahmins do not feel painful, racking, piercing feelings due to exertion, they are capable of knowledge and vision and supreme enlightenment.[16] This was the third simile that occurred to me spontaneously, never heard before. These are the three similes that occurred to me spontaneously, never heard before.

20. "I thought: 'Suppose, with my teeth clenched and my tongue pressed against the roof of my mouth, I beat down, constrain, and crush mind with mind.' So, with my teeth clenched and my tongue pressed against the roof of my mouth, I beat down, constrained, and crushed mind with mind. While I did so, sweat ran from my armpits. Just as a strong man might seize a weaker man by the head or shoulders and beat him down, constrain him, and crush him, so too, with my teeth clenched and my tongue pressed against the roof of my mouth, I beat down, constrained, and crushed mind with mind, and sweat ran from my armpits. But although tireless energy was aroused in me and unremitting mindfulness was established, my body was overwrought and strained because I was exhausted by the painful striving. But such painful feeling that arose in me did not invade my mind and remain.[17]

21. "I thought: 'Suppose I practice the breathless meditation.' So I stopped the in-breaths and out-breaths through my mouth and nose. While I did so, there was a loud sound of winds coming out from my ear holes. Just as there is a loud sound when a smith's bellows are blown, so too, while I stopped the in-breaths and out-breaths through my nose and ears, there was a loud sound of winds coming out from my ear holes. But although tireless energy was aroused in me and unremitting mindfulness was established, my body was overwrought and strained because I was exhausted by the painful striving. But such painful feeling that arose in me did not invade my mind and remain.

22. "I thought: 'Suppose I practice further the breathless meditation.' So I stopped the in-breaths and out-breaths through my mouth, nose, and ears. While I did so, violent winds cut through my head. Just as if a strong man were pressing against my head with the tip of a sharp sword, so too, while I stopped the in-breaths and out-breaths through my mouth, nose, and ears, violent winds cut through my head. But although tireless energy was aroused in me and unremitting mindfulness was established, my body was overwrought and strained because I was exhausted by the painful striving. But such painful feeling that arose in me did not invade my mind and remain.

23. "I thought: 'Suppose I practice further the breathless meditation.' So I stopped the in-breaths and out-breaths through my mouth, nose, and ears. While I did so, there were violent pains in my head. Just as if a strong man were tightening a tough leather strap around my head as a headband, so too, while I stopped the in-breaths and out-breaths through my mouth, nose, and ears, there were violent pains in my head. But although tireless energy was aroused in me and unremitting mindfulness was established, my body was overwrought and strained because I was exhausted by the painful striving. But such painful feeling that arose in me did not invade my mind and remain.

24. "I thought: 'Suppose I practice further the breathless meditation.' So I stopped the in-breaths and out-breaths through my mouth, nose, and ears. While I did so, violent winds carved up my belly. Just as if a skilled butcher or his apprentice were to carve up an ox's belly with a sharp butcher's knife, so too, while I stopped the in-breaths and out-breaths through my mouth, nose, and ears, violent winds carved up my belly. But although tireless energy was aroused in me and unremitting mindfulness was established, my body was overwrought and

strained because I was exhausted by the painful striving. But such painful feeling that arose in me did not invade my mind and remain.

25. "I thought: 'Suppose I practice further the breathless meditation.' So I stopped the in-breaths and out-breaths through my mouth, nose, and ears. While I did so, there was a violent burning in my body. Just as if two strong men were to seize a weaker man by both arms and roast him over a pit of hot coals, so too, while I stopped the in-breaths and out-breaths through my mouth, nose, and ears, there was a violent burning in my body. But although tireless energy was aroused in me and unremitting mindfulness was established, my body was overwrought and strained because I was exhausted by the painful striving. But such painful feeling that arose in me did not invade my mind and remain.

26. "Now when deities saw me, some said: 'The ascetic Gotama is dead.' Other deities said: 'The ascetic Gotama is not dead, he is dying.' And other deities said: 'The ascetic Gotama is neither dead nor dying; he is an arahant, for such is the way arahants dwell.'

27. "I thought: 'Suppose I practice entirely cutting off food.' Then deities came to me and said: 'Good sir, do not practice entirely cutting off food. If you do so, we shall infuse heavenly food into the pores of your skin and this will sustain you.' I considered: 'If I claim to be completely fasting while these deities infuse heavenly food into the pores of my skin and this sustains me, then I shall be lying.' So I dismissed those deities, saying: 'There is no need.'

28. "I thought: 'Suppose I take very little food, a handful each time, whether of bean soup or lentil soup or vetch soup or pea soup.' So I took very little food, a handful each time, whether of bean soup or lentil soup or vetch soup or pea soup. While I did so, my body reached a state of extreme emaciation. Because of eating so little my limbs became like the jointed segments of vine stems or bamboo stems. Because of eating so little my backside became like a camel's hoof. Because of eating so little the projections on my spine stood forth like corded beads. Because of eating so little my ribs jutted out as gaunt as the crazy rafters of an old roofless barn. Because of eating so little the gleam of my eyes sank far down in their sockets, looking like the gleam of water that has sunk far down in a deep well. Because of eating so little my scalp shriveled and withered as a green bitter gourd shrivels and withers in the wind and sun. Because of eating so little my belly

skin adhered to my backbone; thus if I touched my belly skin I encountered my backbone and if I touched my backbone I encountered my belly skin. Because of eating so little, if I defecated or urinated, I fell over on my face there. Because of eating so little, if I tried to ease my body by rubbing my limbs with my hands, the hair, rotted at its roots, fell from my body as I rubbed.

29. "Now when people saw me, some said: 'The ascetic Gotama is black.' Other people said: 'The ascetic Gotama is not black; he is brown.' Other people said: 'The ascetic Gotama is neither black nor brown; he is golden-skinned.' So much had the clear, bright color of my skin deteriorated through eating so little.

30. "I thought: 'Whatever ascetics or brahmins in the past have experienced painful, racking, piercing feelings due to exertion, this is the utmost; there is none beyond this. And whatever ascetics and brahmins in the future will experience painful, racking, piercing feelings due to exertion, this is the utmost; there is none beyond this. And whatever ascetics and brahmins at present experience painful, racking, piercing feelings due to exertion, this is the utmost; there is none beyond this. But by this racking practice of austerities I have not attained any superhuman distinction in knowledge and vision worthy of the noble ones. Could there be another path to enlightenment?'

31. "I considered: 'I recall that when my father the Sakyan was occupied, while I was sitting in the cool shade of a rose-apple tree, secluded from sensual pleasures, secluded from unwholesome states, I entered and dwelled in the first jhāna, which is accompanied by thought and examination, with rapture and happiness born of seclusion.[18] Could this be the path to enlightenment?' Then, following on that memory, came the realization: 'This is indeed the path to enlightenment.'

32. "I thought: 'Why am I afraid of that happiness that has nothing to do with sensual pleasures and unwholesome states?' I thought: 'I am not afraid of that happiness that has nothing to do with sensual pleasures and unwholesome states.'

33. "I considered: 'It is not easy to attain that happiness with a body so excessively emaciated. Suppose I ate some solid food—some boiled rice and porridge.' And I ate some solid food—some boiled rice and porridge. Now at that time five monks were waiting upon me, thinking: 'If our ascetic Gotama achieves some higher state, he will inform us.' But when I ate the boiled rice and porridge, the five monks were

disgusted and left me, thinking: 'The ascetic Gotama now lives luxuriously; he has given up his striving and reverted to luxury.'

34. "Now when I had eaten solid food and regained my strength, then secluded from sensual pleasures, secluded from unwholesome states, I entered and dwelled in the first jhāna, which is accompanied by thought and examination, with rapture and happiness born of seclusion. But such pleasant feeling that arose in me did not invade my mind and remain.[19]

35. "With the subsiding of thought and examination, I entered and dwelled in the second jhāna, which has internal confidence and unification of mind, is without thought and examination, and has rapture and happiness born of concentration. But such pleasant feeling that arose in me did not invade my mind and remain.

36. "With the fading away as well of rapture, I dwelled equanimous, and mindful and clearly comprehending, I experienced happiness with the body; I entered and dwelled in the third jhāna of which the noble ones declare: 'He is equanimous, mindful, one who dwells happily.' But such pleasant feeling that arose in me did not invade my mind and remain.

37. "With the abandoning of pleasure and pain, and with the previous passing away of joy and displeasure, I entered and dwelled in the fourth jhāna, which is neither painful nor pleasant and includes the purification of mindfulness by equanimity. But such pleasant feeling that arose in me did not invade my mind and remain.

38. "When my mind was thus concentrated, purified, bright, unblemished, rid of imperfection, malleable, wieldy, steady, and attained to imperturbability, I directed it to knowledge of the recollection of past lives. I recollected my manifold past lives, that is, one birth, two births, three births, four births, five births, ten births, twenty births, thirty births, forty births, fifty births, a hundred births, a thousand births, a hundred thousand births, many eons of world-contraction, many eons of world-expansion, many eons of world-contraction and expansion: 'There I was so named, of such a clan, with such an appearance, such was my nutriment, such my experience of pleasure and pain, such my lifespan; and passing away from there, I was reborn elsewhere; and there too I was so named, of such a clan, with such an appearance, such was my nutriment, such my experience of pleasure and pain, such my lifespan; and passing away from there, I was reborn

here.' Thus with their aspects and particulars I recollected my manifold past lives.

39. "This was the first true knowledge attained by me in the first watch of the night. Ignorance was banished and true knowledge arose, darkness was banished and light arose, as happens in one who dwells diligent, ardent, and resolute. But such pleasant feeling that arose in me did not invade my mind and remain.

40. "When my mind was thus concentrated, purified, bright, unblemished, rid of imperfection, malleable, wieldy, steady, and attained to imperturbability, I directed it to knowledge of the passing away and rebirth of beings. With the divine eye, which is purified and surpasses the human, I saw beings passing away and being reborn, inferior and superior, beautiful and ugly, fortunate and unfortunate, and I understood how beings fare on according to their actions thus: 'These beings who behaved wrongly by body, speech, and mind, who reviled the noble ones, held wrong view, and undertook actions based on wrong view, with the breakup of the body, after death, have been reborn in a state of misery, in a bad destination, in the lower world, in hell; but these beings who behaved well by body, speech, and mind, who did not revile the noble ones, who held right view, and undertook action based on right view, with the breakup of the body, after death, have been reborn in a good destination, in a heavenly world.' Thus with the divine eye, which is purified and surpasses the human, I saw beings passing away and being reborn, inferior and superior, beautiful and ugly, fortunate and unfortunate, and I understood how beings fare on according to their actions.

41. "This was the second true knowledge attained by me in the middle watch of the night. Ignorance was banished and true knowledge arose, darkness was banished and light arose, as happens in one who dwells diligent, ardent, and resolute. But such pleasant feeling that arose in me did not invade my mind and remain.

42. "When my mind was thus concentrated, purified, bright, unblemished, rid of imperfection, malleable, wieldy, steady, and attained to imperturbability, I directed it to knowledge of the destruction of the taints. I directly knew as it actually is: 'This is suffering. This is the origin of suffering. This is the cessation of suffering. This is the way leading to the cessation of suffering.' I directly knew as it actually is: 'These are the taints. This is the origin of the taints. This is

the cessation of the taints. This is the way leading to the cessation of the taints.'

43. "When I knew and saw thus, my mind was liberated from the taint of sensual desire, from the taint of existence, and from the taint of ignorance. When it was liberated, there came the knowledge: 'It is liberated.' I directly knew: 'Birth is destroyed, the spiritual life has been lived, what had to be done has been done, there is no more coming back to any state of being.'

44. "This was the third true knowledge attained by me in the last watch of the night. Ignorance was banished and true knowledge arose, darkness was banished and light arose, as happens in one who dwells diligent, ardent, and resolute. But such pleasant feeling that arose in me did not invade my mind and remain."

(from MN 36: *Mahāsaccaka Sutta*; I 240–49)

(3) The Ancient City

"Monks, before my enlightenment, while I was still a bodhisatta, not yet fully enlightened, it occurred to me: 'Alas, this world has fallen into trouble, in that it is born, ages, and dies, it passes away and is reborn, yet it does not understand the escape from this suffering headed by aging-and-death. When now will an escape be discerned from this suffering headed by aging-and-death?'

"Then, monks, it occurred to me: 'When what exists does aging-and-death come to be? By what is aging-and-death conditioned?' Then, monks, through careful attention, there took place in me a breakthrough by wisdom: 'When there is birth, aging-and-death comes to be; aging-and-death has birth as its condition.'

"Then, monks, it occurred to me: 'When what exists does birth come to be?… existence?… clinging?… craving?… feeling?… contact?… the six sense bases?… name-and-form? By what is name-and-form conditioned?' Then, monks, through careful attention, there took place in me a breakthrough by wisdom: 'When there is consciousness, name-and-form comes to be; name-and-form has consciousness as its condition.'

"Then, monks, it occurred to me: 'When what exists does consciousness come to be? By what is consciousness conditioned?' Then, monks, through careful attention, there took place in me a breakthrough by wisdom: 'When there is name-and-form, consciousness comes to be; consciousness has name-and-form as its condition.'[20]

"Then, monks, it occurred to me: 'This consciousness turns back; it does not go further than name-and-form. It is to this extent that one may be born and age and die, pass away and be reborn, that is, when there is consciousness with name-and-form as its condition, and name-and-form with consciousness as its condition.[21] With name-and-form as condition, the six sense bases; with the six sense bases as condition, contact.... Such is the origin of this whole mass of suffering.'

"'Origination, origination'—thus, monks, in regard to things unheard before there arose in me vision, knowledge, wisdom, penetration, and light.

"Then, monks, it occurred to me: 'When what does not exist does aging-and-death not come to be? With the cessation of what does the cessation of aging-and-death come about?' Then, monks, through careful attention, there took place in me a breakthrough by wisdom: 'When there is no birth, aging-and-death does not come to be; with the cessation of birth comes cessation of aging-and-death.'

"It occurred to me: 'When what does not exist does birth not come to be?... existence?... clinging?... craving?... feeling?... contact?... the six sense bases?... name-and-form? With the cessation of what does the cessation of name-and-form come about?' Then, monks, through careful attention, there took place in me a breakthrough by wisdom: 'When there is no consciousness, name-and-form does not come to be; with the cessation of consciousness comes cessation of name-and-form.'

"It occurred to me: 'When what does not exist does consciousness not come to be? With the cessation of what does the cessation of consciousness come about?' Then, monks, through careful attention, there took place in me a breakthrough by wisdom: 'When there is no name-and-form, consciousness does not come to be; with the cessation of name-and-form comes cessation of consciousness.'

"Then, monks, it occurred to me: 'I have discovered this path to enlightenment, that is, with the cessation of name-and-form comes cessation of consciousness; with the cessation of consciousness comes cessation of name-and-form; with the cessation of name-and-form, cessation of the six sense bases; with the cessation of the six sense bases, cessation of contact.... Such is the cessation of this whole mass of suffering.'[22]

"'Cessation, cessation'—thus, monks, in regard to things unheard before there arose in me vision, knowledge, wisdom, penetration, and light.

"Suppose, monks, a man wandering through a forest would see an ancient path, an ancient road traveled upon by people in the past. He would follow it and would see an ancient city, an ancient capital that had been inhabited by people in the past, with parks, groves, ponds, and ramparts, a delightful place. Then the man would inform the king or a royal minister: 'Sire, know that while wandering through the forest I saw an ancient path, an ancient road traveled upon by people in the past. I followed it and saw an ancient city, an ancient capital that had been inhabited by people in the past, with parks, groves, ponds, and ramparts, a delightful place. Renovate that city, sire!' Then the king or the royal minister would renovate the city, and some time later that city would become successful and prosperous, well populated, filled with people, attained to growth and expansion.

"So too, monks, I saw the ancient path, the ancient road traveled by the Perfectly Enlightened Ones of the past. And what is that ancient path, that ancient road? It is just this Noble Eightfold Path; that is, right view, right intention, right speech, right action, right livelihood, right effort, right mindfulness, right concentration. I followed that path and by doing so I have directly known aging-and-death, its origin, its cessation, and the way leading to its cessation. I have directly known birth ... existence ... clinging ... craving ... feeling ... contact ... the six sense bases ... name-and-form ... consciousness ... volitional formations, their origin, their cessation, and the way leading to their cessation.[23] Having directly known them, I have explained them to the monks, the nuns, the male lay followers, and the female lay followers. This spiritual life, monks, has become successful and prosperous, extended, popular, widespread, well proclaimed among devas and humans."

(SN 12:65; II 104–7)

4. The Decision to Teach

19. "I considered: 'This Dhamma that I have attained is profound, hard to see and hard to understand, peaceful and sublime, unattainable by mere reasoning, subtle, to be experienced by the wise. But this

population delights in attachment, takes delight in attachment, rejoices in attachment.[24] It is hard for such a population to see this truth, namely, specific conditionality, dependent origination. And it is hard to see this truth, namely, the stilling of all formations, the relinquishing of all acquisitions, the destruction of craving, dispassion, cessation, Nibbāna.[25] If I were to teach the Dhamma, others would not understand me, and that would be wearying and troublesome for me.' Thereupon there came to me spontaneously these stanzas never heard before:

> Enough with teaching the Dhamma
> That even I found hard to reach;
> For it will never be perceived
> By those who live in lust and hate.
>
> Those dyed in lust, wrapped in darkness
> Will never discern this abstruse Dhamma,
> Which goes against the worldly stream,
> Subtle, deep, and difficult to see.

"Considering thus, my mind inclined to inaction rather than to teaching the Dhamma.[26]

20. "Then, monks, the Brahmā Sahampati knew with his mind the thought in my mind and he considered: 'The world will be lost, the world will perish, since the mind of the Tathāgata, the Arahant, the Perfectly Enlightened One, inclines to inaction rather than to teaching the Dhamma.' Then, just as quickly as a strong man might extend his flexed arm or flex his extended arm, the Brahmā Sahampati vanished in the brahma world and appeared before me. He arranged his upper robe on one shoulder, and extending his hands in reverential salutation toward me, said: 'Venerable sir, let the Blessed One teach the Dhamma, let the Sublime One teach the Dhamma. There are beings with little dust in their eyes who are perishing through not hearing the Dhamma. There will be those who will understand the Dhamma.' The Brahmā Sahampati spoke thus, and then he said further:

> 'In Magadha there have appeared till now
> Impure teachings devised by those still stained.

'Open the doors to the Deathless! Let them hear
The Dhamma that the stainless one has found.

'Just as one who stands on a mountain peak
Can see below the people all around,
So, O wise one, all-seeing sage,
Ascend the palace of the Dhamma.
Let the sorrowless one survey this human breed,
Engulfed in sorrow, overcome by birth and old age.

'Arise, victorious hero, caravan leader,
Debtless one, and wander in the world.
Let the Blessed One teach the Dhamma,
There will be those who will understand.'

21. "Then I listened to the Brahmā's pleading, and out of compassion for beings I surveyed the world with the eye of a Buddha. Surveying the world with the eye of a Buddha, I saw beings with little dust in their eyes and with much dust in their eyes, with keen faculties and with dull faculties, with good qualities and with bad qualities, easy to teach and hard to teach, and some who dwelled seeing fear and blame in the other world. Just as in a pond of blue or red or white lotuses, some lotuses that are born and grow in the water thrive immersed in the water without rising out of it, and some other lotuses that are born and grow in the water rest on the water's surface, and some other lotuses that are born and grow in the water rise out of the water and stand clear, unwetted by it; so too, surveying the world with the eye of a Buddha, I saw beings with little dust in their eyes and with much dust in their eyes, with keen faculties and with dull faculties, with good qualities and with bad qualities, easy to teach and hard to teach, and some who dwelled seeing fear and blame in the other world. Then I replied to the Brahmā Sahampati in stanzas:

'Open for them are the doors to the Deathless,
Let those with ears now show their faith.
Thinking it would be troublesome, O Brahmā,
I did not speak the Dhamma subtle and sublime.'

"Then the Brahmā Sahampati thought: 'The Blessed One has consented to my request that he teach the Dhamma.' And after paying homage to me, keeping me on the right, he thereupon departed at once.

22. "I considered thus: 'To whom should I first teach the Dhamma? Who will understand this Dhamma quickly?' It then occurred to me: 'Āḷāra Kālāma is wise, intelligent, and discerning; he has long had little dust in his eyes. Suppose I taught the Dhamma first to Āḷāra Kālāma. He will understand it quickly.' Then deities approached me and said: 'Venerable sir, Āḷāra Kālāma died seven days ago.' And the knowledge and vision arose in me: 'Āḷāra Kālāma died seven days ago.' I thought: 'Āḷāra Kālāma's loss is a great one. If he had heard this Dhamma, he would have understood it quickly.'

23. "I considered thus: 'To whom should I first teach the Dhamma? Who will understand this Dhamma quickly?' It then occurred to me: 'Uddaka Rāmaputta is wise, intelligent, and discerning; he has long had little dust in his eyes. Suppose I taught the Dhamma first to Uddaka Rāmaputta. He will understand it quickly.' Then deities approached me and said: 'Venerable sir, Uddaka Rāmaputta died last night.' And the knowledge and vision arose in me: 'Uddaka Rāmaputta died last night.' I thought: 'Uddaka Rāmaputta's loss is a great one. If he had heard this Dhamma, he would have understood it quickly.'

24. "I considered thus: 'To whom should I first teach the Dhamma? Who will understand this Dhamma quickly?' It then occurred to me: 'The monks of the group of five who attended upon me while I was engaged in my striving were very helpful.[27] Suppose I taught the Dhamma first to them.' Then I thought: 'Where are the monks of the group of five now living?' And with the divine eye, which is purified and surpasses the human, I saw that they were living at Bārāṇasī in the Deer Park at Isipatana.

25. "Then, monks, when I had stayed at Uruvelā as long as I chose, I set out to wander by stages to Bārāṇasī. Between Gayā and the Bodhi, the Ājīvaka Upaka saw me on the road and said: 'Friend, your faculties are clear, the color of your skin is pure and bright. Under whom have you gone forth, friend? Who is your teacher? Whose Dhamma do you profess?' I replied to the Ājīvaka Upaka in stanzas:

'I am one who has transcended all, a knower of all,
Unsullied among all things, renouncing all,
By craving's ceasing freed. Having known this all
For myself, to whom should I point as teacher?

'I have no teacher, and one like me
Exists nowhere in all the world
With all its devas, because I have
No person for my counterpart.

'For I am the arahant in the world,
I am the teacher supreme.
I alone am a Perfectly Enlightened One
Whose fires are quenched and extinguished.

'I go now to the city of Kāsi
To set in motion the wheel of Dhamma.
In a world that has become blind
I go to beat the drum of the Deathless.'

'By your claims, friend, you ought to be the universal victor.'[28]

'The victors are those like me
Who have won the destruction of taints.
I have vanquished all evil states,
Therefore, Upaka, I am a victor.'

"When this was said, the Ājīvaka Upaka said: 'May it be so, friend.' Shaking his head, he took a bypath and departed.

26. "Then, monks, wandering by stages, I eventually came to Bārāṇasī, to the Deer Park at Isipatana, and I approached the monks of the group of five. The monks saw me coming in the distance, and they agreed among themselves thus: 'Friends, here comes the ascetic Gotama who lives luxuriously, who gave up his striving and reverted to luxury. We should not pay homage to him or rise up for him or receive his bowl and outer robe. But a seat may be prepared for him. If he likes, he may sit down.' However, as I approached, those monks found themselves unable to keep their pact. One came to meet me and

took my bowl and outer robe, another prepared a seat, and another set out water for my feet; however, they addressed me by name and as 'friend.'[29]

27. "Thereupon I told them: 'Monks, do not address the Tathāgata by name and as "friend." The Tathāgata is an Arahant, a Perfectly Enlightened One. Listen, monks, the Deathless has been attained. I shall instruct you, I shall teach you the Dhamma. Practicing as you are instructed, by realizing it for yourselves here and now through direct knowledge you will soon enter and dwell in that supreme goal of the holy life for the sake of which clansmen rightly go forth from the home life into homelessness.'

"When this was said, the monks of the group of five answered me thus: 'Friend Gotama, by the conduct, the practice, and the performance of austerities that you undertook, you did not achieve any superhuman distinction in knowledge and vision worthy of the noble ones. Since you now live luxuriously, having given up your striving and reverted to luxury, how could you have achieved any superhuman distinction in knowledge and vision worthy of the noble ones?' When this was said, I told them: 'The Tathāgata does not live luxuriously, nor has he given up his striving and reverted to luxury. The Tathāgata is an Arahant, a Perfectly Enlightened One. Listen, monks, the Deathless has been attained ... from the home life into homelessness.'

"A second time the monks of the group of five said to me: 'Friend Gotama ... how could you have achieved any superhuman distinction in knowledge and vision worthy of the noble ones?' A second time I told them: 'The Tathāgata does not live luxuriously ... from the home life into homelessness.' A third time the monks of the group of five said to me: 'Friend Gotama ... how could you have achieved any superhuman distinction in knowledge and vision worthy of the noble ones?'

28. "When this was said I asked them: 'Monks, have you ever known me to speak like this before?'—'No, venerable sir.'[30]—'Monks, the Tathāgata is an Arahant, a Perfectly Enlightened One. Listen, monks, the Deathless has been attained. I shall instruct you, I shall teach you the Dhamma. Practicing as you are instructed, by realizing it for yourselves here and now through direct knowledge, you will soon enter and dwell in that supreme goal of the holy life for the sake of which clansmen rightly go forth from the home life into homelessness.'

29. "I was able to convince the monks of the group of five.[31] Then I sometimes instructed two monks while the other three went for alms, and the six of us lived on what those three monks brought back from their almsround. Sometimes I instructed three monks while the other two went for alms, and the six of us lived on what those two monks brought back from their almsround.

30. "Then the monks of the group of five, thus taught and instructed by me, being themselves subject to birth, having understood the danger in what is subject to birth, seeking the unborn supreme security from bondage, Nibbāna, attained the unborn supreme security from bondage, Nibbāna; being themselves subject to aging, sickness, death, sorrow, and defilement, having understood the danger in what is subject to aging, sickness, death, sorrow, and defilement, seeking the unaging, unailing, deathless, sorrowless, and undefiled supreme security from bondage, Nibbāna, they attained the unaging, unailing, deathless, sorrowless, and undefiled supreme security from bondage, Nibbāna. The knowledge and vision arose in them: 'Our liberation is unshakable; this is our last birth; now there is no more renewed existence.'"

(from MN 26: *Ariyapariyesana Sutta*; I 167–73)

5. The First Discourse

Thus have I heard. On one occasion the Blessed One was dwelling at Bārāṇasī in the Deer Park at Isipatana. There the Blessed One addressed the monks of the group of five thus:

"Monks, these two extremes should not be followed by one who has gone forth into homelessness. What two? The pursuit of sensual happiness in sensual pleasures, which is low, vulgar, the way of worldlings, ignoble, unbeneficial; and the pursuit of self-mortification, which is painful, ignoble, unbeneficial. Without veering toward either of these extremes, the Tathāgata has awakened to the middle way, which gives rise to vision, which gives rise to knowledge, and leads to peace, to direct knowledge, to enlightenment, to Nibbāna.

"And what, monks, is that middle way awakened to by the Tathāgata? It is this Noble Eightfold Path; that is, right view, right intention, right speech, right action, right livelihood, right effort, right mindfulness, right concentration. This, monks, is that middle way awakened to by the Tathāgata, which gives rise to vision, which gives rise to knowledge, and leads to peace, to direct knowledge, to enlightenment, to Nibbāna.

"Now this, monks, is the noble truth of suffering: birth is suffering, aging is suffering, illness is suffering, death is suffering; union with what is displeasing is suffering; separation from what is pleasing is suffering; not to get what one wants is suffering; in brief, the five aggregates subject to clinging are suffering.

"Now this, monks, is the noble truth of the origin of suffering: it is this craving that leads to renewed existence, accompanied by delight and lust, seeking delight here and there; that is, craving for sensual pleasures, craving for existence, craving for extermination.

"Now this, monks, is the noble truth of the cessation of suffering: it is the remainderless fading away and cessation of that same craving, the giving up and relinquishing of it, freedom from it, nonattachment.

"Now this, monks, is the noble truth of the way leading to the cessation of suffering: it is this Noble Eightfold Path; that is, right view ... right concentration.

"'This is the noble truth of suffering': thus, monks, in regard to things unheard before, there arose in me vision, knowledge, wisdom, penetration, and light.[32]

"'This noble truth of suffering is to be fully understood': thus, monks, in regard to things unheard before, there arose in me vision, knowledge, wisdom, penetration, and light.[33]

"'This noble truth of suffering has been fully understood': thus, monks, in regard to things unheard before, there arose in me vision, knowledge, wisdom, penetration, and light.[34]

"'This is the noble truth of the origin of suffering': thus, monks, in regard to things unheard before, there arose in me vision, knowledge, wisdom, penetration, and light.

"'This noble truth of the origin of suffering is to be abandoned': thus, monks, in regard to things unheard before, there arose in me vision, knowledge, wisdom, penetration, and light.

"'This noble truth of the origin of suffering has been abandoned': thus, monks, in regard to things unheard before, there arose in me vision, knowledge, wisdom, penetration, and light.

"'This is the noble truth of the cessation of suffering': thus, monks, in regard to things unheard before, there arose in me vision, knowledge, wisdom, penetration, and light.

"'This noble truth of the cessation of suffering is to be realized': thus, monks, in regard to things unheard before, there arose in me vision, knowledge, wisdom, penetration, and light.

"'This noble truth of the cessation of suffering has been realized': thus, monks, in regard to things unheard before, there arose in me vision, knowledge, wisdom, penetration, and light.

"'This is the noble truth of the way leading to the cessation of suffering': thus, monks, in regard to things unheard before, there arose in me vision, knowledge, wisdom, penetration, and light.

"'This noble truth of the way leading to the cessation of suffering is to be developed': thus, monks, in regard to things unheard before, there arose in me vision, knowledge, wisdom, penetration, and light.

"'This noble truth of the way leading to the cessation of suffering has been developed': thus, monks, in regard to things unheard before, there arose in me vision, knowledge, wisdom, penetration, and light.

"So long, monks, as my knowledge and vision of these Four Noble Truths as they really are in their three phases and twelve aspects was not thoroughly purified in this way,[35] I did not claim to have awakened to the unsurpassed perfect enlightenment in this world with its devas, Māra, and Brahmā, in this population with its ascetics and brahmins, its devas and humans. But when my knowledge and vision of these Four Noble Truths as they really are in their three phases and twelve aspects was thoroughly purified in this way, then I claimed to have awakened to the unsurpassed perfect enlightenment in this world with its devas, Māra, and Brahmā, in this population with its ascetics and brahmins, its devas and humans. The knowledge and vision arose in me: 'Unshakable is the liberation of my mind. This is my last birth. Now there is no more renewed existence.'"

This is what the Blessed One said. Elated, the monks of the group of five delighted in the Blessed One's statement. And while this discourse was being spoken, there arose in the Venerable Koṇḍañña the dust-free, stainless vision of the Dhamma: "Whatever is subject to origination is all subject to cessation."[36]

And when the wheel of the Dhamma had been set in motion by the Blessed One, the earth-dwelling devas raised a cry: "At Bārāṇasī, in the Deer Park at Isipatana, this unsurpassed wheel of the Dhamma has been set in motion by the Blessed One, which cannot be stopped by any ascetic or brahmin or deva or Māra or Brahmā or by anyone in the world." Having heard the cry of the earth-dwelling devas, the devas of the realm of the Four Great Kings raised a cry: "At Bārāṇasī ... this unsurpassed wheel of the Dhamma has been set in motion by the Blessed One, which cannot be stopped ... by anyone in the world." Having heard the cry of the devas of the realm of the Four Great Kings, the Tāvatiṃsa devas ... the Yāma devas ... the Tusita devas ... the devas who delight in creating ... the devas who wield power over others' creations ... the devas of Brahmā's company[37] raised a cry: "At Bārāṇasī, in the Deer Park at Isipatana, this unsurpassed wheel of the Dhamma has been set in motion by the Blessed One, which cannot be stopped by any ascetic or brahmin or deva or Māra or Brahmā or by anyone in the world."

Thus at that moment, at that instant, at that second, the cry spread as far as the brahma world, and this ten-thousand-fold world system shook, quaked, and trembled, and an immeasurable great radiance surpassing the divine majesty of the devas appeared in the world.

Then the Blessed One uttered this inspired utterance: "Koṇḍañña has indeed understood! Koṇḍañña has indeed understood!" In this way the Venerable Koṇḍañña acquired the name "Aññā Koṇḍañña—Koṇḍañña Who Has Understood."

(SN 56:11: *Dhammacakkappavattana Sutta;* V 420–24)

III. Approaching the Dhamma

Introduction

One of the most distressing predicaments any earnest, open-minded spiritual seeker might face is the sheer difficulty of choosing from among the bewildering diversity of religious and spiritual teachings available. By their very nature, spiritual teachings make claims upon our allegiance that are absolute and all-encompassing. Adherents of a particular creed are prone to assert that their religion *alone* reveals the final truth about our place in the universe and our ultimate destiny; they boldly propose that their path *alone* offers the sure means to eternal salvation. If we could suspend all belief commitments and compare the competing doctrines impartially, submitting them to empirical tests, we would have a sure-fire method of deciding between them, and then our ordeal would be over. But it isn't that simple. Rival religions all propose—or presuppose—doctrines that we cannot directly validate by personal experience; they advocate tenets that call for some degree of trust. So, as their tenets and practices clash, we run up against the problem of finding some way to decide between them and negotiate their competing claims to truth.

One solution to this problem is to deny that there is any real conflict between alternative belief systems. The adherents of this approach, which we might call religious universalism, say that at their core all spiritual traditions teach essentially the same thing. Their formulations may differ but their inner core is the same, expressed differently merely to accord with different sensibilities. What we need to do, the universalist says, when faced with different spiritual traditions, is to extract the kernel of inner truth from the pods of their exoteric creeds. From ground level our goals look different, but from the heights we will find the goal is the same; it is like the view of the moon from different mountain peaks. Universalists in matters of doctrine often endorse eclecticism in practice, holding that we can select whatever practices we prefer and combine them like dishes at a buffet.

This solution to the problem of religious diversity has an immediate appeal to those disillusioned with the exclusive claims of dogmatic religion. Honest critical reflection, however, would show that on the most vital issues the different religions and spiritual traditions take different standpoints. They give us very different answers to our questions concerning the basic grounds and goals of the spiritual quest and often these differences are not merely verbal. To sweep them away as being merely verbal may be an effective way of achieving harmony between followers of different belief systems, but it cannot withstand close examination. In the end, it is as little tenable as saying that, because they have beaks and wings, eagles, sparrows, and chickens are essentially the same type of creature, the differences between them being merely verbal.

It is not only theistic religions that teach doctrines beyond the range of immediate empirical confirmation. The Buddha too taught doctrines that an ordinary person cannot directly confirm by everyday experience, and these doctrines are fundamental to the structure of his teaching. We saw, for example, in the introductions to chapters I and II, that the Nikāyas envisage a universe with many domains of sentient existence spread out in boundless space and time, a universe in which sentient beings roam and wander from life to life on account of their ignorance, craving, and kamma. The Nikāyas presuppose that throughout beginningless time, Buddhas without number have arisen and turned the wheel of the Dhamma, and that each Buddha attains enlightenment after cultivating spiritual perfections over long periods of cosmic time. When we approach the Dhamma we are likely to resist such beliefs and feel that they make excessive demands on our capacity for trust. Thus we inevitably run up against the question whether, if we wish to follow the Buddha's teaching, we must take on board the entire package of classical Buddhist doctrine.

For Early Buddhism, all the problems we face in deciding how far we should go in placing faith can be disposed of at a single stroke. That single stroke involves reverting to direct experience as the ultimate basis for judgment. One of the distinctive features of the Buddha's teaching is the respect it accords to direct experience. The texts of Early Buddhism do not teach a secret doctrine, nor do they leave scope for anything like an esoteric path reserved for an élite of initiates and withheld from others. According to **Text III,1**, secrecy in a religious teaching is the hallmark of wrong views and confused thinking. The teaching of the Buddha shines openly, as radiant and brilliant as the light of the sun and moon. Freedom from the cloak of secrecy is integral to a teaching that gives primacy to direct experience, inviting each individual to test its principles in the crucible of his or her own experience.

This does not mean that an ordinary person can fully validate the Buddha's doctrine by direct experience without special effort. To the contrary, the teaching can only be fully realized through the achievement of certain extraordinary types of experience that are far beyond the range of the ordinary person enmeshed in the concerns of mundane life. However, in sharp contrast to revealed religion, the Buddha does not demand that we *begin* our spiritual quest by placing faith in doctrines that lie beyond the range of our immediate experience. Rather than ask us to wrestle with issues that, *for us in our present condition*, no amount of experience can decide, he instead asks us to consider a few simple questions pertaining to our immediate welfare and happiness, questions that we *can* answer on the basis of personal experience. I highlight the expression "for us in our present condition," because the fact that we cannot presently validate such matters does not constitute grounds for rejecting them as invalid or even as irrelevant. It only means that we should put them aside for the time being and concern ourselves with issues that come within the range of direct experience.

The Buddha says that his teaching is about suffering and the cessation of suffering. This statement does not mean that the Dhamma is concerned *only* with our experience of suffering in the present life, but it does imply that we can use our present experience, backed by intelligent observation, as a criterion for determining what is beneficial and what detrimental to our spiritual progress. Our most insistent existential demand, springing up deep within us, is the need for freedom from harm, sorrow, and distress; or, positively stated, the need to achieve well-being and happiness. However, to avoid harm and to secure our well-being, it is not sufficient for us merely to hope. We first have to understand the conditions on which they depend. According to the Buddha, whatever arises, arises through appropriate causes and conditions, and this applies with equal force to suffering and happiness. Thus we must ascertain the causes and conditions that lead to harm and suffering, and likewise the causes and conditions that lead to well-being and happiness. Once we have extracted these two principles—

the conditions leading to harm and suffering, and the conditions leading to well-being and happiness—we have at our disposal an outline of the entire process that leads to the ultimate goal, final liberation from suffering.

One text offering an excellent example of this approach is a short discourse in the Aṅguttara Nikāya popularly known as the Kālāma Sutta, included as **Text III,2**. The Kālāmas were a people living in a remote area of the Ganges plain. Various religious teachers would come to visit them and each would extol his own doctrine and tear down the doctrines of his rivals. Confused and perplexed by this conflict of belief systems, the Kālāmas did not know whom to trust. When the Buddha passed through their town, they approached him and asked him to clear away their doubts. Though the text does not specify what particular issues were troubling the Kālāmas, the later part of the discourse makes it clear that their perplexities revolved around the questions of rebirth and kamma.

The Buddha began by assuring the Kālāmas that under such circumstances it was proper for them to doubt, for the issues that troubled them were indeed common sources of doubt and perplexity. He then told them not to rely on ten sources of belief. Four of these pertain to established scriptural authority (oral tradition, lineage of teaching, hearsay, and collections of texts); four to rational grounds (logic, inferential reasoning, reasoned cogitation, and the acceptance of a view after pondering it); and two to authoritative persons (impressive speakers and respected teachers). This advice is sometimes quoted to prove that the Buddha rejected all external authorities and invited each individual to fashion his or her own personal path to truth. Read in context, however, the message of the Kālāma Sutta is quite different. The Buddha is not advising the Kālāmas—who, it must be stressed, had at this point not yet become his own disciples—to reject all authoritative guides to spiritual understanding and fall back solely on their personal intuition. Rather, he is offering them a simple and pragmatic outlet from the morass of doubt and perplexity in which they are immersed. By the use of skillful methods of inquiry, he leads them to understand a number of basic principles that they can verify by their own experience and thereby acquire a sure starting point for further spiritual development.[1]

Always underlying the Buddha's questions and their replies is the tacit premise that people are primarily motivated to act by a concern for their own welfare and happiness. In asking this particular set of questions, the Buddha's purpose is to lead the Kālāmas to see that, even when we suspend all concern with future lives, unwholesome mental states such as greed, hatred, and delusion, and unwholesome actions such as killing and stealing, eventually redound to one's own harm and suffering right here and now. Conversely, wholesome mental states and wholesome actions promote one's long-term welfare and happiness here and now. Once this much is seen, the immediately visible harmful consequences to which unwholesome mental states lead become a sufficient reason for abandoning them, while the visible benefits to which wholesome mental states lead become a sufficient motivation for cultivating them. Then, whether or not there is a life after death, one has adequate reasons *in the present life* to abandon unwholesome mental states and cultivate wholesome mental states. If there is an afterlife, one's recompense is simply that much greater.

A similar approach underlies **Text III,3**, in which the Buddha demonstrates how present suffering arises and ceases in correlation with present craving. This short sutta, addressed to a lay follower, concisely articulates the causal principle that lies behind the Four Noble Truths, but rather than doing so in the abstract, it adopts a concrete, down-to-earth approach that has a remarkably contemporary appeal. By using powerful examples drawn from the life of a layman deeply attached to his wife and son, the sutta makes a deep and lasting impression on us.

The fact that such texts as this sutta and the Kālāma Sutta do not dwell on the doctrines of kamma and rebirth does not mean, as is sometimes assumed, that such teachings are mere cultural accretions to the Dhamma that can be deleted or explained away without losing anything essential. It means only that, *at the outset*, the Dhamma can be approached in ways that do not require reference to past and future lives. The Buddha's teaching has many sides, and thus, from certain angles, it can be directly evaluated against our concern for our present well-being and happiness. Once we see that the practice of the teaching does indeed bring peace, joy, and inner security in this very life, this will inspire our trust and confidence in the Dhamma as a whole, including those aspects that lie beyond our present capacity for personal verification. If we were to undertake certain practices—practices that require highly refined skills and determined effort—we would be able to acquire the faculties needed to validate those other aspects, such as the law of kamma, the reality of rebirth, and the existence of supersensible realms (see **Text VII,4** §§23–24 and **Text VII,5** §§19–20).

Another major problem that often besets spiritual seekers is the demands that teachers place upon their capacity for trust. This problem has become especially acute in our own time, when the news media gleefully spotlight the frailties of numberless gurus and jump at the chance to show up any modern-day saint as nothing better than a swindler in robes. But the problem of rogue gurus is a perennial one by no means peculiar to our age. Whenever one person exercises spiritual authority over others, it is only too easy for that person to be tempted to exploit the trust others place in him in ways that can be seriously detrimental to himself and his disciples. When a pupil approaches a teacher who claims to be perfectly enlightened and thus capable of teaching the path to final liberation, the pupil must have some criteria at hand for testing the teacher to determine whether the teacher truly measures up to the lofty claims he makes about himself—or that others make about him.

In the Vīmaṃsaka Sutta—**Text III,4**—the Buddha lays down guidelines by which a monk can test "the Tathāgata," that is, the Buddha, to evaluate his claim to be perfectly enlightened. One benchmark of perfect enlightenment is freedom of the mind from all defilements. If a monk cannot directly see into the Buddha's own mind, he can nevertheless rely on indirect evidence to ascertain that the Buddha is freed from defilements; that is, by evaluating the Buddha's bodily deeds and speech he can infer that the Buddha's mental states are exclusively pure, uninfluenced by greed, hatred, and delusion. In addition to such observational inference, the Buddha further encourages the monk to approach him and directly inquire about his mental states.

Once the pupil gains confidence that the Buddha is a qualified teacher, he then puts the Master to the ultimate test. He learns his teaching, enters upon the practice, and penetrates the Dhamma by direct knowledge. This act of penetration—here equivalent at minimum to the attainment of stream-entry—brings the gain of "invincible faith," the faith of one who is established upon the irreversible path leading to final release.

Taken in isolation, the Vīmaṃsaka Sutta might give the impression that one acquires faith only after gaining realization of the teaching, and since realization is self-validating, faith would then become redundant. This impression, however, would be one-sided. The point the sutta is making is that faith becomes *invincible* as a result of realization, not that faith first enters the spiritual path only when one attains realization. Faith is the first of the five spiritual faculties, and in some degree, as trusting confidence in the Buddha's enlightenment and in the main principles of his teaching, it is a prerequisite for the higher training. We see faith functioning in this preparatory role in **Text III,5**, a long excerpt from the Caṅkī Sutta. Here, the Buddha explains that a person who has faith in something "preserves truth" when he says "this is my faith." He "preserves truth" because he merely states what he believes without jumping to the conclusion that what he believes is definitely true and anything else contrary to it false. The Buddha contrasts the "preservation of truth" (*saccānurakkhanā*) with the "discovery of truth" (*saccānubodha*), which begins by placing faith in a teacher who has proved himself worthy of trust. Having gained faith in such a teacher, one then approaches him for instruction, learns the Dhamma, practices it (according to a series of steps more finely calibrated than in the preceding text), and finally sees the supreme truth for oneself.

This does not yet mark the end of the road for the disciple, but only the initial breakthrough to the truth, again corresponding to the attainment of stream-entry. Having achieved the vision of truth, to reach the "final arrival at truth" (*saccānupatti*)—that is, the attainment of arahantship or final liberation—one must repeat, develop, and cultivate the same series of steps until one has fully absorbed and assimilated the supreme truth disclosed by that initial vision. Thus the entire process of training in the Dhamma is rooted in personal experience. Even faith should be rooted in investigation and inquiry and not based solely upon emotional leanings and blind belief. Faith alone is insufficient but is the door to deeper levels of experience. Faith serves as a spur to practice; practice leads to experiential understanding; and when one's understanding matures, it blossoms in full realization.

III. Approaching the Dhamma

1. Not a Secret Doctrine

"These three things, monks, are conducted in secret, not openly. What three? Affairs with women, the mantras of the brahmins, and wrong view.

"But these three things, monks, shine openly, not in secret. What three? The moon, the sun, and the Dhamma and Discipline proclaimed by the Tathāgata."

(AN 3:129; I 282–83)

2. No Dogmas or Blind Belief

Thus have I heard. On one occasion the Blessed One was wandering on tour together with a large Saṅgha of monks when he arrived at a town of the Kālāmas named Kesaputta.[2] Now the Kālāmas of Kesaputta heard: "It is said that the ascetic Gotama, the Sakyan son who went forth from a Sakyan family, has arrived at Kesaputta. Now a good report about that master Gotama has been circulating thus: 'That Blessed One is an arahant, perfectly enlightened, accomplished in true knowledge and conduct, fortunate, knower of the world, unsurpassed leader of persons to be tamed, teacher of devas and humans, the Enlightened One, the Blessed One. Having realized with his own direct knowledge this world with its devas, Māra, and Brahmā, this population with its ascetics and brahmins, with its devas and humans, he makes it known to others. He teaches a Dhamma that is good in the beginning, good in the middle, and good in the end, with the right meaning and expression; he reveals a spiritual life that is perfectly complete and purified.' Now it is good to see such arahants."[3]

Then the Kālāmas of Kesaputta approached the Blessed One. Some paid homage to him and sat down to one side; some exchanged greetings with him and, after their greetings and cordial talk, sat down to one side; some saluted him reverentially and sat down to one side; some remained silent and sat down to one side. Then the Kālāmas said to the Blessed One:

"Venerable sir, some ascetics and brahmins who come to Kesaputta explain and elucidate their own doctrines, but disparage, debunk, revile, and vilify the doctrines of others. But then some other ascetics and brahmins come to Kesaputta, and they too explain and elucidate their own doctrines, but disparage, debunk, revile, and vilify the doctrines of the others. For us, venerable sir, there is perplexity and doubt as to which of these good ascetics speak truth and which speak falsehood."

"It is fitting for you to be perplexed, O Kālāmas, it is fitting for you to be in doubt. Doubt has arisen in you about a perplexing matter. Come, Kālāmas. Do not go by oral tradition, by lineage of teaching, by hearsay, by a collection of texts, by logic, by inferential reasoning, by reasoned cogitation, by the acceptance of a view after pondering it, by the seeming competence of a speaker, or because you think, 'The ascetic is our teacher.'[4] But when you know for yourselves, 'These things are unwholesome; these things are blamable; these things are censured by the wise; these things, if undertaken and practiced, lead to harm and suffering,' then you should abandon them.

"What do you think, Kālāmas? When greed, hatred, and delusion arise in a person, is it for his welfare or harm?"[5]—"For his harm, venerable sir."—"Kālāmas, a person who is greedy, hating, and deluded, overpowered by greed, hatred, and delusion, his thoughts controlled by them, will destroy life, take what is not given, engage in sexual misconduct, and tell lies; he will also prompt others to do likewise. Will that conduce to his harm and suffering for a long time?"—"Yes, venerable sir."

"What do you think, Kālāmas? Are these things wholesome or unwholesome?—"Unwholesome, venerable sir."—"Blamable or blameless?"—"Blamable, venerable sir."—"Censured or praised by the wise?"—"Censured, venerable sir."—"Undertaken and practiced, do they lead to harm and suffering or not, or how is it in this case?"—"Undertaken and practiced, these things lead to harm and suffering. So it appears to us in this case."

"It was for this reason, Kālāmas, that we said: Do not go by oral tradition....

"Come, Kālāmas. Do not go by oral tradition, by lineage of teaching, by hearsay, by a collection of texts, by logic, by inferential reasoning, by reasoned cogitation, by the acceptance of a view after pondering it, by the seeming competence of a speaker, or because you think, 'The ascetic is our teacher.' But when you know for yourselves, 'These things are wholesome; these things are blameless; these things are praised by the wise; these things, if undertaken and practiced, lead to welfare and happiness,' then you should engage in them.

"What do you think, Kālāmas? When nongreed, nonhatred, and nondelusion arise in a person, is it for his welfare or harm?"—"For his welfare, venerable sir."—"Kālāmas, a person who is without greed, without hatred, without delusion, not overpowered by greed, hatred, and delusion, his thoughts not controlled by them, will abstain from the destruction of life, from taking what is not given, from sexual misconduct, and from false speech; he will also prompt others to do likewise. Will that conduce to his welfare and happiness for a long time?"—"Yes, venerable sir."

"What do you think, Kālāmas? Are these things wholesome or unwholesome?—"Wholesome, venerable sir."—"Blamable or blameless?"—"Blameless, venerable sir."—"Censured or praised by the wise?"—"Praised, venerable sir."—"Undertaken and practiced, do they lead to welfare and happiness or not, or how is it in this case?"—"Undertaken and practiced, these things lead to welfare and happiness. So it appears to us in this case."

"It was for this reason, Kālāmas, that we said: Do not go upon oral tradition....

"Then, Kālāmas, that noble disciple—devoid of covetousness, devoid of ill will, unconfused, clearly comprehending, ever mindful—dwells pervading one quarter with a mind imbued with loving-kindness, likewise the second quarter, the third, and the fourth.[6] Thus above, below, across, and everywhere, and to all as to himself, he dwells pervading the entire world with a mind imbued with loving-kindness, vast, exalted, measureless, without hostility and without ill will.

"He dwells pervading one quarter with a mind imbued with compassion ... with altruistic joy ... with equanimity, likewise the second quarter, the third, and the fourth. Thus above, below, across, and everywhere, and to all as to himself, he dwells pervading the entire world with a mind imbued with equanimity, vast, exalted, measureless, without hostility and without ill will.

"When, Kālāmas, this noble disciple has thus made his mind free of enmity, free of ill will, uncorrupted and pure, he has won four assurances in this very life.

"The first assurance he has won is this: 'If there is another world, and if good and bad deeds bear fruit and yield results, it is possible that with the breakup of the body, after death, I shall arise in a good destination, in a heavenly world.'

"The second assurance he has won is this: 'If there is no other world, and if good and bad deeds do not bear fruit and yield results, still right here, in this very life, I live happily, free of enmity and ill will.

"The third assurance he has won is this: 'Suppose evil befalls the evil-doer. Then, as I do not intend evil for anyone, how can suffering afflict me, one who does no evil deed?'

"The fourth assurance he has won is this: 'Suppose evil does not befall the evil-doer. Then right here I see myself purified in both respects.'[7]

"When, Kālāmas, this noble disciple has thus made his mind free of enmity, free of ill will, uncorrupted, and pure, he has won these four assurances in this very life."

"So it is, Blessed One! So it is, Fortunate One! When this noble disciple has thus made his mind free of enmity, free of ill will, uncorrupted and pure, he has won these four assurances in this very life.

"Magnificent, venerable sir! Magnificent, venerable sir! The Blessed One has made the Dhamma clear in many ways, as though he were turning upright what had been overthrown, revealing what was hidden, showing the way to one who was lost, or holding up a lamp in the darkness so those with good eyesight can see forms. We now go for refuge to the Blessed One, to the Dhamma, and to the Saṅgha of monks. Let the Blessed One accept us as lay followers who have gone for refuge from today until life's end."[8]

(AN 3:65; I 188–93)

3. The Visible Origin and Passing Away of Suffering

On one occasion the Blessed One was dwelling at a town of the Mallans named Uruvelakappa. Then Bhadraka the headman[9] approached the Blessed One, paid homage to him, sat down to one side, and said to him: "It would be good, venerable sir, if the Blessed One would teach me about the origin and the passing away of suffering."

"If, headman, I were to teach you about the origin and the passing away of suffering with reference to the past, saying, 'So it was in the past,' perplexity and uncertainty about that might arise in you. And if I were to teach you about the origin and the passing away of suffering with reference to the future, saying, 'So it will be in the future,' perplexity and uncertainty about that might arise in you. Instead, headman, while I am sitting right here, and you are sitting right there, I will teach you about the origin and the passing away of suffering. Listen and attend closely, I will speak."

"Yes, venerable sir," Bhadraka replied. The Blessed One said this:

"What do you think, headman? Are there any people in Uruvelakappa on whose account sorrow, lamentation, pain, dejection, and despair would arise in you if they were to be executed, imprisoned, fined, or censured?"

"There are such people, venerable sir."

"But are there any people in Uruvelakappa on whose account sorrow, lamentation, pain, dejection, and despair would not arise in you in such an event?"

"There are such people, venerable sir."

"Why is it, headman, that in relation to some people in Uruvelakappa sorrow, lamentation, pain, dejection, and despair would arise in you if they were to be executed, imprisoned, fined, or censured, while in regard to others they would not arise in you?"

"Those people in Uruvelakappa, venerable sir, in relation to whom sorrow, lamentation, pain, dejection, and despair would arise in me if they were to be executed, imprisoned, fined, or censured—these are the ones for whom I have desire and attachment. But those people in Uruvelakappa in relation to whom they would not arise in me—these are the ones for whom I have no desire and attachment."

"Headman, by means of this principle that is seen, understood, immediately attained, fathomed, apply the method to the past and to the future thus: 'Whatever suffering arose in the past, all that arose rooted in desire, with desire as its source; for desire is the root of suffering. Whatever suffering will arise in the future, all that will arise rooted in desire, with desire as its source; for desire is the root of suffering.'"

"It is wonderful, venerable sir! It is amazing, venerable sir! How well that has been stated by the Blessed One: 'Whatever suffering arises, all that is rooted in desire, has desire as its source; for desire is the root of suffering.'[10] Venerable sir, I have a son named Ciravāsī, who stays at an outside residence. I rise early and send a man, saying, 'Go, man, and find out how Ciravāsī is.' Until that man returns, venerable sir, I am upset, thinking, 'I hope Ciravāsī has not met with any affliction!'"

"What do you think, headman? If Ciravāsī were to be executed, imprisoned, fined, or censured, would sorrow, lamentation, pain, dejection, and despair arise in you?"

"Venerable sir, if Ciravāsī were to be executed, imprisoned, fined, or censured, even my life would seem futile, so how could sorrow, lamentation, pain, dejection, and despair not arise in me?"

"In this way too, headman, it can be understood: 'Whatever suffering arises, all that arises rooted in desire, with desire as its source; for desire is the root of suffering.'

"What do you think, headman? Before you saw your wife or heard about her, did you have any desire, attachment, or affection for her?"

"No, venerable sir."

"Then was it, headman, only when you saw her or heard about her that this desire, attachment, and affection arose in you?"

"Yes, venerable sir."

"What do you think, headman? If your wife were to be executed, imprisoned, fined, or censured, would sorrow, lamentation, pain, dejection, and despair arise in you?"

"Venerable sir, if my wife were to be executed, imprisoned, fined, or censured, even my life would seem futile, so how could sorrow, lamentation, pain, dejection, and despair not arise in me?"

"In this way too, headman, it can be understood: 'Whatever suffering arises, all that arises rooted in desire, with desire as its source; for desire is the root of suffering.'"

(SN 42:11; IV 327–30)

4. Investigate the Teacher Himself

1. Thus have I heard. On one occasion the Blessed One was living at Sāvatthī in Jeta's Grove, Anāthapiṇḍika's Park. There he addressed the

monks thus: "Monks!"—"Venerable sir!" they replied. The Blessed One said this:

2. "Monks, a monk who is an inquirer, not knowing how to gauge another's mind,[11] should make an investigation of the Tathāgata in order to find out whether or not he is perfectly enlightened."

3. "Venerable sir, our teachings are rooted in the Blessed One, guided by the Blessed One, have the Blessed One as their resort. It would be good if the Blessed One would explain the meaning of these words. Having heard it from him, the monks will remember it."

"Then listen, monks, and attend closely to what I shall say."

"Yes, venerable sir," the monks replied. The Blessed One said this:

4. "Monks, a monk who is an inquirer, not knowing how to gauge another's mind, should investigate the Tathāgata with respect to two kinds of states, states cognizable through the eye and through the ear thus: 'Are there found in the Tathāgata or not any defiled states cognizable through the eye or through the ear?'[12] When he investigates him, he comes to know: 'No defiled states cognizable through the eye or through the ear are found in the Tathāgata.'

5. "When he comes to know this, he investigates him further thus: 'Are there found in the Tathāgata or not any mixed states cognizable through the eye or through the ear?'[13] When he investigates him, he comes to know: 'No mixed states cognizable through the eye or through the ear are found in the Tathāgata.'

6. "When he comes to know this, he investigates him further thus: 'Are there found in the Tathāgata or not cleansed states cognizable through the eye or through the ear?' When he investigates him, he comes to know: 'Cleansed states cognizable through the eye or through the ear are found in the Tathāgata.'

7. "When he comes to know this, he investigates him further thus: 'Has this venerable one attained this wholesome state over a long time or did he attain it recently?' When he investigates him, he comes to know: 'This venerable one has attained this wholesome state over a long time; he did not attain it only recently.'

8. "When he comes to know this, he investigates him further thus: 'Has this venerable one acquired renown and attained fame, so that the dangers [connected with renown and fame] are found in him?' For, monks, as long as a monk has not acquired renown and attained fame, the dangers [connected with renown and fame] are not found in him;

but when he has acquired renown and attained fame, those dangers are found in him.[14] When he investigates him, he comes to know: 'This venerable one has acquired renown and attained fame, but the dangers [connected with renown and fame] are not found in him.'

9. "When he comes to know this, he investigates him further thus: 'Is this venerable one restrained without fear, not restrained by fear, and does he avoid indulging in sensual pleasures because he is without lust through the destruction of lust?' When he investigates him, he comes to know: 'This venerable one is restrained without fear, not restrained by fear, and he avoids indulging in sensual pleasure because he is without lust through the destruction of lust.'

10. "Now, monks, if others should ask that monk thus: 'What are the venerable one's reasons and what is his evidence whereby he says: "That venerable one is restrained without fear, not restrained by fear, and he avoids indulging in sensual pleasures because he is without lust through the destruction of lust"?'—answering rightly, that monk would answer thus: 'Whether that venerable one dwells in the Saṅgha or alone, while some there are well behaved and some are ill behaved and some there teach a group, while some here are seen concerned about material things and some are unsullied by material things, still that venerable one does not despise anyone because of that.[15] And I have heard and learned this from the Blessed One's own lips: "I am restrained without fear, not restrained by fear, and I avoid indulging in sensual pleasures because I am without lust through the destruction of lust."'

11. "The Tathāgata, monks, should be questioned further about that thus: 'Are there found in the Tathāgata or not any defiled states cognizable through the eye or through the ear?' The Tathāgata would answer thus: 'No defiled states cognizable through the eye or through the ear are found in the Tathāgata.'

12. "If asked, 'Are there found in the Tathāgata or not any mixed states cognizable through the eye or through the ear?' the Tathāgata would answer thus: 'No mixed states cognizable through the eye or through the ear are found in the Tathāgata.'

13. "If asked, 'Are there found in the Tathāgata or not cleansed states cognizable through the eye or through the ear?' the Tathāgata would answer thus: 'Cleansed states cognizable through the eye or through the ear are found in the Tathāgata. They are my pathway and my domain, yet I do not identify with them.'

14. "Monks, a disciple should approach the Teacher who speaks thus in order to hear the Dhamma. The Teacher teaches him the Dhamma with its successively higher levels, with its successively more sublime levels, with its dark and bright counterparts. As the Teacher teaches the Dhamma to a monk in this way, through direct knowledge of a certain teaching here in that Dhamma, the monk comes to a conclusion about the teachings.[16] He places confidence in the Teacher thus: 'The Blessed One is perfectly enlightened, the Dhamma is well proclaimed by the Blessed One, the Saṅgha is practicing the good way.'

15. "Now if others should ask that monk thus: 'What are the venerable one's reasons and what is his evidence whereby he says, "The Blessed One is perfectly enlightened, the Dhamma is well proclaimed by the Blessed One, the Saṅgha is practicing the good way"?'—answering rightly, that monk would answer thus: 'Here, friends, I approached the Blessed One in order to hear the Dhamma. The Blessed One taught me the Dhamma with its successively higher levels, with its successively more sublime levels, with its dark and bright counterparts. As the Blessed One taught the Dhamma to me in this way, through direct knowledge of a certain teaching here in that Dhamma, I came to a conclusion about the teachings. I placed confidence in the Teacher thus: "The Blessed One is perfectly enlightened, the Dhamma is well proclaimed by the Blessed One, the Saṅgha is practicing the good way."'

16. "Monks, when anyone's faith has been planted, rooted, and established in the Tathāgata through these reasons, terms, and phrases, his faith is said to be supported by reasons, rooted in vision, firm; it is invincible by any ascetic or brahmin or deva or Māra or Brahmā or by anyone in the world.[17] That is how, monks, there is an investigation of the Tathāgata in accordance with the Dhamma, and that is how the Tathāgata is well investigated in accordance with the Dhamma."

That is what the Blessed One said. The monks were satisfied and delighted in the Blessed One's words.

(MN 47: *Vīmaṃsaka Sutta*; I 317–20)

5. Steps toward the Realization of Truth

10. Then the brahmin Caṅkī,[18] together with a large company of brahmins, went to the Blessed One, exchanged greetings with him, and sat down at one side.

11. Now on that occasion the Blessed One was seated finishing some amiable talk with some very senior brahmins. At the time, sitting in the assembly, was a brahmin student named Kāpaṭhika. Young, shaven-headed, sixteen years old, he was a master of the three Vedas with their vocabularies, liturgy, phonology, and etymology, and the histories as a fifth; skilled in philology and grammar, he was fully versed in natural philosophy and in the marks of a great man. While the very senior brahmins were conversing with the Blessed One, he repeatedly broke in and interrupted their talk. Then the Blessed One rebuked the brahmin student Kāpaṭhika thus: "The honorable Bhāradvāja[19] shouldn't break in and interrupt the talk of the very senior brahmins while they are conversing. He should wait until the talk is finished."

When this was said, the brahmin Caṅkī said to the Blessed One: "Master Gotama shouldn't rebuke the brahmin student Kāpaṭhika. This brahmin student is very learned; he has a good delivery; he is wise. He can well take part in this discussion with Master Gotama."

12. Then the Blessed One thought: "Surely, since the brahmins honor him thus, the brahmin student Kāpaṭhika must be accomplished in the scriptures of the three Vedas."

Then the brahmin student Kāpaṭhika thought: "When the ascetic Gotama catches my eye, I shall ask him a question."

Then, knowing with his own mind the thought in the brahmin student Kāpaṭhika's mind, the Blessed One turned his eye toward him. Then the brahmin student Kāpaṭhika thought: "The ascetic Gotama has turned toward me. Suppose I ask him a question." Then he said to the Blessed One: "Master Gotama, in regard to the ancient brahmin hymns that have come down through oral transmission, preserved in the collections, the brahmins come to the definite conclusion: 'Only this is true, anything else is wrong.' What does Master Gotama say about this?"

13. "How then, Bhāradvāja, among the brahmins is there even a single brahmin who says thus: 'I know this, I see this: only this is true, anything else is wrong'?"—"No, Master Gotama."

"How then, Bhāradvāja, among the brahmins is there even a single teacher or a single teacher's teacher back to the seventh generation of teachers who says thus: 'I know this, I see this: only this is true, anything else is wrong'?"—"No, Master Gotama."

"How then, Bhāradvāja, the ancient brahmin seers, the creators of the hymns, the composers of the hymns, whose ancient hymns that were formerly chanted, uttered, and compiled, the brahmins nowadays still chant and repeat, repeating what was spoken and reciting what was recited—that is, Aṭṭhaka, Vāmaka, Vāmadeva, Vessāmitta, Yamataggi, Angirasa, Bhāradvāja, Vāseṭṭha, Kassapa, and Bhagu[20]—did even these ancient brahmin seers say thus: 'We know this, we see this: only this is true, anything else is wrong'?"—"No, Master Gotama."

"So, Bhāradvāja, it seems that among the brahmins there is not even a single brahmin who says thus: 'I know this, I see this: only this is true, anything else is wrong.' And among the brahmins there is not even a single teacher or a single teacher's teacher back to the seventh generation of teachers, who says thus: 'I know this, I see this: only this is true, anything else is wrong.' And the ancient brahmin seers, the creators of the hymns, the composers of the hymns ... even these ancient brahmin seers did not say thus: 'We know this, we see this: only this is true, anything else is wrong.' Suppose there were a file of blind men each in touch with the next: the first one does not see, the middle one does not see, and the last one does not see. So too, Bhāradvāja, in regard to their statement the brahmins seem to be like a file of blind men: the first one does not see, the middle one does not see, and the last one does not see. What do you think, Bhāradvāja, that being so, does not the faith of the brahmins turn out to be groundless?"

14. "The brahmins honor this not only out of faith, Master Gotama. They also honor it as oral tradition."

"Bhāradvāja, first you took your stand on faith, now you speak of oral tradition. There are five things, Bhāradvāja, that may turn out in two different ways here and now. What five? Faith, approval, oral tradition, reasoned cogitation, and acceptance of a view as a result of pondering it.[21] These five things may turn out in two different ways here and now. Now something may be fully accepted out of faith, yet it may be empty, hollow, and false; but something else may not be fully accepted out of faith, yet it may be factual, true, and unmistaken. Again, something may be fully approved of ... well transmitted ... well cogitated ... well pondered, yet it may be empty, hollow, and false; but something else may not be well pondered, yet it may be factual, true, and unmistaken. [Under these conditions] it is not proper for a wise man who preserves truth to come to the definite conclusion: 'Only this is true, anything else is wrong.'"[22]

15. "But, Master Gotama, in what way is there the preservation of truth?[23] How does one preserve truth? We ask Master Gotama about the preservation of truth."

"If a person has faith, Bhāradvāja, he preserves truth when he says: 'My faith is thus'; but he does not yet come to the definite conclusion: 'Only this is true, anything else is wrong.' In this way, Bhāradvāja, there is the preservation of truth; in this way he preserves truth; in this way we describe the preservation of truth. But as yet there is no discovery of truth.[24]

"If a person approves of something ... if he receives an oral tradition ... if he [reaches a conclusion based on] reasoned cogitation ... if he accepts a view as a result of pondering it, he preserves truth when he says: 'The view that I accept as a result of pondering it is thus'; but he does not yet come to the definite conclusion: 'Only this is true, anything else is wrong.' In this way too, Bhāradvāja, there is the preservation of truth; in this way he preserves truth; in this way we describe the preservation of truth. But as yet there is no discovery of truth."

16. "In that way, Master Gotama, there is the preservation of truth; in that way one preserves truth; in that way we recognize the preservation of truth. But in what way, Master Gotama, is there the discovery of truth? In what way does one discover truth? We ask Master Gotama about the discovery of truth."

17. "Here, Bhāradvāja, a monk may be living in dependence on some village or town. Then a householder or a householder's son goes to him and investigates him in regard to three kinds of states: in regard to states based on greed, in regard to states based on hate, and in regard to states based on delusion: 'Are there in this monk any states based on greed such that, with his mind obsessed by those states, while not knowing he might say, "I know," or while not seeing he might say, "I see," or he might urge others to act in a way that would lead to their harm and suffering for a long time?' As he investigates him he comes to know: 'There are no such states based on greed in this monk. The bodily and verbal behavior of this monk are not those of one affected by greed. And the Dhamma that he teaches is profound, hard to see and hard to understand, peaceful and sublime, unattainable by mere reasoning, subtle, to be experienced by the wise. This Dhamma cannot easily be taught by one affected by greed.'

18. "When he has investigated him and has seen that he is purified

from states based on greed, he next investigates him in regard to states based on hate: 'Are there in this monk any states based on hate such that, with his mind obsessed by those states ... he might urge others to act in a way that would lead to their harm and suffering for a long time?' As he investigates him, he comes to know: 'There are no such states based on hate in this monk. The bodily and verbal behavior of this monk are not those of one affected by hate. And the Dhamma that he teaches is profound ... to be experienced by the wise. This Dhamma cannot easily be taught by one affected by hate.'

19. "When he has investigated him and has seen that he is purified from states based on hate, he next investigates him in regard to states based on delusion: 'Are there in this monk any states based on delusion such that, with his mind obsessed by those states ... he might urge others to act in a way that would lead to their harm and suffering for a long time?' As he investigates him, he comes to know: 'There are no such states based on delusion in this monk. The bodily and verbal behavior of this monk are not those of one affected by delusion. And the Dhamma that he teaches is profound ... to be experienced by the wise. This Dhamma cannot easily be taught by one affected by delusion.'

20. "When he has investigated him and has seen that he is purified from states based on delusion, then he places faith in him; filled with faith he visits him and pays respect to him; having paid respect to him, he gives ear; when he gives ear, he hears the Dhamma; having heard the Dhamma, he memorizes it and examines the meaning of the teachings he has memorized; when he examines their meaning, he accepts those teachings as a result of pondering them; when he has accepted those teachings as a result of pondering them, desire springs up; when desire has sprung up, he applies his will; having applied his will, he scrutinizes; having scrutinized, he strives; resolutely striving, he realizes with the body the supreme truth and sees it by penetrating it with wisdom.[25] In this way, Bhāradvāja, there is the discovery of truth; in this way one discovers truth; in this way we describe the discovery of truth. But as yet there is no final arrival at truth."[26]

21. "In that way, Master Gotama, there is the discovery of truth; in that way one discovers truth; in that way we recognize the discovery of truth. But in what way, Master Gotama, is there the final arrival at truth? In what way does one finally arrive at truth? We ask Master Gotama about the final arrival at truth."

"The final arrival at truth, Bhāradvāja, lies in the repetition, development, and cultivation of those same things. In this way, Bhāradvāja, there is the final arrival at truth; in this way one finally arrives at truth; in this way we describe the final arrival at truth."

22. "In that way, Master Gotama, there is the final arrival at truth; in that way one finally arrives at truth; in that way we recognize the final arrival at truth. But what, Master Gotama, is most helpful for the final arrival at truth? We ask Master Gotama about the thing most helpful for the final arrival at truth."

"Striving is most helpful for the final arrival at truth, Bhāradvāja. If one does not strive, one will not finally arrive at truth; but because one strives, one does finally arrive at truth. That is why striving is most helpful for the final arrival at truth."

23. "But what, Master Gotama, is most helpful for striving? We ask Master Gotama about the thing most helpful for striving."

"Scrutiny is most helpful for striving, Bhāradvāja. If one does not scrutinize, one will not strive; but because one scrutinizes, one strives. That is why scrutiny is most helpful for striving."

24. "But what, Master Gotama, is most helpful for scrutiny? We ask Master Gotama about the thing most helpful for scrutiny."

"Application of the will is most helpful for scrutiny, Bhāradvāja. If one does not apply one's will, one will not scrutinize; but because one applies one's will, one scrutinizes. That is why application of the will is most helpful for scrutiny."

25. "But what, Master Gotama, is most helpful for application of the will? We ask Master Gotama about the thing most helpful for application of the will."

"Desire is most helpful for application of the will, Bhāradvāja. If one does not arouse desire, one will not apply one's will; but because one arouses desire, one applies one's will. That is why desire is most helpful for application of the will."

26. "But what, Master Gotama, is most helpful for desire? We ask Master Gotama about the thing most helpful for desire."

"Accepting the teachings as a result of pondering them is most helpful for desire, Bhāradvāja. If one does not accept the teachings as a result of pondering them, desire will not spring up; but because one accepts the teachings as a result of pondering them, desire springs up. That is why accepting the teachings as a result of pondering them is most helpful for desire."

27. "But what, Master Gotama, is most helpful for accepting the teachings as a result of pondering them? We ask Master Gotama about the thing most helpful for accepting the teachings as a result of pondering them."

"Examination of the meaning is most helpful for accepting the teachings as a result of pondering them, Bhāradvāja. If one does not examine their meaning, one will not accept the teachings as a result of pondering them; but because one examines their meaning, one accepts the teachings as a result of pondering them. That is why examination of the meaning is most helpful for accepting the teachings as a result of pondering them."

28. "But what, Master Gotama, is most helpful for examination of the meaning? We ask Master Gotama about the thing most helpful for examination of meaning."

"Memorizing the teachings is most helpful for examining the meaning, Bhāradvāja. If one does not memorize a teaching, one will not examine its meaning; but because one memorizes a teaching, one examines its meaning."

29. "But what, Master Gotama, is most helpful for memorizing the teachings? We ask Master Gotama about the thing most helpful for memorizing the teachings."

"Hearing the Dhamma is most helpful for memorizing the teachings, Bhāradvāja. If one does not hear the Dhamma, one will not memorize the teachings; but because one hears the Dhamma, one memorizes the teachings. That is why hearing the Dhamma is most helpful for memorizing the teachings."

30. "But what, Master Gotama, is most helpful for hearing the Dhamma? We ask Master Gotama about the thing most helpful for hearing the Dhamma."

"Giving ear is most helpful for hearing the Dhamma, Bhāradvāja. If one does not give ear, one will not hear the Dhamma; but because one gives ear, one hears the Dhamma. That is why giving ear is most helpful for hearing the Dhamma."

31. "But what, Master Gotama, is most helpful for giving ear? We ask Master Gotama about the thing most helpful for giving ear."

"Paying respect is most helpful for giving ear, Bhāradvāja. If one does not pay respect, one will not give ear; but because one pays respect, one gives ear. That is why paying respect is most helpful for giving ear."

32. "But what, Master Gotama, is most helpful for paying respect? We ask Master Gotama about the thing most helpful for paying respect."

"Visiting is most helpful for paying respect, Bhāradvāja. If one does not visit a teacher, one will not pay respect to him; but because one visits a teacher, one pays respect to him. That is why visiting is most helpful for paying respect."

33. "But what, Master Gotama, is most helpful for visiting? We ask Master Gotama about the thing most helpful for visiting."

"Faith is most helpful for visiting, Bhāradvāja. If faith in a teacher does not arise, one will not visit him; but because faith in a teacher arises, one visits him. That is why faith is most helpful for visiting."

34. "We asked Master Gotama about the preservation of truth, and Master Gotama answered about the preservation of truth; we approve of and accept that answer, and so we are satisfied. We asked Master Gotama about the discovery of truth, and Master Gotama answered about the discovery of truth; we approve of and accept that answer, and so we are satisfied. We asked Master Gotama about the final arrival at truth, and Master Gotama answered about the final arrival at truth; we approve of and accept that answer, and so we are satisfied. We asked Master Gotama about the thing most helpful for the final arrival at truth, and Master Gotama answered about the thing most helpful for the final arrival at truth; we approve of and accept that answer, and so we are satisfied. Whatever we asked Master Gotama about, that he has answered us; we approve of and accept that answer, and so we are satisfied. Formerly, Master Gotama, we used to think: 'Who are these bald-headed ascetics, these dark menial offspring of the Lord's feet, that they would understand the Dhamma?'[27] But Master Gotama has indeed inspired in me love for ascetics, confidence in ascetics, reverence for ascetics.

35. "Magnificent, Master Gotama! Magnificent, Master Gotama!... [as in Text III,2] ... From today let Master Gotama remember me as a lay follower who has gone to him for refuge for life."

(from MN 95: *Caṅkī Sutta*; II 168–77)

IV. The Happiness Visible in This Present Life

Introduction

Is it the case, as some scholars hold, that the Buddha's original message was exclusively one of world-transcending liberation, with little relevance for people stuck in the routines of worldly life? Did the ancient Buddhists believe that it was only in the monastery that the real practice of the Dhamma began and that only those who left the world were considered proper receptacles of the teaching? Did the Buddha's teachings for the laity have no more than a token significance? Were they mainly injunctions to acquire merit by offering material support to the monastic order and its members so that they could become monks and nuns (preferably monks) in future lives and then get down to the real practice?

At certain periods, in almost all traditions, Buddhists have lent support to the assumptions that underlie these questions. They have spurned concern with the present life and dismissed the world as a valley of tears, a deceptive illusion, convinced that the sign of spiritual maturity is an exclusive focus on emancipation from the round of birth and death. Monks have sometimes displayed little interest in showing those still stuck in the world how to use the wisdom of the Dhamma to deal with the problems of ordinary life. Householders in turn have seen little hope of spiritual progress in their own chosen mode of life and have thus resigned themselves merely to gaining merit by offering material support to the monks.

While the Nikāyas reveal the crown of the Buddha's teachings to lie in the path to final release from suffering, it would be a mistake to reduce the teachings, so diverse in the original sources, to their transcendent pinnacle. We must again recall the statement that a Buddha arises "for the welfare of the multitude, for the happiness of the multitude ... out of compassion for the world, for the good, welfare, and happiness of devas and humans" (p. 50). The function of a Buddha is to discover, realize, and proclaim the Dhamma in its full range and depth, and this involves a comprehensive understanding of the varied applications of the Dhamma in all its multiple dimensions. A Buddha not only penetrates to the unconditioned state of perfect bliss that lies beyond saṃsāra, outside the pale of birth, aging, and death; he not only proclaims the path to full enlightenment and final liberation; but he also illuminates the many ways the Dhamma applies to the complex conditions of human life for people still immersed in the world.

The Dhamma, in its broadest sense, is the immanent, invariable order of the universe in which truth, lawful regularity, and virtue are inextricably merged. This cosmic Dhamma is reflected in the human mind as the aspiration for truth, spiritual beauty, and goodness; it is expressed in human conduct as wholesome bodily, verbal, and mental action. The Dhamma has institutional embodiments as well as expressions in the lives of individuals who look upon it as their source of guidance in the proper conduct of life. These embodiments are both secular and spiritual. Buddhist tradition sees the responsibility for upholding the Dhamma in the secular domain as falling to the legendary wheel-turning monarch (*rājā cakkavattī*). The wheel-turning monarch is the benevolent ruler who governs his kingdom in accordance with the highest ethical norms (*dhammiko dhammarājā*) and thereby peacefully unites the world under a reign of universal justice and prosperity. As **Text IV,1(1)** shows, within the spiritual domain, the Buddha is the counterpart of the wheel-turning monarch. Like the latter, the Buddha relies on the Dhamma and reveres the Dhamma, but whereas the wheel-turning monarch relies upon the Dhamma as principle of righteousness to rule his kingdom, the Buddha relies upon the Dhamma as ethical and spiritual norm to teach and transform human beings and guide them toward proper conduct of body, speech, and mind. Neither the wheel-turning monarch nor the Buddha creates the Dhamma they uphold, yet neither can perform their respective functions without it; for the Dhamma is the objective, impersonal, ever-existent principle of order that serves as the source and standard for their respective policies and promulgations.

As the king of the Dhamma, the Buddha takes up the task of promoting the true good, welfare, and happiness of the world. He does so by teaching the people of the world how to live in accordance with the Dhamma and behave in such a way that they can attain realization of the same liberating Dhamma that he realized through his enlightenment. The Pāli commentaries demonstrate the broad scope of the Dhamma by distinguishing three types of benefit that the Buddha's teaching is intended to promote, graded hierarchically according to their relative merit:

1. welfare and happiness directly visible in this present life (*diṭṭha-dhamma-hitasukha*), attained by fulfilling one's moral commitments and social responsibilities;
2. welfare and happiness pertaining to the next life (*samparāyika-hitasukha*), attained by engaging in meritorious deeds;
3. the ultimate good or supreme goal (*paramattha*), Nibbāna, final release from the cycle of rebirths, attained by developing the Noble Eightfold Path.

While many Western writers on Early Buddhism have focused on this last aspect as almost exclusively representing the Buddha's original teaching, a balanced presentation should give consideration to all three aspects. Therefore, in this chapter and those to follow, we will be exploring texts from the Nikāyas that illustrate each of these three facets of the Dhamma.

The present chapter includes a variety of texts on the Buddha's teachings that pertain to the happiness directly visible in this present life. The most comprehensive Nikāya text in this genre is the Sigālaka Sutta (DN 31, also known as the Siṅgalovāda Sutta), sometimes called "The Layperson's Code of Discipline." The heart of this sutta is the section on "worshipping the six directions"—**Text IV,1(2)**—in which the Buddha freely reinterprets an ancient Indian ritual, infusing it with a new ethical meaning. The practice of "worshipping the six directions," as explained by the Buddha, presupposes that society is sustained by a network of interlocking relationships that bring coherence to the social order when its members fulfill their reciprocal duties and responsibilities in a spirit of kindness, sympathy, and good will. The six basic social relationships that the Buddha draws upon to fill out his metaphor are: parents and children, teacher and pupils, husband and wife, friend and friend, employer and workers, lay follower and religious guides. Each is considered one of the six directions in relation to its counterpart. For a young man like Sigālaka, his parents are the east, his teachers the south, his wife and children the west, his friends the north, his workers the nadir, and religious guides the zenith. With his customary sense of systematic concision, the Buddha ascribes to each member of each pair five obligations with respect to his or her counterpart; when each member fulfills these obligations, the corresponding "direction" comes to be "at peace and free from fear." "Thus, for Early Buddhism, the social stability and security that contribute to human happiness are most effectively achieved when every member of society fulfills the various duties that befall them as determined by their social relationships. Each person rises above the demands of narrow self-interest and develops a sincere, large-hearted concern for the welfare of others and the greater good of the whole."

From this general code of lay Buddhist ethics, we turn to texts that offer more specific points of advice, beginning with a selection of suttas on "The Family." This has separate sections on "Parents and Children" (**IV,2(1)**) and "Husbands and Wives" (**IV,2(2)**). In keeping with the norms of Indian society—in fact, of virtually all traditional agrarian societies—the Buddha regards the family as the basic unit of social integration and acculturation. It is especially the close, loving relationship between parents and children that fosters the virtues and sense of humane responsibility essential to a cohesive social order. Within the family, these values are transmitted from one generation to the next, and thus a harmonious society is highly dependent on harmonious relations between parents and children. The Buddha emphasizes filial piety—**Text IV,2(1)(a)**—and the gratitude of children to their parents, a debt they can adequately repay only by establishing their parents in the proper Dhamma—**Text IV,2(1)(b)**.

Wholesome relations between parents and children depend in turn upon the mutual affection and respect of husband and wife, and thus the Buddha also offers guidelines for proper relationships between married couples. These again emphasize a common commitment to ethical conduct and spiritual ideals. Of special interest to us, at a time when many marriages end so soon in divorce, is the Buddha's advice to the loving couple Nakulapitā and Nakulamātā—**Text IV,2(2)(b)**—on how the love between a husband and his wife can be sustained so strongly that they can be reunited in their future lives. This discourse also shows that far from demanding that his lay disciples spurn the desires of the world, the Buddha was ready to show those still under the sway of worldly desire how to obtain the objects of their desire. The one requirement he laid down was that the fulfillment of desire be regulated by ethical principles.

Next come a number of texts dealing with different aspects of household life united by an emphasis on right livelihood. Two characteristics of the Buddha's injunctions to his lay followers regarding the pursuit of mundane happiness stand out from these texts.

First, in seeking "the good visible in this present life," the lay follower should consistently adhere to principles of right conduct, especially to the five precepts and the rules of right livelihood. Thus, for example, he stipulates that wealth must be "acquired by energetic striving … *righteous* wealth *righteously* gained"—**Text IV,3**. Again, he asks his lay followers to use the wealth they obtain not only to gratify themselves but also to benefit their dependents and others who live on charity, particularly virtuous ascetics and brahmins—**Text IV,4(2).**

Second, the lay follower should not rest content with the mere pursuit of temporal well-being and happiness but should also seek the well-being and happiness pertaining to the future life. This is to be done by fostering those qualities that lead to a happy rebirth and the attainment of Nibbāna. According to **Texts IV,3** and **IV,5**, the principal virtues a lay follower should possess, leading to future welfare, are: (1) *faith* (in the Buddha as the Enlightened One), (2) *moral discipline* (as unbroken observance of the five precepts), (3) *generosity* (as application to charity, giving, and sharing), and (4) *wisdom* (as insight into the arising and passing away of phenomena). For Early Buddhism, the ideal householder is not merely a devout supporter of the monastic order but a noble person who has attained at least the first of the four stages of realization, the fruition of stream-entry (*sotāpatti*).

Finally, with section 6, we come to a selection of texts on "the Community." I use this word to refer broadly to both the Saṅgha, the monastic order, and the civil society in which any branch of the monastic order must be rooted. From the Nikāyas, it is clear that while the Buddha principally aimed at guiding people toward moral and spiritual progress, he was fully aware that their capacity for moral and spiritual development depends upon the material conditions of the society in which they live. He acutely realized that when people are mired in poverty and oppressed by hunger and want, they will find it hard to hold to a path of moral rectitude. The sheer pain of hunger, and the need to ward off the elements and provide for their families, will compel them to stoop to types of behavior they would avoid if they could obtain fair employment and adequate remuneration for their services. Thus he saw that the provision of economic justice is integral to social harmony and political stability.

The first two texts included here prescribe two sets of guidelines for the monastic order. Both are excerpts from a long discourse the Buddha spoke shortly after the death of Mahāvīra, the leader of the Jains. According to the Nikāyas, following their leader's death, the Jain monastic order was already beginning to split up, and the Buddha must have felt compelled to lay down guidelines to protect his own order from sharing the same fate after his passing. **Text IV,6(1)** enumerates six qualities that lead to quarrels and disputes, which the monks should be wary of and strive to eliminate when they discover them within themselves. Although these guidelines are laid down for the monks, they can easily be given a wider application to any organization, secular or religious, for it is the same six factors that lie at the bottom of all conflicts. The positive counterpart to this set of cautionary guidelines is **Text IV,6(2)**, which enumerates "six principles of cordiality" that lead to love, respect, and harmony among the members of the community. Again, with appropriate adaptation, these principles—loving acts of body, speech, and mind; sharing of possessions; common observance of precepts; and unity of views—can be given an extended application beyond a monastic order to the wider community. The same sutta provides more detailed guidelines for preserving harmony in the monastic order after the Buddha's death, but these deal with aspects of monastic discipline too specialized for the present anthology.

Text IV,6(3), a long excerpt from the Assalāyana Sutta, captures the Buddha in debate with a precocious brahmin pundit about the brahmins' claims on behalf of the caste system. In the Buddha's age the caste system was only beginning to take shape in northeast India and had not yet spawned the countless subdivisions and rigid regulations that were to manacle Indian society through the centuries. Society was divided into four broad social classes: the *brahmins*, who performed the priestly functions prescribed in the Vedas; the *khattiyas*, the nobles, warriors, and administrators; the *vessas*, the merchants and agriculturalists; and the *suddas*, the menials and serfs. There were also those outside the pale of the four main classes, who were regarded as even lower than the suddas. From the Nikāyas it appears that the brahmins, while vested with authority in religious matters, had not yet attained the unchallengeable hegemony they were to gain after the appearance of such works as the *Laws of Manu*, which laid down the fixed rules of the caste system. They had, however, already embarked on their drive for domination over the rest of Indian society and did so by propagating the thesis that brahmins are the highest caste, the divinely blessed offspring of Brahmā who are alone capable of purification.

Contrary to certain popular notions, the Buddha did not agitate for the abolition of the Indian class system and attempt to establish a classless society. Within the Saṅgha, however, all caste distinctions were abrogated from the moment of ordination. People from any of the four social classes who went forth under the Buddha renounced their class titles and prerogatives, becoming known simply as disciples of the Sakyan son (that is, of the Buddha, who was from the Sakyan clan). Whenever the Buddha and his disciples confronted the brahmins' claim to superiority, they argued vigorously against them. As our text shows, the Buddha maintained that all such claims were groundless. Purification, he contended, was the result of conduct, not of birth, and was thus accessible to those of all four castes. The Buddha even stripped the term "brahmin" of its hereditary accretions, and hearkening back to its original connotation of holy man, defined the true brahmin as the arahant (see MN 98, not included in this anthology).

The next two selections suggest guidelines for political administration. During the Buddha's time two distinct forms of government prevailed among the states of northern India in which the Buddha moved and taught, monarchical kingdoms and tribal republics. As a spiritual teacher, the Buddha did not prefer one type of government to the other, nor did he actively interfere in affairs of state. But his followers included leaders from both types of state, and thus he occasionally offered them guidance intended to ensure that they would govern their realms in accordance with ethical norms.

The opening scene of the Mahāparinibbāna Sutta, the narrative of the Buddha's last days—**Text IV,6(4)**—gives us a glimpse into this tumultuous phase of Indian history when Magadha, the rising star among the northern monarchies, was expanding in influence and absorbing its neighboring tribal republics. In the passage reproduced here we see King Ajātasattu, the ruler of Magadha, setting his sights on the Vajjian confederacy, the largest and best organized of the tribal republics. When the sutta opens, he sends his chief minister to inquire from the Buddha whether he has any chance of success in waging war against the Vajjians. The Buddha questions Ānanda about seven conditions of social stability that he had earlier taught the Vajjians, concluding that "as long as they keep to these seven principles, as long as these principles remain in force, the Vajjians may be expected to prosper and not decline." He then convenes a meeting of the monks and teaches them seven analogous principles of stability applicable to the monastic order.

Since the eventual triumph of the monarchical type of government seemed inevitable, the Buddha sought to establish a model of kingship that could curb the arbitrary exercise of power and subordinate the king to a higher authority. He did so by setting up the ideal of the "wheel-turning monarch," the righteous king who rules in compliance with the Dhamma, the impersonal law of righteousness (see **Text IV,1(1)**). The Dhamma that he obeys is the ethical basis for his rule. Symbolized by the sacred wheel-treasure, the Dhamma enables him to subdue without force all the nations of the world and establish a universal reign of peace and virtue based on observance of the five precepts—see **Text IV,6(5)**.

The wheel-turning monarch rules for the welfare and happiness of his subjects and extends protection to all within his realm, even to the birds and beasts. Among his duties is to prevent crime from erupting in his kingdom, and to keep the kingdom safe from crime he must give wealth to those in need, for in the view of the Nikāyas poverty is the breeding ground of criminality. This theme, mentioned among the duties of the wheel-turning monarch in **Text IV,6(5)**, is elaborated in **Text IV,6(6)**. We here see a wise chaplain advise a king that the correct way to end the plague of theft and brigandage in his realm is not by imposing harsher punishments and stricter law enforcement, but by giving the citizens the means to earn their living. Once the people enjoy a satisfactory standard of living, they will lose all interest in harming others, and the country will enjoy peace and tranquillity.

IV. The Happiness Visible in This Present Life

1. Upholding the Dhamma in Society

(1) The King of the Dhamma

The Blessed One said: "Monks, even a wheel-turning monarch, a just and righteous king, does not govern his realm without a co-regent."

When he had spoken, a certain monk addressed the Blessed One thus: "But who, venerable sir, is the co-regent of the wheel-turning monarch, the just and righteous king?"

"It is the Dhamma, the law of righteousness, O monk," replied the Blessed One.[1]

"In this case, the wheel-turning monarch, the just and righteous king, relying on the Dhamma, honoring the Dhamma, esteeming and respecting it, with the Dhamma as his standard, banner, and sovereign, provides lawful protection, shelter, and safety for his own dependents. He provides lawful protection, shelter, and safety for the khattiyas attending on him; for his army, for the brahmins and householders, for the inhabitants of town and countryside, for ascetics and brahmins, for the beasts and birds.

"A wheel-turning monarch, a just and righteous king, who thus provides lawful protection, shelter, and safety for all, is the one who rules by Dhamma only. And that rule cannot be overthrown by any hostile human being.

"Even so, O monk, the Tathāgata, the Arahant, the Perfectly Enlightened One, the just and righteous king of the Dhamma, relying on the Dhamma, honoring the Dhamma, esteeming and respecting it, with the Dhamma as his standard, banner, and sovereign, provides lawful protection, shelter, and safety in regard to action by body, speech, and mind. [He teaches thus:] 'Such bodily action should be undertaken and such should not be undertaken. Such verbal action should be undertaken and such should not be undertaken. Such mental action should be undertaken and such should not be undertaken.'

"The Tathāgata, the Arahant, the Fully Enlightened One, the just and righteous king of the Dhamma, who thus provides lawful protection, shelter, and safety in regard to action by body, speech, and mind, is the one who turns the incomparable wheel of the Dhamma in accordance with the Dhamma only. And that wheel of the Dhamma cannot be turned back by any ascetic or brahmin, by any deva or Māra or Brahmā or by anyone in the world."[2]

(AN 3:14; I 109–10)

(2) Worshipping the Six Directions

1. Thus have I heard. On one occasion the Blessed One was dwelling at Rājagaha, at the Bamboo Grove, in the Squirrels' Sanctuary. Then Sigālaka the householder's son, having got up early and gone out of Rājagaha, was paying homage, with wet clothes and hair and with joined palms, to the different directions: to the east, the south, the west, the north, the nadir, and the zenith.

2. And the Blessed One, having risen early and dressed, took his robe and bowl and went to Rājagaha for alms. And seeing Sigālaka paying homage to the different directions, he said: "Householder's son, why have you got up early to pay homage to the different directions?"

"Venerable sir, my father, when he was dying, told me to do so. And so, out of respect for my father's words, which I revere, honor, and hold sacred, I have got up early to pay homage in this way to the six directions."

"But, householder's son, that is not the right way to pay homage to the six directions according to the Noble One's discipline."

"Well, venerable sir, how should one pay homage to the six directions according to the Noble One's discipline? It would be good if the Blessed One would teach me the proper way to pay homage to the six directions according to the Noble One's discipline."

"Then listen and attend carefully, householder's son, I will speak."

"Yes, venerable sir," Sigālaka said. The Blessed One said this: ...

27. "And how, householder's son, does the noble disciple protect the six directions? These six things are to be regarded as the six directions. The east denotes mother and father. The south denotes teachers. The west denotes wife and children. The north denotes friends and

companions. The nadir denotes servants, workers, and helpers. The zenith denotes ascetics and brahmins.

28. "There are five ways in which a son should minister to his mother and father as the eastern direction. [He should think:] 'Having been supported by them, I will support them. I will perform their duties for them. I will keep up the family tradition. I will be worthy of my heritage. After my parents' deaths I will distribute gifts on their behalf.' And there are five ways in which the parents, so ministered to by their son as the eastern direction, will reciprocate: they will restrain him from evil, support him in doing good, teach him some skill, find him a suitable wife, and, in due time, hand over his inheritance to him. In this way the eastern direction is covered, making it at peace and free from fear.

29. "There are five ways in which pupils should minister to their teachers as the southern direction: by rising to greet them, by waiting on them, by being attentive, by serving them, by mastering the skills they teach. And there are five ways in which their teachers, thus ministered to by their pupils as the southern direction, will reciprocate: they will give thorough instruction, make sure they have grasped what they should have duly grasped, give them a thorough grounding in all skills, recommend them to their friends and colleagues, and provide them with security in all directions. In this way the southern direction is covered, making it at peace and free from fear.

30. "There are five ways in which a husband should minister to his wife as the western direction: by honoring her, by not disparaging her, by not being unfaithful to her, by giving authority to her, by providing her with adornments. And there are five ways in which a wife, thus ministered to by her husband as the western direction, will reciprocate: by properly organizing her work, by being kind to the servants, by not being unfaithful, by protecting stores, and by being skillful and diligent in all she has to do. In this way the western direction is covered, making it at peace and free from fear.

31. "There are five ways in which a man should minister to his friends and companions as the northern direction: by gifts, by kindly words, by looking after their welfare, by treating them like himself, and by keeping his word. And there are five ways in which friends and companions, thus ministered to by a man as the northern direction, will reciprocate:

by looking after him when he is inattentive, by looking after his property when he is inattentive, by being a refuge when he is afraid, by not deserting him when he is in trouble, and by showing concern for his children. In this way the northern direction is covered, making it at peace and free from fear.

32. "There are five ways in which a master should minister to his servants and workers as the nadir: by arranging their work according to their strength, by supplying them with food and wages, by looking after them when they are ill, by sharing special delicacies with them, and by letting them off work at the right time. And there are five ways in which servants and workers, thus ministered to by their master as the nadir, will reciprocate: they will get up before him, go to bed after him, take only what they are given, do their work properly, and be bearers of his praise and good repute. In this way the nadir is covered, making it at peace and free from fear.

33. "There are five ways in which a man should minister to ascetics and brahmins as the zenith: by kindness in bodily deed, speech, and thought, by keeping open house for them, and by supplying their bodily needs. And the ascetics and brahmins, thus ministered to by him as the zenith, will reciprocate in five ways: they will restrain him from evil, encourage him to do good, be benevolently compassionate toward him, teach him what he has not heard, and point out to him the way to heaven. In this way the zenith is covered, making it at peace and free from fear."

(from DN 31: *Sigālaka Sutta*; III 180–81, 187–91)

2. The Family

(1) Parents and Children

(a) Respect for Parents

"Monks, those families dwell with Brahmā where at home the parents are respected by their children. Those families dwell with the ancient teachers where at home the parents are respected by their children. Those families dwell with the ancient deities where at home the parents are respected by the children. Those families dwell with the holy ones where at home the parents are respected by their children.

"'Brahmā,' monks, is a term for father and mother. 'The ancient teachers' is a term for father and mother. 'The ancient deities' is a term for father and mother. 'The holy ones' is a term for father and mother. And why? Parents are of great help to their children; they bring them up, feed them, and show them the world."

(AN 4:63; II 70)

(b) Repaying One's Parents

"Monks, I declare that there are two persons one can never repay. What two? One's mother and father.

"Even if one should carry about one's mother on one shoulder and one's father on the other, and while doing so should live a hundred years, reach the age of a hundred years; and if one should attend to them by anointing them with balms, by massaging, bathing, and rubbing their limbs, and they should even void their excrements there—even by that would one not do enough for one's parents, nor would one repay them. Even if one were to establish one's parents as the supreme lords and rulers over this earth so rich in the seven treasures, one would not do enough for them, nor would one repay them. For what reason? Parents are of great help to their children; they bring them up, feed them, and show them the world.

"But, monks, one who encourages his unbelieving parents, settles and establishes them in faith; who encourages his immoral parents, settles and establishes them in moral discipline; who encourages his stingy parents, settles and establishes them in generosity; who encourages his ignorant parents, settles and establishes them in wisdom—such a one, monks, does enough for his parents: he repays them and more than repays them for what they have done."

(AN 2: iv, 2; I 61–62)

(2) Husbands and Wives

(a) Different Kinds of Marriages

On one occasion the Blessed One was traveling along the highway between Madhurā and Verañjā, and a number of householders and their wives were traveling along the same road. Then the Blessed One left the road and sat down on a seat at the foot of a tree. The householders and their wives saw the Blessed One sitting there and approached him. Having paid homage to him, they sat down to one side, and the Blessed One then said to them:

"Householders, there are these four kinds of marriages. What four? A wretch lives together with a wretch; a wretch lives together with a goddess; a god lives together with a wretch; a god lives together with a goddess.

"And how does a wretch live together with a wretch? Here, householders, the husband is one who destroys life, takes what is not given, engages in sexual misconduct, speaks falsely, and indulges in wines, liquor, and intoxicants, the basis for negligence; he is immoral, of bad character; he dwells at home with a heart obsessed by the stain of stinginess; he abuses and reviles ascetics and brahmins. And his wife is exactly the same in all respects. It is in such a way that a wretch lives together with a wretch.

"And how does a wretch live together with a goddess? Here, householders, the husband is one who destroys life ... who abuses and reviles ascetics and brahmins. But his wife is one who abstains from the destruction of life ... from wines, liquor, and intoxicants; she is virtuous, of good character; she dwells at home with a heart free from the stain of stinginess; she does not abuse or revile ascetics and brahmins. It is in such a way that a wretch lives together with a goddess.

"And how does a god live together with a wretch? Here, householders, the husband is one who abstains from the destruction of life ... who does not abuse or revile ascetics and brahmins. But his wife is one who destroys life ... who abuses and reviles ascetics and brahmins. It is in such a way that a god lives together with a wretch.

"And how does a god live together with a goddess? Here, householders, the husband is one who abstains from the destruction of life ... from wines, liquor, and intoxicants; he is virtuous, of good character; he dwells at home with a heart free from the stain of stinginess; he does not abuse or revile ascetics and brahmins. And his wife is exactly the same in all respects. It is in such a way that a god lives together with a goddess.

"These, householders, are the four kinds of marriages."

(AN 4:53; II 57–59)

(b) How to Be United in Future Lives

On one occasion the Blessed One was dwelling among the Bhagga people, near Suṃsumāragiri, in the Deer Park of the Bhesakalā Grove. One morning the Blessed One dressed, took his upper robe and bowl, and went to the dwelling of the householder Nakulapitā.[3] Having arrived there, he sat down on the seat prepared for him. Then the householder Nakulapitā and the housewife Nakulamātā approached the Blessed One and, after paying homage to him, sat down to one side. So seated, the householder Nakulapitā said to the Blessed One:

"Venerable sir, ever since the young housewife Nakulamātā was brought home to me when I too was still young, I am not aware of having wronged her even in my thoughts, still less in my deeds. Our wish is to be in one another's sight so long as this life lasts and in the future life as well."

Then Nakulamātā the housewife addressed the Blessed One thus: "Venerable sir, ever since I was taken to the home of my young husband Nakulapitā, while being a young girl myself, I am not aware of having wronged him even in my thoughts, still less in my deeds. Our wish is to be in one another's sight so long as this life lasts and in the future life as well."

Then the Blessed One spoke thus: "If, householders, both wife and husband wish to be in one another's sight so long as this life lasts and in the future life as well, they should have the same faith, the same moral discipline, the same generosity, the same wisdom; then they will be in one another's sight so long as this life lasts and in the future life as well."

When both are faithful and generous,
Self-restrained, of righteous living,
They come together as husband and wife
Full of love for each other.

Many blessings come their way,
They dwell together in happiness,
Their enemies are left dejected,
When both are equal in virtue.

Having lived by Dhamma in this world,
The same in virtue and observance,
They rejoice after death in the deva-world,
Enjoying abundant happiness.

(AN 4:55; II 61–62)

(c) Seven Kinds of Wives

On one occasion the Blessed One was dwelling at Sāvatthī in Jeta's Grove, Anāthapiṇḍika's monastery. In the morning the Blessed One dressed, took his bowl and robe, and went to Anāthapiṇḍika's house, where he sat down in a seat prepared for him. On that occasion people in the house were making an uproar and a racket. The householder Anāthapiṇḍika approached the Blessed One, paid homage to him, and sat down to one side.[4] The Blessed One then said to him: "Why are people in your house making this uproar and racket, householder? One would think they were fishermen making a haul of fish."

"That, venerable sir, is our daughter-in-law Sujātā. She is rich and has been brought here from a rich family. She does not obey her father-in-law and mother-in-law, nor her husband. She does not even honor, respect, esteem, and venerate the Blessed One."

Then the Blessed One called the daughter-in-law Sujātā, saying, "Come, Sujātā."

"Yes, venerable sir," she replied, and she went to the Blessed One, paid homage to him, and sat down to one side. The Blessed One then said to her: "There are these seven kinds of wives, Sujātā. What seven? One like a slayer, one like a thief, one like a tyrant, one like a mother, one like a sister, one like a friend, and one like a handmaid. These are the seven kinds of wives. Now which of these seven are you?"

"I do not understand in detail the meaning of the Blessed One's brief statement. It would be good, venerable sir, if the Blessed One would teach me the Dhamma in such a way that I might understand the meaning in detail."

"Then listen, Sujātā, and attend carefully. I will speak."

"Yes, venerable sir," Sujātā replied. The Blessed One said this:

"With hateful mind, cold and heartless,
Lusting for others, despising her husband;
Who seeks to kill the one who bought her—
Such a wife is called *a slayer*.

"When her husband acquires wealth
By his craft or trade or farm work,
She tries to filch a little for herself—
Such a wife is called *a thief*.

"The slothful glutton, bent on idling,
Harsh, fierce, rough in speech,
A woman who bullies her own supporter—
Such a wife is called *a tyrant*.

"One who is always helpful and kind,
Who guards her husband as a mother her son,
Who carefully protects the wealth he earns—
Such a wife is called *a mother*.

"She who holds her husband in high regard
As younger sister holds the elder born,
Who humbly submits to her husband's will—
Such a wife is called *a sister*.

"One who rejoices at her husband's sight
As one friend might welcome another,
Well raised, virtuous, devoted—
Such a wife is called *a friend*.

"One without anger, afraid of punishment,
Who bears with her husband free of hate,
Who humbly submits to her husband's will—
Such a wife is called *a handmaid*.[5]

"The types of wives here called a slayer,
A thief, and the wife like a tyrant,
These kinds of wives, with the body's breakup,
Will be reborn deep in hell.

"But wives like mother, sister, friend,
And the wife called a handmaid,
Steady in virtue, long restrained,
With the body's breakup go to heaven.

"These, Sujātā, are the seven kinds of wives. Now which of these are you?"

"Beginning today, venerable sir, you should consider me a wife who is like a handmaid."

(AN 7:59; IV 91–94)

3. Present Welfare, Future Welfare

On one occasion the Blessed One was dwelling among the Koliyans where there was a market town of the Koliyans named Kakkarapatta. Then the Koliyan family man Dīghajānu approached the Blessed One, paid homage to him, and sat down to one side. So seated, he said to the Blessed One:

"Venerable sir, we are laypeople who enjoy sensual pleasures, dwelling at home in a bed crowded with children, enjoying fine sandalwood, wearing garlands, scents, and unguents, accepting gold and silver. Let the Blessed One teach the Dhamma to us in a way that will lead to our welfare and happiness both in the present life and in the future life as well."

"There are, Byagghapajja, four things that lead to the welfare and happiness of a family man in this very life. What four? The accomplishment of persistent effort, the accomplishment of protection, good friendship, and balanced living.

"And what is the accomplishment of persistent effort? Here, Byagghapajja, whatever may be the means by which a family man earns his living—whether by farming, trade, cattle raising, archery or civil service, or by some other craft—he is skillful and diligent; he investigates the appropriate means, and is able to act and arrange everything properly. This is called the accomplishment of persistent effort.

"And what is the accomplishment of protection? Here, Byagghapajja, a family man sets up protection and guard over the wealth acquired by energetic striving, amassed by the strength of his arms, earned by the sweat of his brow, righteous wealth righteously gained, thinking: 'How can I prevent kings and bandits from taking this away, fire from burning it, floods from sweeping it off, and unloved heirs from taking it?' This is called the accomplishment of protection.

"And what is good friendship? Here, Byagghapajja, in whatever village or town a family man dwells, he associates with householders or their sons, whether young or old, who are of mature virtue, accomplished in faith, moral discipline, generosity, and wisdom; he converses with them and engages in discussions with them. He emulates them in regard to their accomplishment in faith, moral discipline, generosity, and wisdom. This is called good friendship.

"And what is balanced living? Here, Byagghapajja, a family man knows his income and expenditures and leads a balanced life, neither extravagant nor miserly, so that his income exceeds his expenditures rather than the reverse. Just as a goldsmith or his apprentice, holding up a scale, knows, 'By so much it has dipped down, by so much it has tilted up,' so a family man leads a balanced life.

"The wealth thus amassed has four sources of dissipation: womanizing, drunkenness, gambling, and evil friendship. Just as in the case of a tank with four inlets and outlets, if one should close the inlets and open the outlets, and there would not be adequate rainfall, a decrease rather than an increase of the water could be expected in the tank, so these four things bring about the dissipation of amassed wealth.

"Similarly, there are four sources for the increase of amassed wealth: abstinence from womanizing, from drunkenness, from gambling, and from evil friendship. Just as in the case of a tank with four inlets and outlets, if one should open the inlets and close the outlets, and there would be adequate rainfall, an increase rather than a decrease of the water could be expected in the tank, so these four things bring about the increase of amassed wealth.

"These four things, Byagghapajja, lead to a family man's welfare and happiness in the present life.

"Four other things lead to a family man's welfare and happiness in the future life. What four? Accomplishment in faith, moral discipline, generosity, and wisdom.

"And how is a family man accomplished in faith? Here, Byagghapajja, a family man has faith; he places faith in the enlightenment of the Tathāgata: 'So the Blessed One is an arahant, perfectly enlightened, accomplished in true knowledge and conduct, fortunate, knower of the world, unsurpassed leader of persons to be tamed, teacher of devas and humans, the Enlightened One, the Blessed One.' In this way a family man is accomplished in faith.

"And how is a family man accomplished in moral discipline? Here,

Byagghapajja, a family man abstains from the destruction of life, from stealing, from sexual misconduct, from false speech, and from wines, liquors, and intoxicants, the basis for negligence. In this way a family man is accomplished in moral discipline.

"And how is a family man accomplished in generosity? Here, Byagghapajja, a family man dwells at home with a mind devoid of the stain of stinginess, freely generous, open-handed, delighting in relinquishment, one devoted to charity, delighting in giving and sharing. In this way a family man is accomplished in generosity.

"And how is a family man accomplished in wisdom? Here, Byagghapajja, a family man possesses the wisdom that sees into the arising and passing away of phenomena, that is noble and penetrative and leads to the complete destruction of suffering. In this way a family man is accomplished in wisdom.

"These four things, Byagghapajja, lead to a family man's welfare and happiness in the future life."

(AN 8:54; IV 281–85)

4. Right Livelihood

(1) Avoiding Wrong Livelihood

"These five trades, O monks, should not be taken up by a lay follower: trading in weapons, trading in living beings, trading in meat, trading in intoxicants, trading in poison."

(AN 5:177; III 208)

(2) The Proper Use of Wealth

[The Blessed One addressed the householder Anāthapiṇḍika:] "With the wealth acquired by energetic striving, amassed by the strength of his arms, earned by the sweat of his brow, righteous wealth righteously gained, the noble disciple undertakes four worthy deeds. What four?

"With the wealth thus gained he makes himself happy and pleased and properly maintains himself in happiness; he makes his parents happy and pleased and properly maintains them in happiness; he makes his wife and children, his slaves, workers, and servants happy and pleased and properly maintains them in happiness; he makes his friends and colleagues happy and pleased and properly maintains them in happiness. This is the first case of wealth gone to good use, fruitfully applied and used for a worthy cause.

"Further, householder, with the wealth thus gained the noble disciple makes provisions against the losses that might arise on account of fire and floods, kings and bandits and unloved heirs; he makes himself secure against them. This is the second case of wealth gone to good use....

"Further, householder, with the wealth thus gained the noble disciple makes the five kinds of offerings: to relatives, guests, ancestors, the king, and the devas. This is the third case of wealth gone to good use....

"Further, householder, with the wealth thus gained the noble disciple establishes a lofty offering of alms to those ascetics and brahmins who refrain from vanity and negligence, who are settled in patience and gentleness, who are devoted to taming themselves, to calming themselves, and to attaining Nibbāna—an offering that is heavenly, resulting in happiness, conducive to heaven. This is the fourth case of wealth gone to good use, fruitfully employed and used for a worthy cause.

"These, householder, are the four worthy deeds that the noble disciple undertakes with the wealth acquired by energetic striving, amassed by the strength of his arms, earned by the sweat of his brow, righteous wealth righteously gained.

"For anyone whose wealth is expended on other things apart from these four worthy deeds, that wealth is said to have gone to waste, to have been squandered and used frivolously. But for anyone whose wealth is expended on these four worthy deeds, that wealth is said to have gone to good use, to have been fruitfully employed and used for a worthy cause."

(AN 4:61; II 65–68)

(3) A Family Man's Happiness

The Blessed One said to the householder Anāthapiṇḍika: "There are, householder, these four kinds of happiness which may be achieved by a layperson who enjoys sensual pleasures, depending on time and occasion. What four? The happiness of possession, the happiness of enjoyment, the happiness of freedom from debt, and the happiness of blamelessness.

"And what, householder, is the happiness of possession? Here, a family man possesses wealth acquired by energetic striving, amassed by the strength of his arms, earned by the sweat of his brow, righteous wealth righteously gained. When he thinks, 'I possess wealth acquired by energetic striving ... righteously gained,' he experiences happiness and joy. This is called the happiness of possession.

"And what, householder, is the happiness of enjoyment? Here, with the wealth acquired by energetic striving, amassed by the strength of his arms, earned by the sweat of his brow, righteous wealth righteously gained, a family man enjoys his wealth and does meritorious deeds. When he thinks, 'With the wealth acquired by energetic striving ... righteously gained, I enjoy my wealth and do meritorious deeds,' he experiences happiness and joy. This is called the happiness of enjoyment.

"And what, householder, is the happiness of freedom from debt? Here, a family man is not indebted to anyone to any degree, whether small or great. When he thinks, 'I am not indebted to anyone to any degree, whether small or great,' he experiences happiness and joy. This is called the happiness of freedom from debt.

"And what, householder, is the happiness of blamelessness? Here, householder, a noble disciple is endowed with blameless conduct of body, speech, and mind. When he thinks, 'I am endowed with blameless conduct of body, speech, and mind,' he experiences happiness and joy. This is called the happiness of blamelessness.

"These, householder, are the four kinds of happiness that a layperson who enjoys sensual pleasures may achieve, depending on time and occasion."

(AN 4:62; II 69–70)

5. The Woman of the Home

On one occasion the Blessed One was dwelling at Sāvatthī in the Eastern Park, in the Mansion of Migāra's Mother. Then Visākhā, Migāra's mother, approached the Blessed One, paid homage to him, and sat down to one side.[6] The Blessed One then said to her:

"Visākhā, when a woman possesses four qualities she is heading for victory in the present world and is successful in this world. What four?

"Here, Visākhā, a woman is capable at her work; she manages her domestic help; she behaves in a way that is agreeable to her husband; and she safeguards his earnings.

"And how is a woman capable at her work? Here, Visākhā, she is skillful and diligent in regard to her husband's household chores, whether with wool or cotton; she investigates the appropriate means and is able to act and arrange everything properly. In this way a woman is capable at her work.

"And how is a woman one who manages the domestic help? Here, Visākhā, in regard to her husband's domestic helpers—slaves, servants, or workers—she knows by direct inspection what they have done and failed to do; she knows when they are sick and healthy; and she distributes to each the appropriate share of food. In this way a woman manages the domestic help.

"And how does a woman behave in a way that is agreeable to her husband? Here, Visākhā, a woman would not commit any misdeed that her husband would consider disagreeable, even at the cost of her life. In this way a woman behaves in a way that is agreeable to her husband.

"And how does a woman safeguard her husband's earnings? Here, Visākhā, whatever her husband brings home—whether money or grain, silver or gold—she succeeds in protecting and guarding it, and she is not a spendthrift, thief, wastrel, or squanderer of his wealth. In this way a woman safeguards her husband's earnings.

"When, Visākhā, a woman possesses these four qualities, she is heading for victory in the present world and is successful in this world. But when she possesses four other qualities, she is heading for victory in the other world and is successful in regard to the other world. What four?

"Here, Visākhā, a woman is accomplished in faith, moral discipline, generosity, and wisdom.

"And how is a woman accomplished in faith? Here, Visākhā, a woman has faith; she places faith in the enlightenment of the Tathāgata thus: 'So the Blessed One is an arahant … [as in Text IV,3] … teacher of devas and humans, the Enlightened One, the Blessed One.' In this way a woman is accomplished in faith.

"And how is a woman accomplished in moral discipline? Here, Visākhā, a woman abstains from the destruction of life, from stealing, from sexual misconduct, from false speech, and from wines, liquors, and intoxicants, the basis for negligence. In this way a woman is accomplished in moral discipline.

"And how is a woman accomplished in generosity? Here, Visākhā, a woman dwells at home with a mind devoid of the stain of stinginess, freely generous, open-handed, delighting in relinquishment, one devoted to charity, delighting in giving and sharing. In this way a woman is accomplished in generosity.

"And how is a woman accomplished in wisdom? Here, Visākhā, a woman possesses the wisdom that sees into the arising and passing away of phenomena, that is noble and penetrative and leads to the complete destruction of suffering.

"When a woman possesses these four qualities, she is heading for victory in the other world and is successful in regard to the other world."

(AN 8:49; IV 269–71)

6. The Community

(1) Six Roots of Dispute

6. "There are, Ānanda, these six roots of disputes. What six? Here, Ānanda, a monk is angry and resentful. Such a monk dwells without respect and deference toward the Teacher, the Dhamma, and the Saṅgha, and he does not fulfill the training. A monk who dwells without respect and deference toward the Teacher, the Dhamma, and the Saṅgha, and who does not fulfill the training, creates a dispute in the Saṅgha, which would be for the harm and unhappiness of many, for the loss, harm, and suffering of devas and humans. Now if you see any such root of dispute either in yourselves or externally, you should strive to abandon that same evil root of dispute. And if you do not see any such root of dispute either in yourselves or externally, you should practice in such a way that that same evil root of dispute does not erupt in the future. Thus there is the abandoning of that evil root of dispute; thus there is the non-eruption of that evil root of dispute in the future.

7–11. "Again, a monk is contemptuous and insolent ... envious and niggardly ... deceitful and fraudulent ... has evil wishes and wrong view ... adheres to his own views, holds on to them tenaciously, and relinquishes them with difficulty. Such a monk dwells without respect and deference toward the Teacher, the Dhamma, and the Saṅgha, and he does not fulfill the training. A monk who dwells without respect and deference toward the Teacher, the Dhamma, and the Saṅgha, and who does not fulfill the training, creates a dispute in the Saṅgha, which would be for the harm and unhappiness of many, for the loss, harm, and suffering of devas and humans. Now if you see any such root of dispute either in yourselves or externally, you should strive to abandon that same evil root of dispute. And if you do not see any such root of dispute either in yourselves or externally, you should practice in such a way that that same evil root of dispute does not erupt in the future. Thus there is the abandoning of that evil root of dispute; thus there is the non-eruption of that evil root of dispute in the future. These are the six roots of dispute."

(from MN 104: *Sāmagāma Sutta*; II 245–47)

(2) Six Principles of Cordiality

21. "Ānanda, there are these six principles of cordiality that create love and respect, and conduce to cohesion, nondispute, concord, and unity. What are the six?

"Here a monk maintains bodily acts of loving-kindness both in public and in private toward his companions in the holy life. This is a principle of cordiality that creates love and respect, and conduces to cohesion, nondispute, concord, and unity.

"Again, a monk maintains verbal acts of loving-kindness both in public and in private toward his companions in the holy life. This too is a principle of cordiality that creates love and respect, and conduces to … unity.

"Again, a monk maintains mental acts of loving-kindness both in public and in private toward his companions in the holy life. This too is a principle of cordiality that creates love and respect, and conduces to … unity.

"Again, a monk enjoys things in common with his virtuous companions in the holy life; without making reservations, he shares with them any righteous gain that has been obtained in a righteous way, including even the mere content of his alms bowl. This too is a principle of cordiality that creates love and respect, and conduces to … unity.

"Again, a monk dwells both in public and in private possessing in common with his companions in the holy life those virtues that are unbroken, untorn, unblemished, unmottled, freeing, praised by the wise, ungrasped, leading to concentration. This too is a principle of cordiality that creates love and respect and conduces to ... unity.

"Again, a monk dwells both in public and in private possessing in common with his companions in the holy life that view that is noble and emancipating, and leads the one who practices in accordance with it to the complete destruction of suffering. This too is a principle of cordiality that creates love and respect, and conduces to cohesion, to nondispute, to concord, and to unity.

"These are the six principles of cordiality that create love and respect, and conduce to cohesion, to nondispute, to concord, and to unity.

(from MN 104: *Sāmagāma Sutta*; II 250–51)

(3) Purification Is for All Four Castes

1. Thus have I heard. On one occasion the Blessed One was living at Sāvatthī in Jeta's Grove, Anāthapiṇḍika's Park.

2. Now at that time five hundred brahmins from diverse provinces were staying at Sāvatthī for some business or other. Then those brahmins thought: "This ascetic Gotama describes purification for all the four castes. Who is there able to dispute with him about this assertion?"

3. Now on that occasion a brahmin student named Assalāyana was staying at Sāvatthī. Young, shaven-headed, sixteen years old, he was a master of the three Vedas with their vocabularies, liturgy, phonology, and etymology, and the histories as a fifth; skilled in philology and grammar, he was fully versed in natural philosophy and in the marks of a great man. So the brahmins thought he would be able to debate with the Blessed One.

4. They went to the brahmin student Assalāyana and said to him: "Master Assalāyana, this ascetic Gotama describes purification for all the four castes. Let Master Assalāyana come and dispute with the ascetic Gotama about this assertion."

When this was said, the brahmin student Assalāyana replied: "Sirs, the ascetic Gotama is one who speaks the Dhamma. Now those who speak the Dhamma are difficult to dispute with. I cannot dispute with the ascetic Gotama about this assertion."

A second time and a third time the brahmins urged him to go. A second time the brahmin student Assalāyana refused, but after the third urging he consented.

5. Then the brahmin student Assalāyana went with a large number of brahmins to the Blessed One and exchanged greetings with him. When this courteous and amiable talk was finished, he sat down at one side and said to the Blessed One: "Master Gotama, the brahmins say thus: 'Brahmins are the highest caste, those of any other caste are inferior; brahmins are the fairest caste, those of any other caste are dark; only brahmins are purified, not non-brahmins; brahmins alone are the sons of Brahmā, the offspring of Brahmā, born of his mouth, born of Brahmā, created by Brahmā, heirs of Brahmā.' What does Master Gotama say about that?"

"Now, Assalāyana, the brahmin women are seen having their periods, becoming pregnant, giving birth, and nursing.[7] And yet those brahmins, though born from the womb, say thus: 'Brahmins are the highest caste ... brahmins alone are the sons of Brahmā, the offspring of Brahmā, born of his mouth, born of Brahmā, created by Brahmā, heirs of Brahmā.'"

6. "Although Master Gotama says this, still the brahmins think thus: 'Brahmins are the highest caste ... heirs of Brahmā.'"

"What do you think, Assalāyana? Have you heard that in Yona and Kamboja[8] and in other outland countries there are only two castes, masters and slaves, and that masters become slaves and slaves become masters?"

"So I have heard, sir."

"Then on the strength of what [argument] or with the support of what [authority] do the brahmins in this case say thus: 'Brahmins are the highest caste ... heirs of Brahmā'?"

7. "Although Master Gotama says this, still the brahmins think thus: 'Brahmins are the highest caste ... heirs of Brahmā.'"

"What do you think, Assalāyana? Suppose a khattiya were to kill living beings, take what is not given, commit sexual misconduct, speak falsely, speak maliciously, speak harshly, gossip, be covetous, have a mind of ill will, and hold wrong view. With the breakup of the body, after death, would only he be reborn in a state of misery, in a bad destination, in the lower world, in hell—and not a brahmin? Suppose a merchant ... a worker were to kill living beings ... and hold wrong view. With the breakup of the body, after death, would only he be reborn in a state of misery, in a bad destination, in the lower world, in hell—and not a brahmin?"

"No, Master Gotama. Whether it be a khattiya, or a brahmin, or a merchant, or a worker—those of all four castes who kill living beings ... and hold wrong view, with the breakup of the body, after death, would be reborn in a state of misery, in a bad destination, in the lower world, in hell."

"Then on the strength of what [argument] or with the support of what [authority] do the brahmins in this case say thus: 'Brahmins are the highest caste ... heirs of Brahmā'?"

8. "Although Master Gotama says this, still the brahmins think thus: 'Brahmins are the highest caste ... heirs of Brahmā.'"

"What do you think, Assalāyana? Suppose a brahmin were to abstain from killing living beings, from taking what is not given, from sexual misconduct, from false speech, from malicious speech, from harsh speech, and from gossip, and were to be without covetousness, to have a mind without ill will, and to hold right view. With the breakup of the body, after death, would only he be reborn in a good destination, in the heavenly world—and not a khattiya, or a merchant, or a worker?"

"No, Master Gotama. Whether a khattiya, a brahmin, a merchant, or a worker—those of all four castes who abstain from killing living beings ... and hold right view, with the breakup of the body, after death, will be reborn in a good destination, in the heavenly world."

"Then on the strength of what [argument] or with the support of what [authority] do the brahmins in this case say thus: 'Brahmins are the highest caste ... heirs of Brahmā'?"

9. "Although Master Gotama says this, still the brahmins think thus: 'Brahmins are the highest caste ... heirs of Brahmā.'"

"What do you think, Assalāyana? Is only a brahmin capable of developing a mind of loving-kindness toward this region, without hostility and without ill will, and not a khattiya, or a merchant, or a worker?"

"No, Master Gotama. Whether a khattiya, a brahmin, a merchant, or a worker—those of all four castes are capable of developing a mind of loving-kindness toward this region, without hostility and without ill will."

"Then on the strength of what [argument] or with the support of what [authority] do the brahmins in this case say thus: 'Brahmins are the highest caste ... heirs of Brahmā'?"

10. "Although Master Gotama says this, still the brahmins think thus: 'Brahmins are the highest caste ... heirs of Brahmā.'"

"What do you think, Assalāyana? Is only a brahmin capable of taking a bathing brush and bath powder, going to the river, and washing off dust and dirt, and not a khattiya, or a merchant, or a worker?"

"No, Master Gotama. Whether a khattiya, a brahmin, a merchant, or a worker—those of all four castes are capable of taking a bathing brush and bath powder, going to the river, and washing off dust and dirt."

"Then on the strength of what [argument] or with the support of what [authority] do the brahmins in this case say thus: 'Brahmins are the highest caste ... heirs of Brahmā'?"

11. "Although Master Gotama says this, still the brahmins think thus: 'Brahmins are the highest caste ... heirs of Brahmā.'"

"What do you think, Assalāyana? Suppose a consecrated khattiya king were to assemble here a hundred men of different birth and say to them: 'Come, sirs, let any here who have been born into a khattiya clan or a brahmin clan or a royal clan take an upper fire-stick of fine quality wood and light a fire and produce heat. And also let any who have been born into an outcast clan, a trapper clan, a wicker workers' clan, a cartwrights' clan, or a scavengers' clan take an upper fire-stick made from a dog's drinking trough, from a pig's trough, from a dustbin, or from castor-oil wood and light a fire and produce heat.'

"What do you think, Assalāyana? When a fire is lit and heat is produced by someone in the first group, would that fire have a flame, a color, and radiance, and would it be possible to use it for the purposes of fire, while when a fire is lit and heat is produced by someone of the second group, that fire would have no flame, no color, and no radiance, and it would not be possible to use it for the purposes of fire?"

"No, Master Gotama. When a fire is lit and heat is produced by someone of the first group, that fire would have a flame, a color, and radiance, and it would be possible to use it for the purposes of fire. And when a fire is lit and heat is produced by someone of the second group, that fire too would have a flame, a color, and radiance, and it would be possible to use it for the purposes of fire. For all fire has a flame, a color, and a radiance, and it is possible to use all fire for the purposes of fire."

"Then on the strength of what [argument] or with the support of what [authority] do the brahmins in this case say thus: 'Brahmins are the highest caste ... heirs of Brahmā'?"

12. "Although Master Gotama says this, still the brahmins think thus: 'Brahmins are the highest caste ... heirs of Brahmā.'"

"What do you think, Assalāyana? Suppose a khattiya youth were to unite with a brahmin girl, and a son was born from their union. Should a son born from a khattiya youth and a brahmin girl be called a khattiya after the father or a brahmin after the mother?"

"He could be called both, Master Gotama."

13. "What do you think, Assalāyana? Suppose a brahmin youth here were to unite with a khattiya girl, and a son were to be born from their union. Should the son born from a brahmin youth and a khattiya girl be called a khattiya after the mother or a brahmin after the father?"

"He could be called both, Master Gotama."

14. "What do you think, Assalāyana? Suppose a mare were to be mated with a male donkey, and a foal were to be born as the result. Should the foal be called a horse after the mother or a donkey after the father?"

"It is a mule, Master Gotama, since it does not belong to either kind. I see the difference in this last case, but I see no difference in either of the former cases."

15. "What do you think, Assalāyana? Suppose there were two brahmin students who were brothers, born of the same mother, one studious and intelligent, and one neither studious nor intelligent. Which of them would brahmins feed first at a funeral feast, or at a ceremonial offering, or at a sacrificial feast, or at a feast for guests?"

"On such occasions, brahmins would feed first the one who was studious and intelligent, Master Gotama; for how could what is given to one who is neither studious nor intelligent bring great fruit?"

16. "What do you think, Assalāyana? Suppose there were two brahmin students who were brothers, born of the same mother, one studious and intelligent, but immoral and of bad character, and one neither studious nor intelligent, but virtuous and of good character. Which of them would brahmins feed first at a funeral feast, or at a ceremonial offering, or at a sacrificial feast, or at a feast for guests?"

"On such occasions, brahmins would feed first the one who was neither studious nor intelligent, but virtuous and of good character, Master Gotama; for how could what is given to one who is immoral and of bad character bring great fruit?"

17. "First, Assalāyana, you took your stand on birth, and after that you took your stand on scriptural learning, and after that you have come to take your stand on the very ground that purification is for all four castes, as I describe it."

When this was said, the brahmin student Assalāyana sat silent and dismayed, his shoulders drooping and head down, glum and without response.

(MN 93: *Assalāyana Sutta*, abridged; II 147–54)

(4) Seven Principles of Social Stability

1.1. Thus have I heard. Once the Blessed One was staying at Rājagaha on Mount Vulture Peak. Now just then King Ajātasattu Vedehiputta of Magadha wanted to attack the Vajjians.[9] He said: "I will strike the Vajjians who are so powerful and strong, I will cut them off and destroy them, I will bring them to ruin and destruction!"

1.2. And King Ajātasattu said to his chief minister, the brahmin Vassakāra: "Brahmin, go to the Blessed One, worship him with your head to his feet in my name, ask if he is free from sickness or disease, if he is living at ease, vigorously and comfortably, and then say: 'Lord, King Ajātasattu Vedehiputta of Magadha wishes to attack the Vajjians and says: "I will strike the Vajjians ... bring them to ruin and destruction!"' And whatever the Blessed One declares to you, report that faithfully back to me, for Tathāgatas never lie."

1.3. "Very good, Sire," said Vassakāra, and having had the state carriages harnessed, he mounted one of them and drove in state from Rājagaha to Vultures' Peak, riding as far as the ground would allow, then continuing on foot to where the Blessed One was. He exchanged courtesies with the Blessed One, then sat down to one side and delivered the king's message.

1.4. Now the Venerable Ānanda was standing behind the Blessed One, fanning him. And the Blessed One said:

(1) "Ānanda, have you heard that the Vajjians hold regular and frequent assemblies?"—"I have heard, venerable sir, that they do."

"Ānanda, as long as the Vajjians hold regular and frequent assemblies, they may be expected to prosper and not decline.

(2) "Have you heard that the Vajjians meet in harmony, break up in harmony, and carry on their business in harmony?"—"I have heard, venerable sir, that they do."

"Ānanda, as long as the Vajjians meet in harmony, break up in harmony, and carry on their business in harmony, they may be expected to prosper and not decline.

(3) "Have you heard that the Vajjians do not authorize what has not been authorized already, and do not abolish what has been authorized, but proceed according to what has been authorized by their ancient tradition?"—"I have, venerable sir."... (4) "Have you heard that they honor, respect, revere, and salute the elders among them, and consider them worth listening to?... (5) that they do not forcibly abduct others' wives and daughters and compel them to live with them?... (6) that they honor, respect, revere, and salute the Vajjian shrines at home and abroad, not withdrawing the proper support made and given before?... (7) that proper provision is made for the safety of arahants, so that such arahants may come in future to live there and those already there may dwell in comfort?"—"I have, Lord."

"Ānanda, so long as such proper provision is made ... the Vajjians may be expected to prosper and not decline."

1.5. Then the Lord said to the brahmin Vassakāra: "Once, brahmin, when I was at the Sārandada Shrine in Vesāli, I taught the Vajjians these seven principles for preventing decline, and as long as they keep to these seven principles, as long as these principles remain in force, the Vajjians may be expected to prosper and not decline."

At this, Vassakāra replied: "Master Gotama, if the Vajjians keep to even one of these principles, they may be expected to prosper and not decline—far less all seven. Certainly the Vajjians will never be conquered by King Ajātasattu by force of arms, but only by means of propaganda and setting them against one another. And now, Master Gotama, I must depart. I am busy and have much to do."

"Brahmin, do as you think fit." Then Vassakāra, rejoicing and delighted at the Blessed One's words, rose from his seat and departed.

1.6. Soon after Vassakāra had gone, the Blessed One said: "Ānanda, go to whatever monks there are living around Rājagaha, and summon them to the assembly hall."

"Yes, venerable sir," said Ānanda, and he did so. Then he came to the Blessed One, saluted him, stood to one side, and said: "Venerable sir, the Saṅgha of monks is assembled. Now is the time for the Blessed One to do as he sees fit." Then the Blessed One rose from his seat, went to the assembly hall, sat down on the prepared seat, and said: "Monks, I will teach you seven things that are conducive to welfare. Listen, pay careful attention, and I will speak."

"Yes, venerable sir," said the monks, and the Blessed One said:

"As long as the monks hold regular and frequent assemblies, they may be expected to prosper and not decline. As long as they meet in harmony, break up in harmony, and carry on their business in harmony, they may be expected to prosper and not decline. As long as they do not authorize what has not been authorized already, and do not abolish what has been authorized, but proceed according to what has been authorized by the rules of training...; as long as they honor, respect, revere, and salute the elders of long standing who are long ordained, fathers and leaders of the order...; as long as they do not fall prey to the craving that arises in them and leads to rebirth...; as long as they are devoted to forest-lodgings...; as long as they preserve their mindfulness regarding the body, so that in future the good among their companions will come to them, and those who have already come will feel at ease with them...; as long as the monks hold to these seven things and are seen to do so, they may be expected to prosper and not decline."

(from DN 16: *Mahāparinibbāna Sutta*; II 72–77)

(5) The Wheel-Turning Monarch

3. "And, after many hundreds and thousands of years, King Daḷhanemi said to a certain man: 'My good man, whenever you see that the sacred wheel-treasure has slipped from its position, report it to me.' 'Yes, Sire,' the man replied. And after many hundreds and thousands of years the man saw that the sacred wheel-treasure had slipped from its position. Seeing this, he reported the fact to the king. Then King Daḷhanemi sent for his eldest son, the crown prince, and said: 'My son, the sacred wheel-treasure has slipped from its position. And I have heard say that when this happens to a wheel-turning monarch, he has not much longer to live. I have had my fill of human pleasures, now is

the time to seek heavenly pleasures. You, my son, take over control of this land. I will shave off my hair and beard, put on ochre robes, and go forth from the household life into homelessness.' And, having installed his eldest son in due form as king, King Daḷhanemi shaved off his hair and beard, put on ochre robes, and went forth from the household life into homelessness. And, seven days after the royal sage had gone forth, the sacred wheel-treasure vanished.

4. "Then a certain man came to the consecrated khattiya king and said: 'Sire, you should know that the sacred wheel-treasure has disappeared.' At this the king was grieved and felt sad. He went to the royal sage and told him the news. And the royal sage said to him: 'My son, you should not grieve or feel sad at the disappearance of the wheel-treasure. The wheel-treasure is not an heirloom from your fathers. But now, my son, you must turn yourself into a noble wheel-turner. And then it may come about that, if you perform the duties of a noble wheel-turning monarch, on the uposatha day of the fifteenth,[10] when you have washed your head and gone up to the verandah on top of your palace for the uposatha day, the sacred wheel-treasure will appear to you, thousand-spoked, complete with rim, hub, and all accessories.'

5. "'But what, Sire, is the duty of a noble wheel-turning monarch?'—'It is this, my son: Yourself depending on the Dhamma, honoring it, revering it, cherishing it, doing homage to it, and venerating it, having the Dhamma as your badge and banner, acknowledging the Dhamma as your master, you should establish righteous guard, ward, and protection for your own household, your troops, your khattiyas and vassals, for brahmins and householders, town and country folk, ascetics and brahmins, for beasts and birds. Let no crime prevail in your kingdom, and to those who are in need, give wealth. And whatever ascetics and brahmins in your kingdom have renounced the life of sensual infatuation and are devoted to forbearance and gentleness, each one taming himself, each one calming himself, and each one striving for the end of craving, from time to time you should approach them and ask: "What, venerable sirs, is wholesome and what is unwholesome, what is blameworthy and what is blameless, what is to be followed and what is not to be followed? What action will in the long run lead to harm and sorrow, and what to welfare and happiness?"[11] Having listened to them, you should avoid what is unwholesome and do what is wholesome. That, my son, is the duty of a noble wheel-turning monarch.'

"'Yes, Sire,' said the king, and he performed the duties of a noble wheel-turning monarch. And as he did so, on the uposatha day of the fifteenth, when he had washed his head and gone up to the verandah on top of his palace for the uposatha day, the sacred wheel-treasure appeared to him, thousand-spoked, complete with rim, hub, and all accessories. Then the king thought: 'I have heard that when a duly anointed khattiya king sees such a wheel on the uposatha day of the fifteenth, he will become a wheel-turning monarch. May I become such a monarch?'

6. "Then, rising from his seat, covering one shoulder with his robe, the king took a gold vessel in his left hand, sprinkled the wheel with his right hand, and said: 'May the noble wheel-treasure turn, may the noble wheel-treasure conquer!' The wheel turned to the east, and the king followed it with his fourfold army. And in whatever country the wheel stopped, the king took up residence with his fourfold army. And those who opposed him in the eastern region came and said: 'Come, Your Majesty, welcome. We are yours, Your Majesty. Rule us, Your Majesty.' And the king said: 'Do not take life. Do not take what is not given. Do not commit sexual misconduct. Do not tell lies. Do not drink intoxicating drinks. Enjoy your possessions as before.'[12] And those who had opposed him in the eastern region became his subjects.

7. "Then the wheel turned south, west, and north ... [as section 6] ... Then the wheel-treasure, having conquered the lands from sea to sea, returned to the royal capital and stopped before the king's palace as he was trying a case, as if to adorn the royal palace."

(from DN 26: *Cakkavatti-Sīhanāda Sutta*; III 59–63)

(6) Bringing Tranquillity to the Land

9. Sitting to one side, the brahmin Kūṭadanta addressed the Blessed One: "Master Gotama, I have heard that you understand how to conduct successfully the triple sacrifice with its sixteen requisites. Now I do not understand all this, but I want to make a big sacrifice. It would be good if Master Gotama would explain this to me."

"Then listen, brahmin, pay proper attention, and I will explain."

"Yes, sir," replied Kūṭadanta, and the Blessed One continued:

10. "Brahmin, once upon a time there was a king called Mahāvijita. He was rich, of great wealth and resources, with an abundance of gold

and silver, of possessions and requisites, of money and money's worth, with a full treasury and granary. And when King Mahāvijita was reflecting in private, the thought came to him: 'I have acquired extensive wealth in human terms, I occupy a wide extent of land which I have conquered. Let me now make a great sacrifice that would be to my benefit and happiness for a long time.' And calling his chaplain,[13] he told him his thought. 'I want to make a great sacrifice. Instruct me, venerable sir, how this may be to my lasting benefit and happiness.'

11. "The chaplain replied: 'Your Majesty's country is beset by thieves. It is ravaged; villages and towns are being destroyed; the countryside is infested with brigands. If Your Majesty were to tax this region, that would be the wrong thing to do. Suppose Your Majesty were to think: "I will get rid of this plague of robbers by executions and imprisonment, or by confiscation, threats, and banishment," the plague would not be properly ended. Those who survived would later harm Your Majesty's realm. However, with this plan you can completely eliminate the plague. To those in the kingdom who are engaged in cultivating crops and raising cattle, let Your Majesty distribute grain and fodder; to those in trade, give capital; to those in government service assign proper living wages. Then those people, being intent on their own occupations, will not harm the kingdom. Your Majesty's revenues will be great; the land will be tranquil and not beset by thieves; and the people, with joy in their hearts, playing with their children, will dwell in open houses.'

"And saying: 'So be it!,' the king accepted the chaplain's advice: he gave grain and fodder to those engaged in cultivating crops and raising cattle, capital to those in trade, proper living wages to those in government service. Then those people, being intent on their own occupations, did not harm the kingdom. The king's revenues became great; the land was tranquil and not beset by thieves; and the people, with joy in their hearts, playing with their children, dwelled in open houses."

(from DN 5: *Kūṭadanta Sutta*; I 134–36)

V. The Way to a Fortunate Rebirth

Introduction

In his account of his "noble quest," the Buddha says that when he gazed out upon the world soon after his enlightenment, he saw that sentient beings are like lotus flowers at various stages of growth within a pond (see p. 71). While some beings are like lotuses at or near the surface of the pond, capable of awakening merely by being exposed to his world-transcending teachings, the vast majority of people who encounter the Dhamma are like the lotuses growing deep below the surface. These lotuses benefit from the sunlight and use its energy to sustain their life, yet still need time to reach the surface and blossom. So too, the great multitude of people who hear the Buddha's teachings and establish faith must still nurture their wholesome qualities with the radiant energy of the Dhamma before their mindstreams become mature enough to attain direct realization. This process ordinarily requires many lives, and thus such people have to take a long-term approach to their spiritual development. While practicing the way to liberation, they must avoid a rebirth in the unfortunate realms and win successive rebirths blessed with material security, happiness, and opportunities for further spiritual progress.

These benefits, the enhancing conditions for spiritual development in the Dhamma, come about by the acquisition of *puñña* or "merit," a word that signifies the capacity of wholesome action to yield beneficial results within the cycle of rebirths. According to the Buddha's teaching, the cosmos, with its many realms of sentient existence, is governed at all levels by immutable laws, physical, biological, psychological, and ethical. The process by which sentient beings migrate from one state of existence to another is likewise lawful. It is regulated by a law that works in two principal ways: first, it connects our actions with a particular realm of rebirth that corresponds to our actions; and second, it determines the relations between our actions and the quality of our experience within the particular realm into which we have been reborn.

The governing factor in this process, the factor that makes the entire process a lawful one, is a force called *kamma* (Skt: *karma*). The word "kamma" literally means action, but technically it refers to volitional action. As the Buddha says: "It is volition (*cetanā*) that I call kamma; for having willed (*cetayitvā*), one acts by body, speech, and mind."[1] Kamma thus denotes deeds that originate from volition. Such volition may remain purely mental, generating mental kamma that occurs as thoughts, plans, and desires; or it may come to expression outwardly through manifest bodily and verbal actions.

It may seem that our deeds, once performed, perish and vanish without leaving behind any traces apart from their visible impact on other people and our environment. However, according to the Buddha, all morally determinate volitional actions create a potential to bring forth results (*vipāka*) or fruits (*phala*) that correspond to the ethical quality of those actions. This capacity of our deeds to produce the morally appropriate results is what is meant by *kamma*. Our deeds generate kamma, a potential to produce fruits that correspond to their own intrinsic tendencies. Then, when internal and external conditions are suitable, the kamma ripens and produces the appropriate fruits. In ripening, the kamma rebounds upon us for good or for harm depending on the moral quality of the original action. This may happen either later in the same life in which the action was done, in the next life, or in some distant future life.[2] The one thing that is certain is that as long as we remain within saṃsāra any stored-up kamma of ours will be capable of ripening so long as it has not yet produced its due results.

On the basis of its ethical quality, the Buddha distinguishes kamma into two major categories: the unwholesome (*akusala*) and the wholesome (*kusala*). Unwholesome kamma is action that is spiritually detrimental to the agent, morally reprehensible, and potentially productive of an unfortunate rebirth and painful results. The criterion for judging an action to be unwholesome is its underlying motives, the "roots" from which it springs. There are three unwholesome roots: greed, hatred, and delusion. From these there arises a wide variety of secondary defilements—states such as anger, hostility, envy, selfishness, arrogance, pride, presumption, and laziness—and from the root defilements and secondary defilements arise defiled actions.

Wholesome kamma, on the other hand, is action that is spiritually beneficial and morally commendable; it is action that ripens in happiness and good fortune. Its underlying motives are the three wholesome roots: nongreed, nonhatred, and nondelusion, which may be expressed more positively as generosity, loving-kindness, and wisdom. Whereas actions springing from the unwholesome roots are necessarily bound to the world of repeated birth and death, actions springing from the wholesome roots may be of two kinds, mundane and world-transcending. The mundane (*lokiya*) wholesome actions have the potential to produce a fortunate rebirth and pleasant results within the round of rebirths. The world-transcending or supramundane (*lokuttara*) wholesome actions—namely, the kamma generated by developing the Noble Eightfold Path and the other aids to enlightenment—lead to enlightenment and to liberation from the round of rebirths. This is the kamma that dismantles the entire process of karmic causation.

The correlation between kamma and its results is indicated in a general way in **Text V,1(1)**. This sutta refers to unwholesome action as "dark kamma" and mundane wholesome action as "bright kamma." It also refers to a type of kamma that is both dark and bright. Strictly speaking, this does not denote a single action that simultaneously partakes of both unwholesome and wholesome characteristics; technically such a thing is impossible, for an action must be one or the other. The combined kamma refers to the conduct of a person who intermittently engages in both unwholesome and wholesome behavior. Finally, the sutta speaks of a fourth type of kamma that is neither dark nor bright. This is the action of developing the Noble Eightfold Path, the wholesome world-transcending kamma.

It cannot be emphasized strongly enough that for Early Buddhism an understanding and acceptance of this principle of kamma and its fruit is an essential component of *right view*. Right view has two aspects, the world-bound or mundane aspect, which pertains to life within the world, and the supramundane or world-transcending aspect, which pertains to the path to liberation.[3] The world-transcending right view includes an understanding of the Four Noble Truths, dependent origination, and the three marks of impermanence, suffering, and nonself. For Early Buddhism this world-transcending right view cannot be taken up in isolation from mundane right view. Rather, it presupposes and depends upon the sound support of mundane right view, which means a firm conviction in the validity of the law of kamma and its unfolding through the process of rebirths.

To accept the law of kamma entails a radical transformation in our understanding of our relationship to the world. The twin doctrines of kamma and rebirth enable us to see that the world in which we live is, in important respects, an external reflection of the internal cosmos of the mind. This does not mean that the external world can be reduced to a mental projection in the way proposed by certain types of philosophical idealism. However, taken in conjunction, these two doctrines do show that the conditions under which we live closely correspond to the karmic tendencies of our minds. The reason why a living being is reborn into a particular realm is because in a previous life that being has generated the kamma, or volitional action, that leads to rebirth into that realm. Thus, in the final analysis, all the realms of existence have been formed, fashioned, and sustained by the mental activity of living beings. As the Buddha says: "For beings obstructed by ignorance and hindered by craving, kamma is the field, consciousness the seed, and craving the moisture, for consciousness to be established in a new realm of existence—either inferior, middling, or superior" (AN 3:76; I 223).[4]

The next selection, **Text V,1(2)**, draws a finer distinction among the types of unwholesome and wholesome kamma. The text enumerates ten primary instances of each class. Here they are called respectively "unrighteous conduct, conduct not in accordance with the Dhamma" and "righteous conduct, conduct in accordance with the Dhamma" but they are usually known as the ten pathways of unwholesome and wholesome kamma.[5] The ten are subdivided by way of the three "doors of action"—body, speech, and mind. Taking the *unwholesome* first, there are three kinds of *bodily* misconduct: killing, stealing, and sexual misconduct; four kinds of *verbal* misconduct: lying, malicious speech, harsh speech, and idle chatter (or gossip); and three kinds of *mental* misconduct: covetousness, ill will, and wrong view. The ten courses of *wholesome* action are their exact opposites: abstinence from the three kinds of bodily misconduct; abstinence from the four kinds of verbal misconduct; and noncovetousness, goodwill, and right view. According to the sutta, the ten types of unwholesome kamma are the reason that beings are reborn in the bad destinations after death; the ten types of wholesome kamma are the reason that beings are reborn in the good destinations after death. As the sutta shows, the ten types of wholesome kamma are the support, not only for a heavenly rebirth, but also for "the destruction of the taints," the attainment of liberation.

The concluding paragraphs of this sutta give us a brief survey of Buddhist cosmology. The Buddhist cosmos is divided into three broad realms—the sense-sphere realm (*kāmadhātu*), the form realm (*rūpadhātu*), and the formless realm (*arūpadhātu*)—each comprising a range of subsidiary planes.

The sense-sphere realm, our realm, is so called because the beings reborn here are strongly driven by sensual desire. The realm is divided into two levels, the bad destinations and the good destinations. The bad destinations or "states of misery" (*apāya*) are three in number: the hells, states of intense torment (see MN 129 and 130, not included in this anthology); the animal kingdom; and the sphere of spirits (*pettivisaya*), beings afflicted with incessant hunger, thirst, and other sufferings. These are the realms of retribution for the ten unwholesome paths of kamma.[6]

The good destinations in the sense-sphere realm are the human world and the six sensual heavenly planes. The latter are: the devas in the heaven of the Four Great Kings, who are presided over by four powerful devas (namely, the Four Great Kings); the Tāvatiṃsa devas presided over by Sakka, a devotee of the Buddha who is faithful but prone to negligence (see the Sakkasaṃyutta, SN chapter 11); the Yāma devas; the devas of the Tusita heaven, the abode of a bodhisatta before his final birth; the Nimmānaratī devas ("the gods who delight in creating"); and the Paranimmitavasavattī devas ("the gods who control what is created by others"). The karmic cause for rebirth into the good destinations of the sense-sphere realm is the practice of the ten courses of wholesome action.

In the form realm the grosser types of material form are absent. Its denizens, known as *brahmās*, enjoy bliss, power, luminosity, and vitality far superior to the beings in the sense-sphere realm. The form realm consists of sixteen planes. These are the objective counterparts of the four jhānas. Attainment of the first jhāna leads to rebirth among Brahmā's assembly, the ministers of Brahmā, and the Mahābrahmās, according to whether it is developed to an inferior, middling, or superior degree. The second jhāna, attained in the same three degrees, leads respectively to rebirth among the devas of limited radiance, of measureless radiance, and of streaming radiance. The third jhāna, attained in the same three degrees, leads respectively to rebirth among the devas of limited glory, of measureless glory, and of refulgent glory. The fourth jhāna ordinarily leads to rebirth among the devas of great fruit, but if developed with a feeling of disgust for perception, it will conduce to rebirth among the "nonpercipient beings," beings who lack perception. The form realm also comprises five planes reserved exclusively for the rebirth of nonreturners (see pp. 379–80), called the pure abodes: *aviha, atappa, sudassa, sudassī,* and *akaniṭṭha.* In each of the subtle form planes, the lifespan is said to be of enormous duration and to increase significantly with each higher plane.[7]

In the third realm of existence, material form is nonexistent and bare mental processes exist; hence it is called the formless realm. This realm consists of four planes, which are the objective counterparts of the four formless meditative attainments, after which they are named: the base of the infinity of space, the base of the infinity of consciousness, the base of nothingness, and the base of neither-perception-nor-nonperception. The lifespans ascribed to these realms are respectively 20,000; 40,000; 60,000; and 84,000 great eons. (For the duration of one eon, see **Text I,4(3)**.)

For Buddhist cosmology, existence in every realm, being the product of a kamma with a finite potency, is necessarily impermanent. Beings take rebirth into a realm appropriate for their kamma or deeds, experience the good or bad results, and then, when the generative kamma has spent its force, they pass away to take rebirth elsewhere as determined by still another kamma that has found the opportunity to ripen. Hence the torments of hell as well as the joys of heaven, no matter how long they may last, are bound to pass. The Buddha guides those whose spiritual faculties are still tender to aspire for a human or heavenly rebirth and teaches them the lines of conduct that conduce to the fulfillment of their aspirations. But he urges those with mature faculties to make a determined effort to put an end to the aimless wandering of saṃsāra and reach the Deathless, Nibbāna, which transcends all conditioned planes of being.

While the first two texts in this chapter establish a general correlation between kamma and spheres of rebirth, **Text V,1(3)** specifies the underlying karmic causes for the manifest differences in human life. It does so with reference to a well-known saying of the Buddha: "Beings are owners of their kamma, heirs of their kamma; they originate from their kamma, are bound to their kamma, have their kamma as their refuge. It is kamma that distinguishes beings as inferior and superior." The sutta proposes to explain this statement with regard to seven pairs of contrasting qualities observed among people. This text also introduces a distinction between two types of consequences that an unwholesome kamma can have: the more powerful is rebirth in a bad destination; the other is unpleasant fruits within the human state, for example, a short lifespan for one who in an earlier life killed living beings. An analogous distinction obtains among the consequences that a wholesome kamma can have: the more powerful is rebirth in a heavenly world; the other is pleasant fruits within the human state.

The next section deals with merit (*puñña*), wholesome kamma capable of yielding favorable results within the cycle of rebirths. Merit produces mundane benefits, such as a good rebirth, wealth, beauty, and success. It also serves as an enhancing condition for supramundane benefits, that is, for attaining the stages along the path to enlightenment. Hence, as seen in **Text V,2(1)**, the Buddha urges his disciples to cultivate merit, referring to his own cultivation of merit over many previous lives as an example.

The Nikāyas concisely organize the types of merit into three "bases of meritorious deeds" (*puññakiriyavatthu*): giving, moral discipline, and meditation. **Text V,2(2)** connects the bases of merit with the types of rebirth to which they lead. In the Indian religious context, the practice of meritorious deeds revolves around faith in certain objects regarded as sacred and spiritually empowering, capable of serving as a support for the acquisition of merit. For followers of the Buddha's teaching these are the Three Jewels: the Buddha, the Dhamma, and the Saṅgha. **Text V,2(3)** extols these as each supreme in its particular sphere: the Buddha is supreme among persons, the Dhamma among teachings, and the Saṅgha among religious communities. The text proposes an interesting twofold distinction of the Dhamma Jewel: among all conditioned things (*dhammā saṅkhatā*), the Noble Eightfold Path is supreme; among all things conditioned or unconditioned (*dhammā saṅkhatā vā asaṅkhatā vā*), Nibbāna is supreme. Merely having confidence in the Three Jewels, that is, reverential trust and devotion toward them, is itself a basis of merit; but as the verses attached to the sutta make clear, the Buddha and the Saṅgha additionally function as the recipients of gifts, and in this role they further enable donors to acquire merit leading to the fulfillment of their virtuous wishes. More will be said about this aspect of merit just below.

The following sections of this chapter elaborate on the three bases of merit individually, beginning in section 3 with giving or generosity (*dāna*). The Buddha often treated giving as the most rudimentary virtue of the spiritual life, for giving serves to break down the egocentric frame of mind on the basis of which we habitually interact with others. Contrary to what a Western reader might expect, however, "giving" for Early Buddhism does not mean simply philanthropic charity directed toward the poor and disadvantaged. While it includes this, the practice of giving has a more context-specific meaning rooted in the social structure of Indian religiosity. In India during the Buddha's time, those who sought to fathom the deepest truths of existence and attain release from the round of birth and death usually renounced home and family, relinquished their secure place in the cohesive Indian social order, and adopted the precarious life of the homeless wanderer. With shaved heads or matted locks, clad in ochre or white robes or going naked, they would move from place to place without fixed abode, except during the three months of the rainy season, when they would settle in simple huts, caves, or other lodgings. Such homeless wanderers, known as *samaṇas* ("ascetics") or *paribbājakas* ("wanderers"), did not perform any remunerative services but depended upon the charity of householders for their livelihood. The lay devotees provided them with their material requisites—robes, food, lodgings, and medicines—doing so in the confidence that such services were a source of merit that would help them advance a few steps farther in the direction of final emancipation.

When the Buddha appeared on the scene, he adopted this mode of life for himself. Once he commenced his work as a spiritual teacher, he established his Saṅgha on the same principle: the *bhikkhus* and *bhikkhunīs*, the monks and nuns, would depend on the charity of others for their material support, and they would reciprocate by offering their donors the more precious gift of the Dhamma, the teaching of the lofty path that leads to happiness, peace, and final liberation. **Text V,3(5)** testifies to this principle of mutual support. By accepting the gifts of lay people, the monastics give them the opportunity to acquire merit. Since the volume of merit generated by the act of giving is considered to be proportional to the worthiness of the recipient, when the recipients are the Buddha and those following in his footsteps, the merit becomes immeasurable (see MN 142, not included in this anthology). For this reason, the *sāvakasaṅgha,* the spiritual community of noble disciples, is called "the unsurpassed field of merit for the world" (*anuttaraṃ puññakhettaṃ lokassa*).[8] Gifts to the Saṅgha, it is said, conduce to great blessings; they lead to one's welfare and happiness for a long time and can bring rebirth in the heavenly worlds. But as **Text V,3(6)** reminds us, this is true "only for the morally pure, not for the immoral."

This leads to the next base of merit, "moral discipline" (*sīla*), which for Early Buddhism requires the undertaking of precepts. The most basic moral guidelines inculcated in the Nikāyas are the five precepts, the training rules to abstain from taking life, stealing, sexual misconduct, false speech, and the use of intoxicants. These are mentioned in **Text V,4(1)**, which, by an interesting twist in terminology, speaks of them as "pristine, traditional, ancient *gifts*," thus implicitly subsuming *sīla* under *dāna*. The reason the observance of precepts is a form of giving is because one who undertakes precepts will be "giving to immeasurable beings freedom from fear, hostility, and oppression," and as a karmic consequence "he himself will enjoy immeasurable freedom from fear, hostility, and oppression."

While the Buddha enjoins observance of the five precepts upon lay followers as a full-time obligation, he recommends a more stringent type of moral practice for the uposatha, the observance days determined by the lunar calendar: the full-moon day, the new-moon day, and the two half-moon days. (Of the four, in Buddhist countries today it is the full-moon day that is given priority.) On these occasions, devout lay Buddhists undertake eight precepts: the usual five, but with the third changed to complete sexual abstinence, augmented by three other precepts that emulate the training rules of a novice monk or nun. The eight precepts, enumerated in **Text V,4(2)**, augment the training in *sīla* as a moral observance with a training in self-restraint, simplicity, and contentment. In this respect they prepare the disciple for the training of the mind undertaken in the practice of meditation, the third base of merit.

The practice of meditation is not only the heart of the path to liberation but a source of merit in its own right. Wholesome meditation practices, even those that do not directly lead to insight, help to purify the grosser levels of mental defilement and uncover deeper dimensions of the mind's potential purity and radiance. **Text V,5(1)** declares that the type of meditation that is most fruitful for the production of mundane merit is the development of loving-kindness (*mettābhāvanā*). The practice of loving-kindness, however, is only one among a set of four meditations called the "divine abodes" (*brahmavihāra*) or "immeasurable states" (*appamaññā*): the development of loving-kindness, compassion, altruistic joy, and equanimity, which are to be extended boundlessly to all sentient beings. Briefly, loving-kindness (*mettā*) is the wish for the welfare and happiness of all beings; compassion (*karuṇā*), the feeling of empathy for all those afflicted with suffering; altruistic joy (*muditā*), the feeling of happiness at the success and good fortune of others; and equanimity (*upekkhā*), a balanced reaction to joy and misery, which protects one from emotional agitation.

These meditations are said to be the means to rebirth in the brahma world; see **Text V,5(2)**. While the brahmins regarded the brahma world as the highest attainment, for the Buddha it was just one exalted sphere of rebirth. The concentration arisen from these meditations, however, can also be used as a basis for cultivating the wisdom of insight, and insight culminates in liberation. **Text V,5(3)**, the last selection of this chapter, thus grades the different types of merit according to their fruits: from giving (with the various kinds of gifts ranked according to the spiritual status of the recipients) through the going for refuge and the five precepts to the meditation on loving-kindness. Then, at the very end, it declares that the most fruitful deed among them all is the perception of impermanence. The perception of impermanence, however, belongs to a different order. It is so fruitful not because it yields pleasant mundane results within the round of rebirths, but because it leads to the wisdom of insight that cuts the chains of bondage and brings the realization of complete emancipation, Nibbāna.

V. The Way to a Fortunate Rebirth

1. The Law of Kamma

(1) Four Kinds of Kamma

"There are, O monks, these four kinds of kamma declared by me after I had realized them for myself by direct knowledge. What four?

"There is dark kamma with dark results; there is bright kamma with bright results; there is kamma that is dark and bright with dark and bright results; there is kamma that is neither dark nor bright, with neither dark nor bright results, which leads to the destruction of kamma.

"And what, monks, is dark kamma with dark results? Here, monks, someone generates an afflictive volitional formation of body, speech, or mind. Having done so, he is reborn in an afflictive world. When he is reborn in an afflictive world, afflictive contacts touch him. Being touched by afflictive contacts, he experiences an afflictive feeling, extremely painful, as for example the beings in hell experience. This is called dark kamma with dark results.

"And what, monks, is bright kamma with bright results? Here, monks, someone generates a non-afflictive volitional formation of body, speech, or mind. Having done so, he is reborn in a non-afflictive world. When he is reborn in a non-afflictive world, non-afflictive contacts touch him. Being touched by non-afflictive contacts, he experiences a non-afflictive feeling, extremely pleasant, as for example the devas of refulgent glory experience.[9] This is called bright kamma with bright results.

"And what, monks, is dark and bright kamma with dark and bright results? Here, monks, someone generates both an afflictive volitional formation of body, speech, or mind and a non-afflictive volitional formation of body, speech, or mind. Having done so, he is reborn in a world that is both afflictive and non-afflictive. When he is reborn in such a world, both afflictive and non-afflictive contacts touch him. Being touched by such contacts, he experiences both an afflictive feeling and a non-afflictive feeling, a mixture and conglomeration of pleasure and pain, as for example human beings and some devas and some beings in the lower world experience. This is called dark and bright kamma with dark and bright results.

"And what, monks, is kamma that is neither dark nor bright, with neither dark nor bright results, which leads to the destruction of kamma? The volition to abandon this dark kamma with dark results, and to abandon the bright kamma with bright results, and to abandon the dark and bright kamma with dark and bright results—this is called the kamma that is neither dark nor bright, with neither dark nor bright results, which leads to the destruction of kamma.[10]

"These, monks, are the four kinds of kamma declared by me after I had realized them for myself by direct knowledge."

(AN 4:232; II 230–32)

(2) Why Beings Fare as They Do After Death

1. Thus have I heard. On one occasion the Blessed One was wandering by stages in the Kosalan country with a large Saṅgha of monks, and eventually he arrived at a Kosalan brahmin village named Sālā.

2. The brahmin householders of Sālā heard: "It is said that the ascetic Gotama, the Sakyan son who went forth from a Sakyan clan, has been wandering in the Kosalan country with a large Saṅgha of monks and has come to Sālā. Now a good report of Master Gotama has been circulating thus: 'That Blessed One is an arahant ... [as in Text III,2] ... that is perfectly complete and purified.' Now it is good to see such arahants."

3. Then the brahmin householders of Sālā went to the Blessed One. Some paid homage to him and sat down to one side; some exchanged greetings with him and, after their greetings and cordial talk, sat down to one side; some saluted him reverentially and sat down to one side; some remained silent and sat down to one side.

4. When they were seated, they said to the Blessed One: "Master Gotama, what is the cause and condition why some beings here, on the breakup of the body, after death, are reborn in a state of misery, in a bad destination, in the lower world, in hell? And what is the cause and condition why some beings here, on the breakup of the body, after death, are reborn in a good destination, in a heavenly world?"

5. "Householders, it is by reason of unrighteous conduct, conduct not in accordance with the Dhamma, that some beings here, on the

breakup of the body, after death, are reborn in a state of misery, in a bad destination, in the lower world, in hell. It is by reason of righteous conduct, conduct in accordance with the Dhamma, that some beings here, on the breakup of the body, after death, are reborn in a good destination, in a heavenly world."

6. "We do not understand the detailed meaning of Master Gotama's statement, which he has spoken in brief without expounding the detailed meaning. It would be good if Master Gotama would teach us the Dhamma so that we might understand the detailed meaning of his statement."

"Then, householders, listen and attend closely to what I shall say."

"Yes, venerable sir," they replied. The Blessed One said this:

7. "Householders, there are three kinds of unrighteous bodily conduct, conduct not in accordance with the Dhamma. There are four kinds of unrighteous verbal conduct, conduct not in accordance with the Dhamma. There are three kinds of unrighteous mental conduct, conduct not in accordance with the Dhamma.

8. "And how, householders, are there three kinds of unrighteous bodily conduct, conduct not in accordance with the Dhamma? Here someone kills living beings; he is murderous, bloody-handed, given to blows and violence, merciless to living beings. He takes what is not given; he takes by way of theft the wealth and property of others in the village or forest. He commits sexual misconduct; he has intercourse with women who are protected by their mother, father, mother and father, brother, sister, or relatives, who have a husband, who are protected by law, and even with those already engaged. That is how there are three kinds of unrighteous bodily conduct, conduct not in accordance with the Dhamma.

9. "And how, householders, are there four kinds of unrighteous verbal conduct, conduct not in accordance with the Dhamma? Here someone speaks falsehood; when summoned to a court, or to a meeting, or to his relatives' presence, or to his guild, or to the royal family's presence, and questioned as a witness thus: 'So, good man, tell what you know,' not knowing, he says, 'I know,' or knowing, he says, 'I do not know'; not seeing, he says, 'I see,' or seeing, he says, 'I do not see'; in full awareness he speaks falsehood for his own ends, or for another's ends, or for some trifling worldly end. He speaks maliciously; he repeats elsewhere what he has heard here in order to

divide [those people] from these, or he repeats to these people what he has heard elsewhere in order to divide [these people] from those; thus he is one who divides those who are united, a creator of divisions, who enjoys discord, rejoices in discord, delights in discord, a speaker of words that create discord. He speaks harshly; he utters such words as are rough, hard, hurtful to others, offensive to others, bordering on anger, not conducive to concentration. He engages in idle chatter; he speaks at the wrong time, speaks what is not fact, speaks what is useless, speaks contrary to the Dhamma and the Discipline; at the wrong time he speaks such words as are worthless, unreasonable, immoderate, and unbeneficial. That is how there are four kinds of unrighteous verbal conduct, conduct not in accordance with the Dhamma.

10. "And how, householders, are there three kinds of unrighteous mental conduct, conduct not in accordance with the Dhamma? Here someone is covetous; he covets the wealth and property of others thus: 'Oh, may what belongs to another be mine!' Or he has a mind of ill will and intentions of hate thus: 'May these beings be slain and slaughtered, may they be cut off, perish, or be annihilated!' Or he has wrong view, distorted vision, thus: 'There is nothing given, nothing offered, nothing sacrificed; no fruit or result of good and bad actions; no this world, no other world; no mother, no father; no beings who are reborn spontaneously; no good and virtuous ascetics and brahmins in the world who have themselves realized by direct knowledge and declare this world and the other world.'[11] That is how there are three kinds of unrighteous mental conduct, conduct not in accordance with the Dhamma. So, householders, it is by reason of such unrighteous conduct, such conduct not in accordance with the Dhamma, that some beings here on the breakup of the body, after death, are reborn in a state of misery, in a bad destination, in the lower world, in hell.

11. "Householders, there are three kinds of righteous bodily conduct, conduct in accordance with the Dhamma. There are four kinds of righteous verbal conduct, conduct in accordance with the Dhamma. There are three kinds of righteous mental conduct, conduct in accordance with the Dhamma.

12. "And how, householders, are there three kinds of righteous bodily conduct, conduct in accordance with the Dhamma? Here someone, abandoning the destruction of life, abstains from the destruction of life; with rod and weapon laid aside, conscientious, merciful, he dwells

compassionate to all living beings. Abandoning the taking of what is not given, he abstains from taking what is not given; he does not take by way of theft the wealth and property of others in the village or in the forest. Abandoning sexual misconduct, he abstains from sexual misconduct; he does not have intercourse with women who are protected by their mother, father, mother and father, brother, sister, or relatives, who have a husband, who are protected by law, or with those already engaged. That is how there are three kinds of righteous bodily conduct, conduct in accordance with the Dhamma.

13. "And how, householders, are there four kinds of righteous verbal conduct, conduct in accordance with the Dhamma? Here someone, abandoning false speech, abstains from false speech; when summoned to a court, or to a meeting, or to his relatives' presence, or to his guild, or to the royal family's presence, and questioned as a witness thus: 'So, good man, tell what you know,' not knowing, he says, 'I do not know,' or knowing, he says, 'I know'; not seeing, he says, 'I do not see,' or seeing, he says, 'I see'; he does not in full awareness speak falsehood for his own ends, or for another's ends, or for some trifling worldly end. Abandoning malicious speech, he abstains from malicious speech; he does not repeat elsewhere what he has heard here in order to divide [those people] from these, nor does he repeat to these people what he has heard elsewhere in order to divide [these people] from those; thus he is one who reunites those who are divided, a promoter of friendships, who enjoys concord, rejoices in concord, delights in concord, a speaker of words that promote concord. Abandoning harsh speech, he abstains from harsh speech; he speaks such words as are gentle, pleasing to the ear, and loveable, as go to the heart, are courteous, desired by many, and agreeable to many. Abandoning idle chatter, he abstains from idle chatter; he speaks at the right time, speaks what is fact, speaks on what is good, speaks on the Dhamma and the Discipline; at the right time he speaks such words as are worth recording, reasonable, moderate, and beneficial. That is how there are four kinds of righteous verbal conduct, conduct in accordance with the Dhamma.

14. "And how, householders, are there three kinds of righteous mental conduct, conduct in accordance with the Dhamma? Here someone is not covetous; he does not covet the wealth and property of others thus: 'Oh, may what belongs to another be mine!' His mind is without ill will, and he has intentions free from hate thus: 'May these beings be

free from enmity, affliction, and anxiety! May they live happily!' He has right view, undistorted vision, thus: 'There is what is given and what is offered and what is sacrificed; there is fruit and result of good and bad actions; there is this world and the other world; there is mother and father; there are beings who are reborn spontaneously; there are good and virtuous ascetics and brahmins in the world who have themselves realized by direct knowledge and declare this world and the other world.' That is how there are three kinds of righteous mental conduct, conduct in accordance with the Dhamma. So, householders, it is by reason of such righteous conduct, such conduct in accordance with the Dhamma that some beings here, on the breakup of the body, after death, are reborn in a good destination, even in a heavenly world.

15. "If, householders, one who observes righteous conduct, conduct in accordance with the Dhamma, should wish: 'Oh, that on the breakup of the body, after death, may I be reborn in the company of well-to-do nobles!' it is possible that, on the breakup of the body, after death, he will be reborn in the company of well-to-do nobles. Why is that? Because he observes righteous conduct, conduct in accordance with the Dhamma.

16–17. "If, householders, one who observes righteous conduct, conduct in accordance with the Dhamma, should wish: 'Oh, that on the breakup of the body, after death, may I be reborn in the company of well-to-do brahmins!... in the company of well-to-do householders!' it is possible that, on the breakup of the body, after death, he will be reborn in the company of well-to-do householders. Why is that? Because he observes righteous conduct, conduct in accordance with the Dhamma.

18–42. "If, householders, one who observes righteous conduct, conduct in accordance with the Dhamma, should wish: 'Oh, that on the breakup of the body, after death, may I be reborn in the company of the devas of the realm of the Four Great Kings!... in the company of the Tāvatiṃsa devas ... the Yāma devas ... the Tusita devas ... the devas who delight in creating ... the devas who wield power over others' creations ... the devas of Brahmā's company ... the devas of radiance[12] ... the devas of limited radiance ... the devas of immeasurable radiance ... the devas of streaming radiance ... the devas of glory ... the devas of limited glory ... the devas of immeasurable glory ... the devas of refulgent glory ... the devas of great fruit ... the *aviha* devas ... the *atappa* devas ... the *sudassa* devas ... the *sudassī* devas ... the *akaniṭṭha* devas ... the devas of the base of the infinity of space ... the devas of the base of the infinity of consciousness ... the devas of the base of nothingness ... the devas of the base of neither-perception-nor-non-perception!' it is possible that on the breakup of the body, after death, he will be reborn in the company of the devas of the base of neither-perception-nor-non-perception. Why is that? Because he observes righteous conduct, conduct in accordance with the Dhamma.

43. "If, householders, one who observes conduct in accordance with the Dhamma, righteous conduct, should wish: 'Oh, by realizing it for myself with direct knowledge, may I in this very life enter upon and dwell in the liberation of mind, liberation by wisdom, that is taintless with the destruction of the taints!' it is possible that, by realizing it for himself with direct knowledge, in this very life he will enter upon and dwell in the liberation of mind, liberation by wisdom, that is taintless with the destruction of the taints. Why is that? Because he observes righteous conduct, conduct in accordance with the Dhamma."[13]

44. When this was said, the brahmin householders of Sālā said to the Blessed One: "Magnificent, Master Gotama! Magnificent, Master Gotama! Master Gotama has made the Dhamma clear in many ways, as though he were turning upright what had been overthrown, revealing what was hidden, showing the way to one who was lost, or holding up a lamp in the darkness so those with good eyesight can see forms. We now go for refuge to Master Gotama, to the Dhamma, and to the Saṅgha of monks. Let Master Gotama accept us as lay followers who have gone for refuge from today until life's end."

(MN 41: *Sāleyyaka Sutta*; I 286–90)

(3) Kamma and Its Fruits

1. Thus have I heard. On one occasion the Blessed One was living at Sāvatthī in Jeta's Grove, Anāthapiṇḍika's Park.

2. Then the brahmin student Subha, Todeyya's son, went to the Blessed One and exchanged greetings with him. When this courteous and amiable talk was finished, he sat down at one side and asked the Blessed One:

3. "Master Gotama, why is it that human beings are seen to be inferior and superior? For people are seen to be short-lived and long-lived, sickly and healthy, ugly and beautiful, without influence and influential, poor and wealthy, low born and high born, stupid and wise. Why is it, Master Gotama, that human beings are seen to be inferior and superior?"

4. "Student, beings are owners of their actions, heirs of their actions; they originate from their actions, are bound to their actions, have their actions as their refuge. It is action that distinguishes beings as inferior and superior."

"I do not understand in detail the meaning of Master Gotama's statement, which he spoke in brief without expounding the meaning in detail. It would be good if Master Gotama would teach me the Dhamma so that I might understand in detail the meaning of his statement."

"Then, student, listen and attend closely to what I shall say."

"Yes, sir," Subha replied. The Blessed One said this:

5. "Here, student, some man or woman kills living beings and is murderous, bloody-handed, given to blows and violence, merciless to living beings. Because of performing and undertaking such action, on the breakup of the body, after death, he is reborn in a state of misery, in a bad destination, in the lower world, in hell. But if on the breakup of the body, after death, he is not reborn in a state of misery, in a bad destination, in the lower world, in hell, but instead comes back to the human state, then wherever he is reborn he is short-lived.[14] This is the way, student, that leads to short life, namely, one kills living beings and is murderous, bloody-handed, given to blows and violence, merciless to living beings.

6. "But here, student, some man or woman, abandoning the destruction of life, abstains from the destruction of life; with rod and weapon laid aside, conscientious, merciful, he dwells compassionate to all living beings. Because of performing and undertaking such action, on the breakup of the body, after death, he is reborn in a good destination, in a heavenly world. But if on the breakup of the body, after death, he is not reborn in a good destination, in a heavenly world, but instead comes back to the human state, then wherever he is reborn he is long-lived.[15] This is the way, student, that leads to long life, namely, abandoning the destruction of life, one abstains from the destruction of life;

with rod and weapon laid aside, conscientious, merciful, one dwells compassionate to all living beings.

7. "Here, student, some man or woman is given to injuring beings with the hand, with a clod, with a stick, or with a knife. Because of performing and undertaking such action, on the breakup of the body, after death, he is reborn in a state of misery.... But if instead he comes back to the human state, then wherever he is reborn he is sickly. This is the way, student, that leads to sickliness, namely, one is given to injuring beings with the hand, with a clod, with a stick, or with a knife.

8. "But here, student, some man or woman is not given to injuring beings with the hand, with a clod, with a stick, or with a knife. Because of performing and undertaking such action, on the breakup of the body, after death, he is reborn in a good destination.... But if instead he comes back to the human state, then wherever he is reborn he is healthy. This is the way, student, that leads to health, namely, one is not given to injuring beings with the hand, with a clod, with a stick, or with a knife.

9. "Here, student, some man or woman is of an angry and irritable character; even when criticized a little, he is offended, becomes angry, hostile, and resentful, and displays anger, hate, and bitterness. Because of performing and undertaking such action ... he is reborn in a state of misery.... But if instead he comes back to the human state, then wherever he is reborn he is ugly. This is the way, student, that leads to ugliness, namely, one is of an angry and irritable character ... and displays anger, hate, and bitterness.

10. "But here, student, some man or woman is not of an angry and irritable character; even when criticized a little, he is not offended, does not become angry, hostile, and resentful, and does not display anger, hate, and bitterness. Because of performing and undertaking such action ... he is reborn in a good destination.... But if instead he comes back to the human state, then wherever he is reborn he is beautiful. This is the way, student, that leads to being beautiful, namely, one is not of an angry and irritable character ... and does not display anger, hate, and bitterness.

11. "Here, student, some man or woman is envious, one who envies, resents, and begrudges the gains, honor, respect, reverence, salutations, and veneration received by others. Because of performing and undertaking such action ... he is reborn in a state of misery.... But if instead

he comes back to the human state, then wherever he is reborn he is without influence. This is the way, student, that leads to being without influence, namely, one is envious ... toward the gains, honor, respect, reverence, salutations, and veneration received by others.

12. "But here, student, some man or woman is not envious, one who does not envy, resent, and begrudge the gains, honor, respect, reverence, salutations, and veneration received by others. Because of performing and undertaking such action ... he is reborn in a good destination.... But if instead he comes back to the human state, then wherever he is reborn he is influential. This is the way, student, that leads to being influential, namely, one is not envious ... toward the gains, honor, respect, reverence, salutations, and veneration received by others.

13. "Here, student, some man or woman does not give food, drink, clothing, carriages, garlands, scents, unguents, beds, dwelling, and lamps to ascetics or brahmins. Because of performing and undertaking such action ... he is reborn in a state of misery.... But if instead he comes back to the human state, then wherever he is reborn he is poor. This is the way, student, that leads to poverty, namely, one does not give food ... and lamps to ascetics or brahmins.

14. "But here, student, some man or woman gives food ... and lamps to ascetics or brahmins. Because of performing and undertaking such action ... he is reborn in a good destination.... But if instead he comes back to the human state, then wherever he is reborn he is wealthy. This is the way, student, that leads to wealth, namely, one gives food ... and lamps to ascetics or brahmins.

15. "Here, student, some man or woman is obstinate and arrogant; he does not pay homage to one who should receive homage, does not rise up for one in whose presence he should rise up, does not offer a seat to one who deserves a seat, does not make way for one for whom he should make way, and does not honor, respect, revere, and venerate one who should be honored, respected, revered, and venerated. Because of performing and undertaking such action ... he is reborn in a state of misery.... But if instead he comes back to the human state, then wherever he is reborn he is low born. This is the way, student, that leads to low birth, namely, one is obstinate and arrogant ... and does not honor, respect, revere, and venerate one who should be honored, respected, revered, and venerated.

16. "But here, student, some man or woman is not obstinate and arrogant; he pays homage to one who should receive homage, rises up for one in whose presence he should rise up, offers a seat to one who deserves a seat, makes way for one for whom he should make way, and honors, respects, reveres, and venerates one who should be honored, respected, revered, and venerated. Because of performing and undertaking such action ... he is reborn in a good destination.... But if instead he comes back to the human state, then wherever he is reborn he is high born. This is the way, student, that leads to high birth, namely, one is not obstinate and arrogant ... and honors, respects, reveres, and venerates one who should be honored, respected, revered, and venerated.

17. "Here, student, some man or woman does not visit an ascetic or a brahmin and ask: 'Venerable sir, what is wholesome? What is unwholesome? What is blamable? What is blameless? What should be cultivated? What should not be cultivated? What kind of action will lead to my harm and suffering for a long time? What kind of action will lead to my welfare and happiness for a long time?' Because of performing and undertaking such action ... he is reborn in a state of misery.... But if instead he comes back to the human state, then wherever he is reborn he is stupid. This is the way, student, that leads to stupidity, namely, one does not visit an ascetic or brahmin and ask such questions.

18. "But here, student, some man or woman visits an ascetic or a brahmin and asks: 'Venerable sir, what is wholesome?... What kind of action will lead to my welfare and happiness for a long time?' Because of performing and undertaking such action ... he is reborn in a good destination.... But if instead he comes back to the human state, then wherever he is reborn he is wise. This is the way, student, that leads to wisdom, namely, one visits an ascetic or brahmin and asks such questions.

19. "Thus, student, the way that leads to short life makes people short-lived, the way that leads to long life makes people long-lived; the way that leads to sickliness makes people sickly, the way that leads to health makes people healthy; the way that leads to ugliness makes people ugly, the way that leads to beauty makes people beautiful; the way that leads to being uninfluential makes people uninfluential, the way that leads to being influential makes people influential; the way

that leads to poverty makes people poor, the way that leads to wealth makes people wealthy; the way that leads to low birth makes people low born, the way that leads to high birth makes people high born; the way that leads to stupidity makes people stupid, the way that leads to wisdom makes people wise.

20. "Beings are owners of their actions, heirs of their actions; they originate from their actions, are bound to their actions, have their actions as their refuge. It is action that distinguishes beings as inferior and superior."

21. When this was said, the brahmin student Subha, Todeyya's son, said to the Blessed One: "Magnificent, Master Gotama! Magnificent, Master Gotama!... [as in preceding text] ... Let Master Gotama accept me as a lay follower who has gone for refuge from today until life's end."

(MN 135: *Cūḷakammavibhaṅga Sutta*; III 202–6)

2. Merit: The Key to Good Fortune

(1) Meritorious Deeds

"Monks, do not fear meritorious deeds. This is an expression denoting happiness, what is desirable, wished for, dear, and agreeable, that is, meritorious deeds. For I know full well, monks, that for a long time I experienced desirable, wished for, dear, and agreeable results from often performing meritorious deeds.

"Having cultivated for seven years a mind of loving-kindness, for seven eons of contraction and expansion I did not return to this world. Whenever the eon contracted I reached the plane of streaming radiance, and when the eon expanded I arose in an empty divine mansion. And there I was Brahmā, the great Brahmā, the unvanquished victor, the all-seeing, the all-powerful. Thirty-six times I was Sakka, ruler of the devas. And many hundreds of times I was a wheel-turning monarch, righteous, a king of righteousness, conqueror of the four regions of the earth, maintaining stability in the land, in possession of the seven treasures. What need is there to speak of mere local kingship?

"It occurred to me, monks, to wonder: 'Of what kind of deed of mine is this the fruit? Of what deed's ripening am I now of such great accomplishment and power?' And then it occurred to me: 'It is the fruit of three kinds of deeds of mine, the ripening of three kinds of deeds that I am now of such great accomplishment and power: deeds of giving, of self-mastery, and of refraining.'"

(It 22; 14–15)

(2) Three Bases of Merit

"There are, O monks, three ways of making merit. What three? There are ways of making merit by giving, by moral discipline, and by the development of meditation.

"There is a person who has practiced the making of merit by giving only to a limited degree; and, likewise to a limited degree, he has practiced the making of merit by moral discipline; but he has not undertaken the making of merit by meditation. With the breakup of the body, after death, he will be reborn among humans in an unfavorable condition.

"Another person has practiced the making of merit by giving as well as by moral discipline to a high degree; but he has not undertaken the making of merit by meditation. With the breakup of the body, after death, he will be reborn among humans in a favorable condition.

"Or he will be reborn in the company of the devas of the Four Great Kings. And there, the Four Great Kings, who had practiced to a very high degree the making of merit by giving and by moral discipline, surpass the devas of their realm in ten respects: in divine lifespan, divine beauty, divine happiness, divine fame, divine power; and in divine sights, sounds, smells, tastes, and touches.

"Or he will be reborn in the company of the Tāvatiṃsa devas. And there, Sakka, ruler of the devas, who had practiced the making of merit by giving and by moral discipline to a very high degree, surpasses the devas of their realm in ten respects: in divine lifespan, divine beauty, divine happiness, divine fame, divine power; and in divine sights, sounds, smells, tastes, and touches.

[*Similar statements are made for rebirth among the Yāma devas, Tusita devas, the devas who delight in creating, the devas who wield power over others' creations, and for the respective rulers of these realms.*]

"These, monks, are the three ways of making merit."

(AN 8:36; IV 241–43)

(3) *The Best Kinds of Confidence*

"Monks, there are these four best kinds of confidence. What four?

"To whatever extent there are beings, whether footless or with two feet, four feet, or many feet, whether having form or formless, whether percipient, non-percipient, or neither percipient nor non-percipient, the Tathāgata, the Arahant, the Perfectly Enlightened One is declared the best among them. Those who have confidence in the Buddha have confidence in the best, and for those who have confidence in the best, the result is best.

"To whatever extent there are things that are conditioned, the Noble Eightfold Path is declared the best among them. Those who have confidence in the Noble Eightfold Path have confidence in the best, and for those who have confidence in the best, the result is best.

"To whatever extent there are things whether conditioned or unconditioned, dispassion is declared the best among them, that is, the crushing of pride, the removal of thirst, the uprooting of attachment, the termination of the round, the destruction of craving, dispassion, cessation, Nibbāna. Those who have confidence in the Dhamma have confidence in the best, and for those who have confidence in the best, the result is best.

"To whatever extent there are communities or groups, the Tathāgata's Saṅgha of disciples is declared the best among them, that is, the four pairs of persons, the eight types of individuals—this Saṅgha of the Blessed One's disciples is worthy of gifts, worthy of hospitality, worthy of offerings, worthy of reverential salutation, the unsurpassed field of merit for the world. Those who have confidence in the Saṅgha have confidence in the best, and for those who have confidence in the best, the result is best."

For those who have confidence as the best,
For those who understand the best Dhamma,
For those who have confidence in the Buddha,
The unsurpassed one worthy of offerings;
For those who have confidence in the Dhamma,
In blissful dispassion, perfect peace;
For those who have confidence in the Saṅgha,
The field of merit unsurpassed;

For those giving gifts to the best,
The best kind of merit increases:
The best lifespan, beauty, and fame,
Good reputation, happiness, and strength.
Whether he becomes a deva or a human being,
The wise one who gives of the best,
Concentrated upon the best Dhamma,
Rejoices when he has attained to the best.

(AN 4:34; II 34–35)

3. Giving

(1) If People Knew the Result of Giving

"O monks, if people knew, as I know, the result of giving and sharing, they would not eat without having given, nor would they allow the stain of niggardliness to obsess them and take root in their minds. Even if it were their last morsel, their last mouthful, they would not eat without having shared it, if there were someone to share it with. But, monks, as people do not know, as I know, the result of giving and sharing, they eat without having given, and the stain of niggardliness obsesses them and takes root in their minds."

(It 26; 18–19)

(2) Reasons for Giving

"There are, O monks, eight reasons for giving. What eight? People may give out of affection; or in an angry mood; or out of stupidity; or out of fear; or with the thought: 'Such gifts have been given before by my father and grandfather and it was done by them before; hence it would be unworthy of me to give up this old family tradition'; or with the thought, 'By giving this gift, I shall be reborn in a good destination, in a heavenly world, after death'; or with the thought, 'When giving this gift, my heart will be glad, and happiness and joy will arise in me'; or one gives because it ennobles and adorns the mind."

(AN 8:33; IV 236–37)

(3) The Gift of Food

On one occasion the Blessed One was dwelling among the Koliyans, at a town called Sajjanela. One morning the Blessed One dressed, took his upper robe and bowl, and went to the dwelling of Suppavāsā, a Koliyan lady. Having arrived there, he sat down on the seat prepared for him. The Koliyan lady Suppavāsā attended to the Blessed One personally and served him with various kinds of delicious food. When the Blessed One had finished his meal and had withdrawn his hand from the bowl, the Koliyan lady Suppavāsā sat down to one side, and the Blessed One addressed her as follows:

"Suppavāsā, a noble female disciple, by giving food, gives four things to those who receive it. What four? She gives long life, beauty, happiness, and strength. By giving long life, she herself will be endowed with long life, human or divine. By giving beauty, she herself will be endowed with beauty, human or divine. By giving happiness, she herself will be endowed with happiness, human or divine. By giving strength, she herself will be endowed with strength, human or divine. A noble female disciple, by giving food, gives those four things to those who receive it."

(AN 4:57; II 62–63)

(4) A Superior Person's Gifts

"There are, O monks, these five gifts of a superior person. What five?

"He gives a gift out of faith; he gives a gift respectfully; he gives a gift at the right time; he gives a gift with a generous heart; he gives a gift without denigration.

"Because he gives a gift out of faith, wherever the result of that gift ripens he becomes rich, affluent, and wealthy, and he is handsome, comely, graceful, endowed with supreme beauty of complexion.

"Because he gives a gift respectfully, wherever the result of that gift ripens he becomes rich, affluent, and wealthy, and his children and wives, his slaves, messengers, and workers are obedient, lend their ears to him, and apply their minds to understand him.

"Because he gives a gift at the right time, wherever the result of that gift ripens he becomes rich, affluent, and wealthy, and benefits come to him at the right time, in abundant measure.

"Because he gives a gift with a generous heart, wherever the result of that gift ripens he becomes rich, affluent, and wealthy, and his mind inclines to the enjoyment of excellent things among the five cords of sensual pleasure.

"Because he gives a gift without denigrating himself and others, wherever the result of that gift ripens he becomes rich, affluent, and wealthy, and no loss of his wealth takes place from any quarter, whether from fire, floods, the king, bandits, or unloved heirs.

"These, monks, are the five gifts of a superior person."

(AN 5:148; III 172–73)

(5) Mutual Support

"Monks, brahmins and householders are very helpful to you. They provide you with the requisites of robes, almsfood, lodgings, and medicines in time of sickness. And you, monks, are very helpful to brahmins and householders, as you teach them the Dhamma that is good in the beginning, the middle, and the end, with the correct meaning and wording, and you proclaim the spiritual life in its fulfillment and complete purity. Thus, monks, this spiritual life is lived with mutual support for the purpose of crossing the flood and making a complete end of suffering."

(It 107; 111)

(6) Rebirth on Account of Giving

"There are, O monks, eight kinds of rebirth on account of giving. What eight?

"Here, monks, a certain person makes a gift to an ascetic or a brahmin, offering him food, drink, clothing, and vehicles; garlands, scents, and unguents; bedding, lodging, and lighting. In making the gift, he hopes for a reward. He now notices affluent nobles, brahmins, or householders enjoying themselves provided and furnished with the five objects of sensual pleasure, and he thinks: 'Oh, with the breakup of the body, after death, may I be reborn among them!' And he sets his mind on that thought, keeps to it firmly, and fosters it. This thought of his aims at what is low, and if not developed to what is higher it will lead him to just such a rebirth. With the breakup of the body, after death, he will be reborn among affluent nobles, brahmins, or householders. This, however, I declare only for the morally pure, not for the immoral; for it is due to his purity, monks, that the heart's desire of the morally pure succeeds.[16]

"Then again, a certain person makes a gift to an ascetic or a brahmin, offering him food ... or lighting. In making the gift, he hopes for a reward. He now hears of the long life, the beauty, and the great happiness of the devas in the realm of the Four Great Kings ... the Tāvatiṃsa devas ... the Yāma devas ... the Tusita devas ... the devas who delight in creating ... the devas who wield power over others' creations, and he wishes to be reborn among them. He sets his mind on that thought, keeps to it firmly, and fosters it. This thought of his aims at what is low, and if not developed to what is higher, it will lead him to just such a rebirth. After his death, when his body breaks up, he will be reborn among the devas in the realm of the Four Great Kings ... or among the devas who wield power over others' creations. This, however, I declare only for the morally pure, not for the immoral; for it is due to his purity, monks, that the heart's desire of the morally pure succeeds.

"Then again, a certain person makes a gift to an ascetic or a brahmin, offering him food ... or lighting. He now hears of the long life, the beauty, and the great happiness of the devas of Brahmā's company, and he wishes to be reborn among them. He sets his mind on that thought, keeps to it firmly, and fosters it. This thought of his aims at what is low, and if not developed to what is higher, it will lead him to just such a rebirth. After his death, when his body breaks up, he will be reborn among the devas of Brahmā's company. This, however, I declare only for the morally pure, not for the immoral; only for one free of lust, not for one who is lustful.[17] Because he is without lust, monks, the heart's desire of the morally pure succeeds.

"These, monks, are the eight kinds of rebirth on account of giving."

(AN 8:35; IV 239–41)

4. Moral Discipline

(1) The Five Precepts

"There are, O monks, eight streams of merit, streams of the wholesome, nourishments of happiness, that are heavenly, ripening in happiness, conducive to heaven, and that lead to whatever is wished for, loved, and agreeable, to one's welfare and happiness. What are the eight?

"Here, monks, a noble disciple has gone for refuge to the Buddha. This is the first stream of merit, stream of the wholesome, nourishment of happiness, that is heavenly, ripening in happiness, conducive to heaven, and that leads to whatever is wished for, loved, and agreeable, to one's welfare and happiness.

"Further, a noble disciple has gone for refuge to the Dhamma. This is the second stream of merit ... that leads to whatever is wished for, loved, and agreeable, to one's welfare and happiness.

"Further, a noble disciple has gone for refuge to the Saṅgha. This is the third stream of merit ... that leads to whatever is wished for, loved, and agreeable, to one's welfare and happiness.

"There are further, monks, these five gifts—pristine, of long standing, traditional, ancient, unadulterated and never before adulterated, that are not being adulterated and that will not be adulterated, not despised by wise ascetics and brahmins. What are these five gifts?

"Here, monks, a noble disciple gives up the destruction of life and abstains from it. By abstaining from the destruction of life, the noble disciple gives to immeasurable beings freedom from fear, hostility, and oppression. By giving to immeasurable beings freedom from fear, hostility, and oppression, he himself will enjoy immeasurable freedom from fear, hostility, and oppression. This is the first of those great gifts and the fourth stream of merit.

"Further, monks, a noble disciple gives up the taking of what is not given and abstains from it. By abstaining from taking what is not given, the noble disciple gives to immeasurable beings freedom from fear.... This is the second of those great gifts and the fifth stream of merit.

"Further, monks, a noble disciple gives up sexual misconduct and abstains from it. By abstaining from sexual misconduct, the noble disciple gives to immeasurable beings freedom from fear.... This is the third of those great gifts and the sixth stream of merit.

"Further, monks, a noble disciple gives up false speech and abstains from it. By abstaining from false speech, the noble disciple gives to immeasurable beings freedom from fear.... This is the fourth of those great gifts and the seventh stream of merit.

"Further, monks, a noble disciple gives up wines, liquors, and intoxicants, the basis for negligence, and abstains from them. By abstaining from wines, liquors, and intoxicants, the noble disciple gives to immeasurable beings freedom from fear, hostility, and oppression. By giving to immeasurable beings freedom from fear, hostility, and oppression, he himself will enjoy immeasurable freedom from fear, hostility, and oppression. This is the fifth of those great gifts and the eighth stream of merit.

"These, monks, are the eight streams of merit, streams of the wholesome, nourishments of happiness, which are heavenly, ripening in happiness, conducive to heaven, and which lead to whatever is wished for, loved, and agreeable, to one's welfare and happiness."

(AN 8:39; IV 245–47)

(2) The Uposatha Observance

"When, O monks, the uposatha observance is complete in eight factors, it is of great fruit and benefit, luminous and pervasive. And how is the uposatha observance complete in eight factors?[18]

"Here, monks, a noble disciple reflects thus: 'As long as they live the arahants abandon the destruction of life, abstain from the destruction of life; with the rod and weapon laid aside, they are conscientious and merciful and dwell compassionate toward all living beings. Today I too, for this day and night, will do likewise. I will imitate the arahants in this respect, and the uposatha observance will be fulfilled by me.' This is the first factor it possesses.

"Further, he reflects: 'As long as they live the arahants abandon the taking of what is not given, abstain from taking what is not given; they accept only what is given, expect only what is given, and dwell with honest hearts devoid of theft. Today I too, for this day and night, will do likewise....' This is the second factor it possesses.

"'As long as they live the arahants abandon sexual relations and observe celibacy, living apart, refraining from the coarse practice of sexual intercourse. Today I too, for this day and night, will do likewise....' This is the third factor it possesses.

"'As long as they live the arahants abandon false speech, abstain from false speech; they are speakers of truth, adherents of truth, trustworthy and reliable, no deceivers of the world. Today I too, for this day and night, will do likewise....' This is the fourth factor it possesses.

"'As long as they live the arahants abandon wines, liquors, and intoxicants, the basis of negligence, and abstain from them. Today I too, for this day and night, will do likewise....' This is the fifth factor it possesses.

"'As long as they live the arahants eat only one meal a day and refrain from eating at night, outside the proper time.[19] Today I too, for this day and night, will do likewise....' This is the sixth factor it possesses.

"'As long as they live the arahants abstain from dancing, singing, instrumental music, and unsuitable shows, and from adorning themselves by wearing garlands and applying scents and ointments. Today I too, for this day and night, will do likewise....' This is the seventh factor it possesses.

"'As long as they live the arahants abandon the use of high and luxurious beds and seats and abstain from using them; they make use of low resting places, either small beds or straw mats. Today I too, for this day and night, will do likewise. I will imitate the arahants in this respect, and the uposatha observance will be fulfilled by me.' This is the eighth factor it possesses.

"When, monks, the uposatha observance is complete in these eight factors, it is of great fruit and benefit, luminous and pervasive. And to what extent is it of great fruit and benefit, luminous and pervasive?

"Suppose, monks, someone were to exercise sovereignty and dominion over these sixteen great countries abounding in the seven precious treasures, that is, Aṅga, Magadha, Kāsi, Kosala, the Vajjis, the Mallas, the Cetis, Vaṃsa, the Kurus, the Pañcālas, Maccha, Sūrasena, Assaka, Avanti, Gandhāra, and Kamboja:[20] this would not be worth a sixteenth part of the uposatha observance complete in those eight factors. For what reason? Because human kingship is poor compared to divine happiness.

"For the devas in the realm of the Four Great Kings a single day and night is equivalent to fifty human years; thirty such days make up a month, and twelve such months make up a year. The lifespan of the devas in the realm of the Four Great Kings is five hundred such celestial years. It is possible, monks, that if some man or woman here observes the uposatha complete in these eight factors, with the breakup of the body, after death, they will be reborn in the company of the devas in the realm of the Four Great Kings. It was with reference to this that I said human kingship is poor compared to divine happiness.

"For the Tāvatiṃsa devas a single day and night is equivalent to a hundred human years.... The lifespan of the Tāvatiṃsa devas is a thousand such celestial years.... For the Yāma devas a single day and night is equivalent to two hundred human years.... The lifespan of the Yāma devas is two thousand such celestial years.... For the Tusita devas, a single day and night is equivalent to four hundred human years.... The lifespan of the Tusita devas is four thousand such celestial years.... For the devas who delight in creating, a single day and night is equivalent to eight hundred human years.... The lifespan of the devas who delight in creating is eight thousand such celestial years.... For the devas who wield power over others' creations a single day and night is equivalent to sixteen hundred human years; thirty such days make up a month, and twelve such months make up a year. The lifespan of the devas who wield power over others' creations is sixteen thousand celestial years. It is possible, monks, that if some man or woman here observes the uposatha complete in these eight factors, with the breakup of the body, after death, they will be reborn in the company of the devas who wield power over others' creations. It was with reference to this that I said human kingship is poor compared to divine happiness."

(AN 8:41; IV 248–51)

5. Meditation

(1) The Development of Loving-Kindness

"Monks, whatever grounds there are for making merit productive of a future birth, all these do not equal a sixteenth part of the liberation of mind by loving-kindness. The liberation of mind by loving-kindness surpasses them and shines forth, bright and brilliant.

"Just as the radiance of all the stars does not equal a sixteenth part of the moon's radiance, but the moon's radiance surpasses them and shines forth, bright and brilliant, even so, whatever grounds there are for making merit productive of a future birth, all these do not equal a sixteenth part of the liberation of mind by loving-kindness. The liberation of mind by loving-kindness surpasses them and shines forth, bright and brilliant.

"Just as in the last month of the rainy season, in the autumn, when the sky is clear and free of clouds, the sun, on ascending, dispels the darkness of space and shines forth, bright and brilliant, even so, whatever grounds there are for making merit productive of a future birth, all these do not equal a sixteenth part of the liberation of mind by loving-kindness. The liberation of mind by loving-kindness surpasses them and shines forth, bright and brilliant.

"And just as in the night, at the moment of dawn, the morning star shines forth, bright and brilliant, even so, whatever grounds there are for making merit productive of a future birth, all these do not equal a sixteenth part of the liberation of mind by loving-kindness. The liberation of mind by loving-kindness surpasses them and shines forth, bright and brilliant."

(It 27; 19–21)

(2) The Four Divine Abodes

22. The brahmin student Subha, Todeyya's son, said to the Blessed One: "Master Gotama, I have heard that the ascetic Gotama knows the path to the company of Brahmā."

"What do you think, student? Is the village of Naḷakāra near here, not far from here?"

"Yes, sir, the village of Naḷakāra is near here, not far from here."

"What do you think, student? Suppose there was a man born and raised in the village of Naḷakāra, and as soon as he had left Naḷakāra they asked him about the path to the village. Would that man be slow or hesitant in answering?"

"No, Master Gotama. Why is that? Because that man has been born and raised in Naḷakāra, and is well acquainted with all the paths to the village."

"Still, a man born and raised in the village of Naḷakāra might be slow or hesitant in answering when asked about the path to the village, but a Tathāgata, when asked about the brahma world or the way leading to the brahma world, would never be slow or hesitant in answering. I understand Brahmā, and I understand the brahma world, and I understand the way leading to the brahma world, and I understand how one should practice to be reborn in the brahma world."

23. "Master Gotama, I have heard that the ascetic Gotama teaches the path to the company of Brahmā. It would be good if Master Gotama would teach me the path to the company of Brahmā."

"Then, student, listen and attend closely to what I shall say."

"Yes, sir," he replied. The Blessed One said this:

24. "What, student, is the path to the company of Brahmā? Here a monk dwells pervading one quarter with a mind imbued with loving-kindness, likewise the second, likewise the third, likewise the fourth; so above, below, around, and everywhere, and to all as to himself, he dwells pervading the all-encompassing world with a mind imbued with loving-kindness, abundant, exalted, immeasurable, without hostility, and without ill will. When the liberation of mind by loving-kindness is developed in this way, no limiting action remains there, none persists there. Just as a vigorous trumpeter could make himself heard without difficulty in the four quarters, so too, when the liberation of mind by loving-kindness is developed in this way, no limiting action remains there, none persists there.[21] This is the path to the company of Brahmā.

25–27. "Again, a monk dwells pervading one quarter with a mind imbued with compassion ... with a mind imbued with altruistic joy ... with a mind imbued with equanimity, likewise the second, likewise the third, likewise the fourth; so above, below, around, and everywhere, and to all as to himself, he dwells pervading the all-encompassing world with a mind imbued with equanimity, abundant, exalted, immeasurable, without hostility, and without ill will. When the liberation of mind by equanimity is developed in this way, no limiting action remains there, none persists there. Just as a vigorous trumpeter could make himself heard without difficulty in the four quarters, so too, when the liberation of mind by equanimity is developed in this way, no limiting action remains there, none persists there. This too is the path to the company of Brahmā."

(from MN 99: *Subha Sutta*; II 206–8)

(3) Insight Surpasses All

[The Buddha said to Anāthapiṇḍika:] "In the past, householder, there was a brahmin named Velāma. He gave such a great alms offering as this: eighty-four thousand bowls of gold filled with silver; eighty-four thousand bowls of silver filled with gold; eighty-four thousand bronze bowls filled with bullion; eighty-four thousand elephants, chariots, milch cows, maidens, and couches, many millions of fine cloths, and indescribable amounts of food, drink, ointment, and bedding.

"As great as was the alms offering that the brahmin Velāma gave, it would be even more fruitful if one would feed a single person possessed of right view.[22] As great as the brahmin Velāma's alms offering was, and though one would feed a hundred persons possessed of right view, it would be even more fruitful if one would feed a single once-returner. As great as the brahmin Velāma's alms offering was, and though one would feed a hundred once-returners, it would be even more fruitful if one would feed a single nonreturner. As great as the brahmin Velāma's alms offering was, and though one would feed a hundred nonreturners, it would be even more fruitful if one would feed a single arahant. As great as the brahmin Velāma's alms offering was, and though one would feed a hundred arahants, it would be even more fruitful if one would feed a single paccekabuddha.[23] As great as the brahmin Velāma's alms offering was, and though one would feed a hundred paccekabuddhas, it would be even more fruitful if one would feed a single Perfectly Enlightened Buddha ... it would be even more fruitful if one would feed the Saṅgha of monks headed by the Buddha and build a monastery for the sake of the Saṅgha of the four quarters ... it would be even more fruitful if, with a trusting mind, one would go for refuge to the Buddha, the Dhamma, and the Saṅgha, and would undertake the five precepts: abstaining from the destruction of life, from taking what is not given, from sexual misconduct, from false speech, and from the use of intoxicants. As great as all this might be, it would be even more fruitful if one would develop a mind of loving-kindness even for the time it takes to pull a cow's udder. And as great as all this might be, it would be even more fruitful still if one would develop the perception of impermanence just for the time it takes to snap one's fingers."

(AN 9:20, abridged; IV 393–96)

VI. Deepening One's Perspective on the World

Introduction

In interpreting suttas, we have to take account of the circumstances under which they were spoken and the persons to whom they were addressed. During the course of his long ministry, the Buddha had to adjust his teaching to people with different capacities and needs. He taught those given to reckless behavior to abandon their self-defeating ways and engage in wholesome actions that yield pleasant fruits. He taught those inclined to resign themselves to fate that present effort determines our present quality of life as well as our future destiny. He taught those convinced that personal existence ceases with bodily death that living beings survive the breakup of the body and re-arise in accordance with their kamma. He taught those not yet ripe enough for higher attainments to aspire for rebirth among the devas, the celestial beings, and to enjoy the bliss and glory of the heavens.

A blissful heavenly rebirth, however, is not the final purpose for which the Buddha taught the Dhamma. At best it is only a temporary waystation. The ultimate goal is the cessation of suffering, and the bliss of the heavens, no matter how blissful, is not the same as the cessation of suffering. According to the Buddha's teaching, all states of existence within the round of rebirths, even the heavens, are transient, unreliable, bound up with pain. Thus the ultimate aim of the Dhamma is nothing short of liberation, which means total release from the round of birth and death.

What lies beyond the round of rebirths is an unconditioned state called *Nibbāna*. Nibbāna transcends the conditioned world, yet it can be attained within conditioned existence, in this very life, and experienced as the extinction of suffering. The Buddha realized Nibbāna through his enlightenment, and for the next forty-five years of his life he endeavored to help others realize it for themselves. The realization of Nibbāna comes with the blossoming of wisdom and brings perfect peace, untarnished happiness, and the stilling of the mind's compulsive drives. Nibbāna is the destruction of thirst, the thirst of craving. It is also the island of safety amid the raging currents of old age, sickness, and death.

To guide his spiritually mature disciples toward Nibbāna, the Buddha had to steer them beyond the blissful rewards that could be won in a future life by performing wholesome deeds. He did so through the "world-transcending" facets of his teaching, those aspects designed to lead disciples beyond the "triple world" of sense-sphere existence, form-sphere existence, and formless existence. Again and again throughout the discourses, the Buddha offered an uncompromising, razor-sharp exposure of the dangers inherent in all conditioned states of being. He sounded a clear warning signal that all states of existence are perilous and fraught with pain. He insisted, unambiguously, that the one hope of lasting security lies in complete purification and liberation of the mind. He presented a path that cuts through ignorance and craving in their entirety and dispels attachment even to the most refined states of meditative absorption.

In his "graduated discourse on the Dhamma," given to introduce receptive newcomers to his teaching, the Buddha regularly began by discussing such practices as giving and moral discipline. He would extol the beauty of such virtues as generosity, harmlessness, honesty, and self-restraint, explaining how such meritorious deeds lead to the joys of a heavenly rebirth. At this point, he would reveal "the danger, degradation, and defilement in sensual pleasures and the blessings of renunciation." Having thus gradually "ripened" the minds of his audience, he would next expound the doctrine distinctive of his own teaching, the Four Noble Truths: suffering, its origin, its cessation, and the path. When the Buddha himself taught the Four Noble Truths, his purpose was not to give his listeners an introductory course in "basic Buddhism," but to awaken in them the "vision of the Dhamma," the first direct realization of the transcendent truth that sets the disciple on the irreversible path to liberation.

Though we sometimes read in the suttas that disciples attained their first experience of awakening merely by listening to the Buddha preach, this does not mean that the Dhamma is easy to understand. Such disciples could penetrate the truth with such apparent ease because their faculties were mature, perhaps too because they had accumulated sufficient supporting conditions from previous lives. But by its very nature, the world-transcending Dhamma goes against the grain of the mundane mind. The Buddha describes the Dhamma as "subtle, deep, and difficult to see," and one of the things that makes it so difficult to see is its thesis that the highest happiness cannot be won by yielding to the longings of the heart but only by subduing them. This thesis runs utterly counter to the thought, attitudes, and actions of people fully immersed in the world. As long as we are infatuated with the seductive lures of sensual enjoyment, as long as we take delight in being this or becoming that, we will regard the sublime Dhamma as a mystery and a puzzle. The Buddha therefore realized that the first major challenge he would face in establishing his world-transcending Dhamma was to break the grip that sensual pleasure and worldly attachment have upon the mind. He had to knock the mind out of its accustomed ruts and set it moving in an altogether different direction. He had to steer his disciples away from the lures of sensuality and worldly attachment and guide them toward disenchantment, complete dispassion, and awakening.

The requirements of this task drew upon all the Buddha's skills as a teacher. It demanded that he make ample use of his ability to precisely adjust his teaching to the mental proclivities of the people who came to him for instruction. It demanded that he speak up frankly and candidly, even when candor bred resentment. It demanded that he enter the fray of debate, even though he much preferred the peace of seclusion. It demanded that he use similes, metaphors, and parables whenever concrete illustrations could give his arguments stronger appeal. It demanded that he uphold his principles strongly whether his adversaries were hostile ascetics or miscreant monks within the ranks of his own order (see the opening sections of MN 22 and MN 38, not included in this anthology). That the Buddha succeeded so well in fulfilling this difficult task is counted among his truly wonderful and marvelous accomplishments. This is a point to which **Text VI,1** bears eloquent testimony.

The Buddha's task at this stage in the unfolding of his doctrine is to impart to us a radically new education in the art of seeing. To follow the Buddha in the direction he wants to lead us, we have to learn to *see beneath* the surface glitter of pleasure, position, and power that usually enthralls us, and at the same time, to learn to *see through* the deceptive distortions of perception, thought, and views that habitually cloak our vision. Ordinarily, we represent things to ourselves through the refractory prism of subjective biases. These biases are shaped by our craving and attachments, which they in turn reinforce. We see things that we want to see; we blot out things that threaten or disturb us, that shake our complacency, that throw into question our comforting assumptions about ourselves and our lives. To undo this process involves a commitment to truth that is often unsettling, but in the long run proves exhilarating and liberating.

The education that the Buddha imparts to us brings about *a deepening of our perspective on the world.* To help us transform our understanding and deepen our perspective on the world, he offers us three standpoints from which we can appraise the values by which we order our lives. These three standpoints also represent three "moments" or steps in an unfolding process of insight that starts from our commonsense attitudes and moves strategically toward higher knowledge, enlightenment, and release. The three moments are: gratification (*assāda*), danger (*ādīnava*), and escape (*nissaraṇa*). In **Texts VI,2(1)–(3)**, this scheme is applied to the world as a whole. Elsewhere in the Nikāyas, the scheme is applied more specifically to the four material elements (SN 14:31–33), the five aggregates (SN 22:26–28), and the six internal and external sense bases (SN 35:13–18). The Buddha underscores the importance of this scheme with the bold pronouncement that until he was able to fully evaluate the world (or, in the texts referred to just above, the elements, aggregates, and sense bases) in this way, he did not claim that he had attained the unsurpassed perfect enlightenment.

In advancing systematically through this scheme, one begins by recognizing the indubitable fact that such worldly phenomena as sense objects, forms, and feelings give us some degree of *gratification*. This gratification consists in the pleasure and joy (*sukha-somanassa*) we experience when we succeed in fulfilling our desires. Once we acknowledge this fact, we can then probe deeper by asking whether such pleasure and joy are entirely satisfactory. If we address this question with utter honesty, in a dispassionate frame of mind, we will realize that such pleasure and joy are far from satisfactory. To the contrary, they are saddled with drawbacks and defects ranging from the trifling to the catastrophic, defects that we perpetually hide from ourselves so that we can continue unhindered in our quest for gratification. This is their *danger*, the second moment or step of observation. The most pervasive danger lurking behind the innocent façade of our worldly pleasures is their inherent nature of being impermanent (*anicca*), bound up with suffering and discontent (*dukkha*), and subject to inevitable change and decay (*vipariṇāmadhamma*).

The third moment, the moment of *escape*, follows from the second. "Escape" here is not *escapism*, a word that implies an anxious attempt to avoid facing one's problems by pretending they don't exist and losing oneself in distractions. True escape is quite the opposite: the sanest, most rational, most judicious course of action we can take when we accurately recognize a genuine danger. It is our search for an exit from a burning building, our visit to the doctor when we're beset by a persistent fever, our decision to give up smoking when we understand how it jeopardizes our health. Once we see that the objects of our attachment are flawed, beset with hidden dangers, we then realize that the way of escape lies in dropping our attachment to them. This is "the removal of desire and lust, the abandoning of desire and lust" (*chandarāga-vinaya, chandarāga-pahāna*) referred to in the texts.

The Pāli commentators, not surprisingly, connect these three moments with the Four Noble Truths. "Gratification" implies the second noble truth, for pleasure and joy arouse craving, the origin of suffering. "Danger" is the truth of suffering itself. And "escape" is the truth of the cessation of suffering, which also implies the Noble Eightfold Path, the fourth truth, the way to the cessation of suffering.

In **Text VI,3** the Buddha uses this threefold scheme to make a detailed appraisal of three major objects of attachment: sensual pleasures, bodily form, and feelings. The major portion of the sutta is devoted to an examination of the dangers in sensual pleasures. It begins with a close-up view of the tribulations that a "clansman"—a young householder pursuing the ancient Indian counterpart of a professional career—might undergo in his quest for sensual gratification. As the discourse unfolds, the scope of the examination widens from the personal to the collective, encompassing the broader social and political consequences of this quest. It reaches its climax in striking images of the warfare and human devastation that follow from the frenzied mass drive for sensual gratification. "Form" is the physical body. The Buddha begins his treatment of form by asking the monks to consider a beautiful young girl. He then traces the progressive stages of her physical decay, through old age, sickness, death, and the eventual disintegration of the corpse until it is reduced to powdered bone. To show the danger in "feeling," the Buddha selects the feelings of a meditating monk in the *jhānas,* the meditative absorptions, the most refined mundane experiences of pleasure and peace. He points out that even these lofty feelings are impermanent, unsatisfactory, and subject to change.

Although the following texts do not explicitly apply the threefold scheme, its underlying presence is obvious. Emphasis falls on the aspect of danger. The two texts presented in section 4 again accentuate the pitfalls in sensual pleasures, but do so differently from the text of the preceding section. In **Text VI,4(1)**, the Buddha appears in dialogue with a pompous householder who imagines that he has "cut off all worldly affairs." To dispel his complacency, the Buddha uses a series of similes that expose the deceptiveness of sensual pleasures to show him what the "cutting off of affairs" means in his own system of training. The use of similes prevails in **Text VI,4(2)** as well, which pits the Buddha against a hedonist named Māgandiya. The Buddha here contends that sensual pleasures seem to be pleasurable only through a distortion of perception, but when seen rightly are like the fire in a burning charcoal pit—"painful to touch, hot, and scorching." This passage includes some of the most powerful similes in the Nikāyas, and there can be little doubt that the Buddha has not used them lightly.

The use of imagery also figures prominently in **Text VI,5**, whose theme is the transience of human life. Buddhist literature frequently advises us to contemplate the certainty of death and the uncertainty of the time of its arrival. This recommendation is not made to induce an attitude of chronic morbidity but to help us break our infatuation with life and develop detachment. For this reason, recollection of death has become one of the most important subjects of Buddhist meditation. The Buddha elsewhere says that the recollection of death "when developed and cultivated, gains a foothold in the Deathless and culminates in the Deathless" (AN 7:46; IV 47–48). Here the transience of life is underscored by counting up the number of days, seasons, and even meals in a single life.

Text VI,6 is an excerpt from the Raṭṭhapāla Sutta, which recounts the life of the disciple the Buddha called "the foremost of those who have gone forth out of faith." Raṭṭhapāla was a young man from a well-established family who was so deeply stirred upon hearing the Buddha preach that he at once decided to embrace the homeless life of a monk. The Buddha asked him to obtain his parents' permission, but his parents, being strongly attached to their only son, adamantly refused to give their consent. Raṭṭhapāla thereupon lay down on the ground and refused to eat or drink, determined to die right there or receive the going forth. His parents finally relented and permitted him to become a monk on the condition that he later return to visit them. Years later, when he visited his parents, they tried to entice him back to the household life, but since he had already attained arahantship he was now beyond any possibility of disrobing. After leaving their home, he went to the royal pleasure garden, where he gave a discourse to King Koravya on "four summaries of the Dhamma." This discourse conveys his profound insights into the depth and universality of suffering, explaining in simple and lucid words why he, like countless other capable men and women in the prime of life, chose to leave the comforts of the household for the uncertainties of the homeless state.

Craving for sensual pleasures is one trap that keeps beings bound to the round of rebirths. Another major trap is attachment to views. Thus, to clear the path to Nibbāna, the Buddha not only had to dispel infatuation with sensual pleasures but also to expose the danger in views. This is the theme of section 7.

The most dangerous of wrong views are those that deny or undermine the foundations of ethics. **Text VI,7(1)** draws together a number of perils posed by this type of wrong view; prominent among them is rebirth in the lower realms. Views also lead to one-sided, biased interpretations of reality that we cling to as accurate and complete. People who cling tenaciously to their own views of a particular situation often come into conflict with those who view the same situation in a different light. Views thus give rise to conflicts and disputes. Perhaps no text in all of world literature has depicted this danger in dogmatic clinging more succinctly than the famous parable of the blind men and the elephant, included here as **Text VI,7(2)**.

Text VI,7(3) draws a contrast between the pair of distorted views known as eternalism (*sassatavāda*) and annihilationism (*ucchedavāda*), also called, respectively, the view of existence (*bhavadiṭṭhi*) and the view of nonexistence (*vibhavadiṭṭhi*). Eternalism affirms an eternal component in the individual, an indestructible self, and an eternal ground of the world, such as an all-powerful creator God. Annihilationism denies that there is any survival beyond death, holding that the individual comes to a complete end with the demise of the physical body. Eternalism, according to the Buddha, leads to delight in existence and binds beings to the cycle of existence. Annihilationism is often accompanied by a disgust with existence that, paradoxically, binds its adherents to the same existence that they loathe. As we will see below, the Buddha's teaching of dependent origination avoids both these futile ends (see IX, pp. 356–57).

Text VI,8 highlights a particular problem posed by eternalist views. Such views can inspire meditators to attain states of deep meditative bliss, which they interpret as union with a divine reality or realization of an eternal self. From the perspective of the Buddha's teaching, however, such attainments merely create the karmic potential for rebirth into a realm in which that meditative experience becomes the fundamental condition of consciousness. In other words, the attainment of these states in the human realm generates rebirth into the corresponding planes in the realm of subtle form or the formless realm. While many religions point to a divine realm as the final answer to the human predicament, the Buddha's teaching holds that these worlds offer no final outlet from the impermanence and misery of saṃsāra.

The text cited here shows that certain meditators attain the four "divine abodes" and take rebirth in the corresponding planes of the brahma world, where they might abide even for as long as five hundred great eons. Eventually, however, they must inevitably pass away and may then fall into the unfortunate realms of rebirth. Similar texts not included here (AN 3:114, 4:124) say the same respectively about realms of rebirth corresponding to the jhānas and the formless attainments.

The two suttas that constitute the final section of this chapter again take up the unsatisfactoriness and insecurity of conditioned existence, reinforcing their message with dramatic imagery. In **Text VI,9(1)**, the Buddha declares that the amount of tears we have shed while wandering through the round of rebirths is greater than the water in the four great oceans. In **Text VI,9(2)**, he tells a group of thirty monks that the amount of blood they have shed when they were slaughtered and executed in the round of rebirths is greater than the water in the four great oceans. According to the compilers of the sutta, the impact of this discourse upon the thirty monks was so powerful that all attained full liberation on the spot.

VI. Deepening One's Perspective on the World

1. Four Wonderful Things

"Monks, on the manifestation of the Tathāgata, the Arahant, the Perfectly Enlightened One, four wonderful and marvelous things appear. What four?

"People for the most part delight in attachment, take delight in attachment, rejoice in attachment. But when the Dhamma of non-attachment is taught by the Tathāgata, people wish to listen to it, lend an ear, and try to understand it. This is the first wonderful and marvelous thing that appears on the manifestation of the Tathāgata, the Arahant, the Perfectly Enlightened One.

"People for the most part delight in conceit, take delight in conceit, rejoice in conceit. But when the Dhamma is taught by the Tathāgata for the abolition of conceit, people wish to listen to it, lend an ear, and try to understand it. This is the second wonderful and marvelous thing that appears on the manifestation of the Tathāgata, the Arahant, the Perfectly Enlightened One.

"People for the most part delight in restlessness, take delight in restlessness, rejoice in restlessness. But when the Dhamma of peace is taught by the Tathāgata, people wish to listen to it, lend an ear, and try to understand it. This is the third wonderful and marvelous thing that appears on the manifestation of the Tathāgata, the Arahant, the Perfectly Enlightened One.

"People for the most part live in ignorance, are blinded by ignorance, fettered by ignorance. But when the Dhamma is taught by the Tathāgata for the abolition of ignorance, people wish to listen to it, lend an ear, and try to understand it. This is the fourth wonderful and marvelous thing that appears on the manifestation of a Tathāgata, an Arahant, a Perfectly Enlightened One.

"On the manifestation of the Tathāgata, the Arahant, the Perfectly Enlightened One, these four wonderful and marvelous things appear."

(AN 4:128; II 131–32)

2. Gratification, Danger, and Escape

(1) Before My Enlightenment

"Before my enlightenment, O monks, while I was still a bodhisatta, it occurred to me: 'What is the gratification in the world, what is the danger in the world, what is the escape from the world?' Then it occurred to me: 'Whatever pleasure and joy there is in the world, this is the gratification in the world; that the world is impermanent, bound up with suffering, and subject to change, this is the danger in the world; the removal and abandoning of desire and lust for the world, this is the escape from the world.'

"So long, monks, as I did not directly know, as they really are, the gratification in the world as gratification, its danger as danger, and the escape from the world as escape, for so long I did not claim to have awakened to the unsurpassed perfect enlightenment in this world with its devas, Māra, and Brahmā, in this population with its ascetics and brahmins, its devas and humans.

"But when I directly knew all this, then I claimed to have awakened to the unsurpassed perfect enlightenment in this world with ... its devas and humans. The knowledge and vision arose in me: 'Unshakable is the liberation of my mind; this is my last birth; there is now no renewed existence.'"

(AN 3:101 §§1–2; I 258–59)

(2) I Set Out Seeking

"O monks, I set out seeking the gratification in the world. Whatever gratification there is in the world, that I have found. I have clearly seen with wisdom just how far the gratification in the world extends.

"I set out seeking the danger in the world. Whatever danger there is in the world, that I have found. I have clearly seen with wisdom just how far the danger in the world extends.

"I set out seeking an escape from the world. Whatever escape there is from the world, that I have found. I have clearly seen with wisdom just how far the escape from the world extends."

(AN 3:101 §3; I 259)

(3) If There Were No Gratification

"If, monks, there were no gratification in the world, beings would not become enamored with the world. But because there is gratification in the world, beings become enamored with it.

"If there were no danger in the world, beings would not become disenchanted with the world. But because there is danger in the world, beings become disenchanted with it.

"If there were no escape from the world, beings could not escape from it. But as there is an escape from the world, beings can escape from it."

(AN 3:102; I 260)

3. Properly Appraising Objects of Attachment

1. Thus have I heard. On one occasion the Blessed One was living at Sāvatthī in Jeta's Grove, Anāthapiṇḍika's Park.

2. Then, when it was morning, a number of monks dressed, and taking their bowls and outer robes, went into Sāvatthī for alms. Then they thought: "It is still too early to wander for alms in Sāvatthī. Suppose we went to the park of the wanderers of other sects." So they went to the park of the wanderers of other sects and exchanged greetings with the wanderers. When this courteous and amiable talk was finished, they sat down at one side. The wanderers said to them:

3. "Friends, the ascetic Gotama describes the full understanding of sensual pleasures, and we do so too; the ascetic Gotama describes the full understanding of form, and we do so too; the ascetic Gotama describes the full understanding of feelings, and we do so too. What then is the distinction here, friends, what is the variance, what is the difference between the ascetic Gotama's teaching of the Dhamma and ours, between his instructions and ours?"[1]

4. Then those monks neither approved nor disapproved of the wanderers' words. Without doing either they rose from their seats and went away, thinking: "We shall come to understand the meaning of these words in the Blessed One's presence."

5. When they had wandered for alms in Sāvatthī and had returned from their almsround, after the meal they went to the Blessed One, and after paying homage to him, they sat down at one side and told him what had taken place. [The Blessed One said:]

6. "Monks, wanderers of other sects who speak thus should be questioned thus: 'But, friends, what is the gratification, what is the danger, and what is the escape in the case of sensual pleasures? What is the gratification, what is the danger, and what is the escape in the case of form? What is the gratification, what is the danger, and what is the escape in the case of feelings?' If they are questioned thus, wanderers of other sects will fail to account for the matter, and what is more, they will get into difficulties. Why is that? Because it is not their province. Monks, I see no one in the world with its devas, Māra, and Brahmā, in this population with its ascetics and brahmins, its devas and humans, who could satisfy the mind with a reply to these questions except for the Tathāgata or his disciple or one who has learned it from them.

[sensual pleasures]

7. (i) "And what, monks, is the gratification in the case of sensual pleasures? Monks, there are these five cords of sensual pleasure. What are the five? Forms cognizable by the eye that are wished for, desired, agreeable and likeable, connected with sensual desire, and provocative of lust. Sounds cognizable by the ear.... Odors cognizable by the nose.... Flavors cognizable by the tongue.... Tactile objects cognizable by the body that are wished for, desired, agreeable and likeable, connected with sensual desire, and provocative of lust. These are the five cords of sensual pleasure. Now the pleasure and joy that arise dependent on these five cords of sensual pleasure are the gratification in the case of sensual pleasures.

8. (ii) "And what, monks, is the danger in the case of sensual pleasures? Here, monks, on account of the craft by which a clansman makes a living—whether checking, accounting, calculating, farming, trading, husbandry, archery, the royal service, or whatever craft it may be—he has to face cold and heat; he is injured by contact with gadflies,

mosquitoes, wind, sun, and creeping things; he risks death by hunger and thirst. Now this is a danger in the case of sensual pleasures, a mass of suffering visible in this present life, having sensual pleasures as its cause, source, and basis, the cause being simply sensual pleasures.

9. "If no property comes to the clansman while he works and strives and makes an effort thus, he sorrows, grieves, and laments, he weeps beating his breast and becomes distraught, crying: 'My work is in vain, my effort is fruitless!' Now this too is a danger in the case of sensual pleasures, a mass of suffering visible in this present life, having sensual pleasures as its cause, source, and basis, the cause being simply sensual pleasures.

10. "If property comes to the clansman while he works and strives and makes an effort thus, he experiences pain and grief in protecting it: 'How shall neither kings nor thieves make off with my property, nor fire burn it, nor water sweep it away, nor unloved heirs make off with it?' And as he guards and protects his property, kings or thieves make off with it, or fire burns it, or water sweeps it away, or unloved heirs make off with it. And he sorrows, grieves, and laments, he weeps beating his breast and becomes distraught, crying: 'I no longer have my property!' Now this too is a danger in the case of sensual pleasures, a mass of suffering visible in this present life, having sensual pleasures as its cause, source, and basis, the cause being simply sensual pleasures.

11. "Again, with sensual pleasures as the cause ... kings quarrel with kings, khattiyas with khattiyas, brahmins with brahmins, householders with householders; mother quarrels with son, son with mother, father with son, son with father; brother quarrels with brother, brother with sister, sister with brother, friend with friend. And here in their quarrels, brawls, and disputes they attack each other with fists, clods, sticks, or knives, whereby they incur death or deadly suffering. Now this too is a danger in the case of sensual pleasures, a mass of suffering visible in this present life, having sensual pleasures as its cause, source, and basis, the cause being simply sensual pleasures.

12. "Again, with sensual pleasures as the cause ... men take swords and shields and buckle on bows and quivers, and they charge into battle massed in double array with arrows and spears flying and swords flashing; and there they are wounded by arrows and spears, and their heads are cut off by swords, whereby they incur death or

deadly suffering. Now this too is a danger in the case of sensual pleasures, a mass of suffering visible in this present life, having sensual pleasures as its cause, source, and basis, the cause being simply sensual pleasures.

13. "Again, with sensual pleasures as the cause ... men take swords and shields and buckle on bows and quivers, and they charge slippery bastions, with arrows and spears flying and swords flashing; and there they are wounded by arrows and spears and splashed with boiling liquids and crushed under heavy weights, and their heads are cut off by swords, whereby they incur death or deadly suffering. Now this too is a danger in the case of sensual pleasures, a mass of suffering visible in this present life, having sensual pleasures as its cause, source, and basis, the cause being simply sensual pleasures.

14. "Again, with sensual pleasures as the cause ... men break into houses, plunder wealth, commit burglary, ambush highways, seduce others' wives, and when they are caught, kings have many kinds of torture inflicted on them ... whereby they incur death or deadly suffering. Now this too is a danger in the case of sensual pleasures, a mass of suffering visible in this present life, having sensual pleasures as its cause, source, and basis, the cause being simply sensual pleasures.

15. "Again, with sensual pleasures as the cause ... people indulge in misconduct of body, speech, and mind. Having done so, on the breakup of the body, after death, they are reborn in a state of misery, in a bad destination, in the lower world, in hell. Now this is a danger in the case of sensual pleasures, a mass of suffering in the life to come,[2] having sensual pleasures as its cause, source, and basis, the cause being simply sensual pleasures.

16. (iii) "And what, monks, is the escape in the case of sensual pleasures? It is the removal of desire and lust, the abandonment of desire and lust for sensual pleasures. This is the escape in the case of sensual pleasures.

17. "That those ascetics and brahmins who do not understand as it really is the gratification as gratification, the danger as danger, and the escape as escape in the case of sensual pleasures, can either themselves fully understand sensual pleasures or instruct others so that they can fully understand sensual pleasures—that is impossible. That those ascetics and brahmins who understand as it really is the gratification as gratification, the danger as danger, and the escape as escape in the

case of sensual pleasures, can themselves fully understand sensual pleasures and instruct others so that they can fully understand sensual pleasures—that is possible.

[form]

18. (i) "And what, monks, is the gratification in the case of form? Suppose there were a girl of the khattiya class or the brahmin class or of householder stock, in her fifteenth or sixteenth year, neither too tall nor too short, neither too thin nor too fat, neither too dark nor too fair. Is her beauty and loveliness then at its height?"—"Yes, venerable sir."—"Now the pleasure and joy that arise in dependence on that beauty and loveliness are the gratification in the case of form.

19. (ii) "And what, monks, is the danger in the case of form? Later on one might see that same woman here at eighty, ninety, or a hundred years, aged, as crooked as a roof bracket, doubled up, supported by a walking stick, tottering, frail, her youth gone, her teeth broken, gray-haired, scanty-haired, bald, wrinkled, with limbs all blotchy. What do you think, monks? Has her former beauty and loveliness vanished and the danger become evident?"—"Yes, venerable sir."—"Monks, this is a danger in the case of form.

20. "Again, one might see that same woman afflicted, suffering, and gravely ill, lying fouled in her own urine and excrement, lifted up by some and set down by others. What do you think, monks? Has her former beauty and loveliness vanished and the danger become evident?"—"Yes, venerable sir."—"Monks, this too is a danger in the case of form.

21. "Again, one might see that same woman as a corpse thrown aside in a charnel ground, one, two, or three days dead, bloated, livid, and oozing matter. What do you think, monks? Has her former beauty and loveliness vanished and the danger become evident?"—"Yes, venerable sir."—"Monks, this too is a danger in the case of form.

22–29. "Again, one might see that same woman as a corpse thrown aside in a charnel ground, being devoured by crows, hawks, vultures, dogs, jackals, or various kinds of worms ... a skeleton with flesh and blood, held together with sinews ... a fleshless skeleton smeared with blood, held together with sinews ... a skeleton without flesh and blood, held together with sinews ... disconnected bones scattered in all directions—here a hand-bone, there a foot-bone, here a thigh-bone, there a rib-bone, here a hip-bone, there a back-bone, here the skull ... bones bleached white, the color of shells ... bones heaped up ... bones more than a year old, rotted and crumbled to dust. What do you think, monks? Has her former beauty and loveliness vanished and the danger become evident?"—"Yes, venerable sir."—"Monks, this too is a danger in the case of form.

30. (iii) "And what, monks, is the escape in the case of form? It is the removal of desire and lust, the abandonment of desire and lust for form. This is the escape in the case of form.

31. "That those ascetics and brahmins who do not understand as it really is the gratification as gratification, the danger as danger, and the escape as escape in the case of form, can either themselves fully understand form or instruct others so that they can fully understand form—that is impossible. That those ascetics and brahmins who understand as it really is the gratification as gratification, the danger as danger, and the escape as escape in the case of form, can themselves fully understand form and instruct others so that they can fully understand form—that is possible.

[feelings]

32. (i) "And what, monks, is the gratification in the case of feelings? Here, monks, quite secluded from sensual pleasures, secluded from unwholesome states, a monk enters upon and dwells in the first jhāna, which is accompanied by thought and examination, with rapture and happiness born of seclusion. On such an occasion he does not choose for his own affliction, or for another's affliction, or for the affliction of both. On that occasion he feels only feeling that is free from affliction. The highest gratification in the case of feelings is freedom from affliction, I say.

33–35. "Again, with the stilling of thought and examination, a monk enters upon and dwells in the second jhāna.... With the fading away as well of rapture ... he enters upon and dwells in the third jhāna.... With the abandoning of pleasure and pain he enters upon and dwells in the fourth jhāna.... On such an occasion he does not choose for his own affliction, or for another's affliction, or for the affliction of both. On that occasion he feels only feeling that is free from affliction. The highest gratification in the case of feelings is freedom from affliction, I say.

36. (ii) "And what, monks, is the danger in the case of feelings? Feelings are impermanent, suffering, and subject to change. This is the danger in the case of feelings.

37. (iii) "And what, monks, is the escape in the case of feelings? It is the removal of desire and lust, the abandonment of desire and lust for feelings. This is the escape in the case of feelings.

38. "That those ascetics and brahmins who do not understand as it really is the gratification as gratification, the danger as danger, and the escape as escape in the case of feelings, can either themselves fully understand feelings or instruct others so that they can fully understand feelings—that is impossible. That those ascetics and brahmins who understand as it really is the gratification as gratification, the danger as danger, and the escape as escape in the case of feelings, can themselves fully understand feelings and instruct others so that they can fully understand feelings—that is possible."

That is what the Blessed One said. The monks were satisfied and delighted in the Blessed One's words.

(MN 13: *Mahādukkhakkhandha Sutta;* I 84–90)

4. The Pitfalls in Sensual Pleasures

(1) Cutting Off All Affairs

[The householder Potaliya asked the Blessed One:] "Venerable sir, how is the cutting off of affairs[3] in the Noble One's discipline achieved entirely and in all ways? It would be good, venerable sir, if the Blessed One would teach me the Dhamma, showing me how the cutting off of affairs in the Noble One's discipline is achieved entirely and in all ways."

"Then listen, householder, and attend closely to what I shall say."

"Yes, venerable sir," Potaliya the householder replied. The Blessed One said this:

15. "Householder, suppose a dog, overcome by hunger and weakness, was waiting by a butcher's shop. Then a skilled butcher or his apprentice would toss the dog a well-hacked, clean-hacked skeleton of meatless bones smeared with blood. What do you think, householder? Would that dog get rid of his hunger and weakness by gnawing such a well-hacked, clean-hacked skeleton of meatless bones smeared with blood?"

"No, venerable sir. Why is that? Because that was a skeleton of well-hacked, clean-hacked meatless bones smeared with blood. Eventually that dog would reap weariness and disappointment."

"So too, householder, a noble disciple considers thus: 'Sensual pleasures have been compared to a skeleton by the Blessed One; they provide much suffering and much despair, while the danger in them is still more.' Having seen this thus as it really is with proper wisdom, he avoids the equanimity that is diversified, based on diversity, and develops the equanimity that is unified, based on unity,[4] where clinging to the carnal things of the world utterly ceases without remainder.

16. "Householder, suppose a vulture, a heron, or a hawk seized a piece of meat and flew away, and then other vultures, herons, and hawks pursued it and pecked and clawed it. What do you think, householder? If that first vulture, heron, or hawk does not quickly let go of that piece of meat, wouldn't it thereby incur death or deadly suffering?"

"Yes, venerable sir."

"So too, householder, a noble disciple considers thus: 'Sensual pleasures have been compared to a piece of meat by the Blessed One; they provide much suffering and much despair, while the danger in them is still more.' Having seen this thus as it really is with proper wisdom ... clinging to the carnal things of the world utterly ceases without remainder.

17. "Householder, suppose a man took a blazing grass torch and went against the wind. What do you think, householder? If that man does not quickly let go of that blazing grass torch, wouldn't that blazing grass torch burn his hand or his arm or some other part of his body, so that he might incur death or deadly suffering because of that?"

"Yes, venerable sir."

"So too, householder, a noble disciple considers thus: 'Sensual pleasures have been compared to a grass torch by the Blessed One; they provide much suffering and much despair, while the danger in them is still more.' Having seen this thus as it really is with proper wisdom ... clinging to the carnal things of the world utterly ceases without remainder.

18. "Householder, suppose there were a charcoal pit deeper than a man's height full of glowing coals without flame or smoke. Then a man came who wanted to live and not to die, who wanted pleasure and recoiled from pain, and two strong men seized him by both arms and dragged him toward that charcoal pit. What do you think, householder? Would that man twist his body this way and that?"

"Yes, venerable sir. Why is that? Because that man knows that if he falls into that charcoal pit, he will incur death or deadly suffering because of that."

"So too, householder, a noble disciple considers thus: 'Sensual pleasures have been compared to a charcoal pit by the Blessed One; they provide much suffering and much despair, while the danger in them is still more.' Having seen this thus as it really is with proper wisdom ... clinging to the carnal things of the world utterly ceases without remainder.

19. "Householder, suppose a man dreamed about lovely parks, lovely groves, lovely meadows, and lovely lakes, and on waking he saw nothing of them. So too, householder, a noble disciple considers thus: 'Sensual pleasures have been compared to a dream by the Blessed One; they provide much suffering and much despair, while the danger in them is still more.' Having seen this thus as it really is with proper wisdom ... clinging to the carnal things of the world utterly ceases without remainder.

20. "Householder, suppose a man borrowed goods on loan—a fancy carriage and fine jewel earrings—and preceded and surrounded by those borrowed goods he went to the marketplace. Then people, seeing him, would say: 'Sirs, that is a rich man! That is how the rich enjoy their wealth!' Then the owners, whenever they saw him, would take back their things. What do you think, householder? Would that be enough for that man to become dejected?"

"Yes, venerable sir. Why is that? Because the owners took back their things."

"So too, householder, a noble disciple considers thus: 'Sensual pleasures have been compared to borrowed goods by the Blessed One; they provide much suffering and much despair, while the danger in them is still more.' Having seen this thus as it really is with proper wisdom ... clinging to carnal things of the world utterly ceases without remainder.

21. "Householder, suppose a dense grove not far from some village or town had a fruit-laden tree, none of whose fruit had fallen to the ground. Then a man came needing fruit, seeking fruit, wandering in search of fruit, and he entered the grove and saw the tree laden with fruit. Thereupon he thought: 'This tree is laden with fruit but none of its fruit has fallen to the ground. I know how to climb a tree, so let me

climb this tree, eat as much fruit as I want, and fill my bag.' And he did so. Then a second man came needing fruit, seeking fruit, wandering in search of fruit, and taking a sharp axe, he too entered the grove and saw that tree laden with fruit. Thereupon he thought: 'This tree is laden with fruit but none of its fruit has fallen to the ground. I do not know how to climb a tree, so let me cut this tree down at its root, eat as much fruit as I want, and fill my bag.' And he did so. What do you think, householder? If that first man who had climbed the tree doesn't come down quickly, when the tree falls, wouldn't he break his hand or foot or some other part of his body, so that he might incur death or deadly suffering because of that?"

"Yes, venerable sir."

"So too, householder, a noble disciple considers thus: 'Sensual pleasures have been compared to fruits on a tree by the Blessed One; they provide much suffering and much despair, while the danger in them is still more.' Having seen this thus as it really is with proper wisdom, he avoids the equanimity that is diversified, based on diversity, and develops the equanimity that is unified, based on unity, where clinging to the carnal things of the world utterly ceases without remainder."

(from MN 54: *Potaliya Sutta*; I 364–66)

(2) The Fever of Sensual Pleasures

10. "Māgandiya, formerly when I lived the household life, I enjoyed myself, provided and endowed with the five cords of sensual pleasure: with forms cognizable by the eye ... with sounds cognizable by the ear ... with odors cognizable by the nose ... with flavors cognizable by the tongue ... with tactile objects cognizable by the body that are wished for, desired, agreeable, and likeable, connected with sensual desire and provocative of lust.[5] I had three palaces, one for the rainy season, one for the winter, and one for the summer. I lived in the rains' palace for the four months of the rainy season, enjoying myself with musicians, none male, and I did not go down to the lower palace.[6]

"On a later occasion, having understood as they really are the origin, the passing away, the gratification, the danger, and the escape in the case of sensual pleasures, I abandoned craving for sensual pleasures, I removed the fever of sensual pleasures, and I dwell without thirst, with a mind inwardly at peace. I see other people who are not free from lust for sensual pleasures being devoured by craving for sensual pleasures, burning with the fever of sensual pleasures, indulging in sensual pleasures, and I do not envy them, nor do I delight therein. Why is that? Because there is, Māgandiya, a delight apart from sensual pleasures, apart from unwholesome states, which surpasses even divine bliss.[7] Since I take delight in that, I do not envy what is inferior, nor do I delight therein.

11. "Suppose, Māgandiya, a householder or a householder's son was rich, affluent, and wealthy, and being provided and endowed with the five cords of sensual pleasure, he might enjoy himself with forms cognizable by the eye … with sounds cognizable by the ear … with odors cognizable by the nose … with flavors cognizable by the tongue … with tactile objects cognizable by the body that are wished for, desired, agreeable and likeable, connected with sensual desire and provocative of lust. Having conducted himself well in body, speech, and mind, on the breakup of the body, after death, he might be reborn in a good destination, in a heavenly world in the retinue of the Tāvatiṃsa devas; and there, surrounded by a group of nymphs in the Nandana Grove,[8] he would enjoy himself provided and endowed with the five cords of divine sensual pleasure. Suppose he saw a householder or a householder's son enjoying himself, provided and endowed with the five cords of [human] sensual pleasure. What do you think, Māgandiya? Would that young deva surrounded by the group of nymphs in the Nandana Grove, enjoying himself provided and endowed with the five cords of divine sensual pleasure, envy the householder or the householder's son for the five cords of human sensual pleasure or would he be enticed by human sensual pleasures?"

"No, Master Gotama. Why not? Because divine sensual pleasures are more excellent and sublime than human sensual pleasures."

12. "So too, Māgandiya, formerly when I lived the household life, I enjoyed myself, provided and endowed with the five cords of sensual pleasure: with forms cognizable by the eye … with tactile objects cognizable by the body that are wished for, desired, agreeable, and likeable, connected with sensual desire and provocative of lust. On a later occasion, having understood as they really are the gratification, the danger, and the escape in the case of sensual pleasures, I abandoned craving for sensual pleasures, I removed the fever of sensual pleasures, and

I dwell without thirst, with a mind inwardly at peace. I see other people who are not free from lust for sensual pleasures being devoured by craving for sensual pleasures, burning with the fever of sensual pleasures, indulging in sensual pleasures, and I do not envy them nor do I delight therein. Why is that? Because there is, Māgandiya, a delight apart from sensual pleasures, apart from unwholesome states, which surpasses even divine bliss. Since I take delight in that, I do not envy what is inferior, nor do I delight therein.

13. "Suppose, Māgandiya, there was a leper with sores and blisters on his limbs, being devoured by worms, scratching the scabs off the openings of his wounds with his nails, cauterizing his body over a burning charcoal pit. Then his friends and companions, his kinsmen and relatives, would bring a physician to treat him. The physician would make medicine for him, and by means of that medicine the man would be cured of his leprosy and would become well and happy, independent, master of himself, able to go where he likes. Then he might see another leper with sores and blisters on his limbs, being devoured by worms, scratching the scabs off the openings of his wounds with his nails, cauterizing his body over a burning charcoal pit. What do you think, Māgandiya? Would that man envy that leper for his burning charcoal pit or his use of medicine?"

"No, Master Gotama. Why is that? Because when there is sickness, there is need for medicine, and when there is no sickness there is no need for medicine."

14. "So too, Māgandiya, formerly when I lived the household life ... [as in §12] ... Since I take delight in that, I do not envy what is inferior, nor do I delight therein.

15. "Suppose, Māgandiya, there was a leper with sores and blisters on his limbs, being devoured by worms, scratching the scabs off the openings of his wounds with his nails, cauterizing his body over a burning charcoal pit. Then his friends and companions, his kinsmen and relatives, brought a physician to treat him. The physician would make medicine for him, and by means of that medicine the man would be cured of his leprosy and would become well and happy, independent, master of himself, able to go where he likes. Then two strong men would seize him by both arms and drag him toward a burning charcoal pit. What do you think, Māgandiya? Would that man twist his body this way and that?"

"Yes, Master Gotama. Why is that? Because that fire is indeed painful to touch, hot, and scorching."

"What do you think, Māgandiya? Is it only now that that fire is painful to touch, hot, and scorching, or previously too was that fire painful to touch, hot, and scorching?"

"Master Gotama, that fire is now painful to touch, hot, and scorching, and previously too that fire was painful to touch, hot, and scorching. For when that man was a leper with sores and blisters on his limbs, being devoured by worms, scratching the scabs off the openings of his wounds with his nails, his faculties were impaired; thus, though the fire was actually painful to touch, he acquired a mistaken perception of it as pleasant."

16. "So too, Māgandiya, in the past sensual pleasures were painful to touch, hot, and scorching; in the future sensual pleasures will be painful to touch, hot, and scorching; and now at present sensual pleasures are painful to touch, hot, and scorching. But these people who are not free from lust for sensual pleasures, who are devoured by craving for sensual pleasures, who burn with the fever of sensual pleasures, have faculties that are impaired; thus, though sensual pleasures are actually painful to touch, they acquire a mistaken perception of them as pleasant.[9]

17. "Suppose, Māgandiya, there was a leper with sores and blisters on his limbs, being devoured by worms, scratching the scabs off the openings of his wounds with his nails, cauterizing his body over a burning charcoal pit; the more he scratches the scabs and cauterizes his body, the fouler, more evil-smelling, and more infected the openings of his wounds would become, yet he would find a certain measure of satisfaction and enjoyment in scratching the openings of his wounds. So too, Māgandiya, people who are not free from lust for sensual pleasures, who are devoured by craving for sensual pleasures, who burn with the fever of sensual pleasures, still indulge in sensual pleasures; the more they indulge in sensual pleasures, the more their craving for sensual pleasures increases and the more they are burned by the fever of sensual pleasures, yet they find a certain measure of satisfaction and enjoyment in dependence on the five cords of sensual pleasure."

(from MN 75: *Māgandiya Sutta*; I 504–8)

5. Life Is Short and Fleeting

"Long ago, O monks, there lived a religious teacher named Araka, who was free of sensual lust. He had many hundreds of disciples, and this was the doctrine he taught to them:

"'Short is the life of human beings, O brahmins, limited and brief; it is full of suffering, full of tribulation. This one should wisely understand. One should do good and live a pure life; for none who is born can escape death.

"'Just as a dew drop on the tip of a blade of grass will quickly vanish at sunrise and will not last long; even so, brahmins, is human life like a dew drop. It is short, limited, and brief; it is full of suffering, full of tribulation. This one should wisely understand. One should do good and live a pure life; for none who is born can escape death.

"'Just as, when rain falls from the sky in thick drops, a bubble appearing on the water will quickly vanish and will not last long; even so, brahmins, is human life like a water bubble. It is short ... for none who is born can escape death.

"'Just as a line drawn on water with a stick will quickly vanish and will not last long; even so, brahmins, is human life like a line drawn on water. It is short ... for none who is born can escape death.

"'Just as a mountain stream, coming from afar, swiftly flowing, carrying along much flotsam, will not stand still for a moment, an instant, a second, but will rush on, swirl and flow forward; even so, brahmins, is human life like a mountain stream. It is short ... for none who is born can escape death.

"'Just as a strong man might form a lump of spittle at the tip of his tongue and spit it out with ease; even so, brahmins, is human life like a lump of spittle. It is short ... for none who is born can escape death.

"'Just as a piece of meat thrown into an iron pan heated all day will quickly burn up and will not last long; even so, brahmins, is human life like this piece of meat. It is short ... for none who is born can escape death.

"'Just as, when a cow to be slaughtered is led to the shambles, whenever she lifts a leg she will be closer to slaughter, closer to death; even so, brahmins, is human life like cattle doomed to slaughter; it is short, limited, and brief. It is full of suffering, full of tribulation. This one should wisely understand. One should do good and live a pure life; for none who is born can escape death.'

"But at that time, O monks, the human lifespan was 60,000 years, and at 500 years girls were ready for marriage. In those days people had but six afflictions: cold, heat, hunger, thirst, excrement, and urine. Though people lived so long and had so few afflictions, that teacher Araka gave to his disciples such a teaching: 'Short is the life of human beings....'

"But nowadays, O monks, one could rightly say, 'Short is the life of human beings ...'; for today one who lives long lives for a hundred years or a little more. And when living for a hundred years, it is just for three hundred seasons: a hundred winters, a hundred summers, and a hundred rains. When living for three hundred seasons, it is just for twelve hundred months: four hundred winter months, four hundred summer months, and four hundred months of the rains. When living for twelve hundred months, it is just for twenty-four hundred fortnights: eight hundred fortnights of winter, eight hundred of summer, and eight hundred of the rains.

"And when living for twenty-four hundred fortnights, it is just for 36,000 days: 12,000 days of winter, 12,000 of summer, and 12,000 of the rains. And when living for 36,000 days, he eats just 72,000 meals: 24,000 meals in winter, 24,000 in summer, and 24,000 in the rains. And this includes the taking of mother's milk and the times without food. These are the times without food: when agitated or grieved or sick, when observing a fast, or when not obtaining anything to eat.

"Thus, O monks, I have reckoned the life of a centenarian: the limit of his lifespan, the number of seasons, years, months, and fortnights, of days and nights, of his meals and foodless times.

"Whatever should be done by a compassionate teacher who, out of compassion, seeks the welfare of his disciples, that I have done for you. These are the roots of trees, O monks, these are empty huts. Meditate, monks, do not be negligent, or else you will regret it later. This is our instruction to you."

(AN 7:70; IV 136–39)

6. Four Summaries of the Dhamma

26. The Venerable Raṭṭhapāla went to King Koravya's Migācira garden and sat down at the root of a tree to pass the day.

27. Then King Koravya addressed his gamekeeper thus: "Good gamekeeper, tidy up the Migācīra Garden so that we may go to the pleasure garden to see a pleasing spot."—"Yes, sire," he replied. Now while he was tidying up the Migācīra Garden, the gamekeeper saw the Venerable Raṭṭhapāla seated at the root of a tree for the day's abiding. When he saw him, he went to King Koravya and told him: "Sire, the Migācīra Garden has been tidied up. The clansman Raṭṭhapāla is there, the son of the leading clan in this same Thullakoṭṭhita, of whom you have always spoken highly; he is seated at the root of a tree for the day's abiding."

"Then, good gamekeeper, enough of the pleasure garden for today. Now we shall go to pay respects to that Master Raṭṭhapāla."

28. Then, saying: "Give away all the food that has been prepared there," King Koravya had a number of state carriages prepared, and mounting one of them, accompanied by the other carriages, he drove out from Thullakoṭṭhita with the full pomp of royalty to see the Venerable Raṭṭhapāla. He drove thus as far as the road was passable for carriages, and then he dismounted from his carriage and went forward on foot with a following of the most eminent officials to where the Venerable Raṭṭhapāla was. He exchanged greetings with the Venerable Raṭṭhapāla, and when this courteous and amiable talk was finished, he stood at one side and said: "Here is an elephant rug. Let Master Raṭṭhapāla be seated on it."

"There is no need, great king. Sit down. I am sitting on my own mat."

King Koravya sat down on a seat made ready and said:

29. "Master Raṭṭhapāla, there are four kinds of loss. Because they have undergone these four kinds of loss, some people here shave off their hair and beard, put on the ochre robe, and go forth from the household life into homelessness. What are the four? They are loss through aging, loss through sickness, loss of wealth, and loss of relatives.

30. "And what is loss through aging? Here, Master Raṭṭhapāla, someone is old, aged, burdened with years, advanced in life, come to the last stage. He considers thus: 'I am old, aged, burdened with years, advanced in life, come to the last stage. It is no longer easy for me to acquire new wealth or to augment wealth already acquired. Suppose I shave off my hair and beard, put on the ochre robe, and go forth from the household life into homelessness.' Because he has undergone that loss through aging, he shaves off his hair and beard, puts on the ochre

robe, and goes forth from the household life into homelessness. This is called loss through aging. But Master Raṭṭhapāla is now still young, a black-haired young man endowed with the blessing of youth, in the prime of life. Master Raṭṭhapāla has not undergone any loss through aging. What has he known, seen, or heard that he has gone forth from the household life into homelessness?

31. "And what is loss through sickness? Here, Master Raṭṭhapāla, someone is afflicted, suffering, and gravely ill. He considers thus: 'I am afflicted, suffering, and gravely ill. It is no longer easy for me to acquire new wealth ... into homelessness.' Because he has undergone that loss through sickness ... he goes forth from the household life into homelessness. This is called loss through sickness. But Master Raṭṭhapāla now is free from illness and affliction; he possesses a good digestion that is neither too cool nor too warm but medium. Master Raṭṭhapāla has not undergone any loss through sickness. What has he known, seen, or heard that he has gone forth from the household life into homelessness?

32. "And what is loss of wealth? Here, Master Raṭṭhapāla, someone is rich, affluent, and wealthy. Gradually his wealth dwindles away. He considers thus: 'Formerly I was rich, affluent, and wealthy. Gradually my wealth has dwindled away. It is no longer easy for me to acquire new wealth ... into homelessness.' Because he has undergone that loss of wealth ... he goes forth from the household life into homelessness. This is called loss of wealth. But Master Raṭṭhapāla is the son of the leading clan in this same Thullakoṭṭhita. Master Raṭṭhapāla has not undergone any loss of wealth. What has he known, seen, or heard that he has gone forth from the household life into homelessness?

33. "And what is loss of relatives? Here, Master Raṭṭhapāla, someone has many friends and companions, kinsmen and relatives. Gradually those relatives of his dwindle away. He considers thus: 'Formerly I had many friends and companions, kinsmen and relatives. Gradually those relatives of mine have dwindled away. It is no longer easy for me to acquire new wealth ... into homelessness.' Because he has undergone that loss of relatives ... he goes forth from the household life into homelessness. This is called loss of relatives. But Master Raṭṭhapāla has many friends and companions, kinsmen and relatives, in this same Thullakoṭṭhita. Master Raṭṭhapāla has not undergone any loss of relatives. What has he known, seen, or heard that he has gone forth from the household life into homelessness?

34. "Master Raṭṭhapāla, these are the four kinds of loss. Because they have undergone these four kinds of loss, some people here shave off their hair and beard, put on the ochre robe, and go forth from the household life into homelessness. Master Raṭṭhapāla has not undergone any of these. What has he known, seen, or heard that he has gone forth from the household life into homelessness?"

35. "Great king, there are four summaries of the Dhamma that have been taught by the Blessed One who knows and sees, the Arahant, the Perfectly Enlightened One. Knowing and seeing and hearing them, I went forth from the household life into homelessness. What are the four?

36. (1) "'[Life in] any world is unstable, it is swept away': this is the first summary of the Dhamma taught by the Blessed One who knows and sees, the Arahant, the Perfectly Enlightened One. Knowing and seeing and hearing this, I went forth from the household life into homelessness.

(2) "'[Life in] any world has no shelter and no protector': this is the second summary of the Dhamma taught by the Blessed One who knows and sees....

(3) "'[Life in] any world has nothing of its own; one has to leave all and pass on': this is the third summary of the Dhamma taught by the Blessed One who knows and sees....

(4) "'[Life in] any world is incomplete, insatiate, the slave of craving': this is the fourth summary of the Dhamma taught by the Blessed One who knows and sees....

37. "Great king, these are the four summaries of the Dhamma that have been taught by the Blessed One who knows and sees, the Arahant, the Perfectly Enlightened One. Knowing and seeing and hearing them, I went forth from the household life into homelessness."

38. "Master Raṭṭhapāla said: '[Life in] any world is unstable, it is swept away.' How should the meaning of that statement be understood?"

"What do you think, great king? When you were twenty or twenty-five years old, were you an expert rider of elephants, an expert horseman, an expert charioteer, an expert archer, an expert swordsman, strong in thighs and arms, sturdy, capable in battle?"

"I certainly was, Master Raṭṭhapāla. Sometimes I wonder if I had supernormal power then. I do not see anyone who could equal me in strength."

"What do you think, great king? Are you now as strong in thighs and arms, as sturdy and as capable in battle?"

"No, Master Raṭṭhapāla. Now I am old, aged, burdened with years, advanced in life, come to the last stage; my years have turned eighty. Sometimes I mean to put my foot here and I put my foot somewhere else."

"Great king, it was on account of this that the Blessed One who knows and sees, the Arahant, the Perfectly Enlightened One, said: '[Life in] any world is unstable, it is swept away'; and when I knew, saw, and heard this, I went forth from the household life into homelessness."

"It is wonderful, Master Raṭṭhapāla, it is marvelous how well that has been expressed by the Blessed One who knows and sees, the Arahant, the Perfectly Enlightened One: '[Life in] any world is unstable, it is swept away.' It is indeed so!

39. "Master Raṭṭhapāla, there exist in this court elephant troops and cavalry and chariot troops and infantry, which will serve to subdue any threats to us. Now Master Raṭṭhapāla said: '[Life in] any world has no shelter and no protector.' How should the meaning of that statement be understood?"

"What do you think, great king? Do you have any chronic ailment?"

"I have a chronic wind ailment, Master Raṭṭhapāla. Sometimes my friends and companions, kinsmen and relatives, stand around me, thinking: 'Now King Koravya is about to die, now King Koravya is about to die!'"

"What do you think, great king? Can you command your friends and companions, your kinsmen and relatives: 'Come, my good friends and companions, my kinsmen and relatives. All of you present share this painful feeling so that I may feel less pain'? Or do you have to feel that pain yourself alone?"

"I cannot command my friends and companions, my kinsmen and relatives thus, Master Raṭṭhapāla. I have to feel that pain alone."

"Great king, it was on account of this that the Blessed One who knows and sees, the Arahant, the Perfectly Enlightened One, said: '[Life in] any world has no shelter and no protector'; and when I knew, saw, and heard this, I went forth from the household life into homelessness."

"It is wonderful, Master Raṭṭhapāla, it is marvelous how well that has been expressed by the Blessed One who knows and sees, the Arahant, the Perfectly Enlightened One: '[Life in] any world has no shelter and no protector.' It is indeed so!

40. "Master Raṭṭhapāla, there exist in this court abundant gold coins and bullion stored away in vaults and lofts. Now Master Raṭṭhapāla said: '[Life in] any world has nothing of its own; one has to leave all and pass on.' How should the meaning of that statement be understood?"

"What do you think, great king? You now enjoy yourself provided and endowed with the five cords of sensual pleasure, but can you be certain that in the life to come you will likewise enjoy yourself provided and endowed with these same five cords of sensual pleasure? Or will others take over this property, while you will have to pass on according to your actions?"

"I cannot be certain of what will happen in the life to come, Master Raṭṭhapāla. On the contrary, others will take over this property while I shall have to pass on according to my actions."

"Great king, it was on account of this that the Blessed One who knows and sees, the Arahant, the Perfectly Enlightened One, said: '[Life in] any world has nothing of its own; one has to leave all and pass on'; and when I knew, saw, and heard this, I went forth from the household life into homelessness."

"It is wonderful, Master Raṭṭhapāla, it is marvelous how well that has been expressed by the Blessed One who knows and sees, the Arahant, the Perfectly Enlightened One: '[Life in] any world has nothing of its own; one has to leave all and pass on.' It is indeed so!

41. "Now Master Raṭṭhapāla said: '[Life in] any world is incomplete, insatiate, the slave of craving.' How should the meaning of that statement be understood?"

"What do you think, great king? Do you reign over the rich Kuru country?"

"Yes, Master Raṭṭhapāla, I do."

"What do you think, great king? Suppose a trustworthy and reliable man came to you from the east and said: 'Please know, great king, that I have come from the east, and there I saw a large country, powerful and rich, very populous and crowded with people. There are plenty of elephant troops there, plenty of cavalry, chariot troops, and infantry; there is plenty of ivory there, and plenty of gold coins and bullion both unworked and worked, and plenty of women for wives. With your present forces you can conquer it. Conquer it then, great king.' What would you do?"

"We would conquer it and reign over it, Master Raṭṭhapāla."

"What do you think, great king? Suppose a trustworthy and reliable man came to you from the west ... from the north ... from the south ... from across the sea and said: 'Please know, great king, that I have come from across the sea, and there I saw a large country, powerful and rich.... Conquer it then, great king.' What would you do?"

"We would conquer it too and reign over it, Master Raṭṭhapāla."

"Great king, it was on account of this that the Blessed One who knows and sees, the Arahant, the Perfectly Enlightened One, said: '[Life in] any world is incomplete, insatiate, the slave of craving'; and when I knew, saw, and heard this, I went forth from the household life into homelessness."

"It is wonderful, Master Raṭṭhapāla, it is marvelous how well that has been expressed by the Blessed One who knows and sees, the Arahant, the Perfectly Enlightened One: '[Life in] any world is incomplete, insatiate, the slave of craving.' It is indeed so!"

(from MN 82: *Raṭṭhapāla Sutta*; II 65–82)

7. The Danger in Views

(1) A Miscellany on Wrong View

"Monks, I do not see even one other thing on account of which unarisen unwholesome qualities of mind arise and arisen unwholesome qualities of mind increase and expand so much as on account of wrong view.[10] For one of wrong view, unarisen unwholesome qualities of mind arise and arisen unwholesome qualities of mind increase and expand.

"Monks, I do not see even one other thing on account of which unarisen wholesome qualities of mind do not arise and arisen wholesome qualities of mind diminish so much as on account of wrong view. For one of wrong view, unarisen wholesome qualities of mind do not arise and arisen wholesome qualities of mind diminish.

"Monks, I do not see even one other thing on account of which, with the breakup of the body, after death, beings are reborn in a state of misery, in a bad destination, in the lower world, in hell, so much as on account of wrong view. Possessing wrong view, with the breakup of the body, after death, beings are reborn in a state of misery, in a bad destination, in the lower world, in hell.

"Monks, for a person of wrong view, whatever bodily, verbal, or mental conduct he undertakes in accordance with that view, and whatever volition, aspiration, wish, and volitional formations he engenders in accordance with that view, all lead to what is undesirable, unwanted, and disagreeable, to harm and suffering. For what reason? Because the view is bad. Just as, when a seed of neem, bitter cucumber, or bitter gourd is planted in moist soil, it transforms any nutriment it obtains from the soil and the water into a fruit with a bitter, harsh, and disagreeable taste, even so is it for a person of wrong view. For what reason? Because the view is bad."

(AN 1: xvii, 1, 3, 7, 9; I 30–32)

(2) The Blind Men and the Elephant

On one occasion the Blessed One was living at Sāvatthī in Jeta's Grove, Anāthapiṇḍika's Park. Now at that time a number of ascetics and brahmins, wanderers of other sects, were living around Sāvatthī. They held various views, beliefs, and opinions, and propagated various views. And they were quarrelsome, disputatious, wrangling, wounding each other with verbal darts, saying, "The Dhamma is like this, the Dhamma is not like that! The Dhamma is not like this, the Dhamma is like that!"

Then a number of monks entered Sāvatthī on almsround. Having returned, after their meal they approached the Blessed One, paid homage to him, sat down to one side, and told him what they had seen. [The Blessed One said:]

"Monks, wanderers of other sects are blind and sightless. They do not know what is beneficial and harmful. They do not know what is the Dhamma and what is not the Dhamma, and thus they are so quarrelsome and disputatious.

"Formerly, monks, there was a king in Sāvatthī who addressed a man and asked him to round up all the persons in the city who were blind from birth. When the man had done so, the king asked the man to show the blind men an elephant. To some of the blind men he presented the head of the elephant, to some the ear, to others a tusk, the trunk, the body, a foot, the hindquarters, the tail, or the tuft at the end of the tail. And to each one he said, 'This is an elephant.'

"When he reported to the king what he had done, the king went to the blind men and asked them, 'Tell me, blind men, what is an elephant like?'

"Those who had been shown the head of the elephant replied, 'An elephant, your majesty, is just like a water jar.' Those who had been shown the ear replied, 'An elephant is just like a winnowing basket.' Those who had been shown the tusk replied, 'An elephant is just like a plowshare.' Those who had been shown the trunk replied, 'An elephant is just like a plow pole.' Those who had been shown the body replied, 'An elephant is just like a storeroom.' And each of the others likewise described the elephant in terms of the part they had been shown.

"Then, saying, 'An elephant is like this, an elephant is not like that! An elephant is not like this, an elephant is like that!' they fought each other with their fists. And the king was delighted. Even so, monks, are the wanderers of other sects blind and sightless, and thus they become quarrelsome, disputatious, and wrangling, wounding each other with verbal darts."

(Ud 6:4; 67–69)

(3) Held by Two Kinds of Views

"Monks, held by two kinds of views, some devas and human beings hold back and some overreach; only those with vision see.

"And how, monks, do some hold back? Devas and human beings delight in existence, are delighted with existence, rejoice in existence. When the Dhamma is taught to them for the cessation of existence, their minds do not enter into it, acquire confidence in it, settle upon it, or resolve upon it. Thus, monks, do some hold back.

"And how, monks, do some overreach? Now some are troubled, ashamed, and disgusted by this very same existence and they rejoice in nonexistence, saying, 'In as much as this self, good sirs, is annihilated and destroyed with the breakup of the body and does not exist after death, this is peaceful, this is excellent, this is just so!' Thus, monks, do some overreach.

"And how, monks do those with vision see? Here, a monk sees what has come to be as having come to be. Having seen it thus, he practices the course for disenchantment, for dispassion, for the cessation of what has come to be. Thus, monks, do those with vision see."

(It 49; 43–44)

8. From the Divine Realms to the Infernal

"Monks, there are these four kinds of persons found existing in the world. What four?

"Here, monks, some person dwells pervading one quarter with a mind imbued with loving-kindness, likewise the second quarter, the third, and the fourth. Thus above, below, across, and everywhere, and to all as to himself, he dwells pervading the entire world with a mind imbued with loving-kindness, vast, exalted, measureless, without hostility, without ill will. He relishes it, takes a liking to it, and is thrilled by it. If he is firm in it, resolves upon it, often dwells in it, and has not lost it when he dies, he is reborn in companionship with the devas of Brahmā's company. The lifespan of those devas is an eon. The worldling remains there all his life, and when he has completed the entire lifespan of those devas, he goes to hell, to the animal realm, and to the domain of spirits. But the Blessed One's disciple remains there all his life, and when he has completed the entire lifespan of those devas, he attains final Nibbāna in that very same state of existence. This is the difference, the disparity, the distinction between the instructed noble disciple and the uninstructed worldling, that is, with regard to destination and rebirth.

"Here, monks, some person dwells pervading one quarter with a mind imbued with compassion, likewise the second quarter, the third, and the fourth. Thus above, below, across, and everywhere, and to all as to himself, he dwells pervading the entire world with a mind imbued with compassion, vast, exalted, measureless, without hostility, without ill will. He relishes it, takes a liking to it, and is thrilled by it. If he is firm in it, resolves upon it, often dwells in it, and has not lost it when he dies, he is reborn in companionship with the devas of streaming radiance. The lifespan of those devas is two eons. The worldling remains there all his life, and when he has completed the entire lifespan of those devas, he goes to hell, to the animal realm, and to the domain of spirits. But the Blessed One's disciple remains there all his life, and when he has completed the entire lifespan of those devas, he attains final Nibbāna in that very same state of existence. This is the difference, the disparity, the distinction between the instructed noble disciple and the uninstructed worldling, that is, with regard to destination and rebirth.

"Here, monks, some person dwells pervading one quarter with a mind imbued with altruistic joy, likewise the second quarter, the third, and the fourth. Thus above, below, across, and everywhere, and to all as to himself, he dwells pervading the entire world with a mind imbued with altruistic joy, vast, exalted, measureless, without hostility, without ill will. He relishes it, takes a liking to it, and is thrilled by it. If he is firm in it, resolves upon it, often dwells in it, and has not lost it when he dies, he is reborn in companionship with the devas of refulgent glory. The lifespan of those devas is four eons. The worldling remains there all his life, and when he has completed the entire lifespan of those devas, he goes to hell, to the animal realm, and to the domain of spirits. But the Blessed One's disciple remains there all his life, and when he has completed the entire lifespan of those devas, he attains final Nibbāna in that very same state of existence. This is the difference, the disparity, the distinction between the instructed noble disciple and the uninstructed worldling, that is, with regard to destination and rebirth.

"Here, monks, some person dwells pervading one quarter with a mind imbued with equanimity, likewise the second quarter, the third, and the fourth. Thus above, below, across, and everywhere, and to all as to himself, he dwells pervading the entire world with a mind imbued with equanimity, vast, exalted, measureless, without hostility, without ill will. He relishes it, takes a liking to it, and is thrilled by it. If he is firm in it, resolves upon it, often dwells in it, and has not lost it when he dies, he is reborn in companionship with the devas of great fruit. The lifespan of those devas is five hundred eons. The worldling remains there all his life, and when he has completed the entire life-span of those devas, he goes to hell, to the animal realm, and to the domain of spirits. But the Blessed One's disciple remains there all his life, and when he has completed the entire lifespan of those devas, he attains final Nibbāna in that very same state of existence. This is the difference, the disparity, the distinction between the instructed noble disciple and the uninstructed worldling, that is, with regard to destination and rebirth.

"These, monks, are the four kinds of persons found existing in the world."

(AN 4:125; II 128–29)

9. The Perils of Saṃsāra

(1) The Stream of Tears

"Monks, this saṃsāra is without discoverable beginning. A first point is not discerned of beings roaming and wandering on hindered by ignorance and fettered by craving. What do you think, monks, which is more: the stream of tears that you have shed as you roamed and wandered through this long course, weeping and wailing because of being united with the disagreeable and separated from the agreeable—this or the water in the four great oceans?"

"As we understand the Dhamma taught by the Blessed One, venerable sir, the stream of tears that we have shed as we roamed and wandered through this long course, weeping and wailing because of being united with the disagreeable and separated from the agreeable—this alone is more than the water in the four great oceans."

"Good, good, monks! It is good that you understand the Dhamma taught by me in such a way. The stream of tears that you have shed as you roamed and wandered through this long course, weeping and wailing because of being united with the disagreeable and separated from the agreeable—this alone is more than the water in the four great oceans. For a long time, monks, you have experienced the death of a mother; as you have experienced this, weeping and wailing because of being united with the disagreeable and separated from the agreeable, the stream of tears that you have shed is more than the water in the four great oceans.

"For a long time, monks, you have experienced the death of a father … the death of a brother … the death of a sister … the death of a son … the death of a daughter … the loss of relatives … the loss of wealth … loss through illness; as you have experienced this, weeping and wailing because of being united with the disagreeable and separated from the agreeable, the stream of tears that you have shed is more than the water in the four great oceans. For what reason? Because, monks, this saṃsāra is without discoverable beginning…. It is enough to experience revulsion toward all formations, enough to become dispassionate toward them, enough to be liberated from them."

(SN 15:3; II 179–80)

(2) The Stream of Blood

While the Blessed One was dwelling at Rājagaha in the Bamboo Grove, thirty monks from Pāvā approached him—all forest dwellers, almsfood eaters, rag-robe wearers, three-robe users, yet all still with fetters.[11] Having approached, they paid homage to the Blessed One and sat down to one side. Then it occurred to the Blessed One: "These thirty monks from Pāvā are all forest dwellers, almsfood eaters, rag-robe wearers, three-robe users, yet all are still with fetters. Let me teach them the Dhamma in such a way that while they are sitting in these very seats their minds will be liberated from the taints by nonclinging."[12]

Then the Blessed One addressed those monks thus: "Monks!"

"Venerable sir!" those monks replied. The Blessed One said this:

"Monks, this saṃsāra is without discoverable beginning. A first point is not discerned of beings roaming and wandering on, hindered by ignorance and fettered by craving. What do you think, monks, which is more: the stream of blood that you have shed when you were beheaded as you roamed and wandered through this long course—this or the water in the four great oceans?"

"As we understand the Dhamma taught by the Blessed One, venerable sir, the stream of blood that we have shed when we were beheaded as we roamed and wandered through this long course—this alone is more than the water in the four great oceans."

"Good, good, monks! It is good that you understand the Dhamma taught by me in such a way. The stream of blood that you have shed as you roamed and wandered through this long course—this alone is more than the water in the four great oceans. For a long time, monks, you have been cows, and when as cows you were beheaded, the stream of blood that you shed is greater than the waters in the four great oceans. For a long time you have been buffalo, sheep, goats, deer, chickens, and pigs.... For a long time you have been arrested as burglars, highwaymen, and adulterers, and when you were beheaded, the stream of blood that you shed is greater than the water in the four great oceans. For what reason? Because, monks, this saṃsāra is without discoverable beginning. A first point is not discerned of beings roaming and wandering on, hindered by ignorance and fettered by craving. For such a long time, monks, you have experienced suffering, anguish, and disaster, and swelled the cemetery. It is enough to become disenchanted with all formations, enough to become dispassionate toward them, enough to be liberated from them."

This is what the Blessed One said. Elated, those monks delighted in the Blessed One's statement. And while this exposition was being spoken, the minds of the thirty monks from Pāvā were liberated from the taints by nonclinging.

(SN 15:13; II 187–89)

VII. The Path to Liberation

Introduction

In this chapter, we come to the unique distinguishing feature of the Buddha's teaching, its "supramundane" or "world-transcending" (*lokuttara*) path to liberation. This path builds upon the transformed understanding and deepened perspective on the nature of the world that arise from our recognition of the perils in sensual pleasures, the inevitability of death, and the vicious nature of saṃsāra, themes that we surveyed in the previous chapter. It aims to lead the practitioner to the state of liberation that lies beyond all realms of conditioned existence, to the same sorrowless and stainless bliss of Nibbāna that the Buddha himself attained on the night of his enlightenment.

This chapter presents texts that offer a broad overview of the Buddha's world-transcending path; the following two chapters will bring together texts that focus more finely on the training of the mind and the cultivation of wisdom, the two major branches of the world-transcending path. I begin, however, with several suttas that are intended to clarify the *purpose* of this path, illuminating it from different angles. **Text VII,1(1)**, The Shorter Discourse to Māluṅkyāputta (MN 63), shows that the Buddhist path is not designed to provide theoretical answers to philosophical questions. In this sutta the monk Māluṅkyāputta approaches the Buddha and demands answers to ten speculative questions, threatening to leave the Saṅgha if this demand is not satisfied. Scholars have debated whether the Buddha refused to answer such questions because they are in principle unanswerable or simply because they are irrelevant to a practical resolution of the problem of suffering. Two collections of suttas in the Saṃyutta Nikāya—SN 33:1–10 and SN 44:7–8—make it clear that the Buddha's "silence" had a deeper basis than mere pragmatic concerns. These suttas show that all such questions are based on an underlying assumption that existence is to be interpreted in terms of a self and a world in which the self is situated. Since these premises are invalid, no answer framed in terms of these premises can be valid, and thus the Buddha must reject the very questions themselves.

However, while the Buddha had philosophical grounds for refusing to answer these questions, he also rejected them because he considered the obsession with their solutions to be irrelevant to the quest for release from suffering. This reason is the evident point of the discourse to Māluṅkyāputta, with its well-known simile of the man shot by the poisoned arrow. Whether any of these views is true or not, the Buddha says, "there is birth, there is aging, there is death, there are sorrow, lamentation, pain, dejection, and despair, the destruction of which I prescribe here and now." Against the picture of the saṃsāric background sketched at the end of the previous chapter, this statement now takes on an expanded meaning: the "destruction of birth, aging, and death" is not merely the end of suffering in a single lifetime, but the end of the immeasurable suffering of repeated birth, aging, and death that we have undergone in the countless eons of saṃsāra.

Text VII,1(2), The Greater Discourse on the Simile of the Heartwood (MN 29), clarifies from a different angle the Buddha's purpose in expounding his world-transcending Dhamma. The sutta is about a "clansman" who has gone forth from the household life into homelessness intent on reaching the end of suffering. Though earnest in purpose at the time of his ordination, once he attains some success, whether a lower achievement like gain and honor or a superior one like concentration and insight, he becomes complacent and neglects his original purpose in entering the Buddha's path. The Buddha declares that none of these stations along the way—not moral discipline, concentration, or even knowledge and vision—is the final goal of the spiritual life. The goal, its heartwood or essential purpose, is "unshakable liberation of the mind," and he urges those who have entered the path not to be satisfied with anything less.

Text VII,1(3) is a selection of suttas from "The Connected Discourses on the Path" (*Maggasaṃyutta*). These suttas state that the purpose of practicing the spiritual life under the Buddha is "the fading away of lust, ... final Nibbāna without clinging," the Noble Eightfold Path being the way to attain each of these aims.

The Noble Eightfold Path is the classical formulation of the way to liberation, as is already clear from the Buddha's first sermon, in which he calls the Eightfold Path the way to the cessation of suffering. **Text VII,2** gives formal definitions of the individual path factors but does not show concretely how their practice is to be integrated into the life of a disciple. The detailed application will be filled out later in this chapter and in chapters VIII and IX.

Text VII,3 throws a different spotlight on the path than we are accustomed to hear in standard Buddhist rhetoric. While we are often told that the practice of the Buddhist path depends entirely on personal effort, this sutta emphasizes the importance of spiritual friendship. The Buddha declares that spiritual friendship is not merely "half the spiritual life" but the whole of it, for the endeavor to attain spiritual perfection is not a purely solitary enterprise but occurs in dependence on close personal ties. Spiritual friendship gives the practice of the Dhamma an inescapably human dimension and welds the body of Buddhist practitioners into a community united both vertically by the relationship of teacher to students and horizontally by friendships among peers treading a shared path.

Contrary to a common assumption, the eight path factors are not steps to be followed in sequence, one after another. They are more appropriately described as components than as steps. Optimally, all eight factors should be present simultaneously, each making its own distinctive contribution, like eight interwoven strands of a cable that give the cable maximum strength. However, until that stage is reached, it is inevitable that the factors of the path exhibit some degree of sequence in their development. The eight factors are commonly distributed into three groups as follows:

1. the moral discipline group (*sīlakkhandha*), made up of right speech, right action, and right livelihood;
2. the concentration group (*samādhikkhandha*), made up of right effort, right mindfulness, and right concentration;
3. the wisdom group (*paññākkhandha*), made up of right view and right intention.

Within the Nikāyas, however, this correlation occurs only once (at MN 44; I 301), where it is ascribed to the nun Dhammadinnā, not to the Buddha himself. It might be said that the two wisdom factors are placed at the beginning because a preliminary right view and right intention are required at the outset of the path, right view providing the conceptual understanding of Buddhist principles that guides the development of the other path factors, right intention the proper motivation and direction for the development of the path.

In the Nikāyas, the Buddha often expounds the practice of the path as a gradual training (*anupubbasikkhā*) that unfolds in stages from the first step to the final goal. This gradual training is a finer subdivision of the threefold division of the path into moral discipline, concentration, and wisdom. Invariably in the suttas the exposition of the gradual training begins with the going forth into homelessness and the adoption of the lifestyle of a *bhikkhu*, a Buddhist monk. This immediately calls attention to the importance of the monastic life in the Buddha's pragmatic vision. In principle the entire practice of the Noble Eightfold Path is open to people from any mode of life, monastic or lay, and the Buddha confirms that many among his lay followers were accomplished in the Dhamma and had attained the first three of the four stages of awakening, up to nonreturning (*anāgāmī*; Theravāda commentators say that lay followers can also attain the fourth stage, arahantship, but they do so either on the verge of death or after attainment immediately seek the going forth). The fact remains, however, that the household life inevitably fosters a multitude of mundane concerns and personal attachments that impede the single-hearted quest for liberation. Thus when the Buddha set out on his own noble quest he did so by going into homelessness, and after his enlightenment, as a practical way to help others, he established the Saṅgha, the order of monks and nuns, for those who want to devote themselves fully to the Dhamma unhindered by the cares of household life.

The gradual training occurs in two versions: a longer version in the Dīgha Nikāya and a middle-length version in the Majjhima Nikāya. The principal differences are: (1) the longer version has a more detailed treatment of the observances that pertain to monastic etiquette and ascetic self-restraint; (2) the longer version includes eight types of higher knowledge while the middle-length version has three types. However, as these three types are the ones mentioned in the Buddha's account of his own enlightenment (see **Text II,3(2)**), they are by far the most important. The main paradigm for the longer version of the gradual training is found at DN 2; the middle-length version is at MN 27 and MN 51, with variants at MN 38, MN 39, MN 53, MN 107, and MN 125. Here, **Text VII,4** includes the whole of MN 27, which embeds the training in the simile of the elephant's footprint that gives the sutta its name. **Text VII,5**, an excerpt from MN 39, repeats the higher stages of the training as described in MN 27, but includes the impressive similes not included in the latter version.

The sequence opens with the appearance of a Tathāgata in the world and his exposition of the Dhamma. Having heard this, the disciple acquires faith and follows the Teacher into homelessness. He then undertakes the rules of discipline that promote the purification of conduct and the right livelihood of an ascetic. The next three steps—contentment, restraint of the sense faculties, and mindfulness and clear comprehension—internalize the process of purification and thereby bridge the transition from moral discipline to concentration.

The section on the abandonment of the five hindrances deals with the preliminary training in concentration. The five hindrances—sensual desire, ill will, dullness and drowsiness, restlessness and remorse, and doubt—are the principal obstacles to meditative development, and thus they must be removed for the mind to become collected and unified. The stock passage on the gradual training treats the overcoming of the hindrances only schematically, but other texts in the Nikāyas provide more practical instructions, while the Pāli commentaries offer even more details. The similes in the version of MN 39—see **Text VII,5**—illustrate the joyful sense of freedom that one wins by overcoming the hindrances.

The next stage in the sequence describes the attainment of the *jhānas*, profound states of concentration in which the mind becomes fully absorbed in its object. The Buddha enumerates four jhānas, named simply after their numerical position in the series, each more refined and elevated than its predecessor. The jhānas are always described by the same formulas, which in several suttas are augmented by similes of great beauty; again, see **Text VII,5**. Although wisdom rather than concentration is the critical factor in the attainment of enlightenment, the Buddha invariably includes the jhānas in the gradual training for at least two reasons: first, because they contribute to the intrinsic perfection of the path; and second, because the deep concentration they induce serves as a basis for the arising of insight. The Buddha calls the jhānas the "footsteps of the Tathāgata" (MN 27.19–22) and shows them to be precursors of the bliss of Nibbāna that lies at the end of the training.

From the fourth jhāna three alternative lines of further development become possible. In a number of texts outside the stock passage on the gradual training the Buddha mentions four meditative states that continue the mental unification established by the jhānas. These states, described as "the liberations that are peaceful and formless," are further refinements of concentration. Distinguished from the jhānas by their transcendence of the subtle mental image that serves as the object in the jhānas, they are named the base of the infinity of space, the base of the infinity of consciousness, the base of nothingness, and the base of neither-perception-nor-nonperception.

A second line of development is the acquisition of supernormal knowledge. The Buddha frequently refers to a set of six types, which come to be called the six kinds of direct knowledge (*chaḷabhiññā*). The last of these, the knowledge of the destruction of the taints, is "supramundane" or world-transcending and thus marks the culmination of the third line of development. But the other five are all mundane, products of the extraordinarily powerful mental concentration achieved in the fourth jhāna: the supernormal powers, the divine ear, the ability to read the minds of others, the recollection of past lives, and the knowledge of the passing away and rebirth of beings (see **Text VIII,4**).

The jhānas and the formless attainments by themselves do not issue in enlightenment and liberation. Though lofty and peaceful, they can only silence the defilements that sustain the round of rebirths but cannot eradicate them. To uproot the defilements at the most fundamental level, and thereby arrive at enlightenment and liberation, the meditative process must be directed to a third line of development. This is the contemplation of "things as they really are," which results in increasingly deeper insights into the nature of existence and culminates in the final goal, the attainment of arahantship.

This line of development is the one the Buddha pursues in the passage on the gradual training. He prefaces it with descriptions of two of the direct knowledges, the recollection of past lives and the knowledge of the passing away and rebirth of beings. The three together figured prominently in the Buddha's own enlightenment—as we saw in **Text II,3(2)**—and are collectively called the three true knowledges (*tevijjā*). Although the first two are not essential to the realization of arahantship, the Buddha probably includes them here because they reveal the truly vast and profound dimensions of suffering in saṃsāra, thereby preparing the mind for the penetration of the Four Noble Truths by which that suffering is diagnosed and surmounted.

The passage on the gradual training does not explicitly show the process of contemplation by which the meditator develops insight. The whole process is only implied by the mention of its final fruit, called the knowledge of the destruction of the taints (*āsavakkhayañāṇa*). The *āsavas* or taints are a classification of defilements considered in their role of sustaining the forward movement of the process of birth and death. The commentaries derive the word from a root *su* meaning "to flow." Scholars differ as to whether the flow implied by the prefix *ā* is inward or outward; hence some have rendered it as "influxes" or "influences," others as "outflows" or "effluents." A stock passage in the suttas indicates the term's real significance independently of etymology when it describes the *āsavas* as states "that defile, bring renewal of existence, give trouble, ripen in suffering, and lead to future birth, aging, and death" (MN 36.47; I 250). Thus other translators, bypassing the literal meaning, have rendered it "cankers," "corruptions," or "taints." The three taints mentioned in the Nikāyas are respectively synonyms for craving for sensual pleasures, craving for existence, and ignorance. When the disciple's mind is liberated from the taints by the completion of the path of arahantship, he reviews his newly won freedom and roars his lion's roar: "Birth is destroyed, the spiritual life has been lived, what had to be done has been done; there is no more coming back to any state of being."

VII. The Path to Liberation

1. Why Does One Enter the Path?

(1) The Arrow of Birth, Aging, and Death

1. Thus have I heard. On one occasion the Blessed One was living at Sāvatthī in Jeta's Grove, Anāthapiṇḍika's Park.

2. Then, while the Venerable Māluṅkyāputta was alone in meditation, the following thought arose in his mind:

"These speculative views have been left undeclared by the Blessed One, set aside and rejected by him, namely: 'the world is eternal' and 'the world is not eternal'; 'the world is finite' and 'the world is infinite'; 'the soul is the same as the body' and 'the soul is one thing and the body another'; and 'after death a Tathāgata exists' and 'after death a Tathāgata does not exist' and 'after death a Tathāgata both exists and does not exist' and 'after death a Tathāgata neither exists nor does not exist.'[1] The Blessed One does not declare these to me, and I do not approve of and accept this fact, so I shall go to the Blessed One and ask him the meaning of this. If he declares to me either 'the world is eternal' ... or 'after death a Tathāgata neither exists nor does not exist,' then I will lead the spiritual life under him; if he does not declare these to me, then I will abandon the training and return to the lower life."

3. Then, when it was evening, the Venerable Māluṅkyāputta rose from meditation and went to the Blessed One. After paying homage to him, he sat down at one side and told him:

"Here, venerable sir, while I was alone in meditation, the following thought arose in my mind: 'These speculative views have been left undeclared by the Blessed One.... If he does not declare these to me, then I will abandon the training and return to the lower life.' If the Blessed One knows 'the world is eternal,' let the Blessed One declare to me 'the world is eternal'; if the Blessed One knows 'the world is not eternal,' let the Blessed One declare to me 'the world is not eternal.' If the Blessed One does not know either 'the world is eternal' or 'the world is not eternal,' then it is straightforward for one who does not know and see to say: 'I do not know and see.'

"If the Blessed One knows 'the world is finite,' … 'the world is infinite,' … 'the soul is the same as the body,' … 'the soul is one thing and the body another,' … 'after death a Tathāgata exists,' … 'after death a Tathāgata does not exist.'… If the Blessed One knows 'after death a Tathāgata both exists and does not exist,' let the Blessed One declare that to me; if the Blessed One knows 'after death a Tathāgata neither exists nor does not exist,' let the Blessed One declare that to me. If the Blessed One does not know either 'after death a Tathāgata both exists and does not exist' or 'after death a Tathāgata neither exists nor does not exist,' then it is straightforward for one who does not know and see to say: 'I do not know and see.'"

4. "How then, Māluṅkyāputta, did I ever say to you: 'Come, Māluṅkyāputta, lead the spiritual life under me and I will declare to you "the world is eternal" … or "after death a Tathāgata neither exists nor does not exist"'?"—"No, venerable sir."—"Did you ever tell me: 'I will lead the spiritual life under the Blessed One, and the Blessed One will declare to me "the world is eternal" … or "after death a Tathāgata neither exists nor does not exist"'?"—"No, venerable sir."—"That being so, misguided man, who are you and what are you abandoning?

5. "If anyone should say thus: 'I will not lead the spiritual life under the Blessed One until the Blessed One declares to me "the world is eternal" … or "after death a Tathāgata neither exists nor does not exist,"' that would still remain undeclared by the Tathāgata and meanwhile that person would die. Suppose, Māluṅkyāputta, a man were wounded by an arrow thickly smeared with poison, and his friends and companions, his kinsmen and relatives, brought a surgeon to treat him. The man would say: 'I will not let the surgeon pull out this arrow until I know whether the man who wounded me was a khattiya, a brahmin, a merchant, or a worker.' And he would say: 'I will not let the surgeon pull out this arrow until I know the name and clan of the man who wounded me;… until I know whether the man who wounded me was tall, short, or of middle height;… until I know whether the man who wounded me was dark, brown, or golden-skinned;… until I know whether the man who wounded me lives in such a village, town, or city;… until I know whether the bow that wounded me was a long bow or a crossbow;… until I know whether the bowstring that

wounded me was fiber, reed, sinew, hemp, or bark;... until I know whether the shaft that wounded me was wild or cultivated;... until I know with what kind of feathers the shaft that wounded me was fitted—whether those of a vulture, a heron, a hawk, a peacock, or a stork;... until I know with what kind of sinew the shaft that wounded me was bound—whether that of an ox, a buffalo, a deer, or a monkey;... until I know what kind of arrowhead it was that wounded me—whether spiked or razor-tipped or curved or barbed or calf-toothed or lancet-shaped.'

"All this would still not be known to that man, and meanwhile he would die. So too, Māluṅkyāputta, if anyone should say thus: 'I will not lead the spiritual life under the Blessed One until the Blessed One declares to me: "the world is eternal" ... or "after death a Tathāgata neither exists nor does not exist,"' that would still remain undeclared by the Tathāgata and meanwhile that person would die.

6. "Māluṅkyāputta, if there is the view 'the world is eternal,' the spiritual life cannot be lived; and if there is the view 'the world is not eternal,' the spiritual life cannot be lived. Whether there is the view 'the world is eternal' or the view 'the world is not eternal,' there is birth, there is aging, there is death, there are sorrow, lamentation, pain, dejection, and despair, the destruction of which I prescribe here and now.

"If there is the view 'the world is finite' ... 'the world is infinite' ... 'the soul is the same as the body' ... 'the soul is one thing and the body another' ... 'after death a Tathāgata exists' ... 'after death a Tathāgata does not exist,' the spiritual life cannot be lived.... If there is the view 'after death a Tathāgata both exists and does not exist,' the spiritual life cannot be lived; and if there is the view 'after death a Tathāgata neither exists nor does not exist,' the spiritual life cannot be lived. Whether there is the view 'after death a Tathāgata both exists and does not exist' or the view 'after death a Tathāgata neither exists nor does not exist,' there is birth, there is aging, there is death, there are sorrow, lamentation, pain, dejection, and despair, the destruction of which I prescribe here and now.

7. "Therefore, Māluṅkyāputta, remember what I have left undeclared as undeclared, and remember what I have declared as declared. And what have I left undeclared? 'The world is eternal'—I have left undeclared. 'The world is not eternal'—I have left undeclared. 'The world is finite'—I have left undeclared. 'The world is infinite'—I have

left undeclared. 'The soul is the same as the body'—I have left undeclared. 'The soul is one thing and the body another'—I have left undeclared. 'After death a Tathāgata exists'—I have left undeclared. 'After death a Tathāgata does not exist'—I have left undeclared. 'After death a Tathāgata both exists and does not exist'—I have left undeclared. 'After death a Tathāgata neither exists nor does not exist'—I have left undeclared.

8. "Why have I left that undeclared? Because it is unbeneficial, it does not belong to the fundamentals of the spiritual life, it does not lead to disenchantment, to dispassion, to cessation, to peace, to direct knowledge, to enlightenment, to Nibbāna. That is why I have left it undeclared.

9. "And what have I declared? 'This is suffering'—I have declared. 'This is the origin of suffering'—I have declared. 'This is the cessation of suffering'—I have declared. 'This is the way leading to the cessation of suffering'—I have declared.

10. "Why have I declared that? Because it is beneficial, it belongs to the fundamentals of the spiritual life, it leads to disenchantment, to dispassion, to cessation, to peace, to direct knowledge, to enlightenment, to Nibbāna. That is why I have declared it.

"Therefore, Māluṅkyāputta, remember what I have left undeclared as undeclared, and remember what I have declared as declared."

That is what the Blessed One said. The Venerable Māluṅkyāputta was satisfied and delighted in the Blessed One's words.[2]

(MN 63: *Cūḷamāluṅkya Sutta*; I 426–32)

(2) The Heartwood of the Spiritual Life

1. Thus have I heard. On one occasion the Blessed One was living at Rājagaha on Mount Vulture Peak; it was soon after Devadatta had left.[3] There, referring to Devadatta, the Blessed One addressed the monks thus:

2. "Monks, here some clansman goes forth out of faith from the household life into homelessness, considering: 'I am a victim of birth, aging, and death, of sorrow, lamentation, pain, dejection, and despair; I am a victim of suffering, a prey to suffering. Surely an ending of this whole mass of suffering can be known.' When he has gone forth thus, he acquires gain, honor, and renown. He is pleased with that gain,

honor, and renown, and his intention is fulfilled. On account of it he lauds himself and disparages others thus: 'I obtain gain and renown, but these other monks are unknown, of no account.' He becomes intoxicated with that gain, honor, and renown, grows negligent, falls into negligence, and being negligent, he lives in suffering.

"Suppose a man needing heartwood, seeking heartwood, wandering in search of heartwood, came to a great tree standing possessed of heartwood. Passing over its heartwood, its sapwood, its inner bark, and its outer bark, he would cut off its twigs and leaves and take them away thinking they were heartwood. Then a man with good sight, seeing him, might say: 'This good man did not know the heartwood, the sapwood, the inner bark, the outer bark, or the twigs and leaves. Thus, while needing heartwood, seeking heartwood, wandering in search of heartwood, he came to a great tree standing possessed of heartwood, and passing over its heartwood, its sapwood, its inner bark, and its outer bark, he cut off its twigs and leaves and took them away thinking they were heartwood. Whatever it was this good man had to make with heartwood, his purpose will not be served.' So too is it with this monk who becomes intoxicated with that gain, honor, and renown. This monk is called one who has taken the twigs and leaves of the spiritual life and stopped short with that.

3. "Here, monks, some clansman goes forth out of faith from the household life into homelessness, considering: 'I am a victim of birth, aging, and death, of sorrow, lamentation, pain, dejection, and despair; I am a victim of suffering, a prey to suffering. Surely an ending of this whole mass of suffering can be known.' When he has gone forth thus, he acquires gain, honor, and renown. He is not pleased with that gain, honor, and renown, and his intention is not fulfilled. He does not, on account of it, laud himself and disparage others. He does not become intoxicated with that gain, honor, and renown; he does not grow negligent and fall into negligence. Being diligent, he achieves the attainment of moral discipline. He is pleased with that attainment of moral discipline and his intention is fulfilled. On account of it he lauds himself and disparages others thus: 'I have moral discipline; I am of good character; but these other monks are immoral, of bad character.' He becomes intoxicated with that attainment of moral discipline, grows negligent, falls into negligence, and being negligent, he lives in suffering.

"Suppose a man needing heartwood, seeking heartwood, wandering in search of heartwood, came to a great tree standing possessed of heartwood. Passing over its heartwood, its sapwood, and its inner bark, he would cut off its outer bark and take it away thinking it was heartwood. Then a man with good sight, seeing him, might say: 'This good man did not know the heartwood ... or the twigs and leaves. Thus, while needing heartwood ... he cut off its outer bark and took it away thinking it was heartwood. Whatever it was this good man had to make with heartwood, his purpose will not be served.' So too is it with this monk who becomes intoxicated with that attainment of moral discipline. This monk is called one who has taken the outer bark of the spiritual life and stopped short with that.

4. "Here, monks, some clansman goes forth out of faith from the household life into homelessness, considering: 'I am a victim of birth, aging, and death, of sorrow, lamentation, pain, dejection, and despair; I am a victim of suffering, a prey to suffering. Surely an ending of this whole mass of suffering can be known.' When he has gone forth thus, he acquires gain, honor, and renown. He is not pleased with that gain, honor, and renown, and his intention is not fulfilled.... Being diligent, he achieves the attainment of moral discipline. He is pleased with that attainment of moral discipline, but his intention is not fulfilled. He does not, on account of it, laud himself and disparage others. He does not become intoxicated with that attainment of moral discipline; he does not grow negligent and fall into negligence. Being diligent, he achieves the attainment of concentration. He is pleased with that attainment of concentration and his intention is fulfilled. On account of it he lauds himself and disparages others thus: 'I am concentrated; my mind is unified; but these other monks are scatter-minded, with their minds astray.' He becomes intoxicated with that attainment of concentration, grows negligent, falls into negligence, and being negligent, he lives in suffering.

"Suppose a man needing heartwood, seeking heartwood, wandering in search of heartwood, came to a great tree standing possessed of heartwood. Passing over its heartwood and its sapwood, he would cut off its inner bark and take it away thinking it was heartwood. Then a man with good sight, seeing him, might say: 'This good man did not know the heartwood ... or the twigs and leaves. Thus, while needing heartwood ... he cut off its inner bark and took it away thinking it was heartwood. Whatever it was this good man had to make with heartwood, his purpose will not be served.' So too is it with this monk who becomes intoxicated with that attainment of concentration. This monk is called one who has taken the inner bark of the spiritual life and stopped short with that.

5. "Here, monks, some clansman goes forth out of faith from the household life into homelessness, considering: 'I am a victim of birth, aging, and death, of sorrow, lamentation, pain, dejection, and despair; I am a victim of suffering, a prey to suffering. Surely an ending of this whole mass of suffering can be known.' When he has gone forth thus, he acquires gain, honor, and renown. He is not pleased with that gain, honor, and renown, and his intention is not fulfilled.... Being diligent, he achieves the attainment of moral discipline. He is pleased with that attainment of moral discipline, but his intention is not fulfilled.... Being diligent, he achieves the attainment of concentration. He is pleased with that attainment of concentration, but his intention is not fulfilled. He does not, on account of it, laud himself and disparage others. He does not become intoxicated with that attainment of concentration; he does not grow negligent and fall into negligence. Being diligent, he achieves knowledge and vision.[4] He is pleased with that knowledge and vision and his intention is fulfilled. On account of it he lauds himself and disparages others thus: 'I live knowing and seeing, but these other monks live unknowing and unseeing.' He becomes intoxicated with that knowledge and vision, grows negligent, falls into negligence, and being negligent, he lives in suffering.

"Suppose a man needing heartwood, seeking heartwood, wandering in search of heartwood, came to a great tree standing possessed of heartwood. Passing over its heartwood, he would cut off its sapwood and take it away thinking it was heartwood. Then a man with good sight, seeing him, might say: 'This good man did not know the heartwood ... or the twigs and leaves. Thus, while needing heartwood ... he cut off its sapwood and took it away thinking it was heartwood. Whatever it was this good man had to make with heartwood, his purpose will not be served.' So too is it with this monk who becomes intoxicated with that knowledge and vision. This monk is called one who has taken the sapwood of the spiritual life and stopped short with that.

6. "Here, monks, some clansman goes forth out of faith from the household life into homelessness, considering: 'I am a victim of birth,

aging, and death, of sorrow, lamentation, pain, dejection, and despair; I am a victim of suffering, a prey to suffering. Surely an ending of this whole mass of suffering can be known.' When he has gone forth thus, he acquires gain, honor, and renown. He is not pleased with that gain, honor, and renown, and his intention is not fulfilled.... When he is diligent, he achieves the attainment of moral discipline. He is pleased with that attainment of moral discipline, but his intention is not fulfilled.... When he is diligent, he achieves the attainment of concentration. He is pleased with that attainment of concentration, but his intention is not fulfilled.... When he is diligent, he achieves knowledge and vision. He is pleased with that knowledge and vision, but his intention is not fulfilled. He does not, on account of it, laud himself and disparage others. He does not become intoxicated with that knowledge and vision; he does not grow negligent and fall into negligence. Being diligent, he attains perpetual emancipation. And it is impossible for that monk to fall away from that perpetual liberation.[5]

"Suppose a man needing heartwood, seeking heartwood, wandering in search of heartwood, came to a great tree standing possessed of heartwood, and cutting off only its heartwood, he would take it away knowing it was heartwood. Then a man with good sight, seeing him, might say: 'This good man knew the heartwood, the sapwood, the inner bark, the outer bark, and the twigs and leaves. Thus, while needing heartwood, seeking heartwood, wandering in search of heartwood, he came to a great tree standing possessed of heartwood, and cutting off only its heartwood, he took it away knowing it was heartwood. Whatever it was this good man had to make with heartwood, his purpose will be served.' So too is it with this monk who attains perpetual liberation.

7. "So this spiritual life, monks, does not have gain, honor, and renown for its benefit, or the attainment of moral discipline for its benefit, or the attainment of concentration for its benefit, or knowledge and vision for its benefit. But it is this unshakable liberation of mind that is the goal of this spiritual life, its heartwood, and its end."[6]

That is what the Blessed One said. The monks were satisfied and delighted in the Blessed One's words.

(MN 29: *Mahāsāropama Sutta*; I 192–97)

(3) The Fading Away of Lust

"Monks, if wanderers of other sects ask you: 'For what purpose, friends, is the spiritual life lived under the ascetic Gotama?'—being asked thus, you should answer them thus: 'It is, friends, for the fading away of lust[7] that the spiritual life is lived under the Blessed One.'

"Then, monks, if the wanderers of other sects ask you: 'But, friends, is there a path, a way for the fading away of lust?'—being asked thus, you should answer them thus: 'There is a path, friends, a way for the fading away of lust.'

"And what, monks, is that path, that way for the fading away of lust? It is this Noble Eightfold Path; that is, right view, right intention, right speech, right action, right livelihood, right effort, right mindfulness, right concentration. This is the path, the way for the fading away of lust.

"Being asked thus, monks, you should answer those wanderers of other sects in such a way.

"[Or else you may answer them:] 'It is, friends, for the abandoning of the fetters ... for the uprooting of the underlying tendencies ... for the full understanding of the course [of saṃsāra] ... for the destruction of the taints ... for the realization of the fruit of true knowledge and liberation ... for the sake of knowledge and vision ... for the sake of final Nibbāna without clinging that the spiritual life is lived under the Blessed One.'

"Then, monks, if the wanderers of other sects ask you: 'But, friends, is there a path, a way for attaining final Nibbāna without clinging?'—being asked thus, you should answer them thus: 'There is a path, friends, a way for attaining final Nibbāna without clinging.'

"And what, monks, is that path, that way for attaining final Nibbāna without clinging? It is this Noble Eightfold Path; that is, right view ... right concentration. This is the path, the way for attaining final Nibbāna without clinging.

"Being asked thus, monks, you should answer those wanderers of other sects in such a way."

(SN 45:41–48, combined; V 27–29)

2. Analysis of the Eightfold Path

"Monks, I will teach you the Noble Eightfold Path, and I will analyze it for you. Listen and attend closely; I will speak."

"Yes, venerable sir," those monks replied. The Blessed One said this:

"And what, monks, is the Noble Eightfold Path? Right view, right intention, right speech, right action, right livelihood, right effort, right mindfulness, and right concentration.

"And what, monks, is right view? Knowledge of suffering, knowledge of the origin of suffering, knowledge of the cessation of suffering, knowledge of the way leading to the cessation of suffering: this is called right view.

"And what, monks, is right intention? Intention of renunciation, intention of non–ill will, intention of harmlessness: this is called right intention.

"And what, monks, is right speech? Abstinence from false speech, abstinence from malicious speech, abstinence from harsh speech, abstinence from idle chatter: this is called right speech.

"And what, monks, is right action? Abstinence from the destruction of life, abstinence from taking what is not given, abstinence from sexual misconduct: this is called right action.

"And what, monks, is right livelihood? Here a noble disciple, having abandoned a wrong mode of livelihood, earns his living by a right livelihood: this is called right livelihood.

"And what, monks, is right effort? Here, monks, a monk generates desire for the nonarising of unarisen evil unwholesome states; he makes an effort, arouses energy, applies his mind, and strives. He generates desire for the abandoning of arisen evil unwholesome states.... He generates desire for the arising of unarisen wholesome states.... He generates desire for the continuation of arisen wholesome states, for their nondecline, increase, expansion, and fulfillment by development; he makes an effort, arouses energy, applies his mind, and strives. This is called right effort.

"And what, monks is right mindfulness? Here, monks, a monk dwells contemplating the body in the body, ardent, clearly comprehending, mindful, having removed longing and dejection in regard to the world. He dwells contemplating feelings in feelings, ardent, clearly comprehending, mindful, having removed longing and dejection in regard to the world. He dwells contemplating mind in mind, ardent, clearly comprehending, mindful, having removed longing and dejection in regard to the world. He dwells contemplating phenomena in phenomena, ardent, clearly comprehending, mindful, having removed longing and dejection in regard to the world. This is called right mindfulness.

"And what, monks, is right concentration? Here, monks, secluded from sensual pleasures, secluded from unwholesome states, a monk enters and dwells in the first jhāna, which is accompanied by thought and examination, with rapture and happiness born of seclusion. With the subsiding of thought and examination, he enters and dwells in the second jhāna, which has internal confidence and unification of mind, is without thought and examination, and has rapture and happiness born of concentration. With the fading away as well of rapture, he dwells equanimous and, mindful and clearly comprehending, he experiences happiness with the body; he enters and dwells in the third jhāna of which the noble ones declare: 'He is equanimous, mindful, one who dwells happily.' With the abandoning of pleasure and pain, and with the previous passing away of joy and dejection, he enters and dwells in the fourth jhāna, which is neither painful nor pleasant and includes the purification of mindfulness by equanimity. This is called right concentration."

(SN 45:8; V 8–10)

3. Good Friendship

Thus have I heard. On one occasion the Blessed One was dwelling among the Sakyans where there was a town of the Sakyans named Nāgaraka. Then the Venerable Ānanda approached the Blessed One, paid homage to him, sat down to one side, and said:

"Venerable sir, this is half of the spiritual life, that is, good friendship, good companionship, good comradeship."[8]

"Not so, Ānanda! Not so, Ānanda! This is the entire spiritual life, Ānanda, that is, good friendship, good companionship, good comradeship. When a monk has a good friend, a good companion, a good comrade, it is to be expected that he will develop and cultivate the Noble Eightfold Path.

"And how, Ānanda, does a monk with a good friend, a good companion, a good comrade, develop and cultivate the Noble Eightfold Path? Here, Ānanda, a monk develops right view, which is based upon seclusion, dispassion, and cessation, maturing in release. He develops right intention ... right speech ... right action ... right livelihood ... right effort ... right mindfulness ... right concentration, which is based upon seclusion, dispassion, and cessation, maturing in release. It is in this way, Ānanda, that a monk with a good friend, a good companion, a good comrade, develops and cultivates the Noble Eightfold Path.

"By the following method too, Ānanda, it may be understood how the entire spiritual life is good friendship, good companionship, good comradeship: by relying upon me as a good friend, Ānanda, beings subject to birth are freed from birth; beings subject to aging are freed from aging; beings subject to death are freed from death; beings subject to sorrow, lamentation, pain, dejection, and despair are freed from sorrow, lamentation, pain, dejection, and despair. By this method, Ānanda, it may be understood how the entire spiritual life is good friendship, good companionship, good comradeship."

(SN 45:2; V 2–3)

4. The Graduated Training

1. Thus have I heard. On one occasion the Blessed One was living at Sāvatthī in Jeta's Grove, Anāthapiṇḍika's Park.

2. Now on that occasion the brahmin Jāṇussoṇi was driving out of Sāvatthī in the middle of the day in an all-white chariot drawn by white mares. He saw the wanderer Pilotika coming in the distance and asked him: "Now where is Master Vacchāyana coming from in the middle of the day?"[9]

"Sir, I am coming from the presence of the ascetic Gotama."

"What does Master Vacchāyana think of the ascetic Gotama's lucidity of wisdom? He is wise, is he not?"

"Sir, who am I to know the ascetic Gotama's lucidity of wisdom? One would surely have to be his equal to know the ascetic Gotama's lucidity of wisdom."

"Master Vacchāyana praises the ascetic Gotama with high praise indeed."

"Sir, who am I to praise the ascetic Gotama? The ascetic Gotama is praised by the praised as best among devas and humans."

"What reasons does Master Vacchāyana see that he has such firm confidence in the ascetic Gotama?"

3. "Sir, suppose a wise elephant hunter were to enter an elephant wood and were to see in the elephant wood a big elephant's footprint, long in extent and broad across. He would come to the conclusion: 'Indeed, this is a big bull elephant.' So too, when I saw four footprints of the ascetic Gotama, I came to the conclusion: 'The Blessed One is perfectly enlightened, the Dhamma is well expounded by the Blessed One, the Saṅgha is practicing the good way.' What are the four?

4. "Sir, I have seen here certain learned nobles who were clever, knowledgeable about the doctrines of others, as sharp as hairsplitting marksmen; they wander about, as it were, demolishing the views of others with their sharp wits. When they hear: 'The ascetic Gotama will visit such and such a village or town,' they formulate a question thus: 'We will go to the ascetic Gotama and ask him this question. If he is asked like this, he will answer like this, and so we will refute his doctrine in this way; and if he is asked like that, he will answer like that, and so we will refute his doctrine in that way.'

"They hear: 'The ascetic Gotama has come to visit such and such a village or town.' They go to the ascetic Gotama, and the ascetic Gotama instructs, urges, rouses, and gladdens them with a talk on the Dhamma. After they have been instructed, urged, roused, and gladdened by the ascetic Gotama with a talk on the Dhamma, they do not so much as ask him the question, so how should they refute his doctrine? In actual fact, they become his disciples. When I saw this first footprint of the ascetic Gotama, I came to the conclusion: 'The Blessed One is perfectly enlightened, the Dhamma is well expounded by the Blessed One, the Saṅgha is practicing the good way.'

5. "Again, I have seen certain learned brahmins who were clever.... In actual fact, they too become his disciples. When I saw this second footprint of the ascetic Gotama, I came to the conclusion: 'The Blessed One is perfectly enlightened....'

6. "Again, I have seen certain learned householders who were clever.... In actual fact, they too become his disciples. When I saw this third footprint of the ascetic Gotama, I came to the conclusion: 'The Blessed One is perfectly enlightened....'

7. "Again, I have seen certain learned ascetics who were clever.... They do not so much as ask him the question, so how should they refute his doctrine? In actual fact, they ask the ascetic Gotama to allow them to go forth from the household life into homelessness, and he gives them the going forth. Not long after they have gone forth, dwelling alone, withdrawn, diligent, ardent, and resolute, by realizing it for themselves with direct knowledge they here and now enter upon and dwell in that supreme goal of the spiritual life for the sake of which clansmen rightly go forth from the household life into homelessness. They say thus: 'We were very nearly lost, we very nearly perished, for formerly we claimed that we were ascetics though we were not really ascetics; we claimed that we were brahmins though we were not really brahmins; we claimed that we were arahants though we were not really arahants. But now we are ascetics, now we are brahmins, now we are arahants.' When I saw this fourth footprint of the ascetic Gotama, I came to the conclusion: 'The Blessed One is perfectly enlightened....'

"When I saw these four footprints of the ascetic Gotama, I came to the conclusion: 'The Blessed One is perfectly enlightened, the Dhamma is well expounded by the Blessed One, the Saṅgha is practicing the good way.'"

8. When this was said, the brahmin Jāṇussoṇi got down from his all-white chariot drawn by white mares, and arranging his upper robe on one shoulder, he extended his hands in reverential salutation toward the Blessed One and uttered this exclamation three times: "Homage to the Blessed One, the Arahant, the Perfectly Enlightened One! Homage to the Blessed One, the Arahant, the Perfectly Enlightened One! Homage to the Blessed One, the Arahant, the Perfectly Enlightened One! Perhaps some time or other I might meet Master Gotama and have some conversation with him."

9. Then the brahmin Jāṇussoṇi went to the Blessed One and exchanged greetings with him. When this courteous and amiable talk was finished, he sat down to one side and related his entire conversation with the wanderer Pilotika. Thereupon the Blessed One told him: "At this point, brahmin, the simile of the elephant's footprint has not yet been completed in detail. As to how it is completed in detail, listen and attend carefully to what I shall say."—"Yes, sir," the brahmin Jāṇussoṇi replied. The Blessed One said this:

10. "Brahmin, suppose an elephant hunter were to enter an elephant wood and were to see in the elephant wood a big elephant's footprint, long in extent and broad across. A wise elephant hunter would not yet come to the conclusion: 'Indeed, this is a big bull elephant.' Why is that? In an elephant wood there are small she-elephants that leave a big footprint, and this might be one of their footprints. He follows it and sees in the elephant wood a big elephant's footprint, long in extent and broad across, and some scrapings high up. A wise elephant hunter would not yet come to the conclusion: 'Indeed, this is a big bull elephant.' Why is that? In an elephant wood there are tall she-elephants that have prominent teeth and leave a big footprint, and this might be one of their footprints. He follows it further and sees in the elephant wood a big elephant's footprint, long in extent and broad across, and some scrapings high up, and marks made by tusks. A wise elephant hunter would not yet come to the conclusion: 'Indeed, this is a big bull elephant.' Why is that? In an elephant wood there are tall she-elephants that have tusks and leave a big footprint, and this might be one of their footprints. He follows it further and sees in the elephant wood a big elephant's footprint, long in extent and broad across, and some scrapings high up, and marks made by tusks, and broken-off branches. And he sees that bull elephant at the root of a tree or in the open, walking about, sitting, or lying down. He comes to the conclusion: 'This is that big bull elephant.'

11. "So too, brahmin, here a Tathāgata appears in the world, an arahant, perfectly enlightened, perfect in true knowledge and conduct, fortunate, knower of the world, unsurpassed leader of persons to be tamed, teacher of devas and humans, the Enlightened One, the Blessed One. Having realized with his own direct knowledge this world with its devas, Māra, and Brahmā, this population with its ascetics and brahmins, with its devas and humans, he makes it known to others. He teaches a Dhamma that is good in the beginning, good in the middle, and good in the end, with the right meaning and expression; he reveals a holy life that is perfectly complete and purified.

12. "A householder or householder's son or one born in some other clan hears that Dhamma. On hearing the Dhamma he acquires faith in the Tathāgata. Possessing that faith, he considers thus: 'Household life is crowded and dusty; life gone forth is wide open. It is not easy, while living in a home, to lead the spiritual life utterly perfect and pure as a

polished shell. Suppose I shave off my hair and beard, put on the ochre robe, and go forth from the household life into homelessness.' On a later occasion, abandoning a small or a large fortune, abandoning a small or a large circle of relatives, he shaves off his hair and beard, puts on the ochre robe, and goes forth from the household life into homelessness.

13. "Having thus gone forth and possessing the monk's training and way of life, abandoning the destruction of life, he abstains from the destruction of life; with rod and weapon laid aside, conscientious, merciful, he dwells compassionate to all living beings. Abandoning the taking of what is not given, he abstains from taking what is not given; taking only what is given, expecting only what is given, by not stealing he dwells in purity. Abandoning sexual relations, he observes celibacy, living apart, refraining from the coarse practice of sexual intercourse.

"Abandoning false speech, he abstains from false speech; he speaks truth, adheres to truth, is trustworthy and reliable, one who is no deceiver of the world. Abandoning malicious speech, he abstains from malicious speech; he does not repeat elsewhere what he has heard here in order to divide [those people] from these, nor does he repeat to these people what he has heard elsewhere in order to divide [these people] from those; thus he is one who reunites those who are divided, a promoter of friendships, who enjoys concord, rejoices in concord, delights in concord, a speaker of words that promote concord. Abandoning harsh speech, he abstains from harsh speech; he speaks such words as are gentle, pleasing to the ear, and loveable, as go to the heart, are courteous, desired by many and agreeable to many. Abandoning idle chatter, he abstains from idle chatter; he speaks at the right time, speaks what is fact, speaks on what is good, speaks on the Dhamma and the Discipline; at the right time he speaks such words as are worth recording, reasonable, moderate, and beneficial.

"He abstains from injuring seeds and plants. He eats only one meal a day, abstaining from eating at night and outside the proper time.[10] He abstains from dancing, singing, music, and unsuitable shows. He abstains from wearing garlands, smartening himself with scent, and embellishing himself with unguents. He abstains from high and large couches. He abstains from accepting gold and silver. He abstains from accepting raw grain. He abstains from accepting raw meat. He abstains from accepting women and girls. He abstains from accepting men and women slaves. He abstains from accepting goats and sheep. He abstains from accepting fowl and pigs. He abstains from accepting elephants, cattle, horses, and mares. He abstains from accepting fields and land. He abstains from going on errands and running messages. He abstains from buying and selling. He abstains from false weights, false metals, and false measures. He abstains from accepting bribes, deceiving, defrauding, and trickery. He abstains from wounding, murdering, binding, brigandage, plunder, and violence.

14. "He becomes content with robes to protect his body and with almsfood to maintain his stomach, and wherever he goes, he sets out taking only these with him. Just as a bird, wherever it goes, flies with its wings as its only burden, so too the monk becomes content with robes to protect his body and with almsfood to maintain his stomach, and wherever he goes, he sets out taking only these with him. Possessing this aggregate of noble moral discipline, he experiences within himself the bliss of blamelessness.

15. "On seeing a form with the eye, he does not grasp at its signs and features.[11] Since, if he left the eye faculty unguarded, evil unwholesome states of longing and dejection might invade him, he practices the way of its restraint, he guards the eye faculty, he undertakes the restraint of the eye faculty. On hearing a sound with the ear ... On smelling an odor with the nose ... On tasting a flavor with the tongue ... On feeling a tactile object with the body ... On cognizing a mental phenomenon with the mind, he does not grasp at its signs and features. Since, if he left the mind faculty unguarded, evil unwholesome states of longing and dejection might invade him, he practices the way of its restraint, he guards the mind faculty, he undertakes the restraint of the mind faculty. Possessing this noble restraint of the sense faculties, he experiences within himself an unsullied bliss.

16. "He becomes one who acts with clear comprehension when going forward and returning; who acts with clear comprehension when looking ahead and looking away; who acts with clear comprehension when flexing and extending his limbs; who acts with clear comprehension when wearing his robes and carrying his outer robe and bowl; who acts with clear comprehension when eating, drinking, chewing, and tasting; who acts with clear comprehension when defecating and urinating; who acts with clear comprehension when walking, standing, sitting, falling asleep, waking up, talking, and keeping silent.

17. "Possessing this aggregate of noble moral discipline, and this noble restraint of the faculties, and possessing this noble mindfulness and clear comprehension, he resorts to a secluded resting place: the forest, the root of a tree, a mountain, a ravine, a hillside cave, a charnel ground, a jungle thicket, an open space, a heap of straw.

18. "On returning from his almsround, after his meal he sits down, folding his legs crosswise, setting his body erect, and establishing mindfulness before him. Abandoning longing for the world, he dwells with a mind free from longing; he purifies his mind from longing.[12] Abandoning ill will and hatred, he dwells with a mind free from ill will, compassionate for the welfare of all living beings; he purifies his mind from ill will and hatred. Abandoning dullness and drowsiness, he dwells free from dullness and drowsiness, percipient of light, mindful and clearly comprehending; he purifies his mind from dullness and drowsiness. Abandoning restlessness and remorse, he dwells free from agitation with a mind inwardly peaceful; he purifies his mind from restlessness and remorse. Abandoning doubt, he dwells having gone beyond doubt, unperplexed about wholesome states; he purifies his mind from doubt.

19. "Having thus abandoned these five hindrances, defilements of the mind that weaken wisdom, secluded from sensual pleasures, secluded from unwholesome states, he enters and dwells in the first jhāna, which is accompanied by thought and examination, with rapture and happiness born of seclusion. This, brahmin, is called a footprint of the Tathāgata, something scraped by the Tathāgata, something marked by the Tathāgata, but a noble disciple does not yet come to the conclusion: 'The Blessed One is perfectly enlightened, the Dhamma is well expounded by the Blessed One, the Saṅgha is practicing the good way.'[13]

20. "Again, with the subsiding of thought and examination, he enters and dwells in the second jhāna, which has internal confidence and unification of mind, is without thought and examination, and has rapture and happiness born of concentration. This too, brahmin, is called a footprint of the Tathāgata ... but a noble disciple does not yet come to the conclusion: 'The Blessed One is perfectly enlightened....'

21. "Again, with the fading away as well of rapture, he dwells equanimous and, mindful and clearly comprehending, he experiences happiness with the body; he enters and dwells in the third jhāna of

which the noble ones declare: 'He is equanimous, mindful, one who dwells happily.' This too, brahmin, is called a footprint of the Tathāgata ... but a noble disciple does not yet come to the conclusion: 'The Blessed One is perfectly enlightened....'

22. "Again, with the abandoning of pleasure and pain, and with the previous passing away of joy and dejection, he enters and dwells in the fourth jhāna, which is neither painful nor pleasant and includes the purification of mindfulness by equanimity. This too, brahmin, is called a footprint of the Tathāgata ... but a noble disciple does not yet come to the conclusion: 'The Blessed One is perfectly enlightened....'

23. "When his mind is thus concentrated, purified, bright, unblemished, rid of defilement, malleable, wieldy, steady, and attained to imperturbability, he directs it to knowledge of the recollection of past lives. He recollects his manifold past lives, that is, one birth, two births, three births, four births, five births, ten births, twenty births, thirty births, forty births, fifty births, a hundred births, a thousand births, a hundred thousand births, many eons of world-contraction, many eons of world-expansion, many eons of world-contraction and expansion: 'There I was so named, of such a clan, with such an appearance, such was my nutriment, such my experience of pleasure and pain, such my life-term; and passing away from there, I was reborn elsewhere; and there too I was so named, of such a clan, with such an appearance, such was my nutriment, such my experience of pleasure and pain, such my life-term; and passing away from there, I was reborn here.' Thus with their aspects and particulars he recollects his manifold past lives. This too, brahmin, is called a footprint of the Tathāgata ... but a noble disciple does not yet come to the conclusion: 'The Blessed One is perfectly enlightened....'

24. "When his mind is thus concentrated, purified, bright, unblemished, rid of defilement, malleable, wieldy, steady, and attained to imperturbability, he directs it to knowledge of the passing away and rebirth of beings. With the divine eye, which is purified and surpasses the human, he sees beings passing away and being reborn, inferior and superior, fair and ugly, fortunate and unfortunate. He understands how beings pass on according to their actions thus: 'These beings who behaved wrongly by body, speech, and mind, who reviled the noble ones, held wrong view, and undertook actions based on wrong view, with the breakup of the body, after death, have been reborn in a state

of misery, in a bad destination, in the lower world, in hell; but these beings who behaved well by body, speech, and mind, who did not revile the noble ones, who held right view, and undertook action based on right view, with the breakup of the body, after death, have been reborn in a good destination, in a heavenly world.' Thus with the divine eye, which is purified and surpasses the human, he sees beings passing away and being reborn, inferior and superior, fair and ugly, fortunate and unfortunate, and he understands how beings pass on according to their actions. This too, brahmin, is called a footprint of the Tathāgata ... but a noble disciple does not yet come to the conclusion: 'The Blessed One is perfectly enlightened....'

25. "When his mind is thus concentrated, purified, bright, unblemished, rid of defilement, malleable, wieldy, steady, and attained to imperturbability, he directs it to knowledge of the destruction of the taints. He understands as it really is: 'This is suffering. This is the origin of suffering. This is the cessation of suffering. This is the way leading to the cessation of suffering.' He understands as it really is: 'These are the taints. This is the origin of the taints. This is the cessation of the taints. This is the way leading to the cessation of the taints.'

"This too, brahmin, is called a footprint of the Tathāgata, something scraped by the Tathāgata, something marked by the Tathāgata, but a noble disciple still has not yet come to the conclusion: 'The Blessed One is perfectly enlightened, the Dhamma is well expounded by the Blessed One, the Saṅgha is practicing the good way.' Rather, he is in the process of coming to this conclusion.[14]

26. "When he knows and sees thus, his mind is liberated from the taint of sensual desire, from the taint of existence, and from the taint of ignorance. When it is liberated there comes the knowledge: 'It is liberated.' He understands: 'Birth is destroyed, the spiritual life has been lived, what had to be done has been done, there is no more coming back to any state of being.'

"This too, brahmin, is called a footprint of the Tathāgata, something scraped by the Tathāgata, something marked by the Tathāgata. It is at this point that a noble disciple has come to the conclusion: 'The Blessed One is perfectly enlightened, the Dhamma is well expounded by the Blessed One, the Saṅgha is practicing the good way.'[15] And it is at this point, brahmin, that the simile of the elephant's footprint has been completed in detail."

27. When this was said, the brahmin Jāṇussoṇi said to the Blessed One: "Magnificent, Master Gotama! Magnificent, Master Gotama! Master Gotama has made the Dhamma clear in many ways, as though he were turning upright what had been overthrown, revealing what was hidden, showing the way to one who was lost, or holding up a lamp in the dark so those with good eyesight can see forms. I now go for refuge to Master Gotama, to the Dhamma, and to the Saṅgha of monks. Let Master Gotama accept me as a lay follower who has gone for refuge from today until life's end."

(MN 27: *Cūḷahatthipadopama Sutta;* I 175–84)

5. The Higher Stages of Training with Similes

12. "Here, monks, a monk resorts to a secluded resting place: the forest, the root of a tree, a mountain, a ravine, a hillside cave, a charnel ground, a jungle thicket, an open space, a heap of straw.

13. "On returning from his almsround, after his meal he sits down, folding his legs crosswise, setting his body erect and establishing mindfulness before him. Abandoning longing for the world ... [as in preceding text, §18] ... he purifies his mind from doubt.

14. "Monks, suppose a man were to take a loan and undertake business, and his business were to succeed so that he could repay all the money of the old loan, and there would remain enough extra to maintain a wife; on considering this, he would be glad and full of joy. Or suppose a man were afflicted, suffering and gravely ill, and his food would not agree with him and his body had no strength, but later he would recover from the affliction and his food would agree with him and his body would regain strength; on considering this, he would be glad and full of joy. Or suppose a man were imprisoned, but later he would be released, safe and secure, with no loss to his property; on considering this, he would be glad and full of joy. Or suppose a man were a slave, not self-dependent but dependent on others, unable to go where he wants, but later on he would be released from slavery, self-dependent, independent of others, a free man able to go where he wants; on considering this, he would be glad and full of joy. Or suppose a man with wealth and property were to enter a road across a desert, but later on he would cross over the desert, safe and secure,

with no loss to his property; on considering this, he would be glad and full of joy. So too, monks, while these five hindrances have not yet been abandoned in himself, a monk sees them respectively as a debt, illness, a prison, slavery, and a road across a desert. But when these five hindrances have been abandoned in himself, he sees that as freedom from debt, recovery from illness, release from prison, freedom from slavery, and a land of safety.

15. "Having abandoned these five hindrances, defilements of the mind that weaken wisdom, secluded from sensual pleasures, secluded from unwholesome states, he enters and dwells in the first jhāna, which is accompanied by thought and examination, with rapture and happiness born of seclusion. He makes the rapture and happiness born of seclusion drench, steep, fill, and pervade this body, so that there is no part of his whole body that is not pervaded by the rapture and happiness born of seclusion. Just as a skilled bath man or a bath man's apprentice heaps bath powder in a metal basin and, sprinkling it gradually with water, kneads it until the moisture wets his ball of bath powder, soaks it, and pervades it inside and out, yet the ball itself does not ooze; so too, a monk makes the rapture and happiness born of seclusion drench, steep, fill, and pervade this body, so that there is no part of his whole body that is not pervaded by the rapture and happiness born of seclusion.

16. "Again, monks, with the subsiding of thought and examination, he enters and dwells in the second jhāna, which has internal confidence and unification of mind, is without thought and examination, and has rapture and happiness born of concentration. He makes the rapture and happiness born of concentration drench, steep, fill, and pervade this body, so that there is no part of his whole body that is not pervaded by the rapture and happiness born of concentration. Just as though there were a lake whose waters welled up from below and it had no inflow from east, west, north, or south, and would not be replenished from time to time by showers of rain, then the cool fount of water welling up in the lake would make the cool water drench, steep, fill, and pervade the lake, so that there would be no part of the whole lake that is not pervaded by cool water; so too, a monk makes the rapture and happiness born of concentration drench, steep, fill, and pervade this body, so that there is no part of his whole body that is not pervaded by the rapture and happiness born of concentration.

17. "Again, monks, with the fading away as well of rapture, he dwells equanimous and, mindful and clearly comprehending, he experiences happiness with the body; he enters and dwells in the third jhāna of which the noble ones declare: 'He is equanimous, mindful, one who dwells happily.' He makes the happiness divested of rapture drench, steep, fill, and pervade this body, so that there is no part of his whole body that is not pervaded by the happiness divested of rapture. Just as, in a pond of blue or red or white lotuses, some lotuses that are born and grow in the water thrive immersed in the water without rising out of it, and cool water drenches, steeps, fills, and pervades them to their tips and their roots, so that there is no part of all those lotuses that is not pervaded by cool water; so too, a monk makes the happiness divested of rapture drench, steep, fill, and pervade this body, so that there is no part of his whole body that is not pervaded by the happiness divested of rapture.

18. "Again, monks, with the abandoning of pleasure and pain, and with the previous disappearance of joy and dejection, a monk enters upon and dwells in the fourth jhāna, which has neither-pain-nor-pleasure and purity of mindfulness due to equanimity. He sits pervading this body with a pure bright mind, so that there is no part of his whole body that is not pervaded by the pure bright mind. Just as though a man were sitting covered from the head down with a white cloth, so that there would be no part of his whole body that is not pervaded by the white cloth; so too, a monk sits pervading this body with a pure bright mind, so that there is no part of his whole body that is not pervaded by the pure bright mind.

19. "When his mind is thus concentrated, purified, bright, unblemished, rid of defilements, malleable, wieldy, steady, and attained to imperturbability, he directs it to knowledge of the recollection of past lives. He recollects his manifold past lives, that is, one birth, two births ... [as in preceding text, §23] ... Thus with their aspects and particulars he recollects his manifold past lives. Just as a man might go from his own village to another village and then back again to his own village, he might think: 'I went from my own village to that village, and there I stood in such a way, sat in such a way, spoke in such a way, kept silent in such a way; and from that village I went to that other village, and there I stood in such a way, sat in such a way, spoke in such a way, kept silent in such a way; and from that village I came back again to my

own village.' So too, a monk recollects his manifold past lives.... Thus with their aspects and particulars he recollects his manifold past lives.

20. "When his mind is thus concentrated, purified, bright, unblemished, rid of defilements, malleable, wieldy, steady, and attained to imperturbability, he directs it to knowledge of the passing away and rebirth of beings ... [as in preceding text, §24] ... Thus with the divine eye, which is purified and surpasses the human, he sees beings passing away and being reborn, inferior and superior, fair and ugly, fortunate and unfortunate, and he understands how beings pass on according to their actions. Just as though there were two houses with doors and a man with good sight standing there between them saw people entering the houses and coming out and passing to and fro, so too, with the divine eye, which is purified and surpasses the human, a monk sees beings passing away and being reborn ... and he understands how beings pass on according to their actions.

21. "When his mind is thus concentrated, purified, bright, unblemished, rid of defilements, malleable, wieldy, steady, and attained to imperturbability, he directs it to knowledge of the destruction of the taints. He understands as it actually is: 'This is suffering' ... [as in preceding text, §§25–26] ... He understands: 'Birth is destroyed, the spiritual life has been lived, what had to be done has been done, there is no more coming back to any state of being.'

"Just as if there were a lake in a mountain recess, clear, limpid, and undisturbed, so that a man with good sight standing on the bank could see shells, gravel, and pebbles, and also shoals of fish swimming about and resting, he might think: 'There is this lake, clear, limpid, and undisturbed, and there are these shells, gravel, and pebbles, and also these shoals of fish swimming about and resting.' So too, a monk understands as it actually is: 'This is suffering.'... He understands: 'Birth is destroyed, the holy life has been lived, what had to be done has been done, there is no more coming back to any state of being.'"

(from MN 39: *Mahā Assapura Sutta*; I 274–80)

VIII. Mastering the Mind

Introduction

Having presented a broad overview of the world-transcending path in the previous chapter, in this chapter and the next I intend to focus more specifically on two aspects of this path as described in the Nikāyas, meditation and wisdom. As we have seen, the gradual training is divided into the three sections of moral discipline, concentration, and wisdom (see pp. 225–26). Moral discipline begins with the observance of precepts, which anchor one's actions in principles of conscientious behavior and moral restraint. The undertaking of precepts—for the Nikāyas, particularly the full code of monastic precepts—is called the training in the higher moral discipline (*adhisīlasikkhā*). Moral discipline, consistently observed, infuses the mind with the purifying force of moral virtue, generating joy and deeper confidence in the Dhamma.

Established upon moral discipline, the disciple takes up the practice of meditation, intended to stabilize the mind and clear away the obstacles to the unfolding of wisdom. Because meditation elevates the mind beyond its normal level, this phase of practice is called the training in the higher mind (*adhicittasikkhā*). Because it brings inner stillness and quietude, it is also called the development of serenity (*samathabhāvanā*). Successful practice results in deep concentration or mental unification (*samādhi*), also known as internal serenity of mind (*ajjhattaṃ ceto-samatha*). The most eminent types of concentration recognized in the Nikāyas are the four *jhānas*, which constitute right concentration (*sammā samādhi*) of the Noble Eightfold Path. Beyond the jhānas lie the four formless attainments (*arūpasamāpatti*), which carry the process of mental unification to still subtler levels.

The third stage of practice is the training in the higher wisdom (*adhipaññāsikkhā*), designed to awaken direct insight into the true nature of things as disclosed by the Buddha's teaching. This will be dealt with in detail in the following chapter.

The first selection below, **Text VIII,1**, is a miscellany of short epigrams that stress the need for mental cultivation. The sayings occur in pairs. In each pair, the first member signals the dangers of the uncultivated mind, the second extols the benefits of the cultivated mind. The uncultivated mind is easy prey to the defilements—greed, hatred, and delusion and their offshoots. The defilements generate unwholesome kamma, which brings painful results both in this life and in future lives. Since the defilements are the cause of our suffering and bondage, the path to liberation necessarily involves a meticulous process of mental training intended to subdue them and ultimately uproot them from their nesting place in the deep recesses of the mind. From development of the mind arise happiness, freedom, and peace.

Development of the mind, for the Nikāyas, means the development of serenity (*samatha*) and insight (*vipassanā*). **Text VIII,2(1)** says that when serenity is developed, it leads to concentration and the liberation of the mind from such emotional defilements as lust and ill will. When insight is developed, it leads to the higher wisdom of insight into the true nature of phenomena and permanently liberates the mind from ignorance. Thus the two things most needed to master the mind are serenity and insight.

Since concentration is the basis for wisdom, the Nikāyas usually treat the development of serenity as the precursor to the development of insight. However, because the aptitudes of meditators differ, several suttas allow for alternative approaches to this sequence. **Text VIII,2(2)** speaks of four approaches to mental cultivation:

1) The first approach, the classical one, is to develop serenity first and insight afterward. By "serenity" is meant the jhānas or (according to the Pāli commentaries) a state bordering on the jhānas called "access" or "threshold" concentration (*upacārasamādhi*).

2) A second approach is to develop insight first and serenity afterward. Since there can be no real insight without concentration, such meditators—presumably people with sharp intellectual faculties—must initially use concentration as the basis for acquiring insight into the true characteristics of phenomena. However, it seems that such concentration, though sufficient for insight, is not strong enough to allow for a breakthrough to the supramundane path. These meditators must therefore return to the task of unifying the mind before resuming the work of insight. Such insight, based on concentration, culminates in the supramundane path.

3) A third approach is to develop serenity and insight in tandem. Meditators who take this approach first attain a particular level of

concentration, such as a jhāna or formless attainment, and then employ it as a basis for insight. Having developed insight, they then return to concentration, attain a different jhāna or formless attainment, and use that as a basis for insight. Thus they proceed until they reach the supramundane path.

4) The description of the fourth approach is somewhat obscure. The sutta says that "a monk's mind is seized by agitation about the teachings," and then, some time later, he gains concentration and attains the supramundane path. This statement suggests a person initially driven by such intense desire to understand the Dhamma that he or she cannot focus clearly upon any meditation object. Later, with the aid of certain supporting conditions, this person manages to subdue the mind, gain concentration, and attain the supramundane path.

Text VIII,2(3) again confirms that both serenity and insight are necessary, and also indicates the skills needed for their respective practice. The cultivation of serenity requires skill in steadying, composing, unifying, and concentrating the mind. The cultivation of insight requires skill in observing, investigating, and discerning conditioned phenomena, spoken of as "formations" (*saṅkhārā*). In line with the preceding text, this sutta confirms that some meditators begin by developing internal serenity of mind, others by developing the higher wisdom of insight into phenomena, others by developing both in tandem. But while meditators may start off differently, eventually they must all strike a healthy balance between serenity and insight. The exact point of balance between the two will differ from one person to another, but when a meditator achieves the appropriate balance, serenity and insight join forces to issue in the knowledge and vision of the Four Noble Truths. This knowledge and vision—the world-transcending wisdom—occurs in four distinct "installments," the four stages of realization which, in sequence, permanently destroy ignorance along with the affiliated defilements.[1] **Text VIII,2(2)** subsumes these defilements under the expression "the fetters and underlying tendencies."

The main impediments to the development of serenity and insight are collectively called the "five hindrances," which we already met in the extended account of the gradual training (see **Text VII,4** §18). **Text VIII,3** states that just as different impurities of water prevent us from clearly seeing the reflection of our face in a bowl of water, so the five hindrances prevent us from properly understanding our own good and the good of others. A meditator's initial efforts therefore have to be devoted to the task of overcoming the hindrances. Once these are overcome, success is assured in the practice of serenity and insight.

Text VIII,4 compares the successive stages in the purification of the mind to the refinement of gold. The meditating monk begins by removing the gross impurities of bodily, verbal, and mental conduct; this is achieved by moral discipline and vigilant introspection. Then he eliminates the middle-level impurities of unwholesome thoughts: thoughts of sensuality, ill will, and harmfulness. Next come the subtle impurities of meandering thoughts. Finally, he must eliminate thoughts about the Dhamma, the subtlest obstacle. When all such distracting thoughts are removed, the monk attains "mental unification" (*ekodibhāva*), the basis for the six "direct knowledges" (*abhiññā*) culminating in arahantship, the knowledge of the destruction of the taints.

The Nikāyas sometimes compare the process of training the mind to the taming of a wild animal. Just as an animal trainer has to use various techniques to bring the animal under control, the meditator has to draw upon various methods to subdue the mind. It is not enough to be acquainted with one meditation technique; one must be skilled in a number of methods intended as antidotes to specific mental obstructions. In **Text VIII,5** the Buddha explains five ancillary techniques—here called "signs" (*nimitta*)—that a monk might deploy to eliminate unwholesome thoughts connected with lust, hatred, and delusion. One who succeeds in overcoming distracting thoughts by the use of these techniques is called "a master of the courses of thought."

The suttas teach various techniques of meditation aimed at inducing concentration. One popular formula pits specific meditation subjects against the unwholesome mental states they are intended to rectify. Thus the meditation on the unattractive nature of the body (see **Text VIII,8** §10) is the remedy for sensual lust; loving-kindness is the remedy for ill will; mindfulness of breathing is the remedy for restlessness; and the perception of impermanence is the remedy for the conceit "I am."[2] The perception of impermanence is a subject of insight meditation, the other three subjects of serenity meditation. Loving-kindness is the first of the four divine abodes (*brahmavihāra*) or immeasurable states (*appamaññā*) briefly discussed in chapter V: boundless loving-kindness, compassion, altruistic joy, and equanimity. These are respectively the antidotes to ill will, harmfulness, discontent, and partiality.

Since we already introduced the standard canonical passage on the divine abodes in connection with meditation as a basis for merit—see **Text V,5(2)**—to shed a different spotlight on this practice I have included here, as **Text VIII,6**, the famous Simile of the Saw, a passage that shows loving-kindness in action.

Through the centuries the most popular meditation subjects among lay Buddhists have probably been the six recollections (*anussati*): of the Buddha, the Dhamma, the Saṅgha, morality, generosity, and the devas. **Text VIII,7** is an important canonical source for these meditations. Their themes are especially close to the hearts and everyday experiences of people living household lives in a culture imbued with Buddhist values. These meditation practices in turn enrich and uplift their lives, bringing them into closer spiritual contact with the ideals of religious faith. The first three are primarily devotional recollections that build upon confidence in the Three Jewels; but while they begin with faith, they temporarily cleanse the mind of defilements and conduce to sustained concentration. The meditation on moral discipline develops from one's observance of the precepts, a practice aimed at self-benefit; the recollection of generosity builds upon one's practice of giving, an altruistic practice; the recollection of the devas is a contemplation of the fruits of one's faith, morality, generosity, and wisdom as they mature in future lives.

The discourse generally considered to offer the most comprehensive instructions on meditation practice is the Satipaṭṭhāna Sutta.[3] Two versions of this sutta exist, a longer version in the Dīgha Nikāya, a middle-length version in the Majjhima Nikāya. The former differs from the latter only by its extended analysis of the Four Noble Truths, which may have originally been an early commentary incorporated into the discourse. The middle-length version is included here as **Text VIII,8**. An entire chapter in the Saṃyutta Nikāya, the Satipaṭṭhānasaṃyutta, is also devoted to this system of meditation.

The Satipaṭṭhāna Sutta does not recommend a single meditation subject nor even a single method of meditation. Its purpose, rather, is to explain how to establish the mode of contemplation needed to arrive at realization of Nibbāna. The appropriate frame of mind to be established, as implied by the title of the sutta, is called an "establishment of mindfulness." The word *satipaṭṭhāna* should probably be understood as a compound of *sati*, mindfulness, and *upaṭṭhāna*, establishment;

hence "establishment of mindfulness" would be the rendering that best captures the original meaning. According to the standard formula that accompanies each exercise, a *satipaṭṭhāna* is a mode of dwelling (*viharati*). This mode of dwelling involves observation of objects in the proper frame of mind. The frame of mind consists of three positive qualities: energy (*ātāpa*, "ardor"), mindfulness (*sati*), and clear comprehension (*sampajañña*). The word *sati* originally meant memory, but in the present context it signifies recollection of the present, a sustained awareness of what is happening to us and within us on each occasion of experience. Mindfulness, in its initial stages, is concerned with keeping the contemplative mind continually on its object, which means keeping the object continually present to the mind. Mindfulness prevents the mind from slipping away, from drifting off under the sway of random thoughts into mental proliferation and forgetfulness. Mindfulness is often said to occur in close conjunction with "clear comprehension," a clear knowledge and understanding of what one is experiencing.

The opening formula of the sutta says that one engages in this practice after "having subdued longing and dejection in regard to the world" (*vineyya loke abhijjhā-domanassaṃ*). The expression "having subdued" need not be taken to imply that one must first overcome longing and dejection—which, according to the commentary, signify greed and aversion and thus represent the five hindrances—before one can start to practice *satipaṭṭhāna*. The expression might be understood to mean that the practice is itself the means of overcoming longing and dejection. Thus, while subduing the obstructive influences of greed and aversion, the meditator arouses the positive qualities of energy, mindfulness, and clear comprehension, and contemplates four objective domains: the body, feelings, states of mind, and phenomena. It is these four objective domains that differentiate mindful observation into four establishments of mindfulness.

The four objective domains divide the expository portion of the Satipaṭṭhāna Sutta into four major sections. Two of these sections, the first and the fourth, have several subdivisions. When the divisions are added up, we obtain altogether twenty-one meditation subjects. Several of these can be used as means to develop serenity (*samatha*), but the *satipaṭṭhāna* system as a whole seems especially designed for the development of insight. The main sections with their divisions are as follows:

1. *Contemplation of the body* (*kāyānupassanā*). This comprises fourteen subjects of meditation: mindfulness of breathing; contemplation of the four postures; clear comprehension of activities; attention to the unattractive nature of the body (viewed by way of its organs and tissues); attention to the elements; and nine charnel ground contemplations, contemplations based on corpses in different stages of decomposition.
2. *Contemplation of feeling* (*vedanānupassanā*). Feeling is differentiated into three primary types—pleasant, painful, and neither-painful-nor-pleasant—which are each further distinguished into carnal and spiritual feelings. However, because these are all merely different types of feeling, the contemplation of feeling is considered one subject.
3. *Contemplation of mind* (*cittānupassanā*). This is one subject of contemplation—the mind—differentiated into eight pairs of contrasting states of mind.
4. *Contemplation of phenomena* (*dhammānupassanā*). The word *dhammā* here probably signifies phenomena, which are classified into five categories governed by the Buddha's teaching, *the* Dhamma. Thus *dhammānupassanā* has a dual meaning, "dhammas (phenomena) contemplated by way of the Dhamma (the teaching)." The five categories are: the five hindrances, the five aggregates, the six internal and external sense bases, the seven factors of enlightenment, and the Four Noble Truths.

Although not specified in the sutta, a progressive sequence seems to be implied by the terms describing each contemplation. In mindfulness of breathing one moves to subtler levels of quiescence; in contemplation of feeling, one moves toward noncarnal feelings that are neither painful nor pleasant; in contemplation of mind, one moves toward states of mind that are concentrated and liberated. These all suggest that progressive contemplation brings enhanced concentration. In the contemplation of phenomena, the emphasis shifts toward insight. One begins by observing and overcoming the five hindrances. The overcoming of the hindrances marks success in concentration. With the concentrated mind, one contemplates the five aggregates and the six sense bases. As contemplation gains momentum, the seven factors of enlightenment become manifest, and the development of the seven enlightenment factors culminates in knowledge of the Four Noble Truths. Knowledge of the Four Noble Truths liberates the mind from the defilements and thus leads to the attainment of Nibbāna. Thus this system of meditation fulfills the potential ascribed to it by the Buddha of leading directly to the realization of Nibbāna.

Each major contemplative exercise is supplemented by an auxiliary section, a "refrain" with four subdivisions. The first states that the meditator contemplates the object internally (within his or her own experience), externally (reflectively considering it as occurring within the experience of others), and both; this ensures that one obtains a comprehensive and balanced view of the object. The second portion states that the meditator contemplates the object as subject to origination, as subject to vanishing, and as subject to both origination and vanishing; this brings to light the characteristic of impermanence and thus leads to insight into the three characteristics: impermanence, suffering, and nonself (*anicca, dukkha, anattā*). The third states that the meditator is simply aware of the bare object to the extent necessary for constant mindfulness and knowledge. And the fourth describes the meditator as dwelling in a state of complete detachment, not clinging to anything in the world.

In the Satipaṭṭhāna Sutta, mindfulness of breathing (*ānāpānasati*) is included as merely one meditation subject among others, but the Nikāyas assign it a position of fundamental importance. The Buddha said that he used mindfulness of breathing as his main meditation subject for the attainment of enlightenment (see SN 54:8; V 317). During his teaching career he occasionally went into seclusion to devote himself to "the concentration gained through mindfulness of breathing" and he confers on it a unique honor by calling it "the Tathāgata's dwelling" (SN 54:11; V 326).

Mindfulness of breathing is the subject of an entire chapter in the Saṃyutta Nikāya (SN 54, Ānāpānasaṃyutta). Whereas the Satipaṭṭhāna Sutta explains mindfulness of breathing by a four-step formula, the suttas in this collection expand its practice to sixteen steps. **Text VIII,9**, from the Ānāpānasaṃyutta, describes the sixteen steps. Since these steps are not necessarily sequential but partly overlap, they might be thought of as facets rather than actual steps. The sixteen facets are grouped into four tetrads each of which corresponds to one of the four establishments of mindfulness. The first tetrad contains the four facets mentioned in the Satipaṭṭhāna Sutta in its section on contemplation of the body, but the other tetrads extend the practice to the contemplations of feelings, mind, and phenomena. Thus the development of mindfulness of breathing can fulfill not just one but *all four* establishments of mindfulness. The four establishments of mindfulness, based on mindfulness of breathing, in turn fulfill the seven factors of enlightenment; and these in turn fulfill true knowledge and liberation. This exposition thus shows mindfulness of breathing to be a complete subject of meditation that begins with simple attention to the breath and culminates in the permanent liberation of the mind.

Finally, in **Text VIII,10**, the Buddha's chief disciple, the Venerable Sāriputta, testifies to his own achievement of mastery over the mind. In reply to questions from the Venerable Ānanda, he explains how he is able to dwell for a whole day in each of the jhānas and formless attainments, as well as in the special attainment called the cessation of perception and feeling (*saññāvedayitanirodha*). In each case, because he is an arahant, he can do so without grasping these attainments with thoughts of "I" and "mine."

VIII. Mastering the Mind

1. The Mind Is the Key

1. "I do not perceive even one other thing, O monks, that is so unwieldy as an undeveloped mind. An undeveloped mind is truly unwieldy.

2. "I do not perceive even one other thing, O monks, that is so wieldy as a developed mind. A developed mind is truly wieldy.

3. "I do not perceive even one other thing, O monks, that leads to such great harm as an undeveloped mind. An undeveloped mind leads to great harm.

4. "I do not perceive even one other thing, O monks, that leads to such great benefit as a developed mind. A developed mind leads to great benefit.

9. "I do not perceive even one other thing, O monks, that when undeveloped and uncultivated entails such great suffering as the mind. The mind when undeveloped and uncultivated entails great suffering.

10. "I do not perceive even one other thing, O monks, that when developed and cultivated entails such great happiness as the mind. The mind when developed and cultivated entails great happiness."

(AN 1: iii, 1, 2, 3, 4, 9, 10; I 5–6)

2. Developing a Pair of Skills

(1) Serenity and Insight

"Two things, O monks, partake of true knowledge. What two? Serenity and insight.

"When serenity is developed, what benefit does one experience? The mind is developed. When the mind is developed, what benefit does one experience? All lust is abandoned.[4]

"When insight is developed, what benefit does one experience? Wisdom is developed. When wisdom is developed, what benefit does one experience? All ignorance is abandoned.[5]

"A mind defiled by lust is not liberated; and wisdom defiled by ignorance is not developed. Thus, monks, through the fading away of lust there is liberation of mind; and through the fading away of ignorance there is liberation by wisdom."[6]

(AN 2: iii, 10; I 61)

(2) Four Ways to Arahantship

Thus have I heard. On one occasion the Venerable Ānanda was dwelling at Kosambī in Ghosita's monastery. There the Venerable Ānanda addressed the monks thus:

"Friends!"

"Yes, friend," the monks replied. Thereupon the Venerable Ānanda said:

"Friends, whatever monks or nuns declare before me that they have attained the final knowledge of arahantship, all these do so in one of four ways. What four?

"Here, friends, a monk develops insight preceded by serenity.[7] While he thus develops insight preceded by serenity, the path arises in him. He now pursues, develops, and cultivates that path, and while he is doing so the fetters are abandoned and the underlying tendencies eliminated.[8]

"Or again, friends, a monk develops serenity preceded by insight.[9] While he thus develops serenity preceded by insight, the path arises in him. He now pursues, develops, and cultivates that path, and while he is doing so the fetters are abandoned and the underlying tendencies eliminated.

"Or again, friends, a monk develops serenity and insight joined in pairs.[10] While he thus develops serenity and insight joined in pairs, the path arises in him. He now pursues, develops, and cultivates that path, and while he is doing so the fetters are abandoned and the underlying tendencies eliminated.

"Or again, friends, a monk's mind is seized by agitation about the teaching.[11] But there comes a time when his mind becomes internally steadied, composed, unified, and concentrated; then the path arises in him. He now pursues, develops, and cultivates that path, and while he is doing so the fetters are abandoned and the underlying tendencies eliminated.

"Friends, whatever monks or nuns declare before me that they have attained the final knowledge of arahantship, all these do so in one of these four ways."

(AN 4:170; II 156–57)

(3) Four Kinds of Persons

"These four kinds of persons, O monks, are found existing in the world. What four?

"Here, monks, a certain person gains internal serenity of mind but does not gain the higher wisdom of insight into phenomena.[12] Another person gains the higher wisdom of insight into phenomena but does not gain internal serenity of mind. Another person gains neither internal serenity of mind nor the higher wisdom of insight into phenomena. And another person gains both internal serenity of mind and the higher wisdom of insight into phenomena.

"Therein, monks, the person who gains internal serenity of mind but not the higher wisdom of insight into phenomena should approach one who gains the higher wisdom and inquire of him: 'How, friend, should formations be seen? How should formations be explored? How should formations be discerned with insight?'[13] The other then answers him as he has seen and understood the matter thus: 'Formations should be seen in such a way; they should be explored in such a way; they should be discerned with insight in such a way.' At a later time this one gains both internal serenity of mind and the higher wisdom of insight into phenomena.

"Therein, monks, the person who gains the higher wisdom of insight into phenomena but not internal serenity of mind should approach one who gains internal serenity and inquire of him: 'How, friend, should the mind be steadied? How should the mind be composed? How should the mind be unified? How should the mind be concentrated?' The other then answers him as he has seen and understood the matter thus: 'The mind should be steadied in such a way, composed in such a way, unified in such a way, concentrated in such a way.' At a later time this one gains both internal serenity of mind and the higher wisdom of insight into phenomena.

"Therein, monks, the person who gains neither internal serenity of mind nor the higher wisdom of insight into phenomena should approach one who gains both and inquire of him: 'How, friend, should the mind be steadied?... How, friend, should formations be seen?...' The other then answers him as he has seen and understood the matter thus: 'The mind should be steadied in such a way.... Formations should be seen in such a way....' At a later time this one gains both internal serenity of mind and the higher wisdom of insight into phenomena.

"Therein, monks, the person who gains both internal serenity of mind and the higher wisdom of insight into phenomena should establish himself in just these wholesome states and make a further effort for the destruction of the taints."

(AN 4:94; II 93–95)

3. The Hindrances to Mental Development

Then the brahmin Saṅgārava approached the Blessed One, exchanged greetings with him, sat down to one side, and said:

"Master Gotama, why is it that sometimes even those texts that have been recited over a long period do not recur to the mind, let alone those that have not been recited? And why is it that sometimes those texts that have not been recited over a long period recur to the mind, let alone those that have been recited?"

"Brahmin, when one dwells with a mind obsessed by sensual lust, overwhelmed by sensual lust, and one does not understand as it really is the escape from arisen sensual lust,[14] on that occasion one neither knows nor sees as it really is one's own good, or the good of others, or the good of both. Then even those texts that have been recited over a long period do not recur to the mind, let alone those that have not been recited.

"Suppose, brahmin, there is a bowl of water mixed with red, yellow, blue, or crimson dye. If a man with good sight were to examine his own facial reflection in it, he would neither know nor see it as it really is. So too, brahmin, when one dwells with a mind obsessed by sensual lust ... even those texts that have been recited over a long period do not recur to the mind, let alone those that have not been recited.

"Again, brahmin, when one dwells with a mind obsessed by ill will, overwhelmed by ill will, and one does not understand as it really is the escape from arisen ill will, on that occasion one neither knows nor sees as it really is one's own good, or the good of others, or the good of both. Then even those texts that have been recited over a long period do not recur to the mind, let alone those that have not been recited.

"Suppose, brahmin, there is a bowl of water being heated over a fire, bubbling and boiling. If a man with good sight were to examine his own facial reflection in it, he would neither know nor see it as it really is. So too, brahmin, when one dwells with a mind obsessed by ill will ... even those texts that have been recited over a long period do not recur to the mind, let alone those that have not been recited.

"Again, brahmin, when one dwells with a mind obsessed by dullness and drowsiness, overwhelmed by dullness and drowsiness, and one does not understand as it really is the escape from arisen dullness and drowsiness, on that occasion one neither knows nor sees as it really is one's own good, or the good of others, or the good of both. Then even those texts that have been recited over a long period do not recur to the mind, let alone those that have not been recited.

"Suppose, brahmin, there is a bowl of water covered over with water plants and algae. If a man with good sight were to examine his own facial reflection in it, he would neither know nor see it as it really is. So too, brahmin, when one dwells with a mind obsessed by dullness and drowsiness ... even those texts that have been recited over a long period do not recur to the mind, let alone those that have not been recited.

"Again, brahmin, when one dwells with a mind obsessed by restlessness and remorse, overwhelmed by restlessness and remorse, and one does not understand as it really is the escape from arisen restlessness and remorse, on that occasion one neither knows nor sees as it really is one's own good, or the good of others, or the good of both. Then even those texts that have been recited over a long period do not recur to the mind, let alone those that have not been recited.

"Suppose, brahmin, there is a bowl of water stirred by the wind, rippling, swirling, churned into wavelets. If a man with good sight were to examine his own facial reflection in it, he would neither know nor see it as it really is. So too, brahmin, when one dwells with a mind obsessed by restlessness and remorse ... even those texts that have been recited over a long period do not recur to the mind, let alone those that have not been recited.

"Again, brahmin, when one dwells with a mind obsessed by doubt, overwhelmed by doubt, and one does not understand as it really is the escape from arisen doubt, on that occasion one neither knows nor sees as it really is one's own good, or the good of others, or the good of both. Then even those texts that have been recited over a long period do not recur to the mind, let alone those that have not been recited.

"Suppose, brahmin, there is a bowl of water that is turbid, unsettled, muddy, placed in the dark. If a man with good sight were to examine his own facial reflection in it, he would neither know nor see it as it really is. So too, brahmin, when one dwells with a mind obsessed by doubt ... even those texts that have been recited over a long period do not recur to the mind, let alone those that have not been recited.

"This, brahmin, is the reason why even those texts that have been recited over a long period do not recur to the mind, let alone those that have not been recited.

"Brahmin, when one dwells with a mind that is not obsessed by sensual lust, ill will, dullness and drowsiness, restlessness and remorse, and doubt, on that occasion even those texts that have not been recited over a long period recur to the mind, let alone those that have been recited.

"Suppose, brahmin, there is a bowl of water that is not mixed with dyes; not bubbling and boiling; not covered over with water plants and algae; not stirred by the wind and churned into wavelets; clear, serene, limpid, set out in the light. If a man with good sight were to examine his own facial reflection in it, he would know and see it as it really is. So too, brahmin, when one dwells with a mind that is not obsessed by sensual lust, ill will, dullness and drowsiness, restlessness and remorse, and doubt on that occasion even those texts that have not been recited over a long period recur to the mind, let alone those that have been recited.

"This, brahmin, is the reason why even those texts that have not been recited over a long period recur to the mind, let alone those that have been recited."...

When this was said, the brahmin Saṅgārava said to the Blessed One: "Magnificent, Master Gotama!... Let Master Gotama accept me as a lay follower who has gone for refuge from today until life's end."

(SN 46:55, abridged; V 121–26)

4. The Refinement of the Mind

"There are, O monks, gross impurities in gold, such as earth and sand, gravel and grit. Now the goldsmith or his apprentice first pours the gold into a trough and washes, rinses, and cleans it thoroughly. When he has done this, there still remain moderate impurities in the gold, such as fine grit and coarse sand. Then the goldsmith or his apprentice washes, rinses, and cleans it again. When he has done this, there still remain minute impurities in the gold, such as fine sand and black dust. Now the goldsmith or his apprentice repeats the washing, and thereafter only the gold dust remains.

"He now pours the gold into a melting pot, smelts it, and melts it together. But he does not yet take it out from the vessel, as the dross has not yet been entirely removed and the gold is not yet quite pliant, workable, and bright; it is still brittle and does not yet lend itself easily to molding. But a time comes when the goldsmith or his apprentice repeats the melting thoroughly, so that the flaws are entirely removed. The gold is now quite pliant, workable, and bright, and it lends itself easily to molding. Whatever ornament the goldsmith now wishes to make of it, be it a diadem, earrings, a necklace, or a golden chain, the gold can now be used for that purpose.

"It is similar, monks, with a monk devoted to the training in the higher mind: there are in him gross impurities, namely, bad conduct of body, speech, and mind. Such conduct an earnest, capable monk abandons, dispels, eliminates, and abolishes.

"When he has abandoned these, there are still impurities of a moderate degree that cling to him, namely, sensual thoughts, thoughts of ill will, and thoughts of harming.[15] Such thoughts an earnest, capable monk abandons, dispels, eliminates, and abolishes.

"When he has abandoned these, there are still some subtle impurities that cling to him, namely, thoughts about his relatives, his home country, and his reputation. Such thoughts an earnest, capable monk abandons dispels, eliminates, and abolishes.

"When he has abandoned these, there still remain thoughts about the teaching.[16] That concentration is not yet peaceful and sublime; it has not attained to full tranquillity, nor has it achieved mental unification; it is maintained by strenuous suppression of the defilements.

"But there comes a time when his mind becomes inwardly steadied, composed, unified, and concentrated. That concentration is then calm and refined; it has attained to full tranquillity and achieved mental unification; it is not maintained by strenuous suppression of the defilements.

"Then, to whatever mental state realizable by direct knowledge he directs his mind, he achieves the capacity of realizing that state by direct knowledge, whenever the necessary conditions obtain.[17]

"If he wishes: 'May I wield the various kinds of spiritual power: having been one, may I become many; having been many, may I become one; may I appear and vanish; go unhindered through a wall, through a rampart, through a mountain as if through space; dive in and out of the earth as if it were water; walk on water without sinking as if it were earth; travel through the sky like a bird while seated cross-legged; touch and stroke with my hand the moon and sun, so powerful and mighty; exercise mastery with my body even as far as the brahma world'—he achieves the capacity of realizing that state by direct knowledge, whenever the necessary conditions obtain.

"If he wishes: 'With the divine ear element, which is purified and surpasses the human, may I hear both kinds of sounds, the divine and human, those that are far as well as near'—he achieves the capacity of realizing that state by direct knowledge, whenever the necessary conditions obtain.

"If he wishes: 'May I understand the minds of other beings, of other persons, having encompassed them with my own mind. May I understand a mind with lust as a mind with lust; a mind without lust as a mind without lust; a mind with hatred as a mind with hatred; a mind without hatred as a mind without hatred; a mind with delusion as a mind with delusion; a mind without delusion as a mind without delusion; a contracted mind as contracted, and a distracted mind as distracted; an exalted mind as exalted, and an unexalted mind as unexalted; a surpassable mind as surpassable, and an unsurpassable mind as unsurpassable; a concentrated mind as concentrated, and an unconcentrated mind as unconcentrated; a liberated mind as liberated, and an unliberated mind as unliberated'—he achieves the capacity of realizing that state by direct knowledge, whenever the necessary conditions obtain.

"If he wishes, 'May I recollect my manifold past lives ... [see Text II,3(2)§38] ... with their modes and details'—he achieves the capacity of realizing that state by direct knowledge, whenever the necessary conditions obtain.

"If he wishes, 'With the divine eye, which is purified and surpasses the human, may I see beings passing away and being reborn, inferior and superior, beautiful and ugly, fortunate and unfortunate ... [see Text II,3(2)§40] ... and understand how beings fare on in accordance with their action'—he achieves the capacity of realizing that state by direct knowledge, whenever the necessary conditions obtain.

"If he wishes, 'By the destruction of the taints, may I in this very life enter and dwell in the taintless liberation of mind, liberation by wisdom, realizing it for myself with direct knowledge'—he achieves the capacity of realizing that state by direct knowledge, whenever the necessary conditions obtain."

(AN 3:100 §§1–10; I 253–56)

5. The Removal of Distracting Thoughts

1. Thus have I heard. On one occasion the Blessed One was living at Sāvatthī in Jeta's Grove, Anāthapiṇḍika's Park. There he addressed the monks thus: "Monks."—"Venerable sir," they replied. The Blessed One said this:

2. "Monks, when a monk is pursuing the higher mind, from time to time he should give attention to five signs.[18] What are the five?

3. (i) "Here, monks, when a monk is giving attention to some sign, and owing to that sign there arise in him evil unwholesome thoughts connected with desire, hate, and delusion, then he should give attention to some other sign connected with what is wholesome.[19] When he gives attention to some other sign connected with what is wholesome, then any evil unwholesome thoughts connected with desire, hate, and delusion are abandoned in him and subside. With their abandoning his mind becomes steadied internally, composed, unified, and concentrated. Just as a skilled carpenter or his apprentice might knock out, remove, and extract a coarse peg by means of a fine one, so too ... when a monk gives attention to some other sign connected with what is wholesome ... his mind becomes steadied internally, composed, unified, and concentrated.

4. (ii) "If, while he is giving attention to some other sign connected with what is wholesome, there still arise in him evil unwholesome

thoughts connected with desire, hate, and delusion, then he should examine the danger in those thoughts thus: 'These thoughts are unwholesome, reprehensible, resulting in suffering.' When he examines the danger in those thoughts, then any evil unwholesome thoughts connected with desire, hate, and delusion are abandoned in him and subside. With their abandoning his mind becomes steadied internally, composed, unified, and concentrated. Just as a man or a woman, young, youthful, and fond of ornaments, would be horrified, humiliated, and disgusted if the carcass of a snake or a dog or a human being were hung around his or her neck, so too ... when a monk examines the danger in those thoughts ... his mind becomes steadied internally, composed, unified, and concentrated.

5. (iii) "If, while he is examining the danger in those thoughts, there still arise in him evil unwholesome thoughts connected with desire, hate, and delusion, then he should try to forget those thoughts and should not give attention to them. When he tries to forget those thoughts and does not give attention to them, then any evil unwholesome thoughts connected with desire, hate, and delusion are abandoned in him and subside. With their abandoning his mind becomes steadied internally, composed, unified, and concentrated. Just as a man with good eyes who did not want to see forms that had come within range of sight would either shut his eyes or look away, so too ... when a monk tries to forget those thoughts and does not give attention to them ... his mind becomes steadied internally, composed, unified, and concentrated.

6. (iv) "If, while he is trying to forget those thoughts and is not giving attention to them, there still arise in him evil unwholesome thoughts connected with desire, hate, and delusion, then he should give attention to stilling the thought-formation of those thoughts.[20] When he gives attention to stilling the thought-formation of those thoughts, then any evil unwholesome thoughts connected with desire, hate, and delusion are abandoned in him and subside. With their abandoning his mind becomes steadied internally, composed, unified, and concentrated. Just as a man walking fast might consider: 'Why am I walking fast? What if I walk slowly?' and he would walk slowly; then he might consider: 'Why am I walking slowly? What if I stand?' and he would stand; then he might consider: 'Why am I standing? What if I sit?' and he would sit; then he might consider:

'Why am I sitting? What if I lie down?' and he would lie down. By doing so he would substitute for each grosser posture one that was subtler. So too ... when a monk gives attention to stilling the thought-formation of those thoughts ... his mind becomes steadied internally, composed, unified, and concentrated.

7. (v) "If, while he is giving attention to stilling the thought-formation of those thoughts, there still arise in him evil unwholesome thoughts connected with desire, hate, and delusion, then, with his teeth clenched and his tongue pressed against the roof of his mouth, he should beat down, constrain, and crush mind with mind. When, with his teeth clenched and his tongue pressed against the roof of his mouth, he beats down, constrains, and crushes mind with mind, then any evil unwholesome thoughts connected with desire, hate, and delusion are abandoned in him and subside. With their abandoning his mind becomes steadied internally, composed, unified, and concentrated. Just as a strong man might seize a weaker man by the head or shoulders and beat him down, constrain him, and crush him, so too ... when, with his teeth clenched and his tongue pressed against the roof of his mouth, a monk beats down, constrains, and crushes mind with mind ... his mind becomes steadied internally, composed, unified, and concentrated.

8. "Monks, when a monk is giving attention to some sign, and owing to that sign there arise in him evil unwholesome thoughts connected with desire, hate, and delusion, then when he gives attention to some other sign connected with what is wholesome, any such evil unwholesome thoughts are abandoned in him and subside, and with their abandoning his mind becomes steadied internally, composed, unified, and concentrated. When he examines the danger in those thoughts ... his mind becomes steadied internally, composed, unified, and concentrated. When he tries to forget those thoughts and does not give attention to them ... his mind becomes steadied internally, composed, unified, and concentrated. When he gives attention to stilling the thought-formation of those thoughts ... his mind becomes steadied internally, composed, unified, and concentrated. When, with his teeth clenched and his tongue pressed against the roof of his mouth, he beats down, constrains, and crushes mind with mind, any such evil unwholesome thoughts are abandoned in him and subside, and with their abandoning, his mind becomes steadied internally, composed,

unified, and concentrated. This monk is then called a master of the courses of thought. He will think whatever thought he wishes to think and he will not think any thought that he does not wish to think. He has severed craving, flung off the fetters, and with the complete penetration of conceit he has made an end of suffering."

That is what the Blessed One said. The monks were satisfied and delighted in the Blessed One's words.

(MN 20: *Vitakkasaṇṭhāna Sutta;* I 118–22)

6. The Mind of Loving-Kindness

11. "Monks, there are these five courses of speech that others may use when they address you: their speech may be timely or untimely, true or untrue, gentle or harsh, connected with good or with harm, spoken with a mind of loving-kindness or in a mood of hate. When others address you, their speech may be timely or untimely; when others address you, their speech may be true or untrue; when others address you, their speech may be gentle or harsh; when others address you, their speech may be connected with good or with harm; when others address you, their speech may be spoken with a mind of loving-kindness or in a mood of hate. Herein, monks, you should train thus: 'Our minds will remain unaffected, and we shall utter no bitter words; we shall abide compassionate for their welfare, with a mind of loving-kindness, never in a mood of hate. We shall abide pervading that person with a mind imbued with loving-kindness, and starting with that person,[21] we shall abide pervading the all-encompassing world with a mind imbued with loving-kindness, abundant, exalted, immeasurable, without hostility, and without ill will.' That is how you should train, monks....

20. "Monks, even if bandits were to sever you savagely limb by limb with a two-handled saw, he who gave rise to a mind of hate toward them would not be carrying out my teaching. Herein, monks, you should train thus: 'Our minds will remain unaffected, and we shall utter no bitter words; we shall abide compassionate for their welfare, with a mind of loving-kindness, never in a mood of hate. We shall abide pervading them with a mind imbued with loving-kindness; and starting with them, we shall abide pervading the all-encompassing

world with a mind imbued with loving-kindness, abundant, exalted, immeasurable, without hostility, and without ill will.' That is how you should train, monks.

21. "Monks, if you keep this advice on the simile of the saw constantly in mind, do you see any course of speech, trivial or gross, that you could not endure?"—"No, venerable sir."—"Therefore, monks, you should keep this advice on the simile of the saw constantly in mind. That will lead to your welfare and happiness for a long time."

(from MN 21: *Kakacūpama Sutta*; I 126–27, 129)

7. The Six Recollections

On one occasion the Blessed One was dwelling at Kapilavatthu in the Banyan-tree Monastery. Then Mahānāma the Sakyan approached the Blessed One, paid homage to him, sat down to one side, and said:[22]

"Venerable sir, in what way does a noble disciple often dwell when he has arrived at the fruit and understood the teaching?"[23]

"When, Mahānāma, a noble disciple has arrived at the fruit and understood the teaching, he often dwells in such a way as this. Here, a noble disciple recollects the Tathāgata thus: 'The Blessed One is an arahant, perfectly enlightened, accomplished in true knowledge and conduct, fortunate, knower of the world, unsurpassed leader of persons to be tamed, teacher of devas and humans, the Enlightened One, the Blessed One.' When a noble disciple recollects the Tathāgata thus, on that occasion his mind is not obsessed by lust, hatred, or delusion; his mind is straight, with the Tathāgata as its object. A noble disciple whose mind is straight gains the inspiration of the meaning, the inspiration of the Dhamma, gains gladness connected with the Dhamma. When he is gladdened rapture arises; for one uplifted by rapture the body becomes calm; one calm in body feels happy; for one who is happy the mind becomes concentrated. This is called a noble disciple who dwells evenly amid an uneven population, who dwells without affliction amid an afflicted population, who has entered upon the stream of the Dhamma and develops recollection of the Buddha.

"Further, Mahānāma, a noble disciple recollects the Dhamma thus: 'The Dhamma is well expounded by the Blessed One, directly visible, immediate, inviting one to come and see, worthy of application, to be personally experienced by the wise.' When a noble disciple recollects the Dhamma thus, on that occasion his mind is not obsessed by lust, hatred, or delusion; his mind is straight, with the Dhamma as its object.... This is called a noble disciple who dwells evenly amid an uneven population, who dwells without affliction amid an afflicted population, who has entered upon the stream of the Dhamma and develops recollection of the Dhamma.

"Further, Mahānāma, a noble disciple recollects the Saṅgha thus: 'The Saṅgha of the Blessed One's disciples is practicing the good way, practicing the straight way, practicing the true way, practicing the proper way; that is, the four pairs of persons, the eight types of individuals—this Saṅgha of the Blessed One's disciples is worthy of gifts, worthy of hospitality, worthy of offerings, worthy of reverential salutation, the unsurpassed field of merit for the world.' When a noble disciple recollects the Saṅgha thus, on that occasion his mind is not obsessed by lust, hatred, or delusion; his mind is straight, with the Saṅgha as its object.... This is called a noble disciple who dwells evenly amid an uneven population, who dwells without affliction amid an afflicted population, who has entered upon the stream of the Dhamma and develops recollection of the Saṅgha.

"Further, Mahānāma, a noble disciple recollects his own moral discipline thus: 'I possess the moral virtues dear to the noble ones, unbroken, untorn, unblemished, unmottled, freeing, praised by the wise, ungrasped, leading to concentration.' When a noble disciple recollects his own moral discipline thus, on that occasion his mind is not obsessed by lust, hatred, or delusion; his mind is straight, with virtue as its object.... This is called a noble disciple who dwells evenly amid an uneven population, who dwells without affliction amid an afflicted population, who has entered upon the stream of the Dhamma and develops recollection of moral discipline.

"Further, Mahānāma, a noble disciple recollects his own generosity thus: 'It is a gain for me, it is well gained by me, that in a population obsessed by the stain of stinginess, I dwell at home with a mind devoid of the stain of stinginess, freely generous, open-handed, delighting in relinquishment, one devoted to charity, delighting in giving and sharing.' When a noble disciple recollects his own generosity thus, on that occasion his mind is not obsessed by lust, hatred, or delusion; his mind is straight, with generosity as its object.... This is called a noble disciple who dwells evenly amid an uneven population, who dwells without affliction amid an afflicted population, who has entered upon the stream of the Dhamma and develops recollection of generosity.

"Further, Mahānāma, a noble disciple develops the recollection of the devas thus: 'There are devas in the various heavenly realms.[24] There is found in me such faith, moral discipline, learning, generosity, and wisdom as those devas possessed because of which, when they passed away from this world, they were reborn there.' When a noble disciple recollects his own faith, moral discipline, learning, generosity, and wisdom, as well as those of the devas, on that occasion his mind is not obsessed by lust, hatred, or delusion; his mind is straight, with the devas as its object.... This is called a noble disciple who dwells evenly amid an uneven population, who dwells without affliction amid an afflicted population, who has entered upon the stream of the Dhamma and develops recollection of the devas.

"A noble disciple, Mahānāma, who has arrived at the fruit and understood the teaching often dwells in just this way."

(AN 6:10; III 284–88)

8. The Four Establishments of Mindfulness

1. Thus have I heard. On one occasion the Blessed One was living in the Kuru country where there was a town of the Kurus named Kammāsadhamma. There he addressed the monks thus: "Monks."—"Venerable sir," they replied. The Blessed One said this:

2. "Monks, this is the one-way path[25] for the purification of beings, for the surmounting of sorrow and lamentation, for the passing away of pain and dejection, for the attainment of the true way, for the realization of Nibbāna—namely, the four establishments of mindfulness.

3. "What are the four? Here, monks, a monk dwells contemplating the body in the body, ardent, clearly comprehending, and mindful, having subdued longing and dejection in regard to the world.[26] He dwells contemplating feelings in feelings, ardent, clearly comprehending, and mindful, having subdued longing and dejection in regard to the world. He dwells contemplating mind in mind, ardent, clearly comprehending, and mindful, having subdued longing and dejection in regard to the world. He dwells contemplating phenomena in phenomena, ardent,

clearly comprehending, and mindful, having subdued longing and dejection in regard to the world.[27]

[contemplation of the body]

[1. Mindfulness of Breathing]

4. "And how, monks, does a monk dwell contemplating the body in the body? Here a monk, gone to the forest, to the foot of a tree, or to an empty hut, sits down; having folded his legs crosswise, straightened his body, and established mindfulness in front of him, just mindful he breathes in, mindful he breathes out. Breathing in long, he understands: 'I breathe in long'; or breathing out long, he understands: 'I breathe out long.' Breathing in short, he understands: 'I breathe in short'; or breathing out short, he understands: 'I breathe out short.'[28] He trains thus: 'I will breathe in experiencing the whole body'; he trains thus: 'I will breathe out experiencing the whole body.'[29] He trains thus: 'I will breathe in tranquilizing the bodily formation'; he trains thus: 'I will breathe out tranquilizing the bodily formation.'[30] Just as a skilled lathe-worker or his apprentice, when making a long turn, understands: 'I make a long turn'; or, when making a short turn, understands: 'I make a short turn'; so too, breathing in long, a monk understands: 'I breathe in long' ... he trains thus: 'I will breathe out tranquilizing the bodily formation.'

5. "In this way he dwells contemplating the body in the body internally, or he dwells contemplating the body in the body externally, or he dwells contemplating the body in the body both internally and externally.[31] Or else he dwells contemplating in the body its nature of arising, or he dwells contemplating in the body its nature of vanishing, or he dwells contemplating in the body its nature of both arising and vanishing.[32] Or else mindfulness that 'there is a body' is simply established in him to the extent necessary for bare knowledge and repeated mindfulness. And he dwells independent, not clinging to anything in the world. That is how a monk dwells contemplating the body in the body.

[2. The Four Postures]

6. "Again, monks, when walking, a monk understands: 'I am walking'; when standing, he understands: 'I am standing'; when sitting, he understands: 'I am sitting'; when lying down, he understands: 'I am lying down'; or he understands accordingly however his body is disposed.[33]

7. "In this way he dwells contemplating the body in the body internally, externally, and both internally and externally.... And he dwells independent, not clinging to anything in the world. That too is how a monk dwells contemplating the body in the body.

[3. Clear Comprehension]

8. "Again, monks, a monk is one who acts with clear comprehension when going forward and returning;[34] who acts with clear comprehension when looking ahead and looking away; who acts with clear comprehension when bending and stretching his limbs; who acts with clear comprehension when wearing his robes and carrying his outer robe and bowl; who acts with clear comprehension when eating, drinking, chewing, and tasting; who acts with clear comprehension when defecating and urinating; who acts with clear comprehension when walking, standing, sitting, falling asleep, waking up, talking, and keeping silent.

9. "In this way he dwells contemplating the body in the body internally, externally, and both internally and externally.... And he dwells independent, not clinging to anything in the world. That too is how a monk dwells contemplating the body in the body.

[4. Unattractiveness of the Body]

10. "Again, monks, a monk reviews this same body up from the soles of the feet and down from the top of the hair, bounded by skin, as full of many kinds of impurity thus: 'In this body there are head-hairs, body-hairs, nails, teeth, skin, flesh, sinews, bones, bone-marrow, kidneys, heart, liver, diaphragm, spleen, lungs, intestines, mesentery, stomach, feces, bile, phlegm, pus, blood, sweat, fat, tears, grease, spittle, snot, oil of the joints, and urine.'[35] Just as though there were a bag with an opening at both ends full of many sorts of grain, such as hill rice, red rice, beans, peas, millet, and white rice, and a man with good eyes were to open it and review it thus: 'This is hill rice, this is red rice, these are beans, these are peas, this is millet, this is white rice'; so too, a monk reviews this same body ... as full of many kinds of impurity thus: 'In this body there are head-hairs ... and urine.'

11. "In this way he dwells contemplating the body in the body internally, externally, and both internally and externally.... And he dwells independent, not clinging to anything in the world. That too is how a monk dwells contemplating the body in the body.

[5. Elements]

12. "Again, monks, a monk reviews this same body, however it is placed, however disposed, as consisting of elements thus: 'In this body there are the earth element, the water element, the fire element, and the air element.'[36] Just as though a skilled butcher or his apprentice had killed a cow and were seated at the crossroads with it cut up into pieces; so too, a monk reviews this same body … as consisting of elements thus: 'In this body there are the earth element, the water element, the fire element, and the air element.'

13. "In this way he dwells contemplating the body in the body internally, externally, and both internally and externally.... And he dwells independent, not clinging to anything in the world. That too is how a monk dwells contemplating the body in the body.

[6–14. The Nine Charnel Ground Contemplations]

14. "Again, monks, as though he were to see a corpse thrown aside in a charnel ground, one, two, or three days dead, bloated, livid, and oozing matter, a monk compares this same body with it thus: 'This body too is of the same nature, it will be like that, it is not exempt from that fate.'[37]

15. "In this way he dwells contemplating the body in the body internally, externally, and both internally and externally.... And he dwells independent, not clinging to anything in the world. That too is how a monk dwells contemplating the body in the body.

16. "Again, as though he were to see a corpse thrown aside in a charnel ground, being devoured by crows, hawks, vultures, dogs, jackals, or various kinds of worms, a monk compares this same body with it thus: 'This body too is of the same nature, it will be like that, it is not exempt from that fate.'

17. "...That too is how a monk dwells contemplating the body in the body.

18–24. "Again, as though he were to see a corpse thrown aside in a charnel ground, a skeleton with flesh and blood, held together with sinews … a fleshless skeleton smeared with blood, held together with sinews … a skeleton without flesh and blood, held together with sinews … disconnected bones scattered in all directions—here a hand-bone, there a foot-bone, here a shin-bone, there a thigh-bone, here a hip-bone, there a back-bone, here the skull—a monk compares this same body with it thus: 'This body too is of the same nature, it will be like that, it is not exempt from that fate.'[38]

25. "...That too is how a monk dwells contemplating the body in the body.

26–30. "Again, as though he were to see a corpse thrown aside in a charnel ground, bones bleached white, the color of shells ... bones heaped up ... bones more than a year old, rotted and crumbled to dust, a monk compares this same body with it thus: 'This body too is of the same nature, it will be like that, it is not exempt from that fate.'

31. "In this way he dwells contemplating the body in the body internally, or he dwells contemplating the body in the body externally, or he dwells contemplating the body in the body both internally and externally. Or else he dwells contemplating in the body its nature of arising, or he dwells contemplating in the body its nature of vanishing, or he dwells contemplating in the body its nature of both arising and vanishing. Or else mindfulness that 'there is a body' is simply established in him to the extent necessary for bare knowledge and repeated mindfulness. And he dwells independent, not clinging to anything in the world. That too is how a monk dwells contemplating the body in the body.

[contemplation of feeling]

32. "And how, monks, does a monk dwell contemplating feelings in feelings?[39] Here, when feeling a pleasant feeling, a monk understands: 'I feel a pleasant feeling'; when feeling a painful feeling, he understands: 'I feel a painful feeling'; when feeling a neither-painful-nor-pleasant feeling, he understands: 'I feel a neither-painful-nor-pleasant feeling.' When feeling a carnal pleasant feeling, he understands: 'I feel a carnal pleasant feeling'; when feeling a spiritual pleasant feeling, he understands: 'I feel a spiritual pleasant feeling'; when feeling a carnal painful feeling, he understands: 'I feel a carnal painful feeling'; when feeling a spiritual painful feeling, he understands: 'I feel a spiritual painful feeling'; when feeling a carnal neither-painful-nor-pleasant feeling, he understands: 'I feel a carnal neither-painful-nor-pleasant feeling'; when feeling a spiritual neither-painful-nor-pleasant feeling, he understands: 'I feel a spiritual neither-painful-nor-pleasant feeling.'

33. "In this way he dwells contemplating feelings in feelings internally, or he dwells contemplating feelings in feelings externally, or he dwells contemplating feelings in feelings both internally and

externally. Or else he dwells contemplating in feelings their nature of arising, or he dwells contemplating in feelings their nature of vanishing, or he dwells contemplating in feelings their nature of both arising and vanishing.[40] Or else mindfulness that 'there is feeling' is simply established in him to the extent necessary for bare knowledge and repeated mindfulness. And he dwells independent, not clinging to anything in the world. That is how a monk dwells contemplating feelings in feelings.

[contemplation of mind]

34. "And how, monks, does a monk dwell contemplating mind in mind?[41] Here a monk understands a mind with lust as a mind with lust, and a mind without lust as a mind without lust. He understands a mind with hatred as a mind with hatred, and a mind without hatred as a mind without hatred. He understands a mind with delusion as a mind with delusion, and a mind without delusion as a mind without delusion. He understands a contracted mind as contracted, and a distracted mind as distracted. He understands an exalted mind as exalted, and an unexalted mind as unexalted. He understands a surpassable mind as surpassable, and an unsurpassable mind as unsurpassable. He understands a concentrated mind as concentrated, and an unconcentrated mind as unconcentrated. He understands a liberated mind as liberated, and an unliberated mind as unliberated.[42]

35. "In this way he dwells contemplating mind in mind internally, or he dwells contemplating mind in mind externally, or he dwells contemplating mind in mind both internally and externally. Or else he dwells contemplating in mind its nature of arising, or he dwells contemplating in mind its nature of vanishing, or he dwells contemplating in mind its nature of both arising and vanishing.[43] Or else mindfulness that 'there is mind' is simply established in him to the extent necessary for bare knowledge and repeated mindfulness. And he dwells independent, not clinging to anything in the world. That is how a monk dwells contemplating mind as mind.

[contemplation of phenomena]

[1. The Five Hindrances]

36. "And how, monks, does a monk dwell contemplating phenomena in phenomena? Here a monk dwells contemplating phenomena in

phenomena in terms of the five hindrances.[44] And how does a monk dwell contemplating phenomena in phenomena in terms of the five hindrances? Here, when there is sensual desire in him, a monk understands: 'There is sensual desire in me'; or when there is no sensual desire in him, he understands: 'There is no sensual desire in me'; and he also understands how unarisen sensual desire arises, and how arisen sensual desire is abandoned, and how abandoned sensual desire does not arise again in the future.'[45]

"When there is ill will in him ... When there is dullness and drowsiness in him ... When there is restlessness and remorse in him ... When there is doubt in him, a monk understands: 'There is doubt in me'; or when there is no doubt in him, he understands: 'There is no doubt in me'; and he also understands how the unarisen doubt arises, and how arisen doubt is abandoned, and how abandoned doubt does not arise again in the future.

37. "In this way he dwells contemplating phenomena in phenomena internally, or he dwells contemplating phenomena in phenomena externally, or he dwells contemplating phenomena in phenomena both internally and externally. Or else he dwells contemplating in phenomena their nature of arising, or he dwells contemplating in phenomena their nature of vanishing, or he dwells contemplating in phenomena their nature of both arising and vanishing. Or else mindfulness that 'there are phenomena' is simply established in him to the extent necessary for bare knowledge and repeated mindfulness. And he dwells independent, not clinging to anything in the world. That is how a monk dwells contemplating phenomena in phenomena in terms of the five hindrances.

[2. The Five Aggregates]

38. "Again, monks, a monk dwells contemplating phenomena in phenomena in terms of the five aggregates subject to clinging.[46] And how does a monk dwell contemplating phenomena in phenomena in terms of the five aggregates affected by clinging? Here a monk understands: 'Such is form, such its origin, such its passing away; such is feeling, such its origin, such its passing away; such is perception, such its origin, such its passing away; such are the volitional formations, such their origin, such their passing away; such is consciousness, such its origin, such its passing away.'[47]

39. "In this way he dwells contemplating phenomena in phenomena internally, externally, and both internally and externally.... And he dwells independent, not clinging to anything in the world. That is how a monk dwells contemplating phenomena in phenomena in terms of the five aggregates subject to clinging.

[3. The Six Sense Bases]

40. "Again, monks, a monk dwells contemplating phenomena in phenomena in terms of the six internal and external sense bases.[48] And how does a monk dwell contemplating phenomena in phenomena in terms of the six internal and external sense bases? Here a monk understands the eye, he understands forms, and he understands the fetter that arises dependent on both; and he also understands how the unarisen fetter arises, and how the arisen fetter is abandoned, and how the abandoned fetter does not arise again in the future.[49]

"He understands the ear, he understands sounds.... He understands the nose, he understands odors.... He understands the tongue, he understands flavors.... He understands the body, he understands tactile objects.... He understands the mind, he understands phenomena, and he understands the fetter that arises dependent on both; and he also understands how the unarisen fetter arises, and how the arisen fetter is abandoned, and how the abandoned fetter does not arise again in the future.

41. "In this way he dwells contemplating phenomena in phenomena internally, externally, and both internally and externally.... And he dwells independent, not clinging to anything in the world. That is how a monk dwells contemplating phenomena in phenomena in terms of the six internal and external sense bases.

[4. The Seven Enlightenment Factors]

42. "Again, monks, a monk dwells contemplating phenomena in phenomena in terms of the seven enlightenment factors.[50] And how does a monk dwell contemplating phenomena in phenomena in terms of the seven enlightenment factors? Here, when there is the mindfulness enlightenment factor in him, a monk understands: 'There is the mindfulness enlightenment factor in me'; or when there is no mindfulness enlightenment factor in him, he understands: 'There is no mindfulness enlightenment factor in me'; and he also understands how the unarisen

mindfulness enlightenment factor arises, and how the arisen mindfulness enlightenment factor comes to fulfillment by development.

"When there is the discrimination of phenomena enlightenment factor in him... When there is the energy enlightenment factor in him ... When there is the rapture enlightenment factor in him ... When there is the tranquillity enlightenment factor in him ... When there is the concentration enlightenment factor in him ... When there is the equanimity enlightenment factor in him, a monk understands: 'There is the equanimity enlightenment factor in me'; or when there is no equanimity enlightenment factor in him, he understands: 'There is no equanimity enlightenment factor in me'; and he also understands how the unarisen equanimity enlightenment factor arises, and how the arisen equanimity enlightenment factor comes to fulfillment by development.[51]

43. "In this way he dwells contemplating phenomena in phenomena internally, externally, and both internally and externally.... And he dwells independent, not clinging to anything in the world. That is how a monk dwells contemplating phenomena in phenomena in terms of the seven enlightenment factors.

[5. The Four Noble Truths]

44. "Again, monks, a monk dwells contemplating phenomena in phenomena in terms of the Four Noble Truths.[52] And how does a monk dwell contemplating phenomena in phenomena in terms of the Four Noble Truths? Here a monk understands as it really is: 'This is suffering. This is the origin of suffering. This is the cessation of suffering. This is the way leading to the cessation of suffering.'

45. "In this way he dwells contemplating phenomena in phenomena internally, or he dwells contemplating phenomena in phenomena externally, or he dwells contemplating phenomena in phenomena both internally and externally. Or else he dwells contemplating in phenomena their nature of arising, or he dwells contemplating in phenomena their nature of vanishing, or he dwells contemplating in phenomena their nature of both arising and vanishing. Or else mindfulness that 'there are phenomena' is simply established in him to the extent necessary for bare knowledge and repeated mindfulness. And he dwells independent, not clinging to anything in the world. That is how a monk dwells contemplating phenomena in phenomena in terms of the Four Noble Truths.

[conclusion]
46. "Monks, if anyone should develop these four establishments of mindfulness in such a way for seven years, one of two fruits could be expected for him: either final knowledge here and now, or if there is a trace of clinging left, nonreturning.[53]

"Let alone seven years, monks. If anyone should develop these four establishments of mindfulness in such a way for six years ... for five years ... for four years ... for three years ... for two years ... for one year, one of two fruits could be expected for him: either final knowledge here and now, or if there is a trace of clinging left, nonreturning.

"Let alone one year, monks. If anyone should develop these four establishments of mindfulness in such a way for seven months ... for six months ... for five months ... for four months ... for three months ... for two months ... for one month ... for half a month, one of two fruits could be expected for him: either final knowledge here and now, or if there is a trace of clinging left, nonreturning.

"Let alone half a month, monks. If anyone should develop these four establishments of mindfulness in such a way for seven days, one of two fruits could be expected for him: either final knowledge here and now, or if there is a trace of clinging left, nonreturning.

47. "So it was with reference to this that it was said: 'Monks, this is the direct path for the purification of beings, for the surmounting of sorrow and lamentation, for the passing away of pain and dejection, for the attainment of the true way, for the realization of Nibbāna—namely, the four establishments of mindfulness.'"

That is what the Blessed One said. The monks were satisfied and delighted in the Blessed One's words.

(MN 10: *Satipaṭṭhāna Sutta*; I 55–63)

9. Mindfulness of Breathing

At Sāvatthī, the Venerable Ānanda approached the Blessed One, paid homage to him, sat down to one side, and said: "Venerable sir, is there one thing which, when developed and cultivated, fulfills four things? And four things which, when developed and cultivated, fulfill seven things? And seven things which, when developed and cultivated, fulfill two things?"

"There is, Ānanda, one thing which, when developed and cultivated, fulfills four things; and four things which, when developed and cultivated, fulfill seven things; and seven things which, when developed and cultivated, fulfill two things."

"But, venerable sir, what is the one thing which, when developed and cultivated, fulfills four things; and the four things which, when developed and cultivated, fulfill seven things; and the seven things which, when developed and cultivated, fulfill two things?"

"Concentration by mindfulness of breathing, Ānanda, is the one thing which, when developed and cultivated, fulfills the four establishments of mindfulness. The four establishments of mindfulness, when developed and cultivated, fulfill the seven factors of enlightenment. The seven factors of enlightenment, when developed and cultivated, fulfill true knowledge and liberation.

[i. Fulfilling the four establishments of mindfulness]

"How, Ānanda, is concentration by mindfulness of breathing developed and cultivated so that it fulfills the four establishments of mindfulness? Here, Ānanda, a monk, having gone to the forest, to the foot of a tree, or to an empty hut, sits down.[54] Having folded his legs crosswise, straightened his body, and set up mindfulness in front of him, just mindful he breathes in, mindful he breathes out. "Breathing in long, he knows: 'I breathe in long'; or breathing out long, he knows: 'I breathe out long.' Breathing in short, he knows: 'I breathe in short'; or breathing out short, he knows: 'I breathe out short.' He trains thus: 'Experiencing the whole body, I will breathe in'; he trains thus: 'Experiencing the whole body, I will breathe out.' He trains thus: 'Tranquilizing the bodily formation, I will breathe in'; he trains thus: 'Tranquilizing the bodily formation, I will breathe out.'

"He trains thus: 'Experiencing rapture, I will breathe in'; he trains thus: 'Experiencing rapture, I will breathe out.' He trains thus: 'Experiencing happiness, I will breathe in'; he trains thus: 'Experiencing happiness, I will breathe out.' He trains thus: 'Experiencing the mental formation, I will breathe in'; he trains thus: 'Experiencing the mental formation, I will breathe out.' He trains thus: 'Tranquilizing the mental formation, I will breathe in'; he trains thus: 'Tranquilizing the mental formation, I will breathe out.'[55]

"He trains thus: 'Experiencing the mind, I will breathe in'; he trains thus: 'Experiencing the mind, I will breathe out.' He trains thus: 'Gladdening the mind, I will breathe in'; he trains thus: 'Gladdening the mind, I will breathe out.' He trains thus: 'Concentrating the mind, I will breathe in'; he trains thus: 'Concentrating the mind, I will breathe out.' He trains thus: 'Liberating the mind, I will breathe in'; he trains thus: 'Liberating the mind, I will breathe out.'[56]

"He trains thus: 'Contemplating impermanence, I will breathe in'; he trains thus: 'Contemplating impermanence, I will breathe out.' He trains thus: 'Contemplating fading away, I will breathe in'; he trains thus: 'Contemplating fading away, I will breathe out.' He trains thus: 'Contemplating cessation, I will breathe in'; he trains thus: 'Contemplating cessation, I will breathe out.' He trains thus: 'Contemplating relinquishment, I will breathe in'; he trains thus: 'Contemplating relinquishment, I will breathe out.'[57]

"Whenever, Ānanda, a monk, when breathing in long, knows: 'I breathe in long' ... [as above] ... when he trains thus: 'Tranquilizing the bodily formation, I will breathe out'—on that occasion the monk dwells contemplating the body in the body, ardent, clearly comprehending, mindful, having subdued longing and dejection in regard to the world. For what reason? I call this a certain kind of body, Ānanda, that is, breathing in and breathing out. Therefore, Ānanda, on that occasion the monk dwells contemplating the body in the body, ardent, clearly comprehending, mindful, having subdued longing and dejection in regard to the world.

"Whenever, Ānanda, a monk trains thus: 'Experiencing rapture, I will breathe in' ... when he trains thus: 'Tranquilizing the mental formation, I will breathe out'—on that occasion the monk dwells contemplating feelings in feelings, ardent, clearly comprehending, mindful, having subdued longing and dejection in regard to the world. For what reason? I call this a certain kind of feeling, Ānanda, that is, close attention to breathing in and breathing out.[58] Therefore, Ānanda, on that occasion the monk dwells contemplating feelings in feelings, ardent, clearly comprehending, mindful, having subdued longing and dejection in regard to the world.

"Whenever, Ānanda, a monk trains thus: 'Experiencing the mind, I will breathe in' ... when he trains thus: 'Liberating the mind, I will breathe out'—on that occasion the monk dwells contemplating mind in mind, ardent, clearly comprehending, mindful, having subdued longing and dejection in regard to the world. For what reason? I say, Ānanda, that there is no development of concentration by mindfulness of breathing for one who is muddled and who lacks clear comprehension. Therefore, Ānanda, on that occasion the monk dwells contemplating mind in mind, ardent, clearly comprehending, mindful, having subdued longing and dejection in regard to the world.

"Whenever, Ānanda, a monk trains thus: 'Contemplating impermanence, I will breathe in' ... when he trains thus: 'Contemplating relinquishment, I will breathe out'—on that occasion the monk dwells contemplating phenomena in phenomena, ardent, clearly comprehending, mindful, having subdued longing and dejection in regard to the world. Having seen with wisdom what is the abandoning of longing and dejection, he is one who looks on closely with equanimity.[59] Therefore, Ānanda, on that occasion the monk dwells contemplating phenomena in phenomena, ardent, clearly comprehending, mindful, having subdued longing and dejection in regard to the world.

"It is, Ānanda, when concentration by mindfulness of breathing is developed and cultivated in this way that it fulfills the four establishments of mindfulness.

[ii. Fulfilling the seven factors of enlightenment]

"And how, Ānanda, are the four establishments of mindfulness developed and cultivated so that they fulfill the seven factors of enlightenment?

"Whenever, Ānanda, a monk dwells contemplating the body in the body, on that occasion unmuddled mindfulness is established in that monk. Whenever, Ānanda, unmuddled mindfulness has been established in a monk, on that occasion the enlightenment factor of mindfulness is aroused by the monk; on that occasion the monk develops the enlightenment factor of mindfulness; on that occasion the enlightenment factor of mindfulness goes to fulfillment by development in the monk.[60]

"Dwelling thus mindfully, he discriminates that phenomenon with wisdom, examines it, makes an investigation of it. Whenever, Ānanda, a monk dwelling thus mindfully discriminates that phenomenon with wisdom, examines it, makes an investigation of it, on that occasion the enlightenment factor of discrimination of phenomena[61] is aroused by the monk; on that occasion the monk develops the enlightenment factor of discrimination of phenomena; on that occasion the enlightenment factor of discrimination of phenomena goes to fulfillment by development in the monk.

"While he discriminates that phenomenon with wisdom, examines it, makes an investigation of it, his energy is aroused without slackening. Whenever, Ānanda, a monk's energy is aroused without slackening as he discriminates that phenomenon with wisdom, examines it, makes an investigation of it, on that occasion the enlightenment factor of energy is aroused by the monk; on that occasion the monk develops the enlightenment factor of energy; on that occasion the enlightenment factor of energy goes to fulfillment by development in the monk.

"When his energy is aroused, there arises in him spiritual rapture. Whenever, Ānanda, spiritual rapture arises in a monk whose energy is aroused, on that occasion the enlightenment factor of rapture is aroused by the monk; on that occasion the monk develops the enlightenment factor of rapture; on that occasion the enlightenment factor of rapture goes to fulfillment by development in the monk.

"For one whose mind is uplifted by rapture the body becomes tranquil and the mind becomes tranquil. Whenever, Ānanda, the body becomes tranquil and the mind becomes tranquil in a monk whose mind is uplifted by rapture, on that occasion the enlightenment factor of tranquillity is aroused by the monk; on that occasion the monk develops the enlightenment factor of tranquillity; on that occasion the enlightenment factor of tranquillity goes to fulfillment by development in the monk.

"For one whose body is tranquil and who is happy the mind becomes concentrated. Whenever, Ānanda, the mind becomes concentrated in a monk whose body is tranquil and who is happy, on that occasion the enlightenment factor of concentration is aroused by the monk; on that occasion the monk develops the enlightenment factor of concentration; on that occasion the enlightenment factor of concentration goes to fulfillment by development in the monk.

"He becomes one who closely looks on with equanimity at the mind thus concentrated. Whenever, Ānanda, a monk becomes one who closely looks on with equanimity at the mind thus concentrated, on that occasion the enlightenment factor of equanimity is aroused by the monk; on that occasion the monk develops the enlightenment factor of equanimity; on that occasion the enlightenment factor of equanimity goes to fulfillment by development in the monk.

"Whenever, Ānanda, a monk dwells contemplating feelings in feelings ... mind in mind ... phenomena in phenomena, on that occasion unmuddled mindfulness is established in that monk. Whenever, Ānanda, unmuddled mindfulness has been established in a monk, on that occasion the enlightenment factor of mindfulness is aroused by the monk; on that occasion the monk develops the enlightenment factor of mindfulness; on that occasion the enlightenment factor of mindfulness goes to fulfillment by development in the monk.

[*All should be elaborated as in the case of the first establishment of mindfulness.*]

"He becomes one who closely looks on with equanimity at the mind thus concentrated. Whenever, Ānanda, a monk becomes one who closely looks on with equanimity at the mind thus concentrated, on that occasion the enlightenment factor of equanimity is aroused by the monk; on that occasion the monk develops the enlightenment factor of equanimity; on that occasion the enlightenment factor of equanimity goes to fulfillment by development in the monk.

"It is, Ānanda, when the four establishments of mindfulness are developed and cultivated in this way that they fulfill the seven factors of enlightenment.

[iii. Fulfilling true knowledge and liberation]

"How, Ānanda, are the seven factors of enlightenment developed and cultivated so that they fulfill true knowledge and liberation?

"Here, Ānanda, a monk develops the enlightenment factor of mindfulness, which is based upon seclusion, dispassion, and cessation, maturing in release. He develops the enlightenment factor of discrimination of phenomena ... the enlightenment factor of energy ... the enlightenment factor of rapture ... the enlightenment factor of tranquillity ... the enlightenment factor of concentration ... the enlightenment factor of equanimity, which is based upon seclusion, dispassion, and cessation, maturing in release.

"It is, Ānanda, when the seven factors of enlightenment are developed and cultivated in this way that they fulfill true knowledge and liberation."

(SN 54:13; V 328–33 ≠ MN 118.15–43; III 82–88)

10. The Achievement of Mastery

On one occasion the Venerable Sāriputta was dwelling at Sāvatthī in Jeta's Grove, Anāthapiṇḍika's Park.[62] Then one morning he dressed and, taking bowl and robe, entered Sāvatthī for alms. When he had walked for alms in Sāvatthī and had returned from the almsround, after his meal he went to the Blind Men's Grove for the day's abiding. Having plunged into the Blind Men's Grove, he sat down at the foot of a tree for the day's abiding.

Then, in the evening, the Venerable Sāriputta emerged from seclusion and went to Jeta's Grove, Anāthapiṇḍika's Park. The Venerable Ānanda saw him coming in the distance and said to him: "Friend Sāriputta, your faculties are serene, your facial complexion is pure and bright. In what dwelling have you spent the day?"

"Here, friend, secluded from sensual pleasures, secluded from unwholesome states, I entered and dwelled in the first jhāna, which is accompanied by thought and examination, with rapture and happiness born of seclusion. Yet, friend, it did not occur to me, 'I am attaining the first jhāna,' or 'I have attained the first jhāna,' or 'I have emerged from the first jhāna.'"

"It must be because I-making, mine-making, and the underlying tendency to conceit have been thoroughly uprooted in your mind for a long time that such thoughts did not occur to you."[63]

[On another occasion the Venerable Sāriputta said:] "Here, friend, with the subsiding of thought and examination, I entered and dwelled in the second jhāna, which has internal confidence and unification of mind, is without thought and examination, and has rapture and happiness born of concentration. Yet, friend, it did not occur to me, 'I am attaining the second jhāna,' or 'I have attained the second jhāna,' or 'I have emerged from the second jhāna.'"

"It must be because I-making, mine-making, and the underlying tendency to conceit have been thoroughly uprooted in your mind for a long time that such thoughts did not occur to you."

[On another occasion the Venerable Sāriputta said:] "Here, friend, with the fading away as well of rapture, I dwelled equanimous and, mindful and clearly comprehending, I experienced happiness with the body; I entered and dwelled in the third jhāna, of which the noble ones declare: 'He is equanimous, mindful, one who dwells happily.' Yet, friend, it did not occur to me, 'I am attaining the third jhāna....'" [*Complete as above.*]

[On another occasion the Venerable Sāriputta said:] "Here, friend, with the abandoning of pleasure and pain, and with the previous passing away of joy and displeasure, I entered and dwelled in the fourth jhāna, which is neither painful nor pleasant and includes the purification of mindfulness by equanimity. Yet, friend, it did not occur to me, 'I am attaining the fourth jhāna....'"

[On another occasion the Venerable Sāriputta said:] "Here, friend, with the complete transcending of perceptions of forms, with the passing away of perceptions of sensory impingement, with nonattention to perceptions of diversity, aware that 'space is infinite,' I entered and dwelled in the base of the infinity of space. Yet, friend, it did not occur to me, 'I am attaining the base of the infinity of space....'"

[On another occasion the Venerable Sāriputta said:] "Here, friend, by completely transcending the base of the infinity of space, aware that 'consciousness is infinite,' I entered and dwelled in the base of the infinity of consciousness. Yet, friend, it did not occur to me, 'I am attaining the base of the infinity of consciousness....'"

[On another occasion the Venerable Sāriputta said:] "Here, friend, by completely transcending the base of the infinity of consciousness, aware that 'there is nothing,' I entered and dwelled in the base of nothingness. Yet, friend, it did not occur to me, 'I am attaining the base of nothingness....'"

[On another occasion the Venerable Sāriputta said:] "Here, friend, by completely transcending the base of nothingness, I entered and dwelled in the base of neither-perception-nor-nonperception. Yet, friend, it did not occur to me, 'I am attaining the base of neither-perception-nor-nonperception....'"

[On another occasion the Venerable Sāriputta said:] "Here, friend, by completely transcending the base of neither-perception-nor-nonperception, I entered and dwelled in the cessation of perception and feeling. Yet, friend, it did not occur to me, 'I am attaining the cessation of perception and feeling,' or 'I have attained the cessation of perception and feeling,' or 'I have emerged from the cessation of perception and feeling.'"[64]

"It must be because I-making, mine-making, and the underlying tendency to conceit have been thoroughly uprooted in your mind for a long time that such thoughts did not occur to you."

(SN 28:1–9, combined; III 235–38)

IX. Shining the Light of Wisdom

Introduction

The texts cited in the last chapter treated meditation as a discipline of mental training aimed at a twofold task: stilling the mind and generating insight. The still mind, calm and collected, is the foundation for insight. The still mind observes phenomena as they arise and pass away, and from sustained observation and probing exploration arises "the higher wisdom of insight into phenomena" (*adhipaññādhammavipassanā*). As wisdom gathers momentum, it penetrates more and more deeply into the nature of things, culminating in the full and comprehensive understanding called enlightenment (*sambodhi*).

The Pāli word translated here as "wisdom" is *paññā*, the Pāli equivalent of Sanskrit *prajñā*, which gives its name to the voluminous *prajñāpāramitā* sūtras of Mahāyāna Buddhism. The idea of *paññā/prajñā* as the principal tool on the path to enlightenment, however, did not originate with the *prajñāpāramitā* literature but is already deeply embedded in the teachings of Early Buddhism. The Nikāyas take *paññā* not only as a point of doctrine but as a rich theme for imagery. Thus, **Texts IX,1(1)–(2)** speak of *paññā* respectively as a light and a knife. It is the supreme light because it illuminates the true nature of things and dispels the darkness of ignorance. It is a knife—a sharp butcher's knife—because it cuts through the tangled mass of the defilements and thereby opens the way to liberation.

The Pāli word *paññā* is derived from the verbal root *ñā* (Skt: *jñā*), meaning "to know," preceded by the prefix *pa* (Skt: *pra*), which merely gives the root meaning a more dynamic nuance. So *paññā/prajñā* means knowing or understanding, not as a possession, but as an action: the act of knowing, the act of understanding, the act of discerning. In Pāli, the verb *pajānāti*, "one understands," conveys this sense more effectively than the correlative noun *paññā*.[1] What is meant by *paññā*, however, is a type of understanding superior to that which occurs when one understands, for instance, a difficult passage in an economics textbook or the implications of a legal argument. *Paññā* signifies the understanding that arises through spiritual training, illuminates the real nature of things, and culminates in the mind's purification and liberation. For this reason, despite its drawbacks, I continue to use the familiar "wisdom."

Contemporary Buddhist literature commonly conveys two ideas about *paññā* that have become almost axioms in the popular understanding of Buddhism. The first is that *paññā* is exclusively nonconceptual and nondiscursive, a type of cognition that defies all the laws of logical thought; the second, that *paññā* arises spontaneously, through an act of pure intuition as sudden and instantaneous as a brilliant flash of lightning. These two ideas about *paññā* are closely connected. If *paññā* defies all the laws of thought, it cannot be approached by any type of conceptual activity but can arise only when the rational, discriminative, conceptual activity of the mind has been stultified. And this stopping of conceptualization, somewhat like the demolition of a building, must be a rapid one, an undermining of thought not previously prepared for by any gradual maturation of understanding. Thus, in the popular understanding of Buddhism, *paññā* defies rationality and easily slides off into "crazy wisdom," an incomprehensible, mind-boggling way of relating to the world that dances at the thin edge between super-rationality and madness.

Such ideas about *paññā* receive no support at all from the teachings of the Nikāyas, which are consistently sane, lucid, and sober. To take the two points in reverse order: First, far from arising spontaneously, *paññā* in the Nikāyas is emphatically conditioned, arisen from an underlying matrix of causes and conditions. And second, *paññā* is not bare intuition, but a careful, discriminative understanding that at certain stages involves precise conceptual operations. *Paññā* is directed to specific domains of understanding. These domains, known in the Pāli commentaries as "the soil of wisdom" (*paññābhūmi*), must be thoroughly investigated and mastered through conceptual understanding before direct, nonconceptual insight can effectively accomplish its work. To master them requires analysis, discrimination, and discernment. One must be able to abstract from the overwhelming mass of facts certain basic patterns fundamental to all experience and use these patterns as templates for close contemplation of one's own experience. I will have more to say about this as we go along.

The conditional basis for wisdom is laid down in the three-tier structure of the Buddhist training. As we have seen, in the three divisions of the Buddhist path, moral discipline functions as the basis for concentration and concentration as the basis for wisdom. Thus the immediate condition for the arising of wisdom is concentration. As the Buddha often says: "Develop concentration, monks. One who is concentrated sees things as they really are."[2] To "see things as they really are" is the work of wisdom; the immediate basis for this correct seeing is concentration. Since concentration depends on proper bodily and verbal conduct, moral discipline too is a condition for wisdom.

Text IX,2 gives a fuller list of eight causes and conditions for obtaining "the wisdom fundamental to the spiritual life" and for bringing such wisdom to maturity. Of particular interest is the fifth condition, which not only emphasizes the contribution that study of the Dhamma makes to the development of wisdom but also prescribes a sequential program of education. First one "learns much" of those "teachings that are good in the beginning, good in the middle, and good in the end." Then one memorizes them; then recites them aloud; then investigates them with the mind; and finally "penetrates them well by view." The last step can be equated with direct insight, but such insight is prepared for by the preceding steps, which provide the "information" necessary for thorough penetration to occur. From this, we can see that wisdom does not arise automatically on the basis of concentration but depends upon a clear and precise conceptual understanding of the Dhamma induced by study, reflection, and deep contemplation of the teachings.

As a factor of the Noble Eightfold Path, wisdom is known as *right view* (*sammādiṭṭhi*). **Text IX,3**, a slightly abridged version of the Sammādiṭṭhi Sutta, the Discourse on Right View (MN 9), gives an excellent overview of the "soil of wisdom." The Venerable Sāriputta, the Buddha's disciple who excelled in wisdom, spoke the discourse to a group of his fellow monks. Since ancient times, the text has served as a primer of Buddhist studies in the monasteries of southern Asia. According to the classical commentary on this sutta, right view is twofold: *conceptual right view*, a clear intellectual grasp of the Dhamma; and *experiential right view*, the wisdom that directly penetrates the Dhamma. Conceptual right view, called "right view in conformity with the truths" (*saccānulomika-sammādiṭṭhi*), is a correct understanding of the Dhamma arrived at by studying and examining the Buddha's teachings in depth. Such understanding, though conceptual rather than experiential, is by no means dry and sterile. When rooted in faith in the Buddha's enlightenment and driven by a strong determination to realize the truth of the Dhamma, it serves as the germ from which experiential right view evolves and thus becomes a critical step in the growth of wisdom.

Experiential right view is the realization of the truth of the Dhamma—above all, of the Four Noble Truths—in one's own immediate experience. For this reason it is called "right view that penetrates the truths" (*saccapaṭivedha-sammādiṭṭhi*). To arrive at direct penetration, one begins with correct conceptual understanding of the teaching and, by practice, transforms this understanding into direct perception. If conceptual right view is compared to a hand—a hand that grasps the truth with the aid of concepts—then experiential right view might be compared to an eye. It is the eye of wisdom, the vision of the Dhamma, that sees directly into the ultimate truth, hidden from us for so long by our greed, hatred, and delusion.

The Discourse on Right View is intended to elucidate the principles that should be comprehended by conceptual right view and penetrated by experiential right view. Sāriputta expounds these principles under sixteen headings: the wholesome and the unwholesome, the four nutriments of life, the Four Noble Truths, the twelve factors of dependent origination, and the taints. It should be noted that from the second section to the end of the sutta, he frames all his expositions in accordance with the same pattern, a pattern that reveals the principle of conditionality to be the scaffolding for the entire teaching. Whatever phenomenon he takes up, he expounds by bringing to light its individual nature, its arising, its cessation, and the way to its cessation. Since this is the pattern that underlies the Four Noble Truths, I shall call it "the four-truth pattern." This pattern recurs throughout the Nikāyas as one of the major templates through which phenomena are to be viewed to arrive at true wisdom. Its application makes it clear that no entity is isolated and self-enclosed but is, rather, inherently linked to other things in a complex web of dependently originated processes. The key to liberation lies in understanding the causes that sustain this web and bringing them to an end within oneself. This is done by practicing the Noble Eightfold Path, the way to extinguish those causes.

The world-transcending right view, arrived at by penetrating any of the sixteen subjects expounded in the sutta, occurs in two main stages.

The first stage is the right view of the trainee (*sekha*), the disciple who has entered irreversibly upon the path to liberation but has not yet reached its end. This stage is indicated by the words that open each section, "(one) who has perfect confidence in the Dhamma and has arrived at this true Dhamma." These words signify right view as a vision of true principles, an insight that has initiated a radical transformation in the disciple but has not yet reached completion. The second stage is the world-transcending right view of the arahant, described by the closing words of each section. These words indicate that the disciple has used right view to eradicate the remaining defilements and has attained complete emancipation.

In section 4 we arrive at what I call "the domain of wisdom," the areas to be explored and penetrated by insight. Many of the texts in this section come from the Saṃyutta Nikāya, whose major chapters are devoted to the principal doctrines of Early Buddhism. I include selections here on the five aggregates; the six sense bases; the elements (in different numerical sets); dependent origination; and the Four Noble Truths. As we survey these selections we will notice certain recurrent patterns.

IX,4(1) *The Five Aggregates.* The five aggregates (*pañcakkhandha*) are the main categories the Nikāyas use to analyze human experience. The five are: (1) form (*rūpa*), the physical component of experience; (2) feeling (*vedanā*), the "affective tone" of experience—either pleasant, painful, or neutral; (3) perception (*saññā*), the identification of things through their distinctive marks and features; (4) volitional formations (*saṅkhārā*), a term for the multifarious mental factors involving volition, choice, and intention; and (5) consciousness (*viññāṇa*), cognition arisen through any of the six sense faculties—eye, ear, nose, tongue, body, and mind.

Examination of the five aggregates, the topic of the Khandhasaṃyutta (Saṃyutta Nikāya, chapter 22), is critical to the Buddha's teaching for at least four reasons. *First,* the five aggregates are the ultimate referent of the first noble truth, the noble truth of suffering (see the exposition of the first truth in **Text II,5**), and since all four truths revolve around suffering, understanding the aggregates is essential for understanding the Four Noble Truths as a whole. *Second,* the five aggregates are the objective domain of clinging and as such contribute to the causal origination of future suffering. *Third,* clinging to the five aggregates must be removed to attain liberation. And *fourth*, the kind of wisdom needed to remove clinging is precisely clear insight into the true nature of the aggregates. The Buddha himself declares that so long as he did not understand the five aggregates in terms of their individual nature, arising, cessation, and the way to their cessation, he did not claim to have attained perfect enlightenment. The full understanding of the five aggregates is a task he likewise enjoins on his disciples. The five aggregates, he says, are the things that must be fully understood; their full understanding brings the destruction of greed, hatred, and delusion (SN 22:23).

The word *khandha* (Skt: *skandha*) means, among other things, a heap or mass (*rāsi*). The five aggregates are so called because they each unite under one label a multiplicity of phenomena that share the same defining characteristic. Thus whatever form there is, "past, future, or present, internal or external, gross or subtle, inferior or superior, far or near," is incorporated into the form aggregate; whatever feeling there is, "past, future, or present, internal or external, gross or subtle, inferior or superior, far or near," is incorporated into the feeling aggregate; and so for each of the other aggregates. **Text IX,4(1)(a)** enumerates in simple terms the constituents of each aggregate and shows that each aggregate arises and ceases in correlation with its own specific condition; the Noble Eightfold Path is the way to bring each aggregate to an end. Here we find the "four-truth pattern" applied to the five aggregates, an application that follows quite logically from the role that the five aggregates play in representing the first noble truth.

This sutta makes a distinction between trainees and arahants similar to that made by the Discourse on Right View. Trainees have directly known the five aggregates by way of the four-truth pattern and are practicing for their fading away and cessation; they have thereby "gained a foothold (*gādhanti*) in this Dhamma and Discipline." Arahants too have directly known the five aggregates by way of the four-truth pattern, but they have gone further than the trainees. They have extirpated all attachment to the aggregates and are liberated by nonclinging; thus they are called "consummate ones" (*kevalino*) who cannot be described by way of the round of rebirths.

A detailed catechism on the aggregates, treating them from diverse angles, can be found in **Text IX,4(1)(b)**. Because the five aggregates that make up our ordinary experience are the objective domain of clinging

The Five Aggregates

(based on SN 22:56–57 and 22:95)

Aggregate	Content	Condition	Simile
form	four great elements and form derived from them	nutriment	a lump of foam
feeling	six classes of feeling: born of contact through eye, ear, nose, tongue, body, and mind	contact	a water bubble
perception	six classes of perception: of forms, sounds, smells, tastes, tactile objects, and mental phenomena	contact	a mirage
volitional formations	six classes of volition: regarding forms, sounds, smells, tastes, tactile objects, and mental phenomena	contact	a banana-tree trunk
consciousness	six classes of consciousness: eye-, ear-, nose-, tongue-, body-, mind-consciousness	name-and-form	a magical illusion

(*upādāna*), they are commonly called the five aggregates subject to clinging (*pañc'upādānakkhandhā*). Clinging to the five aggregates occurs in two principal modes, which we might call *appropriation* and *identification*. One either grasps them and takes possession of them, that is, one *appropriates* them; or one uses them as the basis for views about one's self or for conceit ("I am better than, as good as, inferior to others"), that is, one *identifies* with them. As the Nikāyas put it, we are prone to think of the aggregates thus: "This is mine, this I am, this is my self" (*etaṃ mama, eso 'ham asmi, eso me attā*). In this phrase, the notion "This is mine" represents the act of appropriation, a function of craving (*taṇhā*). The notions "This I am" and "This is my self" represent two types of identification, the former expressing conceit (*māna*), the latter views (*diṭṭhi*).[3]

Giving up craving is so difficult because craving is reinforced by views, which rationalize our identification with the aggregates and thus equip craving with a protective shield. The type of view that lies at the bottom of all affirmation of selfhood is called identity view (*sakkāyadiṭṭhi*). The suttas often mention twenty types of identity view, obtained by considering one's self to stand in any of four relations to each of the five aggregates: either as identical with it, as possessing it, as containing it, or as contained within it. The "uninstructed worldling" holds some kind of identity view; "the instructed noble disciple," having seen with wisdom the selfless nature of the aggregates, no longer regards the aggregates as a self or the belongings of a self. Adopting any of these views is a cause of anxiety and distress. It is also a leash that keeps us bound to the round of rebirths—see above, **Text I,2(3)** and **Text I,4(5)**.

All the defilements ultimately stem from ignorance, which thus lies at the bottom of all suffering and bondage. Ignorance weaves a net of three delusions around the aggregates. These delusions are the notions that the five aggregates are permanent, a source of true happiness, and a self. The wisdom needed to break the spell of these delusions is the insight into the five aggregates as impermanent (*anicca*), suffering (*dukkha*), and nonself (*anattā*). This is called the direct knowledge of the three characteristics of existence (*tilakkhaṇa*).

Some suttas seem to make insight into one or another of the three characteristics alone sufficient for reaching the goal. However, the three characteristics are closely interwoven, and thus the most common formula found in the Nikāyas builds upon their internal relationship. First enunciated in the Buddha's second discourse at Bārāṇasī—**Text IX,4(1)(c)**—the formula uses the characteristic of impermanence to reveal the characteristic of suffering, and both together to reveal the characteristic of nonself. The suttas take this indirect route to the characteristic of nonself because the selfless nature of things is so subtle that often it cannot be seen except when pointed to by the other two characteristics. When we recognize that the things we identify as our self are impermanent and bound up with suffering, we realize that they lack the essential marks of authentic selfhood and we thereby stop identifying with them.

The different expositions of the three characteristics all thus eventually converge on the eradication of clinging. They do so by showing, with regard to each aggregate, "This is not mine, this I am not, this is not my self." This makes the insight into nonself the culmination and consummation of the contemplation of the three characteristics. While the characteristic of nonself is usually approached through the other two characteristics, as in **Text IX,4(1)(d)**, it is sometimes disclosed directly. An example of the direct approach to nonself is **Text IX,4(1)(e)**, the discourse on "the lump of foam," which uses five memorable similes to reveal the empty nature of the five aggregates. According to the standard formula, insight into the five aggregates as impermanent, suffering, and nonself induces disenchantment (*nibbidā*), dispassion (*virāga*), and liberation (*vimutti*). One who attains liberation subsequently wins "the knowledge and vision of liberation," the assurance that the round of rebirths has indeed been stopped and nothing more remains to be done.

Another pattern that the suttas often apply to the five aggregates, and to the other groups of phenomena, is the triad of gratification, danger, and escape. **Texts VI,2(1)–(3)**, from the Aṅguttara Nikāya, apply this triad to the world as a whole. The Saṃyutta Nikāya applies the same scheme individually to the aggregates, sense bases, and elements. The pleasure and joy each aggregate, sense base, and element offers is its gratification; its impermanence, pervasion by suffering, and nature to change is its danger; and the abandoning of desire and lust for it is the escape from it.

IX,4(2) *The Six Sense Bases.* The Saḷāyatanasaṃyutta, the Connected Discourses on the Six Sense Bases (Saṃyutta Nikāya, chapter 35), contains over two hundred short suttas on the sense bases. The six internal and external sense bases provide a perspective on the totality of experience different from, but complementary to, the perspective provided by the aggregates. The six pairs of bases are the sense faculties and their corresponding objects, which support the arising of the respective type of consciousness. Because they mediate between consciousness and its objects, the internal sense bases are spoken of as the

The Six Internal and External Sense Bases

Internal sense bases	External sense bases	Types of consciousness arisen from the sense bases
eye	forms	eye-consciousness
ear	sounds	ear-consciousness
nose	smells	nose-consciousness
tongue	tastes	tongue-consciousness
body	tactile objects	body-consciousness
mind	mental phenomena	mind-consciousness

"bases for contact" (*phassāyatana*), "contact" (*phassa*) being the coming together of sense faculty, object, and consciousness.

What the first five sense bases and their objects signify is obvious enough, but the sixth pair, mind (*mano*) and phenomena (*dhammā*), presents some difficulty. If we treat the two terms as parallel to the other internal and external bases, we would understand the mind base to be the support for the arising of mind-consciousness (*manoviññāṇa*) and the phenomena base to be the objective sphere of mind-consciousness. On this interpretation, "mind" might be taken as the passive flow of consciousness from which active conceptual consciousness emerges, and "phenomena" as purely mental objects such as those apprehended by introspection, imagination, and reflection. The Abhidhamma and the Pāli commentaries, however, interpret the two terms differently. They hold that the mind base comprises all classes of consciousness, that is, they include within it all six types of consciousness. They also hold that all actual entities not comprised in the other sense bases constitute the phenomena base. The phenomena base, then, includes the other three mental aggregates—feeling, perception, and volitional formations—as well as types of subtle material form not implicated in experience through the physical senses. Whether this interpretation conforms to the meaning intended in the oldest Buddhist texts is an open question.

Text IX,4(2)(a) testifies that for Early Buddhism, liberation requires direct knowledge and full understanding of the internal and external sense bases and all the phenomena that arise from them. This seems to establish an apparent correspondence between Buddhism and empirical science, but the type of knowledge sought by the two disciplines differs. Whereas the scientist seeks impersonal, "objective" information, the Buddhist practitioner seeks direct insight into the nature of these phenomena as components of lived experience.

The Nikāyas suggest an interesting difference between the treatment given to the aggregates and the sense bases. Both serve as the soil where clinging takes root and grows, but while the aggregates are primarily the soil for *views about a self,* the sense bases are primarily the soil for *craving.* A necessary step in the conquest of craving is therefore restraint of the senses. Monks and nuns in particular must be vigilant in their encounters with desirable and undesirable sense objects. When one is negligent, experience through the senses invariably becomes a trigger for craving: lust for pleasant objects, aversion toward disagreeable objects (and a craving for pleasant escape routes), and a dull attachment to neutral objects.

In one of his earliest discourses popularly known as "The Fire Sermon"—**Text IX,4(2)(b)**—the Buddha declared that "all is burning." The "all" is just the six senses, their objects, the types of consciousness arisen from them, and the related contacts and feelings. The way to liberation is to see that this "all" is burning with the fires of defilements and suffering. The Saḷāyatanasaṃyutta repeatedly states that to dispel ignorance and generate true knowledge, we must contemplate all the sense bases and the feelings that arise through them as impermanent, suffering, and nonself. This, according to **Text IX,4(2)(c)**, is the direct way to the attainment of Nibbāna. An alternative route, commended by **Text IX,4(2)(d)**, is to see that the six senses are empty—empty of a self or of anything belonging to a self. Since consciousness arises via the six sense bases, it too is devoid of self—**Text IX, 4(2)(e).**

IX,4(3) *The Elements.* The elements are the subject of the Dhātusaṃyutta (Saṃyutta Nikāya, chapter 14). The word "elements" (*dhātu*) is applied to several quite disparate groups of phenomena, and thus the suttas in this chapter fall into separate clusters with little in common but their concern with entities called elements. The most important groups consist of eighteen, four, and six elements.

The *eighteen elements* are an elaboration of the twelve sense bases. They consist of the six sense faculties, the six sense objects, and the six types of sense consciousness. Since six types of consciousness have been extracted from the mind base, the mind element that remains must be a simpler type of cognitive event. The Nikāyas do not specify its precise function. The Abhidhamma identifies it with a type of consciousness that fulfills more rudimentary roles in the process of cognition than the more discriminative mind-consciousness element. **IX,4(3)(a)** contains a simple enumeration of the eighteen elements. Contemplation of these elements helps to dispel the notion that an abiding subject underlies the changing contents of experience. It shows how experience consists of different types of consciousness, each of which is conditioned, arisen in dependence on its own specific sense faculty and object. Thus to ascertain the composite, diversified, conditioned nature of experience dispels the illusion of unity and solidity that ordinarily obscures correct cognition.

The *four elements* are earth, water, heat, and air. These represent four "behavioral modes" of matter: solidity, fluidity, energy, and distension. The four are inseparably united in any unit of matter, from the smallest to the largest and most complex. The elements are not merely properties of the external world, however, but also of one's own body. Thus one must contemplate them in relation to one's body, as the Satipaṭṭhāna Sutta teaches (see **Text VIII, 8** §12). The three suttas combined in **Text IX,4(3)(b)** show that these elements can be viewed: as impermanent and conditioned; from the triple standpoint of gratification, danger, and escape; and by way of the four-truth pattern.

The *six elements* include the four physical elements, the space element, and the element of consciousness. **Text IX,4(3)(c)**, a long excerpt from MN 140, explains in detail how to contemplate the six elements in relation to the physical body, the external world, and conscious experience.

IX,4(4) *Dependent Origination.* Dependent origination (*paṭicca-samuppāda*) is so central to the Buddha's teaching that the Buddha said: "One who sees dependent origination sees the Dhamma, and one who sees the Dhamma sees dependent origination" (MN 28; I 190–91). The ulitmate purpose of the teaching on dependent origination is to reveal the conditions that sustain the round of rebirths and thereby to show what must be done to gain release from the round. To win deliverance is a matter of unraveling the causal pattern that underlies our bondage, and this process begins with understanding the causal pattern itself. It is dependent origination that defines this causal pattern.

An entire chapter of the Saṃyutta Nikāya, the Nidānasaṃyutta (chapter 12), is devoted to dependent origination. The doctrine is usually expounded as a sequence of twelve factors joined into a chain of eleven propositions; see **Text IX,4(4)(a)**. A Buddha discovers this chain of conditions; after his enlightenment, his mission is to explain it to the world. **Text IX,4(4)(b)** declares the sequence of conditions to be a fixed principle, a stable law, the nature of things. The series is expounded in two ways: by way of origination (called *anuloma* or forward order), and by way of cessation (called *paṭiloma* or reverse order). Sometimes the presentation proceeds from the first factor to the last; sometimes it begins at the end and traces the chain of conditions back to the first. Other suttas pick up the chain somewhere in the middle and work either backward to the end or forward to the front.

The Nikāyas themselves do not give any systematic explanation of dependent origination in the way one might expect a college textbook to do. Thus, for a clear explanation, we must rely on the commentaries and expository treatises that have come down from the Early Buddhist schools. Despite minor differences in details, these concur on the general meaning of this ancient formula, which might be briefly summarized as follows: Because of (1) ignorance (*avijjā*), lack of direct knowledge of the Four Noble Truths, we engage in wholesome and unwholesome activities of body, speech, and mind; these are (2) volitional formations (*saṅkhārā*), in other words, kamma. Volitional formations sustain consciousness from one life to the next and determine where it re-arises; in this way volitional formations condition (3) consciousness (*viññāṇa*). Along with consciousness, beginning from the moment of conception, comes (4) "name-and-form" (*nāmarūpa*), the sentient organism with its physical form (*rūpa*) and its sensitive and cognitive capacities (*nāma*). The sentient organism is equipped with (5) six sense bases (*saḷāyatana*), the five physical sense faculties and the mind as organ of cognition. The sense bases allow (6) contact (*phassa*) to occur between consciousness and its objects, and contact conditions (7) feeling (*vedanā*). Called into play by feeling, (8) craving (*taṇhā*) arises, and when craving intensifies it gives rise to (9) clinging (*upādāna*), tight attachment to the objects of desire through sensuality and wrong views. Impelled by our attachments, we again engage in volitional actions pregnant with (10) a new existence (*bhava*). At death this potential for new existence is actualized in a new life beginning with (11) birth (*jāti*) and ending in (12) aging-and-death (*jarāmaraṇa*).[4]

From the above, we can see that the commentarial interpretation treats the twelve factors as spread out over a span of three lives, with ignorance and volitional formations pertaining to the past, birth and aging-and-death to the future, and the intermediate factors to the present. The segment from consciousness through feeling is the resultant phase of the present, the phase resulting from past ignorance and kamma; the segment from craving through existence is the karmically creative phase of the present, leading to renewed existence in the future. But existence is distinguished into two phases: one, called kamma-existence (*kammabhava*), constitutes the active side of existence and belongs to the causal phase of the present life; the other, called rebirth-existence (*upapattibhava*), constitutes the passive side of existence and belongs to the resultant phase of the future life. The twelve factors are also distributed into three "rounds": the round of defilements (*kilesavaṭṭa*) includes ignorance, craving, and clinging; the round of action (*kammavaṭṭa*) includes volitional formations and kamma-existence; and all the other factors belong to the round of results (*vipākavaṭṭa*). Defilements give rise to defiled actions, actions bring forth results, and results serve as the soil for more defilements. In this way the round of rebirths revolves without discernible beginning.

This method of dividing up the factors should not be misconstrued to mean that the past, present, and future factors are mutually exclusive. The distribution into three lives is only an expository device which, for the sake of concision, has to resort to some degree of abstraction. As many suttas in the Nidānasaṃyutta show, groups of factors separated in the formula are inevitably interwoven in their dynamic operation. Whenever there is ignorance, craving and clinging invariably accompany it; and whenever there is craving and clinging, ignorance stands behind them. The formula demonstrates how rebirth can take place without the presence of a substantial self that maintains its identity as it transmigrates from one life to the next. Without a self to hold the sequence together, what connects one life to the next is nothing other than the principle of conditionality. Conditions in one existence initiate the arising of the conditioned phenomena in the next existence; these serve as conditions for still other phenomena, which condition still other phenomena, and so on indefinitely into the future.

The whole process ends only when its underlying springs—ignorance, craving, and clinging—are extirpated by wisdom.

Dependent origination is not a mere theory but a teaching that should be directly known by personal experience, a point clearly made by **Text IX,4(4)(c)**. This sutta instructs the disciple to understand each factor by way of the four-truth pattern: one should understand the factor itself, its origin, its cessation, and the way to its cessation. First one understands this pattern in relation to one's personal experience. Then, on this basis, one infers that all those who correctly understood these things in the past understood them in exactly the same way; then that all those who will correctly understand these things in the future will understand them in exactly the same way. In this way, dependent origination acquires a timeless and universal significance.

Several suttas hold up dependent origination as a "teaching by the middle" (*majjhena tathāgato dhammaṃ deseti*). It is a "teaching by the middle" because it transcends two extreme views that polarize philosophical reflection on the human condition. One extreme, the metaphysical thesis of eternalism (*sassatavāda*), asserts that the core of human identity is an indestructible and eternal self, whether individual or universal. It also asserts that the world is created and maintained by a permanent entity, a God or some other metaphysical reality. The other extreme, annihilationism (*ucchedavāda*), holds that at death the person is utterly annihilated. There is no spiritual dimension to human existence and thus no personal survival of any sort. For the Buddha, both extremes pose insuperable problems. Eternalism encourages an obstinate clinging to the five aggregates, which are really impermanent and devoid of a substantial self; annihilationism threatens to undermine ethics and to make suffering the product of chance.

Dependent origination offers a radically different perspective that transcends the two extremes. It shows that individual existence is constituted by a current of conditioned phenomena devoid of a metaphysical self yet continuing on from birth to birth as long as the causes that sustain it remain effective. Dependent origination thereby offers a cogent explanation of the problem of suffering that on the one hand avoids the philosophical dilemmas posed by the hypothesis of a permanent self, and on the other avoids the dangers of ethical anarchy to which annihilationism eventually leads. As long as ignorance and craving remain, the process of rebirth continues; kamma yields its pleasant and painful fruit, and the great mass of suffering accumulates. When ignorance and craving are destroyed, the inner mechanism of karmic causation is deactivated, and one reaches the end of suffering in saṃsāra. Perhaps the most elegant exposition of dependent origination as the "middle teaching" is the famous Kaccānagotta Sutta, included here as **Text IX,4(4)(d)**.

Though the twelve-factor formula is the most familiar version of the doctrine of dependent origination, the Nidānasaṃyutta introduces a number of little-known variants that help to illuminate the standard version. One such variant, **Text IX,4(4)(e)**, speaks about the conditions for "the continuance of consciousness" (*viññāṇassa ṭhitiyā*), in other words, how consciousness passes on to a new existence. The causes are said to be the underlying tendencies, namely, ignorance and craving, and "what one intends and plans," namely, the volitional formations. Once consciousness becomes established, the production of a new existence begins; thus we here proceed directly from consciousness (the usual third factor) to existence (the usual tenth factor). **Text IX,4(4)(f)** says that from the six internal and external sense bases (the former being the usual fifth factor), consciousness (the third factor) arises, followed by contact, feeling, craving, and all the rest. These variants make it plain that the sequence of factors should not be regarded as a linear causal process in which each preceding factor gives rise to its successor through the simple exercise of efficient causality. Far from being linear, the relationship among the factors is always complex, involving several interwoven strands of conditionality.

IX,4(5) *The Four Noble Truths.* As we have seen in both the "gradual path to liberation" and in the "contemplation of phenomena" section of the Discourse on the Establishment of Mindfulness, the path to liberation culminates in the realization of the Four Noble Truths: see **Text VII,4** §25 and **Text VIII,8** §44. These were the truths that the Buddha discovered on the night of his enlightenment and enunciated in his first discourse: see **Text II,3(2)** §42 and **Text II,5**. The First Discourse is tucked away almost inconspicuously in the Saccasaṃyutta (Saṃyutta Nikāya, chapter 56), the Connected Discourses on the Truths, a chapter replete with many other pithy and thought-provoking suttas.

To highlight the wide-ranging significance of the Four Noble Truths, the Saccasaṃyutta casts them against a universal background. According to **Text IX,4(5)(a)**, not only the Buddha Gotama, but all the Buddhas past, present, and future awaken to these same four truths. These four truths, says **Text IX,4(5)(b)**, are truths because they are "actual, unerring, not otherwise." According to **Text IX,4(5)(c)**, the things the Buddha teaches are as few as a handful of leaves in the forest, and what he teaches are just these Four Noble Truths, taught precisely because they lead to enlightenment and Nibbāna.

Sentient beings roam and wander in saṃsāra because they have not understood and penetrated the Four Noble Truths—**Text IX,4(5)(d)**. As the chain of dependent origination shows, what lies at the base of the causal genesis of suffering is ignorance (*avijjā*), and ignorance is unawareness of the Four Noble Truths. Thus those who fail to understand the four truths generate volitional formations and fall down the precipice of birth, aging, and death—**Text IX,4(5)(e)**.

The antidote to ignorance is knowledge (*vijjā*), which accordingly is defined as knowledge of the Four Noble Truths. The first penetration of the Four Noble Truths occurs with the attainment of stream-entry, called the breakthrough to the Dhamma (*dhammābhisamaya*). To make this breakthrough is by no means easy, but without doing so it is impossible to put an end to suffering—**Text IX,4(5)(f)**. Hence the Buddha again and again urges his disciples to "make an extraordinary effort" to achieve the breakthrough to the truths.

Once the disciple makes the breakthrough and sees the Four Noble Truths, more work still lies ahead, for each truth imposes a task that must be fulfilled in order to win the final fruit. The truth of suffering, which ultimately consists of the five aggregates, must be fully understood (*pariññeyya*). The truth of its origin, craving, must be abandoned (*pahātabba*). The truth of cessation, Nibbāna, must be realized (*sacchikātabba*). And the truth of the way, the Noble Eightfold Path, must be developed (*bhāvetabba*). Developing the path brings to completion all four tasks, at which point one reaches the destruction of the taints. This process begins with penetration of the same Four Noble Truths, and thus **Text IX,4(5)(g)** says that the destruction of the taints is for those who know and see the Four Noble Truths.

IX,5 *The Goal of Wisdom*. The Four Noble Truths not only serve as the objective domain of wisdom but also define its purpose, which is enshrined in the third noble truth, the cessation of suffering. The cessation of suffering is *Nibbāna*, and thus the goal of wisdom, the end toward which the cultivation of wisdom moves, is the attainment of

Nibbāna. But what exactly is meant by Nibbāna? The suttas explain Nibbāna in a number of ways. Some, such as **Text IX,5(1),** define Nibbāna simply as the destruction of lust, hatred, and delusion. Others, such as the series comprised in **Text IX,5(2)**, employ metaphors and images to convey a more concrete idea of the ultimate goal. Nibbāna is still the destruction of lust, hatred, and delusion, but as such it is, among other things, peaceful, deathless, sublime, wonderful, and amazing. Such descriptions indicate that Nibbāna is a state of supreme happiness, peace, and freedom to be experienced in this present life.

A few suttas, most notably a pair in the Udāna—included here as **Texts IX,5(3)** and **IX,5(4)**—suggest that Nibbāna is not simply the destruction of defilements and an exalted feeling of psychological well-being. They speak of Nibbāna almost as if it were a transcendent state or dimension of being. **Text IX,5(3)** refers to Nibbāna as a "base" (*āyatana*) beyond the world of common experience where none of the physical elements or even the subtle formless dimensions of experience are present; it is a state completely quiescent, without arising, perishing, or change. **Text IX,5(4)** calls it the state that is "unborn, unmade, unbecome, [and] unconditioned" (*ajātaṃ, akataṃ, abhūtaṃ, asaṅkhataṃ*), the existence of which makes possible deliverance from all that is born, made, come-to-be, and conditioned.

How are we to correlate these two perspectives on Nibbāna found in the Nikāyas, one treating it as an experiential state of inward purity and sublime bliss, the other as an unconditioned state transcending the empirical world? Commentators, both Buddhists and outsiders, have tried to connect these two aspects of Nibbāna in different ways. Their interpretations generally reflect the proclivity of the interpreter as much as they do the texts themselves. The way that seems most faithful to both aspects of Nibbāna delineated in the texts is to regard the attainment of Nibbāna as a state of freedom and happiness attained by realizing, with profound wisdom, the unconditioned and transcendent element, the state that is intrinsically tranquil and forever beyond suffering. The penetration of this element brings the destruction of defilements, culminating in complete purification of mind. Such purification is accompanied by the experience of perfect peace and happiness in this present life. With the breakup of the body at physical death, it brings irreversible release from the beginningless round of rebirths.

The suttas speak of two "elements of Nibbāna," the Nibbāna element with residue remaining (*sa-upādisesa-nibbānadhātu*) and the Nibbāna element without residue remaining (*anupādisesa-nibbānadhātu*). **Text IX,5(5)** explains the Nibbāna element with residue remaining to be the destruction of lust, hatred, and delusion attained by an arahant while still alive. The "residue" that remains is the composite of the five aggregates that was brought into being by the ignorance and craving of the past life and that must continue on until the end of the lifespan. As to the Nibbāna element without residue remaining, the same text says only that when the arahant passes away, all that is felt, not being delighted in, will become cool right here. Since there is no more clinging to the five aggregates, and no more craving for fresh experience through a new set of aggregates, the occurrence of the aggregates comes to an end and cannot continue. The process of the five aggregates is "extinguished" (the literal meaning of Nibbāna).[5]

The Buddha says nothing at all, however, in terms either of existence or nonexistence, about the condition of the arahant after death. It might seem logical to suppose that since the five aggregates that constitute experience completely cease with the attainment of the Nibbāna element without residue, this element must itself be a state of complete nonexistence, a state of nothingness. Yet no text in the Nikāyas ever states this. To the contrary, the Nikāyas consistently refer to Nibbāna by terms that refer to actualities. It is an element (*dhātu*), a base (*āyatana*), a reality (*dhamma*), a state (*pada*), and so on. However, though so designated, it is qualified in ways that indicate this state ultimately lies beyond all familiar categories and concepts.

In **Text IX,5(6)**, the wanderer Vacchagotta asks the Buddha whether the Tathāgata—here signifying one who has attained the supreme goal—is reborn (*upapajjati*) or not after death. The Buddha refuses to concede any of the four alternatives. To say that the Tathāgata is reborn, is not reborn, both is and is not reborn, neither is nor is not reborn—none of these is acceptable, for all accept the term *Tathāgata* as indicative of a real being, while from an internal point of view a Tathāgata has given up all clinging to notions of a real being. The Buddha illustrates this point with the simile of an extinguished fire. Just as a fire that has been extinguished cannot be said to have gone anywhere but must simply be said to have "gone out," so with the breakup of the body the Tathāgata does not go anywhere but has simply "gone out." The past participle *nibbuta*, used to describe a fire that has been extinguished, is related to the noun *nibbāna*, which literally means "extinguishing."[6]

Yet, if this simile suggests a Buddhist version of the "annihilationist" view of the arahant's fate after his demise, this impression would rest on a misunderstanding, on a wrong perception of the arahant as a "self" or "person" that is annihilated. Our problem in understanding the state of the Tathāgata after death is compounded by our difficulty in understanding the state of the Tathāgata even while alive. The simile of the great ocean underscores this difficulty. Since the Tathāgata no longer identifies with the five aggregates that constitute individual identity, he cannot be reckoned in terms of them, whether individually or collectively. Freed from reckoning in terms of the five aggregates, the Tathāgata transcends our understanding. Like the great ocean, he is "deep, immeasurable, [and] hard to fathom."[7]

IX. Shining the Light of Wisdom

1. Images of Wisdom

(1) Wisdom as a Light

"There are, O monks, these four lights. What four? The light of the moon, the light of the sun, the light of fire, and the light of wisdom. Of these four lights, the light of wisdom is supreme."

(AN 4:143; II 139)

(2) Wisdom as a Knife

11. "Sisters, suppose a skilled butcher or his apprentice were to kill a cow and carve it up with a sharp butcher's knife. Without damaging the inner mass of flesh and without damaging the outer hide, he would cut, sever, and carve away the inner tendons, sinews, and ligaments with the sharp butcher's knife. Then having cut, severed, and carved all this away, he would remove the outer hide and cover the cow again with that same hide. Would he be speaking rightly if he were to say: 'This cow is joined to this hide just as it was before'?"

"No, venerable sir. Why is that? Because if that skilled butcher or his apprentice were to kill a cow … and cut, sever, and carve all that away, even though he covers the cow again with that same hide and says: 'This cow is joined to this hide just as it was before,' that cow would still be disjoined from that hide."

12. "Sisters, I have given this simile in order to convey a meaning. This is the meaning: 'The inner mass of flesh' is a term for the six internal bases. 'The outer hide' is a term for the six external bases. 'The inner tendons, sinews, and ligaments' is a term for delight and lust. 'The sharp butcher's knife' is a term for noble wisdom—the noble wisdom that cuts, severs, and carves away the inner defilements, fetters, and bonds."

(from MN 146: *Nandakovāda Sutta*; III 274–75)

2. The Conditions for Wisdom

"There are, O monks, these eight causes and conditions for obtaining the wisdom fundamental to the spiritual life when it has not been obtained and for bringing about the increase, maturation, and fulfillment by development of the wisdom that has already been obtained. What eight?

(1) "Here, a monk lives in dependence on the Teacher or on a certain fellow monk in the position of a teacher, and he has set up toward him a keen sense of shame and moral dread and regards him with affection and respect. This is the first cause and condition for obtaining the wisdom fundamental to the spiritual life....

(2) "As he is living in dependence on such teachers, he approaches them from time to time and inquires: 'How is this, venerable sir? What is the meaning of this?' Those venerable ones then disclose to him what has not been disclosed, clear up what is obscure, and dispel his perplexity about many perplexing points. This is the second cause and condition for obtaining the wisdom fundamental to the spiritual life....

(3) "Having learned the Dhamma, he dwells withdrawn by way of two kinds of withdrawal: withdrawal of body and withdrawal of mind. This is the third cause and condition for obtaining the wisdom fundamental to the spiritual life....

(4) "He is virtuous, restrained by the restraint of the Pātimokkha,[8] perfect in conduct and resort, seeing danger in the slightest faults. Having undertaken the training rules, he trains himself in them. This is the fourth cause and condition for obtaining the wisdom fundamental to the spiritual life....

(5) "He has learned much, remembers what he has learned, and consolidates what he has learned. Such teachings that are good in the beginning, good in the middle, and good in the end, with the right meaning and phrasing, and which affirm a spiritual life that is perfectly complete and pure—such teachings as these he has learned much of, memorized, recited verbally, investigated with the mind, and penetrated well by view. This is the fifth cause and condition for obtaining the wisdom fundamental to the spiritual life....

(6) "He is energetic; he lives with energy set upon the abandoning of everything unwholesome and the acquiring of everything wholesome; he is steadfast and strong in his effort, not shirking his task in regard

to wholesome qualities. This is the sixth cause and condition for obtaining the wisdom fundamental to the spiritual life....

(7) "When he is in the midst of the Saṅgha, he does not engage in rambling and pointless talk. Either he himself speaks on the Dhamma or he requests others to do so, or he does not shun noble silence. This is the seventh cause and condition for obtaining the wisdom fundamental to the spiritual life....

(8) "He dwells contemplating rise and fall in the five aggregates subject to clinging thus: 'Such is form, such its arising, such its passing away; such is feeling ... such is perception ... such are volitional formations ... such is consciousness, such its arising, such its passing away.' This is the eighth cause and condition for obtaining the wisdom fundamental to the spiritual life....

"For these eight reasons his fellow monks esteem him as one who truly knows and sees, and these qualities lead to affection, esteem, concord, and unity.

"These, monks, are the eight causes and conditions for obtaining the wisdom fundamental to the spiritual life when it has not been obtained and for bringing about the increase, maturation, and fulfillment by development of the wisdom that has already been obtained."

(AN 8:2, abridged; IV 151–55)

3. A Discourse on Right View

1. Thus have I heard. On one occasion the Blessed One was living at Sāvatthī in Jeta's Grove, Anāthapiṇḍika's Park. There the Venerable Sāriputta addressed the monks thus: "Friends, monks."—"Friend," they replied. The Venerable Sāriputta said this:

2. "'One of right view, one of right view,' is said, friends. In what way is a noble disciple one of right view, whose view is straight, who has confirmed confidence in the Dhamma and has arrived at this true Dhamma?"[9]

"Indeed, friend, we would come from far away to learn from the Venerable Sāriputta the meaning of this statement. It would be good if the Venerable Sāriputta would explain the meaning of this statement. Having heard it from him, the monks will remember it."

"Then, friends, listen and attend closely to what I shall say."

"Yes, friend," the monks replied. The Venerable Sāriputta said this:

[the wholesome and the unwholesome]

3. "When, friends, a noble disciple understands the unwholesome and the root of the unwholesome, the wholesome and the root of the wholesome, in that way he is one of right view, whose view is straight, who has confirmed confidence in the Dhamma and has arrived at this true Dhamma.

4. "And what, friends, is the unwholesome, what is the root of the unwholesome, what is the wholesome, what is the root of the wholesome? The destruction of life is unwholesome; taking what is not given is unwholesome; sexual misconduct is unwholesome; false speech is unwholesome; malicious speech is unwholesome; harsh speech is unwholesome; idle chatter is unwholesome; covetousness is unwholesome; ill will is unwholesome; wrong view is unwholesome. This is called the unwholesome.[10]

5. "And what is the root of the unwholesome? Greed is a root of the unwholesome; hatred is a root of the unwholesome; delusion is a root of the unwholesome. This is called the root of the unwholesome.

6. "And what is the wholesome? Abstention from destruction of life is wholesome; abstention from taking what is not given is wholesome; abstention from sexual misconduct is wholesome; abstention from false speech is wholesome; abstention from malicious speech is wholesome; abstention from harsh speech is wholesome; abstention from idle chatter is wholesome; uncovetousness is wholesome; non–ill will is wholesome; right view is wholesome. This is called the wholesome.

7. "And what is the root of the wholesome? Nongreed is a root of the wholesome; nonhatred is a root of the wholesome; nondelusion is a root of the wholesome. This is called the root of the wholesome.

8. "When a noble disciple has thus understood the unwholesome and the root of the unwholesome, the wholesome and the root of the wholesome,[11] he entirely abandons the underlying tendency to lust, he abolishes the underlying tendency to aversion, he extirpates the underlying tendency to the view and conceit 'I am,' and by abandoning ignorance and arousing true knowledge he here and now makes an end of suffering.[12] In that way too a noble disciple is one of right view, whose view is straight, who has confirmed confidence in the Dhamma and has arrived at this true Dhamma."

[nutriment]

9. Saying, "Good, friend," the monks delighted and rejoiced in the Venerable Sāriputta's words. Then they asked him a further question: "But, friend, might there be another way in which a noble disciple is one of right view ... and has arrived at this true Dhamma?"—"There might be, friends.

10. "When, friends, a noble disciple understands nutriment, the origin of nutriment, the cessation of nutriment, and the way leading to the cessation of nutriment, in that way he is one of right view ... and has arrived at this true Dhamma.

11. "And what is nutriment, what is the origin of nutriment, what is the cessation of nutriment, what is the way leading to the cessation of nutriment? There are four kinds of nutriment for the sustenance of beings that already have come to be and for the support of those about to come to be. What four? They are: physical food as nutriment, gross or subtle; contact as the second; mental volition as the third; and consciousness as the fourth.[13] With the arising of craving there is the arising of nutriment. With the cessation of craving there is the cessation of nutriment. The way leading to the cessation of nutriment is just this Noble Eightfold Path; that is, right view, right intention, right speech, right action, right livelihood, right effort, right mindfulness, and right concentration.

12. "When a noble disciple has thus understood nutriment, the origin of nutriment, the cessation of nutriment, and the way leading to the cessation of nutriment, he entirely abandons the underlying tendency to lust ... he here and now makes an end of suffering. In that way too a noble disciple is one of right view, whose view is straight, who has confirmed confidence in the Dhamma and has arrived at this true Dhamma."

[the Four Noble Truths]

13. Saying, "Good, friend," the monks delighted and rejoiced in the Venerable Sāriputta's words. Then they asked him a further question: "But, friend, might there be another way in which a noble disciple is one of right view ... and has arrived at this true Dhamma?"—"There might be, friends.

14. "When, friends, a noble disciple understands suffering, the origin of suffering, the cessation of suffering, and the way leading to the

cessation of suffering, in that way he is one of right view ... and has arrived at this true Dhamma.

15. "And what is suffering, what is the origin of suffering, what is the cessation of suffering, what is the way leading to the cessation of suffering? Birth is suffering; aging is suffering; illness is suffering; death is suffering; sorrow, lamentation, pain, dejection, and despair are suffering; not to get what one wants is suffering; in brief, the five aggregates subject to clinging are suffering. This is called suffering.

16. "And what is the origin of suffering? It is this craving that leads to renewed existence, accompanied by delight and lust, seeking delight here and there; that is, craving for sensual pleasures, craving for existence, craving for extermination. This is called the origin of suffering.

17. "And what is the cessation of suffering? It is the remainderless fading away and cessation of that same craving, the giving up and relinquishing of it, freedom from it, nonattachment.

18. "And what is the way leading to the cessation of suffering? It is just this Noble Eightfold Path; that is, right view ... right concentration. This is called the way leading to the cessation of suffering.

19. "When a noble disciple has thus understood suffering, the origin of suffering, the cessation of suffering, and the way leading to the cessation of suffering ... he here and now makes an end of suffering. In that way too a noble disciple is one of right view ... and has arrived at this true Dhamma."

[aging and death]

20. Saying, "Good, friend," the monks delighted and rejoiced in the Venerable Sāriputta's words. Then they asked him a further question: "But, friend, might there be another way in which a noble disciple is one of right view ... and has arrived at this true Dhamma?"—"There might be, friends.

21. "When, friends, a noble disciple understands aging and death, the origin of aging and death, the cessation of aging and death, and the way leading to the cessation of aging and death, in that way he is one of right view ... and has arrived at this true Dhamma.[14]

22. "And what is aging and death, what is the origin of aging and death, what is the cessation of aging and death, what is the way leading to the cessation of aging and death? The aging of beings in the various orders of beings, their old age, brokenness of teeth, grayness of

hair, wrinkling of skin, decline of life, weakness of faculties—this is called aging. The passing of beings out of the various orders of beings, their passing away, breakup, disappearance, dying, completion of time, the breakup of the aggregates, laying down of the body—this is called death. So this aging and this death are what is called aging and death. With the arising of birth there is the arising of aging and death. With the cessation of birth there is the cessation of aging and death. The way leading to the cessation of aging and death is just this Noble Eightfold Path; that is, right view ... right concentration.

23. "When a noble disciple has thus understood aging and death, the origin of aging and death, the cessation of aging and death, and the way leading to the cessation of aging and death ... he here and now makes an end of suffering. In that way too a noble disciple is one of right view ... and has arrived at this true Dhamma."

[birth]

24. Saying, "Good, friend," the monks delighted and rejoiced in the Venerable Sāriputta's words. Then they asked him a further question: "But, friend, might there be another way in which a noble disciple is one of right view ... and has arrived at this true Dhamma?"—"There might be, friends.

25. "When, friends, a noble disciple understands birth, the origin of birth, the cessation of birth, and the way leading to the cessation of birth, in that way he is one of right view ... and has arrived at this true Dhamma.

26. "And what is birth, what is the origin of birth, what is the cessation of birth, what is the way leading to the cessation of birth? The birth of beings in the various orders of beings, their coming to birth, precipitation [in a womb], generation, manifestation of the aggregates, obtaining the bases for contact—this is called birth. With the arising of existence there is the arising of birth. With the cessation of existence there is the cessation of birth. The way leading to the cessation of birth is just this Noble Eightfold Path; that is, right view ... right concentration.

27. "When a noble disciple has thus understood birth, the origin of birth, the cessation of birth, and the way leading to the cessation of birth ... he here and now makes an end of suffering. In that way too a noble disciple is one of right view ... and has arrived at this true Dhamma."

[existence]

28. Saying, "Good, friend," the monks delighted and rejoiced in the Venerable Sāriputta's words. Then they asked him a further question: "But, friend, might there be another way in which a noble disciple is one of right view ... and has arrived at this true Dhamma?"—"There might be, friends.

29. "When, friends, a noble disciple understands existence, the origin of existence, the cessation of existence, and the way leading to the cessation of existence, in that way he is one of right view ... and has arrived at this true Dhamma.

30. "And what is existence, what is the origin of existence, what is the cessation of existence, what is the way leading to the cessation of existence? There are these three kinds of existence: sense-sphere existence, form-sphere existence, and formless-sphere existence.[15] With the arising of clinging there is the arising of existence. With the cessation of clinging there is the cessation of existence. The way leading to the cessation of existence is just this Noble Eightfold Path; that is, right view ... right concentration.

31. "When a noble disciple has thus understood existence, the origin of existence, the cessation of existence, and the way leading to the cessation of existence ... he here and now makes an end of suffering. In that way too a noble disciple is one of right view ... and has arrived at this true Dhamma."

[clinging]

32. Saying, "Good, friend," the monks delighted and rejoiced in the Venerable Sāriputta's words. Then they asked him a further question: "But, friend, might there be another way in which a noble disciple is one of right view ... and has arrived at this true Dhamma?"—"There might be, friends.

33. "When, friends, a noble disciple understands clinging, the origin of clinging, the cessation of clinging, and the way leading to the cessation of clinging, in that way he is one of right view ... and has arrived at this true Dhamma.

34. "And what is clinging, what is the origin of clinging, what is the cessation of clinging, what is the way leading to the cessation of clinging? There are these four kinds of clinging: clinging to sensual pleasures, clinging to views, clinging to rules and observances, and clinging

to a doctrine of self.[16] With the arising of craving there is the arising of clinging. With the cessation of craving there is the cessation of clinging. The way leading to the cessation of clinging is just this Noble Eightfold Path; that is, right view ... right concentration.

35. "When a noble disciple has thus understood clinging, the origin of clinging, the cessation of clinging, and the way leading to the cessation of clinging ... he here and now makes an end of suffering. In that way too a noble disciple is one of right view ... and has arrived at this true Dhamma."

[craving]

36. Saying, "Good, friend," the monks delighted and rejoiced in the Venerable Sāriputta's words. Then they asked him a further question: "But, friend, might there be another way in which a noble disciple is one of right view ... and has arrived at this true Dhamma?"—"There might be, friends.

37. "When, friends, a noble disciple understands craving, the origin of craving, the cessation of craving, and the way leading to the cessation of craving, in that way he is one of right view ... and has arrived at this true Dhamma.

38. "And what is craving, what is the origin of craving, what is the cessation of craving, what is the way leading to the cessation of craving? There are these six classes of craving: craving for forms, craving for sounds, craving for odors, craving for flavors, craving for tactile objects, craving for mental phenomena.[17] With the arising of feeling there is the arising of craving. With the cessation of feeling there is the cessation of craving. The way leading to the cessation of craving is just this Noble Eightfold Path; that is, right view ... right concentration.

39. "When a noble disciple has thus understood craving, the origin of craving, the cessation of craving, and the way leading to the cessation of craving ... he here and now makes an end of suffering. In that way too a noble disciple is one of right view ... and has arrived at this true Dhamma."

[feeling]

40. Saying, "Good, friend," the monks delighted and rejoiced in the Venerable Sāriputta's words. Then they asked him a further question: "But, friend, might there be another way in which a noble disciple is

one of right view ... and has arrived at this true Dhamma?"—"There might be, friends.

41. "When, friends, a noble disciple understands feeling, the origin of feeling, the cessation of feeling, and the way leading to the cessation of feeling, in that way he is one of right view ... and has arrived at this true Dhamma.

42. "And what is feeling, what is the origin of feeling, what is the cessation of feeling, what is the way leading to the cessation of feeling? There are these six classes of feeling: feeling born of eye-contact, feeling born of ear-contact, feeling born of nose-contact, feeling born of tongue-contact, feeling born of body-contact, feeling born of mind-contact. With the arising of contact there is the arising of feeling. With the cessation of contact there is the cessation of feeling. The way leading to the cessation of feeling is just this Noble Eightfold Path; that is, right view ... right concentration.

43. "When a noble disciple has thus understood feeling, the origin of feeling, the cessation of feeling, and the way leading to the cessation of feeling ... he here and now makes an end of suffering. In that way too a noble disciple is one of right view ... and has arrived at this true Dhamma."

[contact]

44. Saying, "Good, friend," the monks delighted and rejoiced in the Venerable Sāriputta's words. Then they asked him a further question: "But, friend, might there be another way in which a noble disciple is one of right view ... and has arrived at this true Dhamma?"—"There might be, friends.

45. "When, friends, a noble disciple understands contact, the origin of contact, the cessation of contact, and the way leading to the cessation of contact, in that way he is one of right view ... and has arrived at this true Dhamma.

46. "And what is contact, what is the origin of contact, what is the cessation of contact, what is the way leading to the cessation of contact? There are these six classes of contact: eye-contact, ear-contact, nose-contact, tongue-contact, body-contact, mind-contact.[18] With the arising of the six sense bases there is the arising of contact. With the cessation of the six sense bases there is the cessation of contact. The way leading to the cessation of contact is just this Noble Eightfold Path; that is, right view ... right concentration.

47. "When a noble disciple has thus understood contact, the origin of contact, the cessation of contact, and the way leading to the cessation of contact ... he here and now makes an end of suffering. In that way too a noble disciple is one of right view ... and has arrived at this true Dhamma."

[the six sense bases]

48. Saying, "Good, friend," the monks delighted and rejoiced in the Venerable Sāriputta's words. Then they asked him a further question: "But, friend, might there be another way in which a noble disciple is one of right view ... and has arrived at this true Dhamma?"—"There might be, friends.

49. "When, friends, a noble disciple understands the six sense bases, the origin of the six sense bases, the cessation of the six sense bases, and the way leading to the cessation of the six sense bases, in that way he is one of right view ... and has arrived at this true Dhamma.

50. "And what are the six sense bases, what is the origin of the six sense bases, what is the cessation of the six sense bases, what is the way leading to the cessation of the six sense bases? There are these six sense bases: the eye-base, the ear-base, the nose-base, the tongue-base, the body-base, the mind-base. With the arising of name-and-form there is the arising of the six sense bases. With the cessation of name-and-form there is the cessation of the six sense bases. The way leading to the cessation of the six sense bases is just this Noble Eightfold Path; that is, right view ... right concentration.

51. "When a noble disciple has thus understood the six sense bases, the origin of the six sense bases, the cessation of the six sense bases, and the way leading to the cessation of the six sense bases ... he here and now makes an end of suffering. In that way too a noble disciple is one of right view ... and has arrived at this true Dhamma."

[name-and-form]

52. Saying, "Good, friend," the monks delighted and rejoiced in the Venerable Sāriputta's words. Then they asked him a further question: "But, friend, might there be another way in which a noble disciple is one of right view ... and has arrived at this true Dhamma?"—"There might be, friends.

53. "When, friends, a noble disciple understands name-and-form, the origin of name-and-form, the cessation of name-and-form, and the

way leading to the cessation of name-and-form, in that way he is one of right view ... and has arrived at this true Dhamma.

54. "And what is name-and-form, what is the origin of name-and-form, what is the cessation of name-and-form, what is the way leading to the cessation of name-and-form? Feeling, perception, volition, contact, and attention—these are called name. The four great elements and the form derived from the four great elements—these are called form. So this name and this form are what is called name-and-form.[19] With the arising of consciousness there is the arising of name-and-form. With the cessation of consciousness there is the cessation of name-and-form. The way leading to the cessation of name-and-form is just this Noble Eightfold Path; that is, right view ... right concentration.

55. "When a noble disciple has thus understood name-and-form, the origin of name-and-form, the cessation of name-and-form, and the way leading to the cessation of name-and-form ... he here and now makes an end of suffering. In that way too a noble disciple is one of right view ... and has arrived at this true Dhamma."

[consciousness]

56. Saying, "Good, friend," the monks delighted and rejoiced in the Venerable Sāriputta's words. Then they asked him a further question: "But, friend, might there be another way in which a noble disciple is one of right view ... and has arrived at this true Dhamma?"—"There might be, friends.

57. "When, friends, a noble disciple understands consciousness, the origin of consciousness, the cessation of consciousness, and the way leading to the cessation of consciousness, in that way he is one of right view ... and has arrived at this true Dhamma.

58. "And what is consciousness, what is the origin of consciousness, what is the cessation of consciousness, what is the way leading to the cessation of consciousness? There are these six classes of consciousness: eye-consciousness, ear-consciousness, nose-consciousness, tongue-consciousness, body-consciousness, mind-consciousness.[20] With the arising of volitional formations there is the arising of consciousness. With the cessation of volitional formations there is the cessation of consciousness. The way leading to the cessation of consciousness is just this Noble Eightfold Path; that is, right view ... right concentration.

59. "When a noble disciple has thus understood consciousness, the origin of consciousness, the cessation of consciousness, and the way leading to the cessation of consciousness ... he here and now makes an end of suffering. In that way too a noble disciple is one of right view ... and has arrived at this true Dhamma."

[volitional formations]

60. Saying, "Good, friend," the monks delighted and rejoiced in the Venerable Sāriputta's words. Then they asked him a further question: "But, friend, might there be another way in which a noble disciple is one of right view ... and has arrived at this true Dhamma?"—"There might be, friends.

61. "When, friends, a noble disciple understands volitional formations, the origin of volitional formations, the cessation of volitional formations, and the way leading to the cessation of volitional formations, in that way he is one of right view ... and has arrived at this true Dhamma.

62. "And what are volitional formations, what is the origin of volitional formations, what is the cessation of volitional formations, what is the way leading to the cessation of volitional formations? There are these three kinds of volitional formations: the bodily volitional formation, the verbal volitional formation, the mental volitional formation.[21] With the arising of ignorance there is the arising of volitional formations. With the cessation of ignorance there is the cessation of volitional formations. The way leading to the cessation of volitional formations is just this Noble Eightfold Path; that is, right view ... right concentration.

63. "When a noble disciple has thus understood volitional formations, the origin of volitional formations, the cessation of volitional formations, and the way leading to the cessation of volitional formations ... he here and now makes an end of suffering. In that way too a noble disciple is one of right view ... and has arrived at this true Dhamma."

[ignorance]

64. Saying, "Good, friend," the monks delighted and rejoiced in the Venerable Sāriputta's words. Then they asked him a further question: "But, friend, might there be another way in which a noble disciple is one of right view ... and has arrived at this true Dhamma?"—"There might be, friends.

65. "When, friends, a noble disciple understands ignorance, the origin of ignorance, the cessation of ignorance, and the way leading to the cessation of ignorance, in that way he is one of right view ... and has arrived at this true Dhamma.

66. "And what is ignorance, what is the origin of ignorance, what is the cessation of ignorance, what is the way leading to the cessation of ignorance? Not knowing about suffering, not knowing about the origin of suffering, not knowing about the cessation of suffering, not knowing about the way leading to the cessation of suffering—this is called ignorance. With the arising of the taints there is the arising of ignorance. With the cessation of the taints there is the cessation of ignorance. The way leading to the cessation of ignorance is just this Noble Eightfold Path; that is, right view ... right concentration.

67. "When a noble disciple has thus understood ignorance, the origin of ignorance, the cessation of ignorance, and the way leading to the cessation of ignorance ... he here and now makes an end of suffering. In that way too a noble disciple is one of right view ... and has arrived at this true Dhamma."

[taints]

68. Saying, "Good, friend," the monks delighted and rejoiced in the Venerable Sāriputta's words. Then they asked him a further question: "But, friend, might there be another way in which a noble disciple is one of right view, whose view is straight, who has confirmed confidence in the Dhamma, and has arrived at this true Dhamma?"—"There might be, friends.

69. "When, friends, a noble disciple understands the taints, the origin of the taints, the cessation of the taints, and the way leading to the cessation of the taints, in that way he is one of right view, whose view is straight, who has confirmed confidence in the Dhamma, and has arrived at this true Dhamma.

70. "And what are the taints, what is the origin of the taints, what is the cessation of the taints, what is the way leading to the cessation of the taints? There are these three taints: the taint of sensual desire, the taint of existence, and the taint of ignorance. With the arising of ignorance there is the arising of the taints.[22] With the cessation of ignorance there is the cessation of the taints. The way leading to the cessation of the taints is just this Noble Eightfold Path; that is, right view, right

intention, right speech, right action, right livelihood, right effort, right mindfulness, and right concentration.

71. "When a noble disciple has thus understood the taints, the origin of the taints, the cessation of the taints, and the way leading to the cessation of the taints, he entirely abandons the underlying tendency to lust, he abolishes the underlying tendency to aversion, he extirpates the underlying tendency to the view and conceit 'I am,' and by abandoning ignorance and arousing true knowledge he here and now makes an end of suffering. In that way too a noble disciple is one of right view, whose view is straight, who has perfect confidence in the Dhamma, and has arrived at this true Dhamma."

That is what the Venerable Sāriputta said. The monks were satisfied and delighted in the Venerable Sāriputta's words.

(MN 9: *Sammādiṭṭhi Sutta;* I 46–55)

4. The Domain of Wisdom

(1) By Way of the Five Aggregates

(a) Phases of the Aggregates

At Sāvatthī, the Blessed One said: "Monks, there are these five aggregates subject to clinging. What five? The form aggregate subject to clinging, the feeling aggregate subject to clinging, the perception aggregate subject to clinging, the volitional formations aggregate subject to clinging, the consciousness aggregate subject to clinging.

"So long as I did not directly know as they really are the five aggregates subject to clinging in four phases,[23] I did not claim to have awakened to the unsurpassed perfect enlightenment in this world with its devas, Māra, and Brahmā, in this population with its ascetics and brahmins, its devas and humans. But when I directly knew all this as it really is, then I claimed to have awakened to the unsurpassed perfect enlightenment in this world with ... its devas and humans.

"And how, monks, are there four phases? I directly knew form, its origin, its cessation, and the way leading to its cessation. I directly knew feeling ... perception ... volitional formations ... consciousness, its origin, its cessation, and the way leading to its cessation.

"And what, monks, is form? The four great elements and the form derived from the four great elements: this is called form. With the arising of nutriment there is the arising of form. With the cessation of nutriment there is the cessation of form. This Noble Eightfold Path is the way leading to the cessation of form; that is, right view ... right concentration.

"Whatever ascetics and brahmins, having thus directly known form, its origin, its cessation, and the way leading to its cessation, are practicing for the purpose of disenchantment with form, for its fading away and cessation, they are practicing well. Those who are practicing well have gained a foothold in this Dhamma and Discipline.[24]

"And whatever ascetics and brahmins, having thus directly known form, its origin, its cessation, and the way leading to its cessation, through disenchantment with form, through its fading away and cessation, are liberated by nonclinging, they are well liberated. Those who are well liberated are consummate ones. As to those consummate ones, there is no round for their manifestation.[25]

"And what, monks, is feeling? There are these six classes of feeling: feeling born of eye-contact, feeling born of ear-contact, feeling born of nose-contact, feeling born of tongue-contact, feeling born of body-contact, feeling born of mind-contact. This is called feeling. With the arising of contact there is the arising of feeling. With the cessation of contact there is the cessation of feeling. This Noble Eightfold Path is the way leading to the cessation of feeling; that is, right view ... right concentration.

"Whatever ascetics and brahmins, having thus directly known feeling, its origin, its cessation, and the way leading to its cessation, are practicing for the purpose of disenchantment with feeling, for its fading away and cessation, they are practicing well. Those who are practicing well have gained a foothold in this Dhamma and Discipline.

"And whatever ascetics and brahmins, having thus directly known feeling ... and the way leading to its cessation ... As to those consummate ones, there is no round for their manifestation.

"And what, monks, is perception? There are these six classes of perception: perception of forms, perception of sounds, perception of odors, perception of tastes, perception of tactile objects, perception of mental phenomena. This is called perception. With the arising of contact there is the arising of perception. With the cessation of contact there is the cessation of perception. This Noble Eightfold Path is the way leading to the cessation of perception; that is, right view ... right concentration.

"Whatever ascetics and brahmins ... As to those consummate ones, there is no round for their manifestation.

"And what, monks, are volitional formations? There are these six classes of volition:[26] volition regarding forms, volition regarding sounds, volition regarding odors, volition regarding tastes, volition regarding tactile objects, volition regarding mental phenomena. These are called volitional formations. With the arising of contact there is the arising of volitional formations. With the cessation of contact there is the cessation of volitional formations. This Noble Eightfold Path is the way leading to the cessation of volitional formations; that is, right view ... right concentration.

"Whatever ascetics and brahmins ... As to those consummate ones, there is no round for their manifestation.

"And what, monks, is consciousness? There are these six classes of consciousness: eye-consciousness, ear-consciousness, nose-consciousness, tongue-consciousness, body-consciousness, mind-consciousness. This is called consciousness. With the arising of name-and-form there is the arising of consciousness.[27] With the cessation of name-and-form there is the cessation of consciousness. This Noble Eightfold Path is the way leading to the cessation of consciousness; that is, right view ... right concentration.

"Whatever ascetics and brahmins, having thus directly known consciousness, its origin, its cessation, and the way leading to its cessation, are practicing for the purpose of disenchantment with consciousness, for its fading away and cessation, they are practicing well. Those who are practicing well have gained a foothold in this Dhamma and Discipline.

"And whatever ascetics and brahmins, having thus directly known consciousness, its origin, its cessation, and the way leading to its cessation, through disenchantment with consciousness, through its fading away and cessation, are liberated by nonclinging, they are well liberated. Those who are well liberated are consummate ones. As to those consummate ones, there is no round for their manifestation."

(SN 22:56; III 58–61)

(b) A Catechism on the Aggregates

On one occasion the Blessed One was dwelling at Sāvatthī in the Eastern Park, in the Mansion of Migāra's Mother, together with a great Saṅgha of monks. Now on that occasion—the uposatha day of the fifteenth, a full-moon night—the Blessed One was sitting out in the open surrounded by the Saṅgha of monks.

Then a certain monk rose from his seat, arranged his upper robe over one shoulder, raised his joined hands in reverential salutation toward the Blessed One, and said to him: "Venerable sir, I would ask the Blessed One about a certain point, if the Blessed One would grant me the favor of answering my question."

"Well then, monk, sit down in your own seat and ask whatever you wish."

"Yes, venerable sir," that monk replied. Then he sat down in his own seat and said to the Blessed One:

"Aren't these the five aggregates subject to clinging, venerable sir: that is, the form aggregate subject to clinging, the feeling aggregate subject to clinging, the perception aggregate subject to clinging, the volitional formations aggregate subject to clinging, the consciousness aggregate subject to clinging?"

"They are, monk."

Saying, "Good, venerable sir," that monk delighted and rejoiced in the Blessed One's statement. Then he asked the Blessed One a further question:

"But, venerable sir, in what are these five aggregates subject to clinging rooted?"

"These five aggregates subject to clinging, monk, are rooted in desire."[28]

"Venerable sir, is that clinging the same as these five aggregates subject to clinging, or is the clinging something apart from the five aggregates subject to clinging?"

"Monk, that clinging is neither the same as the five aggregates subject to clinging, nor is the clinging something apart from the five aggregates subject to clinging. But rather, the desire and lust for them, that is the clinging there."[29]

Saying, "Good, venerable sir," that monk ... asked the Blessed One a further question:

"But, venerable sir, can there be diversity in the desire and lust for the five aggregates subject to clinging?"

"There can be, monk," the Blessed One said. "Here, monk, it occurs to someone: 'May I be of such form in the future! May I be of such feeling in the future! May I be of such perception in the future! May I be of such volitional formations in the future! May I be of such consciousness in the future!' Thus, monk, there can be diversity in the desire and lust for the five aggregates subject to clinging."

Saying, "Good, venerable sir," that monk ... asked the Blessed One a further question:

"In what way, venerable sir, does the designation 'aggregates' apply to the aggregates?"

"Whatever kind of form there is, monk, whether past, future, or present, internal or external, gross or subtle, inferior or superior, far or near: this is called the form aggregate. Whatever kind of feeling there is, whether past, future, or present, internal or external, gross or subtle, inferior or superior, far or near: this is called the feeling aggregate. Whatever kind of perception there is, whether past, future, or present, internal or external, gross or subtle, inferior or superior, far or near: this is called the perception aggregate. Whatever kind of volitional formations there are, whether past, future, or present, internal or external, gross or subtle, inferior or superior, far or near: this is called the volitional formations aggregate. Whatever kind of consciousness there is, whether past, future, or present, internal or external, gross or subtle, inferior or superior, far or near: this is called the consciousness aggregate. It is in this way, monk, that the designation 'aggregates' applies to the aggregates."

Saying, "Good, venerable sir," that monk ... asked the Blessed One a further question:

"What is the cause and condition, venerable sir, for the manifestation of the form aggregate? What is the cause and condition for the manifestation of the feeling aggregate?... for the manifestation of the perception aggregate?... for the manifestation of the volitional formations aggregate?... for the manifestation of the consciousness aggregate?"

"The four great elements, monk, are the cause and condition for the manifestation of the form aggregate. Contact is the cause and condition for the manifestation of the feeling aggregate, the perception aggregate, and the volitional formations aggregate. Name-and-form is the cause and condition for the manifestation of the consciousness aggregate."

"Venerable sir, how does identity view come to be?"

"Here, monk, the uninstructed worldling, who is not a seer of the noble ones and is unskilled and undisciplined in their Dhamma, who is not a seer of superior persons and is unskilled and undisciplined in their Dhamma, regards form as self, or self as possessing form, or form as in self, or self as in form. He regards feeling as self ... perception as self ... volitional formations as self ... consciousness as self, or self as possessing consciousness, or consciousness as in self, or self as in consciousness. That is how identity view comes to be."

"But, venerable sir, how does identity view not come to be?"

"Here, monk, the instructed noble disciple, who is a seer of the noble ones and is skilled and disciplined in their Dhamma, who is a seer of superior persons and is skilled and disciplined in their Dhamma, does not regard form as self, or self as possessing form, or form as in self, or self as in form. He does not regard feeling as self ... perception as self ... volitional formations as self ... consciousness as self, or self as possessing consciousness, or consciousness as in self, or self as in consciousness. That is how identity view does not come to be."

"What, venerable sir, is the gratification, the danger, and the escape in the case of the five aggregates?"

"The pleasure and joy, monk, that arise in dependence on form: this is the gratification in form. That form is impermanent, suffering, and subject to change: this is the danger in form. The removal and abandonment of desire and lust for form: this is the escape from form. The pleasure and joy that arise in dependence on feeling ... in dependence on perception ... in dependence on volitional formations ... in dependence on consciousness: this is the gratification in consciousness. That consciousness is impermanent, suffering, and subject to change: this is the danger in consciousness. The removal and abandonment of desire and lust for consciousness: this is the escape from consciousness."

Saying, "Good, venerable sir," that monk delighted and rejoiced in the Blessed One's statement. Then he asked the Blessed One a further question:

"Venerable sir, how should one know and see so that, in regard to this body with consciousness and in regard to all external signs, I-making, mine-making, and the underlying tendency to conceit no longer occur within?"[30]

"Any kind of form whatsoever, monk, whether past, future, or present, internal or external, gross or subtle, inferior or superior, far or near—one sees all form as it really is with correct wisdom thus: 'This is not mine, this I am not, this is not my self.'

"Any kind of feeling whatsoever ... Any kind of perception whatsoever ... Any kind of volitional formations whatsoever ... Any kind of consciousness whatsoever, whether past, future, or present, internal or external, gross or subtle, inferior or superior, far or near—one sees all consciousness as it really is with correct wisdom thus: 'This is not mine, this I am not, this is not my self.'

"When one knows and sees thus, monk, then in regard to this body with consciousness and in regard to all external signs, I-making, mine-making, and the underlying tendency to conceit no longer occur within."

(from SN 22: 82, abridged; 100–103 = MN 109, abridged; III 15–19)

(c) The Characteristic of Nonself

Thus have I heard. On one occasion the Blessed One was dwelling at Bārāṇasī in the Deer Park at Isipatana.[31] There the Blessed One addressed the monks of the group of five thus: "Monks!"

"Venerable sir!" those monks replied. The Blessed One said this:

"Monks, form is nonself. For if, monks, form were self, this form would not lead to affliction, and it would be possible to determine form: 'Let my form be thus; let my form not be thus.' But because form is nonself, form leads to affliction, and it is not possible to determine form: 'Let my form be thus; let my form not be thus.'[32]

"Feeling is nonself.... Perception is nonself.... Volitional formations are nonself.... Consciousness is nonself. For if, monks, consciousness were self, this consciousness would not lead to affliction, and it would be possible to determine consciousness: 'Let my consciousness be thus; let my consciousness not be thus.' But because consciousness is nonself, consciousness leads to affliction, and it is not possible to determine consciousness: 'Let my consciousness be thus; let my consciousness not be thus.'

"What do you think, monks, is form permanent or impermanent?"—"Impermanent, venerable sir."—"Is what is impermanent suffering or happiness?"—"Suffering, venerable sir."—"Is what is impermanent, suffering, and subject to change fit to be regarded thus: 'This is mine, this I am, this is my self'?"—"No, venerable sir."

"Is feeling permanent or impermanent?... Is perception permanent or impermanent?... Are volitional formations permanent or impermanent?... Is consciousness permanent or impermanent?"—"Impermanent, venerable sir."—"Is what is impermanent suffering or happiness?"—"Suffering, venerable sir."—"Is what is impermanent, suffering, and subject to change fit to be regarded thus: 'This is mine, this I am, this is my self'?"—"No, venerable sir."

"Therefore, monks, any kind of form whatsoever, whether past, future, or present, internal or external, gross or subtle, inferior or superior, far or near, all form should be seen as it really is with correct wisdom thus: 'This is not mine, this I am not, this is not my self.'

"Any kind of feeling whatsoever ... Any kind of perception whatsoever ... Any kind of volitional formations whatsoever ... Any kind of consciousness whatsoever, whether past, future, or present, internal or external, gross or subtle, inferior or superior, far or near, all consciousness should be seen as it really is with correct wisdom thus: 'This is not mine, this I am not, this is not my self.'

"Seeing thus, monks, the instructed noble disciple becomes disenchanted with form, disenchanted with feeling, disenchanted with perception, disenchanted with volitional formations, disenchanted with consciousness. Becoming disenchanted, he becomes dispassionate. Through dispassion [his mind] is liberated. When it is liberated there comes the knowledge: 'It's liberated.' He understands: 'Destroyed is birth, the spiritual life has been lived, what had to be done has been done, there is no more coming back to any state of being.'"

That is what the Blessed One said. Elated, those monks delighted in the Blessed One's statement. And while this discourse was being spoken, the minds of the monks of the group of five were liberated from the taints by nonclinging.

(SN 22:59; III 66–68)

(d) Impermanent, Suffering, Nonself

"Monks, form is impermanent. What is impermanent is suffering. What is suffering is nonself. What is nonself should be seen as it really is with correct wisdom thus: 'This is not mine, this I am not, this is not my self.' When one sees this thus as it really is with correct wisdom, the mind becomes dispassionate and is liberated from the taints by nonclinging.

"Feeling is impermanent.... Perception is impermanent.... Volitional formations are impermanent.... Consciousness is impermanent. What is impermanent is suffering. What is suffering is nonself. What is nonself should be seen as it really is with correct wisdom thus: 'This is not mine, this I am not, this is not my self.' When one sees this thus as it really is with correct wisdom, the mind becomes dispassionate and is liberated from the taints by nonclinging.

"If, monks, a monk's mind has become dispassionate toward the form element, it is liberated from the taints by nonclinging. If his mind has become dispassionate toward the feeling element ... toward the perception element ... toward the volitional formations element ... toward the consciousness element, it is liberated from the taints by nonclinging.

"By being liberated, it is steady; by being steady, it is content; by being content, he is not agitated. Being unagitated, he personally attains Nibbāna. He understands: 'Destroyed is birth, the spiritual life has been lived, what had to be done has been done, there is no more coming back to any state of being.'"

(SN 22:45; III 44–45)

(e) A Lump of Foam

On one occasion the Blessed One was dwelling at Ayojjhā on the bank of the river Ganges. There the Blessed One addressed the monks thus:

"Monks, suppose that this river Ganges was carrying along a great lump of foam. A man with good sight would inspect it, ponder it, and carefully investigate it, and it would appear to him to be void, hollow, insubstantial. For what substance could there be in a lump of foam? So too, monks, whatever kind of form there is, whether past, future, or present, internal or external, gross or subtle, inferior or superior, far or near: a monk inspects it, ponders it, and carefully investigates it, and it would appear to him to be void, hollow, insubstantial. For what substance could there be in form?[33]

"Suppose, monks, that in the autumn, when it is raining and big rain drops are falling, a water bubble arises and bursts on the surface of the water. A man with good sight would inspect it, ponder it, and carefully investigate it, and it would appear to him to be void, hollow, insubstantial. For what substance could there be in a water bubble? So too, monks, whatever kind of feeling there is, whether past, future, or present, internal or external, gross or subtle, inferior or superior, far or near: a monk inspects it, ponders it, and carefully investigates it, and it would appear to him to be void, hollow, insubstantial. For what substance could there be in feeling?[34]

"Suppose, monks, that in the last month of the hot season, at high noon, a shimmering mirage appears. A man with good sight would inspect it, ponder it, and carefully investigate it, and it would appear to him to be void, hollow, insubstantial. For what substance could there be in a mirage? So too, monks, whatever kind of perception there is, whether past, future, or present, internal or external, gross or subtle, inferior or superior, far or near: a monk inspects it, ponders it, and carefully investigates it, and it would appear to him to be void, hollow, insubstantial. For what substance could there be in perception?[35]

"Suppose, monks, that a man needing heartwood, seeking heartwood, wandering in search of heartwood, would take a sharp axe and enter a forest. There he would see the trunk of a large banana tree, straight, fresh, without a fruit-bud core. He would cut it down at the root, cut off the crown, and unroll the coil. As he unrolls the coil, he would not find even softwood, let alone heartwood. A man with good sight would inspect it, ponder it, and carefully investigate it, and it would appear to him to be void, hollow, insubstantial. For what substance could there be in the trunk of a banana tree? So too, monks, whatever kind of volitional formations there are, whether past, future, or present, internal or external, gross or subtle, inferior or superior, far or near: a monk inspects them, ponders them, and carefully investigates them. As he investigates them, they appear to him to be void, hollow, insubstantial. For what substance could there be in volitional formations?[36]

"Suppose, monks, that a magician or a magician's apprentice would display a magical illusion at a crossroads. A man with good sight would inspect it, ponder it, and carefully investigate it, and it would appear to him to be void, hollow, insubstantial. For what substance could there be in a magical illusion? So too, monks, whatever kind of consciousness there is, whether past, future, or present, internal or external, gross or subtle, inferior or superior, far or near: a monk inspects it, ponders it, and carefully investigates it, and it would appear to him to be void, hollow, insubstantial. For what substance could there be in consciousness?[37]

"Seeing thus, monks, the instructed noble disciple becomes disenchanted with form, disenchanted with feeling, disenchanted with perception, disenchanted with volitional formations, disenchanted with consciousness. Becoming disenchanted, he becomes dispassionate. Through dispassion [his mind] is liberated. When it is liberated there comes the knowledge: 'It's liberated.' He understands: 'Destroyed is birth, the spiritual life has been lived, what had to be done has been done, there is no more coming back to any state of being.'"

(SN 22:95; III 140–42)

(2) By Way of the Six Sense Bases

(a) Full Understanding

"Monks, without directly knowing and fully understanding the all, without developing dispassion toward it and abandoning it, one is incapable of destroying suffering.

"And what, monks, is that all? Without directly knowing and fully understanding the eye, without developing dispassion toward it and abandoning it, one is incapable of destroying suffering. Without directly knowing and fully understanding forms ... eye-consciousness ... eye-contact ... and whatever feeling arises with eye-contact as condition ... without developing dispassion toward it and abandoning it, one is incapable of destroying suffering.

"Without directly knowing and fully understanding the ear ... the mind ... and whatever feeling arises with mind-contact as condition ... without developing dispassion toward it and abandoning it, one is incapable of destroying suffering.

"This, monks, is the all. Without directly knowing and fully understanding this all ... one is incapable of destroying suffering.

"Monks, by directly knowing and fully understanding the all, by developing dispassion toward it and abandoning it, one is capable of destroying suffering.

"And what, monks, is that all? By directly knowing and fully understanding the eye ... the mind ... and whatever feeling arises with mind-contact as condition ... by developing dispassion toward it and abandoning it, one is capable of destroying suffering.

"This, monks, is the all by directly knowing and fully understanding which ... one is capable of destroying suffering."

(SN 35:26; IV 17–18)

(b) Burning

On one occasion the Blessed One was dwelling at Gayā, at Gayā's Head, together with a thousand monks. There the Blessed One addressed the monks thus:[38]

"Monks, all is burning. And what, monks, is the all that is burning? The eye is burning, forms are burning, eye-consciousness is burning, eye-contact is burning, and whatever feeling arises with eye-contact as condition—whether pleasant or painful or neither-painful-nor-pleasant—that too is burning. Burning with what? Burning with the fire of lust, with the fire of hatred, with the fire of delusion; burning with birth, aging, and death; with sorrow, lamentation, pain, dejection, and despair, I say.

"The ear is burning ... The mind is burning ... and whatever feeling arises with mind-contact as condition—whether pleasant or painful or neither-painful-nor-pleasant—that too is burning. Burning with what? Burning with the fire of lust, with the fire of hatred, with the fire of delusion; burning with birth, aging, and death; with sorrow, lamentation, pain, dejection, and despair, I say.

"Seeing thus, monks, the instructed noble disciple becomes disenchanted with the eye, with forms, with eye-consciousness, with eye-contact, with whatever feeling arises with eye-contact as condition—whether pleasant or painful or neither-painful-nor-pleasant; becomes disenchanted with the ear ... with the mind ... with whatever feeling arises with mind-contact as condition.... Becoming disenchanted, he becomes dispassionate. Through dispassion [his mind] is liberated. When it is liberated there comes the knowledge: 'It's liberated.' He understands: 'Destroyed is birth, the spiritual life has been lived, what had to be done has been done, there is no more coming back to any state of being.'"

This is what the Blessed One said. Elated, those monks delighted in the Blessed One's statement. And while this discourse was being spoken, the minds of the thousand monks were liberated from the taints by nonclinging.

(SN 35:28; IV 19–20)

(c) Suitable for Attaining Nibbāna

"Monks, I will teach you the way that is suitable for attaining Nibbāna. Listen...."

"And what, monks, is the way that is suitable for attaining Nibbāna? Here, a monk sees the eye as impermanent, he sees forms as impermanent, he sees eye-consciousness as impermanent, he sees eye-contact as impermanent, he sees as impermanent whatever feeling arises with eye-contact as condition, whether pleasant or painful or neither-painful-nor-pleasant.

"He sees the ear as impermanent ... He sees the mind as impermanent, he sees mental phenomena as impermanent, he sees mind-consciousness as impermanent, he sees mind-contact as impermanent, he sees as impermanent whatever feeling arises with mind-contact as condition, whether pleasant or painful or neither-painful-nor-pleasant. This, monks, is the way that is suitable for attaining Nibbāna."

"He sees the eye as suffering ... he sees as suffering whatever feeling arises with mind-contact as condition, whether pleasant or painful or neither-painful-nor-pleasant. This, monks, is the way that is suitable for attaining Nibbāna.

"He sees the eye as nonself ... he sees as nonself whatever feeling arises with mind-contact as condition, whether pleasant or painful or neither-painful-nor-pleasant. This, monks, is the way that is suitable for attaining Nibbāna."

(SN 35:147–49, combined; IV 133–35)

(d) Empty Is the World

Then the Venerable Ānanda approached the Blessed One ... and said to him: "Venerable sir, it is said, 'Empty is the world, empty is the world.' In what way, venerable sir, is it said, 'Empty is the world'?"

"It is, Ānanda, because it is empty of self and of what belongs to self that it is said, 'Empty is the world.' And what is empty of self and of what belongs to self? The eye, Ānanda, is empty of self and of what belongs to self. Forms are empty of self and of what belongs to self. Eye-consciousness is empty of self and of what belongs to self. Eye-contact is empty of self and of what belongs to self.... Whatever feeling arises with mind-contact as condition—whether pleasant or painful or neither-painful-nor-pleasant—that too is empty of self and of what belongs to self.

"It is, Ānanda, because it is empty of self and of what belongs to self that it is said, 'Empty is the world.'"

(SN 35:85; IV 54)

(e) Consciousness Too Is Nonself

The Venerable Udāyī asked the Venerable Ānanda: "Friend Ānanda, in many ways [the nature of] this body has been declared, disclosed, and revealed by the Blessed One thus: 'For such a reason this body is nonself.' Is it possible to explain [the nature of] this consciousness in a similar way—to teach, proclaim, establish, disclose, analyze, and elucidate it thus: 'For such a reason this consciousness is nonself'?"

"It is possible, friend Udāyī. Doesn't eye-consciousness arise in dependence on the eye and forms?"

"Yes, friend."

"If the cause and condition for the arising of eye-consciousness would cease completely and totally without remainder, could eye-consciousness be discerned?"

"No, friend."

"In this way, friend, this has been declared, disclosed, and revealed by the Blessed One thus: 'For such a reason this consciousness is nonself.'

"Doesn't ear-consciousness arise in dependence on the ear and sounds?... Doesn't mind-consciousness arise in dependence on the mind and mental phenomena?"

"Yes, friend."

"If the cause and condition for the arising of mind-consciousness would cease completely and totally without remainder, could mind-consciousness be discerned?"

"No, friend."

"In this way too, friend, this has been declared, disclosed, and revealed by the Blessed One thus: 'For such a reason this consciousness is nonself.'

"Suppose, friend, a man needing heartwood, seeking heartwood, wandering in search of heartwood, would take a sharp axe and enter a forest. There he would see the trunk of a large banana tree, straight, fresh, without a fruit-bud core. He would cut it down at the root, cut off the crown, and unroll the coil. As he unrolls the coil, he would not find even softwood, let alone heartwood.

"So too, a monk does not recognize either a self or anything belonging to a self in these six bases for contact. Since he does not recognize anything thus, he does not cling to anything in the world. Not clinging, he is not agitated. Being unagitated, he personally attains Nibbāna. He understands: 'Destroyed is birth, the spiritual life has been lived, what had to be done has been done, there is no more coming back to any state of being.'"

(SN 35:234; IV 166–68)

(3) By Way of the Elements

(a) The Eighteen Elements

"Monks, I will teach you the diversity of elements. The eye element, form element, eye-consciousness element; the ear element, sound element, ear-consciousness element; the nose element, odor element, nose-consciousness element; the tongue element, taste element, tongue-consciousness element; the body element, tactile-object element, body-consciousness element; the mind element, mental-phenomena element, mind-consciousness element. This, monks, is called the diversity of elements."

(SN 14:1; II 140)

(b) The Four Elements

"Monks, there are these four elements. What four? The earth element, the water element, the heat element, the air element.

"Those ascetics or brahmins, monks, who do not understand as they really are the gratification, the danger, and the escape in the case of these four elements: these I do not consider to be ascetics among ascetics or brahmins among brahmins, and these venerable ones do not, by realizing it for themselves with direct knowledge, in this very life enter and dwell in the goal of asceticism or the goal of brahminhood.

"But, monks, those ascetics and brahmins who understand as they really are the gratification, the danger, and the escape in the case of these four elements: these I consider to be ascetics among ascetics and brahmins among brahmins, and these venerable ones, by realizing it for themselves with direct knowledge, in this very life enter and dwell in the goal of asceticism and the goal of brahminhood."

"Those ascetics or brahmins, monks, who do not understand as they really are the origin and the passing away, the gratification, the danger, and the escape in the case of these four elements: these I do not consider to be ascetics among ascetics...."

"But, monks, those ascetics and brahmins who understand these things: these I consider to be ascetics among ascetics and brahmins among brahmins, and these venerable ones, by realizing it for themselves with direct knowledge, in this very life enter and dwell in the goal of asceticism and the goal of brahminhood."

"Monks, those ascetics or brahmins who do not understand the earth element, its origin, its cessation, and the way leading to its cessation; who do not understand the water element ... the heat element ... the air element, its origin, its cessation, and the way leading to its cessation: these I do not consider to be ascetics among ascetics....

"But, monks, those ascetics and brahmins who understand these things: these I consider to be ascetics among ascetics and brahmins among brahmins, and these venerable ones, by realizing it for themselves with direct knowledge, in this very life enter and dwell in the goal of asceticism and the goal of brahminhood."

(SN 14:37–39, combined; II 175–77)

(c) The Six Elements

13. "How, monk, does one not neglect wisdom?[39] There are these six elements: the earth element, the water element, the fire element, the air element, the space element, and the consciousness element.

14. "What, monk, is the earth element? The earth element may be either internal or external. What is the internal earth element? Whatever internally, belonging to oneself, is solid, solidified, and clung-to, that is, head-hairs, body-hairs, nails, teeth, skin, flesh, sinews, bones, bone-marrow, kidneys, heart, liver, diaphragm, spleen, lungs, intestines, mesentery, stomach, feces, or whatever else internally, belonging to oneself, is solid, solidified, and clung-to: this is called the internal earth element. Now both the internal earth element and the external earth element are simply earth element. And that should be seen as it really is with correct wisdom thus: 'This is not mine, this I am not, this is not my self.' When one sees it thus as it really is with correct wisdom, one becomes disenchanted with the earth element and makes the mind dispassionate toward the earth element.

15. "What, monk, is the water element? The water element may be either internal or external. What is the internal water element? Whatever internally, belonging to oneself, is water, watery, and clung-to,

that is, bile, phlegm, pus, blood, sweat, fat, tears, grease, spittle, snot, oil-of-the-joints, urine, or whatever else internally, belonging to oneself, is water, watery, and clung-to: this is called the internal water element. Now both the internal water element and the external water element are simply water element. And that should be seen as it really is with correct wisdom thus: 'This is not mine, this I am not, this is not my self.' When one sees it thus as it really is with correct wisdom, one becomes disenchanted with the water element and makes the mind dispassionate toward the water element.

16. "What, monk, is the fire element? The fire element may be either internal or external. What is the internal fire element? Whatever internally, belonging to oneself, is fire, fiery, and clung-to, that is, that by which one is warmed, ages, and is consumed, and that by which what is eaten, drunk, consumed, and tasted gets completely digested, or whatever else internally, belonging to oneself, is fire, fiery, and clung-to: this is called the internal fire element. Now both the internal fire element and the external fire element are simply fire element. And that should be seen as it really is with correct wisdom thus: 'This is not mine, this I am not, this is not my self.' When one sees it thus as it really is with correct wisdom, one becomes disenchanted with the fire element and makes the mind dispassionate toward the fire element.

17. "What, monk, is the air element? The air element may be either internal or external. What is the internal air element? Whatever internally, belonging to oneself, is air, airy, and clung-to, that is, up-going winds, down-going winds, winds in the belly, winds in the bowels, winds that course through the limbs, in-breath and out-breath, or whatever else internally, belonging to oneself, is air, airy, and clung-to: this is called the internal air element. Now both the internal air element and the external air element are simply air element. And that should be seen as it really is with correct wisdom thus: 'This is not mine, this I am not, this is not my self.' When one sees it thus as it really is with correct wisdom, one becomes disenchanted with the air element and makes the mind dispassionate toward the air element.

18. "What, monk, is the space element? The space element may be either internal or external. What is the internal space element? Whatever internally, belonging to oneself, is space, spatial, and clung-to, that is, the holes of the ears, the nostrils, the door of the mouth, and that

[aperture] whereby what is eaten, drunk, consumed, and tasted gets swallowed, and where it collects, and whereby it is excreted from below, or whatever else internally, belonging to oneself, is space, spatial, and clung-to: this is called the internal space element. Now both the internal space element and the external space element are simply space element. And that should be seen as it really is with correct wisdom thus: 'This is not mine, this I am not, this is not my self.' When one sees it thus as it really is with correct wisdom, one becomes disenchanted with the space element and makes the mind dispassionate toward the space element.

19. "Then there remains only consciousness, purified and bright.[40] What does one cognize with that consciousness? One cognizes: '[This is] pleasant'; one cognizes: '[This is] painful'; one cognizes: '[This is] neither-painful-nor-pleasant.' In dependence on a contact to be felt as pleasant there arises a pleasant feeling.[41] When one feels a pleasant feeling, one understands: 'I feel a pleasant feeling.' One understands: 'With the cessation of that same contact to be felt as pleasant, its corresponding feeling—the pleasant feeling that arose in dependence on that contact to be felt as pleasant—ceases and subsides.' In dependence on a contact to be felt as painful there arises a painful feeling. When one feels a painful feeling, one understands: 'I feel a painful feeling.' One understands: 'With the cessation of that same contact to be felt as painful, its corresponding feeling—the painful feeling that arose in dependence on that contact to be felt as painful—ceases and subsides.' In dependence on a contact to be felt as neither-painful-nor-pleasant there arises a neither-painful-nor-pleasant feeling. When one feels a neither-painful-nor-pleasant feeling, one understands: 'I feel a neither-painful-nor-pleasant feeling.' One understands: 'With the cessation of that same contact to be felt as neither-painful-nor-pleasant, its corresponding feeling—the neither-painful-nor-pleasant feeling that arose in dependence on that contact to be felt as neither-painful-nor-pleasant—ceases and subsides.' Monk, just as from the contact and friction of two fire-sticks heat is generated and fire is produced, and with the separation and disjunction of these two fire-sticks the corresponding heat ceases and subsides; so too, in dependence on a contact to be felt as pleasant ... to be felt as painful ... to be felt as neither-painful-nor-pleasant there arises a neither-painful-nor-pleasant feeling.... One understands: 'With the cessation of that same contact to be

felt as neither-painful-nor-pleasant, its corresponding feeling ... ceases and subsides.'"

(from MN 140: *Dhātuvibhaṅga Sutta;* III 240–43)

(4) By Way of Dependent Origination

(a) What Is Dependent Origination?

"Monks, I will teach you dependent origination. Listen to that and attend closely, I will speak."—"Yes, venerable sir," those monks replied. The Blessed One said this:

"And what, monks, is dependent origination? With ignorance as condition, volitional formations [come to be]; with volitional formations as condition, consciousness; with consciousness as condition, name-and-form; with name-and-form as condition, the six sense bases; with the six sense bases as condition, contact; with contact as condition, feeling; with feeling as condition, craving; with craving as condition, clinging; with clinging as condition, existence; with existence as condition, birth; with birth as condition, aging-and-death, sorrow, lamentation, pain, dejection, and despair come to be. Such is the origin of this whole mass of suffering. This, monks, is called dependent origination.

"But with the remainderless fading away and cessation of ignorance comes cessation of volitional formations; with the cessation of volitional formations, cessation of consciousness; with the cessation of consciousness, cessation of name-and-form; with the cessation of name-and-form, cessation of the six sense bases; with the cessation of the six sense bases, cessation of contact; with the cessation of contact, cessation of feeling; with the cessation of feeling, cessation of craving; with the cessation of craving, cessation of clinging; with the cessation of clinging, cessation of existence; with the cessation of existence, cessation of birth; with the cessation of birth, aging-and-death, sorrow, lamentation, pain, dejection, and despair cease. Such is the cessation of this whole mass of suffering."

(SN 12:1; II 1–2)

(b) The Stableness of the Dhamma

"Monks, I will teach you dependent origination and dependently arisen phenomena. Listen and attend closely, I will speak."

"Yes, venerable sir," those monks replied. The Blessed One said this:

"And what, monks, is dependent origination? 'With birth as condition, aging-and-death [comes to be]': whether there is an arising of Tathāgatas or no arising of Tathāgatas, that element still persists, the stableness of the Dhamma, the fixed course of the Dhamma, specific conditionality.[42] A Tathāgata awakens to this and breaks through to it. Having done so, he explains it, teaches it, proclaims it, establishes it, discloses it, analyzes it, elucidates it. And he says: 'See! With birth as condition, monks, aging-and-death arises.'

"'With existence as condition, birth' … 'With clinging as condition, existence' … 'With craving as condition, clinging' … 'With feeling as condition, craving' … 'With contact as condition, feeling' … 'With the six sense bases as condition, contact' … 'With name-and-form as condition, the six sense bases' … 'With consciousness as condition, name-and-form' … 'With volitional formations as condition, consciousness' … 'With ignorance as condition, volitional formations': whether there is an arising of Tathāgatas or no arising of Tathāgatas, that element still persists, the stableness of the Dhamma, the fixed course of the Dhamma, specific conditionality. A Tathāgata awakens to this and breaks through to it. Having done so, he explains it, teaches it, proclaims it, establishes it, discloses it, analyzes it, elucidates it. And he says: 'See! With ignorance as condition, monks, volitional formations arise.'

"Thus, monks, the actuality, the inerrancy, the invariability, the specific conditionality in this: this is called dependent origination.[43]

"And what, monks, are the dependently arisen phenomena? Aging-and-death, monks, is impermanent, conditioned, dependently arisen, subject to destruction, vanishing, fading away, and cessation. Birth is impermanent … Existence is impermanent … Clinging is impermanent … Craving is impermanent … Feeling is impermanent … Contact is impermanent … The six sense bases are impermanent … Name-and-form is impermanent … Consciousness is impermanent … Volitional formations are impermanent … Ignorance is impermanent, conditioned, dependently arisen, subject to destruction, vanishing, fading away, and cessation. These, monks, are called the dependently arisen phenomena.

"When, monks, a noble disciple has clearly seen with correct wisdom as it really is this dependent origination and these dependently arisen phenomena, it is impossible that he will run back into the past, thinking: 'Did I exist in the past? Did I not exist in the past? What was

I in the past? How was I in the past? Having been what, what did I become in the past?' Or that he will run forward into the future, thinking: 'Will I exist in the future? Will I not exist in the future? What will I be in the future? How will I be in the future? Having been what, what will I become in the future?' Or that he will now be inwardly confused about the present thus: 'Do I exist? Do I not exist? What am I? How am I? This being—where has it come from, and where will it go?'

"For what reason? Because the noble disciple has clearly seen with correct wisdom as it really is this dependent origination and these dependently arisen phenomena."

(SN 12:20; II 25–27)

(c) Forty-Four Cases of Knowledge

"Monks, I will teach you forty-four cases of knowledge. Listen to that and attend closely, I will speak."

"Yes, venerable sir," those monks replied. The Blessed One said this:

"Monks, what are the forty-four cases of knowledge? Knowledge of aging-and-death, knowledge of its origin, knowledge of its cessation, knowledge of the way leading to its cessation. Knowledge of birth ... Knowledge of existence ... Knowledge of clinging ... Knowledge of craving ... Knowledge of feeling ... Knowledge of contact ... Knowledge of the six sense bases ... Knowledge of name-and-form ... Knowledge of consciousness ... Knowledge of volitional formations, knowledge of their origin, knowledge of their cessation, knowledge of the way leading to their cessation. These, monks, are the forty-four cases of knowledge.

"And what, monks, is aging-and-death?... [definition as in Text IX,3 §22] ... Thus this aging and this death are together called aging-and-death. With the arising of birth there is the arising of aging-and-death. With the cessation of birth there is the cessation of aging-and-death. This Noble Eightfold Path is the way leading to the cessation of aging-and-death; that is, right view ... right concentration.

"When, monks, a noble disciple thus understands aging-and-death, its origin, its cessation, and the way leading to its cessation, this is his knowledge of the principle.[44] By means of this principle that is seen, understood, immediately attained, fathomed, he applies the method to the past and the future thus: 'Whatever ascetics and brahmins in the past directly knew aging-and-death, its origin, its cessation, and the way leading to its cessation, all these directly knew it in the very same way that I do now. Whatever ascetics and brahmins in the future will directly know aging-and-death, its origin, its cessation, and the way leading to its cessation, all these will directly know it in the very same way that I do now.' This is his knowledge of entailment.[45]

"When, monks, a noble disciple has purified and cleansed these two kinds of knowledge—knowledge of the principle and knowledge of entailment—he is then called a noble disciple who is accomplished in view, accomplished in vision, who has arrived at this true Dhamma, who sees this true Dhamma, who possesses a trainee's knowledge, a trainee's true knowledge, who has entered the stream of the Dhamma, a noble one with penetrative wisdom, one who stands squarely before the door to the Deathless.

"And what, monks, is birth?… What are the volitional formations?… [definitions as in Text IX,3] … This Noble Eightfold Path is the way leading to the cessation of volitional formations; that is, right view … right concentration.

"When, monks, a noble disciple thus understands volitional formations, their origin, their cessation, and the way leading to their cessation, this is his knowledge of the principle. By means of this principle that is seen, understood, immediately attained, fathomed, he applies the method to the past and to the future…. This is his knowledge of entailment.

"When, monks, a noble disciple has purified and cleansed these two kinds of knowledge—knowledge of the principle and knowledge of entailment—he is then called a noble disciple who is accomplished in view … one who stands squarely before the door to the Deathless."

(SN 12:33; II 56–59)

(d) A Teaching by the Middle

At Sāvatthī, the Venerable Kaccānagotta approached the Blessed One, paid homage to him, sat down to one side, and said to him: "Venerable sir, it is said, 'right view, right view.' In what way, venerable sir, is there right view?"

"This world, Kaccāna, for the most part depends upon a duality—upon the idea of existence and the idea of nonexistence.[46] But for one who sees the origin of the world as it really is with correct wisdom, there is no idea of nonexistence in regard to the world. And for one who sees the cessation of the world as it really is with correct wisdom, there is no idea of existence in regard to the world.[47]

"This world, Kaccāna, is for the most part shackled by engagement, clinging, and adherence. But this one [with right view] does not become engaged and cling through that engagement and clinging, mental standpoint, adherence, underlying tendency; he does not take a stand about 'my self.' He has no perplexity or doubt that what arises is only suffering arising, what ceases is only suffering ceasing.[48] His knowledge about this is independent of others. It is in this way, Kaccāna, that there is right view.

"'All exists': Kaccāna, this is one extreme. 'All does not exist': this is the second extreme. Without veering toward either of these extremes, the Tathāgata teaches the Dhamma by the middle: 'With ignorance as condition, volitional formations [come to be]; with volitional formations as condition, consciousness.... Such is the origin of this whole mass of suffering. But with the remainderless fading away and cessation of ignorance comes cessation of volitional formations; with the cessation of volitional formations, cessation of consciousness.... Such is the cessation of this whole mass of suffering.'"

(SN 12:15; II 16–17)

(e) The Continuance of Consciousness

"Monks, what one intends and what one plans and whatever one has a tendency toward: this becomes a basis for the continuance of consciousness. When there is a basis there is a support for the establishing of consciousness. When consciousness is established and has come to growth, there is the production of future renewed existence. When there is the production of future renewed existence, future birth, aging-and-death, sorrow, lamentation, pain, dejection, and despair come to be. Such is the origin of this whole mass of suffering.[49]

"If, monks, one does not intend and does not plan but still has a tendency toward something, this becomes a basis for the continuance of consciousness. When there is a basis, there is a support for the establishing of consciousness.... Such is the origin of this whole mass of suffering.[50]

"But, monks, when one does not intend and does not plan and does not have a tendency toward anything, no basis exists for the continuance of consciousness. When there is no basis, there is no support for the establishing of consciousness. When consciousness is unestablished and does not come to growth, there is no production of future renewed existence. When there is no production of future renewed existence, future birth, aging-and-death, sorrow, lamentation, pain, dejection, and despair cease. Such is the cessation of this whole mass of suffering."[51]

(SN 12:38; II 65–66)

(f) The Origin and Passing of the World

"Monks, I will teach you the origin and the passing away of the world. Listen and attend closely, I will speak."

"Yes, venerable sir," the monks replied. The Blessed One said this:

"And what, monks, is the origin of the world? In dependence on the eye and forms, eye-consciousness arises. The meeting of the three is contact. With contact as condition, feeling [comes to be]; with feeling as condition, craving; with craving as condition, clinging; with clinging as condition, existence; with existence as condition, birth; with birth as condition, aging-and-death, sorrow, lamentation, pain, dejection, and despair come to be. This, monks, is the origin of the world.

"In dependence on the ear and sounds ... In dependence on the nose and odors ... In dependence on the tongue and tastes ... In dependence on the body and tactile objects ... In dependence on the mind and mental phenomena, mind-consciousness arises. The meeting of the three is contact. With contact as condition, feeling [comes to be]; with feeling as condition, craving; with craving as condition, clinging ... existence ... birth; with birth as condition, aging-and-death, sorrow, lamentation, pain, dejection, and despair come to be. This, monks, is the origin of the world.

"And what, monks, is the passing away of the world? In dependence on the eye and forms, eye-consciousness arises. The meeting of the three is contact. With contact as condition, feeling [comes to be]; with feeling as condition, craving. But with the remainderless fading away and cessation of that same craving comes cessation of clinging; with the cessation of clinging, cessation of existence; with the cessation of existence, cessation of birth; with the cessation of birth, aging-and-death, sorrow, lamentation, pain, dejection, and despair cease. Such is the cessation of this whole mass of suffering. This, monks, is the passing away of the world.

"In dependence on the ear and sounds ... In dependence on the mind and mental phenomena, mind-consciousness arises. The meeting of the three is contact. With contact as condition, feeling [comes to be]; with feeling as condition, craving. But with the remainderless fading away and cessation of that same craving comes cessation of clinging ... cessation of existence ... cessation of birth; with the cessation of birth, aging-and-death, sorrow, lamentation, pain, dejection, and despair cease. Such is the cessation of this whole mass of suffering. This, monks, is the passing away of the world."

(SN 12:44; II 73–74)

(5) By Way of the Four Noble Truths

(a) The Truths of All Buddhas

"Monks, whatever Perfectly Enlightened Buddhas in the past fully awakened to things as they really are, all fully awakened to the Four Noble Truths as they really are. Whatever Perfectly Enlightened Buddhas in the future will fully awaken to things as they really are, all will fully awaken to the Four Noble Truths as they really are. Whatever Perfectly Enlightened Buddhas at present have fully awakened to things as they really are, all have fully awakened to the Four Noble Truths as they really are.

"What four? The noble truth of suffering, the noble truth of the origin of suffering, the noble truth of the cessation of suffering, the noble truth of the way leading to the cessation of suffering. Whatever Perfectly Enlightened Buddhas fully awakened ... will fully awaken ... have fully awakened to things as they really are, all have fully awakened to these Four Noble Truths as they really are.

"Therefore, monks, an exertion should be made to understand: 'This is suffering.' An exertion should be made to understand: 'This is the origin of suffering.' An exertion should be made to understand: 'This is the cessation of suffering.' An exertion should be made to understand: 'This is the way leading to the cessation of suffering.'"

(SN 56:24; V 433–34)

(b) These Four Truths Are Actual

"Monks, these four things are actual, unerring, invariable.[52] What four?

"'This is suffering': this, monks, is actual, unerring, invariable. 'This is the origin of suffering': this is actual, unerring, invariable. 'This is the cessation of suffering': this is actual, unerring, invariable. 'This is the way leading to the cessation of suffering': this is actual, unerring, invariable.

"These four things, monks, are actual, unerring, invariable.

"Therefore, monks, an exertion should be made to understand: 'This is suffering.'... An exertion should be made to understand: 'This is the way leading to the cessation of suffering.'"

(SN 56:20; V 430–31)

(c) A Handful of Leaves

On one occasion the Blessed One was dwelling at Kosambī in a siṃsapā grove. Then the Blessed One took up a few siṃsapā leaves in his hand and addressed the monks thus: "What do you think, monks, which is more numerous: these few leaves that I have taken up in my hand or those in the grove overhead?"

"Venerable sir, the leaves that the Blessed One has taken up in his hand are few, but those in the grove overhead are numerous."

"So too, monks, the things I have directly known but have not taught you are numerous, while the things I have taught you are few. And why, monks, have I not taught those many things? Because they are without benefit, irrelevant to the fundamentals of the spiritual life, and do not lead to disenchantment, to dispassion, to cessation, to peace, to direct knowledge, to enlightenment, to Nibbāna. Therefore I have not taught them.

"And what, monks, have I taught? I have taught: 'This is suffering'; I have taught: 'This is the origin of suffering'; I have taught: 'This is the cessation of suffering'; I have taught: 'This is the way leading to the cessation of suffering.' And why, monks, have I taught this? Because this is beneficial, relevant to the fundamentals of the spiritual life, and leads to disenchantment, to dispassion, to cessation, to peace, to direct knowledge, to enlightenment, to Nibbāna. Therefore I have taught this.

"Therefore, monks, an exertion should be made to understand: 'This is suffering.'... An exertion should be made to understand: 'This is the way leading to the cessation of suffering.'"

(SN 56:31; V 437–38)

(d) Because of Not Understanding

On one occasion the Blessed One was dwelling among the Vajjians at Koṭigāma. There the Blessed One addressed the monks thus: "Monks, it is because of not understanding and not penetrating the Four Noble Truths that you and I have roamed and wandered through this long course of saṃsāra. What four?

"It is, monks, because of not understanding and not penetrating the noble truth of suffering that you and I have roamed and wandered through this long course of saṃsāra. It is because of not understanding and not penetrating the noble truth of the origin of suffering ... the noble truth of the cessation of suffering ... the noble truth of the way leading to the cessation of suffering that you and I have roamed and wandered through this long course of saṃsāra.

"That noble truth of suffering, monks, has been understood and penetrated. That noble truth of the origin of suffering has been understood and penetrated. That noble truth of the cessation of suffering has been understood and penetrated. That noble truth of the way leading to the cessation of suffering has been understood and penetrated. Craving for existence has been cut off; the conduit to existence[53] has been destroyed; now there is no more renewed existence."

(SN 56:21; V 431–32)

(e) The Precipice

On one occasion the Blessed One was dwelling at Rājagaha on Mount Vulture Peak. Then the Blessed One addressed the monks thus: "Come, monks, let us go to Inspiration Peak for the day's abiding."

"Yes, venerable sir," those monks replied. Then the Blessed One, together with a number of monks, went to Inspiration Peak. A certain monk saw the steep precipice off Inspiration Peak and said to the Blessed One: "That precipice is indeed steep, venerable sir; that precipice is extremely frightful. But is there, venerable sir, a precipice steeper and more frightful than that one?"

"There is, monk."

"But what precipice, venerable sir, is steeper and more frightful than that one?"

"Those ascetics and brahmins, monk, who do not understand as it really is: 'This is suffering. This is the origin of suffering. This is the cessation of suffering. This is the way leading to the cessation of suffering'—they delight in volitional formations that lead to birth, aging, and death; they delight in volitional formations that lead to sorrow, lamentation, pain, dejection, and despair. Delighting in such volitional formations, they generate volitional formations that lead to birth, aging, and death; they generate volitional formations that lead to sorrow, lamentation, pain, dejection, and despair. Having generated such volitional formations, they tumble down the precipice of birth, aging, and death; they tumble down the precipice of sorrow, lamentation, pain, dejection, and despair. They are not freed from birth, aging, and death; not freed from sorrow, lamentation, pain, dejection, and despair; not freed from suffering, I say.

"But, monk, those ascetics and brahmins who understand as it really is: 'This is suffering' … 'This is the way leading to the cessation of suffering'—they do not delight in volitional formations that lead to birth, aging, and death; they do not generate volitional formations that lead to sorrow, lamentation, pain, dejection, and despair. Not delighting in such volitional formations, they do not generate volitional formations that lead to birth, aging, and death; they do not generate volitional formations that lead to sorrow, lamentation, pain, dejection, and despair. Not having generated such volitional formations, they do not tumble down the precipice of birth, aging, and death; they do not tumble down the precipice of sorrow, lamentation, pain, dejection, and despair. They are freed from birth, aging, and death; freed from sorrow, lamentation, pain, dejection, and despair; freed from suffering, I say.

"Therefore, monks, an exertion should be made to understand: 'This is suffering.'… An exertion should be made to understand: 'This is the way leading to the cessation of suffering.'"

(SN 56:42; V 448–50)

(f) Making the Breakthrough

"Monks, if anyone should speak thus: 'Without having made the breakthrough to the noble truth of suffering as it really is, without having made the breakthrough to the noble truth of the origin of suffering as it really is, without having made the breakthrough to the noble truth of the cessation of suffering as it really is, without having made the breakthrough to the noble truth of the way leading to the cessation of suffering as it really is, I will completely make an end to suffering'—this is impossible.

"Just as, monks, if someone should speak thus: 'Having made a basket of acacia leaves or of pine needles or of myrobalan leaves,[54] I will bring water or a palm fruit,' this would be impossible; so too, if anyone should speak thus: 'Without having made the breakthrough to the noble truth of suffering as it really is ... I will completely make an end to suffering'—this is impossible.

"But, monks, if anyone should speak thus: 'Having made the breakthrough to the noble truth of suffering as it really is, having made the breakthrough to the noble truth of the origin of suffering as it really is, having made the breakthrough to the noble truth of the cessation of suffering as it really is, having made the breakthrough to the noble truth of the way leading to the cessation of suffering as it really is, I will completely make an end to suffering'—this is possible.

"Just as, monks, if someone should speak thus: 'Having made a basket of lotus leaves or of kino leaves or of māluva leaves, I will bring water or a palm fruit,' this would be possible; so too, if anyone should speak thus: 'Having made the breakthrough to the noble truth of suffering as it really is ... I will completely make an end to suffering'—this is possible.

"Therefore, monks, an exertion should be made to understand: 'This is suffering.'... An exertion should be made to understand: 'This is the way leading to the cessation of suffering.'"

(SN 56:32; V 442–43)

(g) The Destruction of the Taints

"Monks, I say that the destruction of the taints is for one who knows and sees, not for one who does not know and does not see. For one who knows what, for one who sees what, does the destruction of the taints come about? The destruction of the taints comes about for one who knows and sees: 'This is suffering. This is the origin of suffering. This is the cessation of suffering. This is the way leading to the cessation of suffering.' It is for one who knows thus, for one who sees thus, that the destruction of the taints comes about.

"Therefore, monks, an exertion should be made to understand: 'This is suffering.'… An exertion should be made to understand: 'This is the way leading to the cessation of suffering.'"

(SN 56:25; V 434)

5. The Goal of Wisdom

(1) What is Nibbāna?

On one occasion the Venerable Sāriputta was dwelling in Magadha at Nālakagāma. Then the wanderer Jambukhādaka[55] approached the Venerable Sāriputta and exchanged greetings with him. When they had concluded their greetings and cordial talk, he sat down to one side and said to the Venerable Sāriputta:

"Friend Sāriputta, it is said, 'Nibbāna, Nibbāna.' What now is Nibbāna?"

"The destruction of lust, the destruction of hatred, the destruction of delusion: this, friend, is called Nibbāna.

"But, friend, is there a path, is there a way for the realization of this Nibbāna?"

"There is a path, friend, there is a way for the realization of this Nibbāna."

"And what, friend, is that path, what is that way for the realization of this Nibbāna?"

"It is, friend, this Noble Eightfold Path; that is, right view, right intention, right speech, right action, right livelihood, right effort, right mindfulness, right concentration. This is the path, friend, this is the way for the realization of this Nibbāna."

"Excellent is the path, friend, excellent is the way for the realization of this Nibbāna. And it is enough, friend Sāriputta, for diligence."

(SN 38:1; IV 251–52)

(2) Thirty-Three Synonyms for Nibbāna

"Monks, I will teach you the unconditioned and the path leading to the unconditioned. Listen ….

"And what, monks, is the unconditioned? The destruction of lust, the destruction of hatred, the destruction of delusion: this is called the unconditioned.

"And what, monks, is the path leading to the unconditioned? Mindfulness directed to the body: this is called the path leading to the unconditioned.

"Monks, I will teach you the uninclined ... the taintless ... the truth ... the far shore ... the subtle ... the very difficult to see ... the unaging ... the stable ... the undisintegrating ... the unmanifest ... the unproliferated[56] ... the peaceful ... the deathless ... the sublime ... the auspicious ... the secure .... the destruction of craving ... the wonderful ... the amazing ... the unailing ... the unailing state ... Nibbāna ... the unafflicted ... dispassion ... purity ... freedom ... nonattachment ... the island ... the shelter ... the asylum ... the refuge ... the destination and the path leading to the destination. Listen ....

"And what, monks, is the destination? The destruction of lust, the destruction of hatred, the destruction of delusion: this is called the destination.

"And what, monks, is the path leading to the destination? Mindfulness directed to the body: this is called the path leading to the destination.

"Thus, monks, I have taught you the unconditioned ... the destination and the path leading to the destination. Whatever should be done, monks, by a compassionate teacher out of compassion for his disciples, desiring their welfare, that I have done for you. These are the roots of trees, monks, these are empty huts. Meditate, monks, do not be negligent, lest you regret it later. This is my instruction to you."

(SN 43:1–44, combined; IV 359–73)

(3) There Is That Base

Thus have I heard. At one time the Blessed One was dwelling at Sāvatthī in Jeta's Grove, Anāthapiṇḍika's Park. Now on that occasion the Blessed One was instructing, rousing, inspiring, and gladdening the monks with a Dhamma talk connected with Nibbāna, and those monks were receptive and attentive, concentrating their whole mind, intent on listening to the Dhamma.

Then, on realizing its significance, the Blessed One on that occasion uttered this inspired utterance:

"There is, monks, that base where there is neither earth, nor water, nor heat, nor air; neither the base of the infinity of space, nor the base of the infinity of consciousness, nor the base of nothingness, nor the base of neither-perception-nor-non-perception; neither this world nor another world; neither sun nor moon.[57] Here, monks, I say there is no coming, no going, no standing still; no passing away and no being reborn. It is not established, not moving, without support. Just this is the end of suffering."

(Ud 8:1; 80)

(4) The Unborn

Thus have I heard. At one time the Blessed One was dwelling at Sāvatthī in Jeta's Grove, Anāthapiṇḍika's Park. Now on that occasion the Blessed One was instructing ... the monks with a Dhamma talk connected with Nibbāna, and those monks were receptive ... intent on listening to the Dhamma.

Then, on realizing its significance, the Blessed One on that occasion uttered this inspired utterance:

"There is, monks, an unborn, unbecome, unmade, unconditioned. If, monks, there were no unborn, unbecome, unmade, unconditioned, no escape would be discerned from what is born, become, made, conditioned. But because there is an unborn, unbecome, unmade, unconditioned, therefore an escape is discerned from what is born, become, made, conditioned."

(Ud 8:3; 80–81)

(5) The Two Nibbāna Elements

"There are, monks, these two Nibbāna elements. What are the two? The Nibbāna element with residue remaining and the Nibbāna element without residue remaining.

"And what, monks, is the Nibbāna element with residue remaining? Here, a monk is an arahant, one whose taints are destroyed, who has lived the holy life, done what had to be done, laid down the burden, reached his own goal, utterly destroyed the fetters of existence, one completely liberated through final knowledge. However, his five sense faculties remain unimpaired, by which he still experiences what is agreeable and disagreeable, still feels pleasure and pain. It is the destruction of lust, hatred, and delusion in him that is called the Nibbāna element with residue remaining.

"And what, monks, is the Nibbāna element without residue remaining? Here, a monk is an arahant, ... one completely liberated through final knowledge. For him, here in this very life, all that is felt, not being delighted in, will become cool right here. That, monks, is called the Nibbāna element without residue remaining.

"These, monks, are the two Nibbāna elements."

(It 44; 38)

(6) The Fire and the Ocean

15. [The wanderer Vacchagotta asked the Blessed One:] "Then does Master Gotama hold any speculative view at all?"

"Vaccha, 'speculative view' is something that the Tathāgata has put away. For the Tathāgata, Vaccha, has seen[58] this: 'Such is form, such its origin, such its passing away; such is feeling, such its origin, such its passing away; such is perception, such its origin, such its passing away; such are volitional formations, such their origin, such their passing away; such is consciousness, such its origin, such its passing away.' Therefore, I say, with the destruction, fading away, cessation, giving up, and relinquishing of all conceiving, all rumination, all I-making, mine-making, and the underlying tendency to conceit, the Tathāgata is liberated through not clinging."

16. "When a monk's mind is liberated thus, Master Gotama, where is he reborn [after death]?"

"'Is reborn' does not apply, Vaccha."

"Then he is not reborn, Master Gotama?"

"'Is not reborn' does not apply, Vaccha."

"Then he both is reborn and is not reborn, Master Gotama?"

"'Both is reborn and is not reborn' does not apply, Vaccha."

"Then he neither is reborn nor is not reborn, Master Gotama?"

"'Neither is reborn nor is not reborn' does not apply, Vaccha."

17. "When Master Gotama is asked these four questions, he replies: '"Is reborn" does not apply, Vaccha; "is not reborn" does not apply, Vaccha; "both is reborn and is not reborn" does not apply, Vaccha; "neither is reborn nor is not reborn" does not apply, Vaccha.' Here I have fallen into bewilderment, Master Gotama, here I have fallen into confusion, and the measure of confidence I had gained through previous conversation with Master Gotama has now disappeared."

18. "It is enough to cause you bewilderment, Vaccha, enough to cause you confusion. For this Dhamma, Vaccha, is profound, hard to see and hard to understand, peaceful and sublime, unattainable by mere reasoning, subtle, to be experienced by the wise. It is hard for you to understand it when you hold another view, accept another teaching, approve of another teaching, pursue a different training, and follow a different teacher. So I shall question you about this in return, Vaccha. Answer as you choose.

19. "What do you think, Vaccha? Suppose a fire were burning before you. Would you know: 'This fire is burning before me'?"

"I would, Master Gotama."

"If someone were to ask you, Vaccha: 'What does this fire burning before you burn in dependence on?'—being asked thus, what would you answer?"

"Being asked thus, Master Gotama, I would answer: 'This fire burning before me burns in dependence on grass and sticks.'"

"If that fire before you were to be extinguished, would you know: 'This fire before me has been extinguished'?"

"I would, Master Gotama."

"If someone were to ask you, Vaccha: 'When that fire before you was extinguished, to which direction did it go: to the east, the west, the north, or the south?'—being asked thus, what would you answer?"

"That does not apply, Master Gotama. The fire burned in dependence on its fuel of grass and sticks. When that is used up, if it does not get any more fuel, being without fuel, it is reckoned as extinguished."

20. "So too, Vaccha, the Tathāgata has abandoned that form by which one describing the Tathāgata might describe him; he has cut it off at the root, made it like a palm stump, done away with it so that it is no longer subject to future arising. Liberated from reckoning in terms of form, the Tathāgata is deep, immeasurable, hard to fathom like the ocean. 'Is reborn' does not apply; 'is not reborn' does not apply; 'both is reborn and is not reborn' does not apply; 'neither is reborn nor is not reborn' does not apply. The Tathāgata has abandoned that feeling by which one describing the Tathāgata might describe him … has abandoned that perception by which one describing the Tathāgata might describe him … has abandoned those volitional formations by which one describing the Tathāgata might describe him … has abandoned that consciousness by which one describing the Tathāgata might

describe him; he has cut it off at the root, made it like a palm stump, done away with it so that it is no longer subject to future arising. Liberated from reckoning in terms of consciousness, the Tathāgata is deep, immeasurable, hard to fathom like the ocean. 'Is reborn' does not apply; 'is not reborn' does not apply; 'both is reborn and is not reborn' does not apply; 'neither is reborn nor is not reborn' does not apply."

(from MN 72: *Aggivacchagotta Sutta*; I 486–88)

X. The Planes of Realization

Introduction

The cultivation of wisdom, as we have seen, aims at the realization of Nibbāna. The Nikāyas stipulate a fixed series of stages through which a person passes on the way toward the attainment of Nibbāna. In passing through these stages one evolves from an "uninstructed worldling," blind to the truths of the Dhamma, into an arahant, a liberated one, who has attained full comprehension of the Four Noble Truths and realized Nibbāna in this present life. I have already referred to several of these stages in the earlier chapters of this book. In the present chapter we will explore them in a more systematic manner.

On entering the irreversible path to the attainment of Nibbāna, one becomes a noble person (*ariyapuggala*), the word "noble" (*ariya*) here denoting spiritual nobility. There are four major types of noble persons. Each stage is divided into two phases: the path (*magga*) and its fruition (*phala*).[1] In the path phase, one is said to be practicing for the attainment of a particular fruition, which one is bound to realize within that same life; in the resultant phase, one is said to be established in that fruition. Thus the four major types of noble persons actually comprise four pairs or eight types of noble individuals. As enumerated in **Text X,1(1)**, these are: (1) one practicing for the realization of the fruit of stream-entry, (2) the stream-enterer, (3) one practicing for the realization of the fruit of once-returning, (4) the once-returner, (5) one practicing for the realization of the fruit of nonreturning, (6) the nonreturner, (7) one practicing for arahantship, (8) the arahant. **Text X,1(2)** grades these eight according to the relative strength of their spiritual faculties, so that those at each subsequent stage possess stronger faculties than those at the preceding stage. The first seven persons are collectively known as *sekhas*, trainees or disciples in the higher training; the arahant is called the *asekha*, the one beyond training.

The four main stages themselves are defined in two ways: (1) by way of the defilements eradicated by the path leading to the corresponding fruit; and (2) by way of the destiny after death that awaits one who has realized that particular fruit. **Text X,1(3)** gives standard definitions of the four types that mention both the defilements abandoned and their future destiny.

The Nikāyas group the defilements abandoned into a set of ten fetters (*saṃyojana*). The stream-enterer abandons the first three fetters: *identity view* (*sakkāyadiṭṭhi*), that is, the view of a truly existent self either as identical with the five aggregates or as existing in some relation to them; *doubt* (*vicikicchā*) about the Buddha, the Dhamma, the Saṅgha, and the training; and the *wrong grasp of rules and observances* (*sīlabbataparāmāsa*), the belief that mere external observances, particularly religious rituals and ascetic practices, can lead to liberation. The stream-enterer is assured of attaining full enlightenment in at most seven more existences, which will all take place either in the human realm or the heavenly worlds. The stream-enterer will never undergo an eighth existence and is forever freed from rebirth in the three lower realms—the hells, the realm of afflicted spirits, and the animal realm.

The once-returner (*sakadāgāmī*) does not eradicate any new fetters. He or she has eliminated the three fetters that the stream-enterer has destroyed and additionally attenuates the three unwholesome roots—lust, hatred, and delusion—so that they do not arise often and, when they do arise, do not become obsessive.[2] As the name implies, the once-returner will come back to this world only one more time and then make an end to suffering.

The nonreturner (*anāgāmī*) eradicates the five "lower fetters." That is, in addition to the three fetters eliminated by the stream-enterer, the nonreturner eradicates two additional fetters, sensual lust and ill will. Because nonreturners have eradicated sensual lust, they have no ties binding them to the sensual realm of existence. They thus take birth in the form realm (*rūpadhātu*), generally in one of five planes called the "pure abodes" (*suddhāvāsa*) reserved exclusively for the rebirth of nonreturners. They attain final Nibbāna there, without ever returning to the sensual realm.

The nonreturner, however, is still bound by the five "higher fetters": desire for existence in the form realm, desire for existence in the formless realm, conceit, restlessness, and ignorance. Those who cut off the five higher fetters have no more ties binding them to conditioned existence. These are the arahants, who have destroyed all defilements and are "completely liberated through final knowledge."

The Four Classes of Noble Disciples

By Way of Fetters Eliminated and Types of Rebirth Remaining

Class of disciple	Fetters newly eliminated	Remaining types of rebirth
stream-enterer	identity view, doubt, wrong grasp of rules and observances	at most seven more births among humans and devas
once-returner	none, but weakens lust, hatred, and delusion	one more birth in the sense-sphere realm
nonreturner	sensual lust and ill will	spontaneous birth in the form realm
arahant	desire for existence in form realm, desire for formless existence, conceit, restlessness, ignorance	none

Besides the four main classes of noble persons, the Nikāyas sometimes mention a pair ranked just below the stream-enterer—see **Text X,1(3)**. These two—called the Dhamma-follower (*dhammānusārī*) and the faith-follower (*saddhānusārī*)—are actually two types belonging to the eighth category of noble disciples, the person practicing for the realization of the fruit of stream-entry. The Nikāyas include this pair to show that those on the way to stream-entry can be distinguished into two classes by way of their dominant faculty. The Dhamma-follower is one for whom wisdom is dominant, the faith-follower one for whom faith is dominant. It may be significant that at this stage prior to the first fruition, it is only faith and wisdom and not the other three faculties—energy, mindfulness, and concentration—that serve to distinguish disciples into different types.[3]

The explanation of the classes of noble disciples found in the above text, an extract from the Alagaddūpama Sutta (MN 22), may convey the impression that all those who attain these stages are monks. This, however, is by no means the case. The Alagaddūpama extract is worded in this way only because it is addressed to monks. **Text X,1(4)** corrects this impression and provides a clearer picture of how the classes of noble disciples are distributed among the groups of the

Buddha's followers. As an abiding state, arahantship is reserved for monks and nuns. This does not mean that only monks and nuns can attain arahantship; the suttas and commentaries do record a few cases of lay disciples attaining the final goal. However, such disciples either attain arahantship on the brink of death or enter the monastic order very soon after their attainment. They do not continue to dwell at home as arahant householders, for dwelling at home is incompatible with the state of one who has severed all craving.

In contrast, nonreturners can continue to dwell as householders. While they continue to live as lay disciples, they have eradicated sensual desire and thus necessarily observe celibacy. They are described as "lay followers ... clothed in white, *leading lives of celibacy,* who, with the destruction of the five lower fetters, will be reborn spontaneously [in the pure abodes] and there attain final Nibbāna without ever returning from that world." Though the suttas do not explicitly say this, it is reasonable to suppose that those disciples practicing to attain the fruit of nonreturning also observe full-time celibacy. Lay stream-enterers and once-returners, however, are not necessarily celibate. In the sutta the Buddha describes them as "lay followers ... clothed in white, *enjoying sensual pleasures,* who carry out my instruction, respond to my advice, have gone beyond doubt, become free from perplexity, gained intrepidity, and become independent of others in the Teacher's dispensation." Thus, while some stream-enterers and once-returners may observe celibacy, this is by no means typical of these two classes.

The Nikāyas occasionally employ another scheme for classifying noble disciples, one that makes the dominant faculty rather than the level of attainment alone the basis for differentiation. The main source for this scheme is a passage in the Kīṭāgiri Sutta included here as **Text X,1(5)**. This method of classification divides arahants into two categories: those liberated in both ways (*ubhatobhāgavimutta*) and those liberated by wisdom (*paññāvimutta*). The former are called "liberated in both ways" because they are liberated from form by their mastery over the formless meditations and liberated from all defilements by their attainment of arahantship. Those arahants "liberated by wisdom" have not mastered the formless attainments but have gained the final fruit by the power of their wisdom combined with degrees of concentration lower than the formless states.

Those who have attained any of the lower stages, from stream-entry up to and including the path to arahantship, are divided into three categories. The "body-witness" (*kāyasakkhī*) is one at any of these stages who has mastered the formless attainments; the "one attained-to-view" (*diṭṭhippatta*), one at any of these stages who lacks the formless attainments and gives prominence to wisdom; and the "one liberated by faith" (*saddhāvimutta*), one at any of these stages who lacks the formless attainments and gives prominence to faith. The last two persons in this typology are the Dhamma-follower and the faith-follower explained above.

It should be noted that this scheme does not mention a person at the path of stream-entry who possesses the formless attainments. This should not be taken to mean that such a type is in principle excluded but only that such a type was considered irrelevant for purposes of classification. It seems that at this preparatory stage, the allotment of a separate category to one with outstanding skills in concentration was deemed unnecessary.

In the selection of texts, I next take up the main types for individual consideration. I begin with the stream-enterer, but first some preliminary comments are necessary. In the Nikāyas, the great majority of human beings are called "uninstructed worldlings" (*assutavā puthujjana*). Uninstructed worldlings have no regard for the Buddha and his teaching, no understanding of the Dhamma or dedication to the practice. The purpose of the Buddha's path is to lead uninstructed worldlings to the attainment of the Deathless, and the stages of realization are the steps toward the completion of this process. The process of transformation generally begins when one encounters the Buddha's teaching and gains confidence in the Buddha as the Enlightened One. One must then acquire a clear understanding of the Dhamma, undertake the precepts, and enter upon the systematic practice of the path. In the suttas such a person is called a noble disciple (*ariyasāvaka*) in a broad sense of the term, not necessarily in the narrow, technical sense of one who has already reached the paths and fruits.

Later tradition calls a person who has faith in the Dhamma and aspires to reach the state of stream-entry a virtuous worldling (*kalyāṇaputhujjana*). To reach the attainment of stream-entry, the aspiring disciple should cultivate the "four factors leading to stream-entry." As **Text X,2(1)** explains, these are: associating with wise and virtuous spiritual guides; listening to the true Dhamma; attending carefully to things (for example, by way of gratification, danger, and escape); and practicing in accordance with the Dhamma (by undertaking the threefold training in moral discipline, concentration, and wisdom). The peak of the training undertaken by the aspiring disciple is the development of insight: the thorough contemplation of the aggregates, sense bases, and elements as impermanent, bound up with suffering, and devoid of a substantial self. At a certain point, when insight reaches its peak, the disciple's understanding will undergo a major transition, which marks the entry upon "the fixed course of rightness," the true Noble Eightfold Path that leads irreversibly to Nibbāna. As **Text X,2(2)** puts it, such a disciple has risen up from the plane of worldlings and reached the plane of the noble ones. Though not yet a stream-enterer, a person at this stage cannot pass away without having realized the fruit of stream-entry.

As we have already seen, among disciples who attain the path there is a distinction between those who arrive through faith, called faith-followers, and those who arrive through wisdom, called Dhamma-followers. But while faith-followers and Dhamma-followers differ by way of their dominant faculty, they are alike in that both must further cultivate the path they have entered. Once they know and see the essence of the Dhamma—when they "obtain the vision of the Dhamma" and "make the breakthrough to the Dhamma"—they become stream-enterers, bound to reach full enlightenment and attain final Nibbāna in a maximum of seven more lives; see **Text X,2(3)**. Stream-enterers eradicate the first three fetters and acquire the eight factors of the Noble Eightfold Path. They also have "four factors of stream-entry": confirmed confidence in the Buddha, the Dhamma, and Saṅgha, and "the moral virtues dear to the noble ones," that is, firm adherence to the five precepts; see **Texts X,2(4)–(5)**.

Having seen the truth of the Dhamma, the stream-enterer faces the challenge of cultivating this vision in order to eliminate the remaining defilements. The next major milestone, the attainment of the plane of the once-returner, does not eliminate any defilements completely. However, it does attenuate the three root defilements—lust, hatred, and delusion—to a degree sufficient to ensure that the disciple will return to "this world," the sense-sphere realm of existence, only one more time and then make an end to suffering.

A disciple who attains either of the first two stages, stream-enterer or once-returner, need not remain fixed there but can advance to the two higher stages. Descriptions of attainment in the Nikāyas suggest that it is also possible for a virtuous worldling with extremely sharp faculties to advance directly to the stage of nonreturner. The state of nonreturner is always said to be attained simply through the destruction of the five lower fetters, the three fetters eradicated by the stream-enterer along with sensual lust and ill will. From the Nikāyas, it appears that one with extremely sharp wisdom can achieve this stage at a single stroke. The commentaries, however, explain that in such a case the person actually passes through the first two paths and fruits in very quick succession before reaching the third path and fruit.

According to **Text X,3(1)**, to abandon the five lower fetters, a monk first attains one of the four jhānas or one of the three lower formless attainments; the constituent factors of the fourth formless attainment are too subtle to serve as objects of insight. Directing his attention to the factors constituting the jhāna or formless attainment,[4] he subsumes them under the five aggregates: as included in form (omitted in relation to the formless attainments), feeling, perception, volitional formations, and consciousness. Having done so, he contemplates these factors, now classified into the five aggregates, as marked by the three characteristics: impermanence, suffering, and nonself (expanded into eleven headings). As contemplation advances, at a certain point his mind turns away from all conditioned things and focuses upon the deathless element, Nibbāna. If he has sharp faculties and can relinquish all attachments on the spot, he attains arahantship, the destruction of the taints; but if he cannot yet give up all attachments, he attains the state of nonreturning.

The Buddha recognized differences in the approaches individuals take to achieving the final goal, and in **Text X,3(2)** he divides persons into four categories with respect to its attainment. The four are obtained through the permutations of two pairs. He first distinguishes disciples on the basis of the strength of their spiritual faculties. Those with strong faculties reach final Nibbāna in this very life. Those with relatively weak faculties attain final Nibbāna in the next life, and thus presumably expire as nonreturners. The other pair distinguishes disciples by their mode of development. One class takes the "difficult" approach, which uses meditation subjects that generate sharp wisdom and lead directly to disenchantment and dispassion. The other class takes the smoother and more pleasant route leading through the four jhānas. These two types correspond roughly to those who give emphasis to insight and those who give emphasis to serenity.

A short sutta in the Sotāpattisaṃyutta, **Text X,3(3)**, relates the story of Dīghāvu, a youth who took the difficult route emphasizing insight to the stage of nonreturner. Dīghāvu was lying on his deathbed when the Buddha came to him and asked him to train in the four factors of stream-entry. Dīghāvu said that he was already endowed with these factors, indicating thereby that he was a stream-enterer. The Buddha then instructed him to develop "six things that partake of true knowledge." He evidently heeded the Buddha's advice, for shortly after he died the Buddha declared him to have expired as a nonreturner. Though it is possible that Dīghāvu had already gained the jhānas and thus did not need to be instructed in their practice, it is also possible that he attained the stage of nonreturner entirely through the power of the deep insight arisen from these six contemplations.

Text X,3(4) makes further distinctions among those who attain arahantship and the stage of nonreturner. Such suttas point to the great variety that can exist even among those at the same spiritual level. It is because he was able to make such distinctions that the Buddha was said to possess perfect understanding of the diversity in the faculties of sentient beings.

Since nonreturners have eradicated the five lower fetters, they are no longer bound to the sensual realm of existence. However, they are still not entirely liberated from the cycle of rebirths but are still bound by the five higher fetters: desire for existence in the form realm, desire for existence in the formless realm, the conceit "I am," subtle restlessness, and ignorance. The conceit "I am" (*asmimāna*) differs from identity view, the view of self (*sakkāyadiṭṭhi*), to which it is partly akin. The view of self affirms an enduring self existing in relation to the five aggregates, either as identical with them, or as their inner core, or as their owner and master. But the conceit "I am" lacks a clear conceptual content. It lurks at the base of the mind as a vague, shapeless, but imperious sense of the "I" as a concrete reality. Though the view of self is already eliminated at the stage of stream-entry, the conceit "I am" persists in noble disciples even up to the stage of nonreturner. This is the point of the incisive Khemaka Sutta—**Text X,4(1)**—with its two beautiful similes of the flower's scent and the laundered cloth. The noble disciples differ from ordinary people in that they do not buy into the conceit "I am." They recognize the conceit "I am" as a mere figment of the imagination, a false notion that does not point to a self, to a truly existent "I." But they have not completely overcome it.

The subtle attachment and the residual sense of "I am" that persist in the nonreturner both stem from ignorance. To reach the end of the path, the nonreturner must obliterate the remaining segment of ignorance and dispel all traces of craving and conceit. The critical point when ignorance, craving, and conceit are eradicated marks the transition from the stage of nonreturner to arahantship. The difference between the two can be a subtle one, and therefore standards for distinguishing them are necessary. In **Text X,4(2)** the Buddha proposes several criteria by which a trainee and an arahant can determine their respective standings. One of particular interest concerns their relationship to the five spiritual faculties: faith, energy, mindfulness, concentration, and wisdom. The trainee sees with wisdom the goal in which the faculties culminate—namely, Nibbāna—but cannot dwell in it. The arahant sees with wisdom the supreme goal and can also dwell in that goal.

The texts that follow offer different perspectives on the arahant. **Text X,4(3)** characterizes the arahant with a series of metaphors, elucidated in the same passage. **Text X,4(4)** enumerates nine things that an arahant cannot do. In **Text X,4(5)**, the Venerable Sāriputta describes the arahant's imperturbability in the face of powerful sense objects, and in **Text X,4(6)** he enumerates the ten powers of an arahant. **Text X,4(7)**, an excerpt from the Dhātuvibhaṅga Sutta, begins as an account of the attainment of arahantship through the contemplation of the elements; the relevant passage was included in the previous chapter as **Text IX,4(3)(c)**. The exposition then turns to the "four foundations" (*cattāro adhiṭṭhāna*) of the arahant, here spoken of as "the sage at peace" (*muni santo*). **Text X,4(8)**, the last in this section, is a poem extolling the arahant's distinguished qualities.

The first and foremost of the arahants is the Buddha himself, to whom the last section of this chapter is devoted. The section is titled "The Tathāgata," the word the Buddha used when referring to himself in his archetypal role as the discoverer and bringer of liberating truth. The word can be resolved in two ways: taken as *tathā āgata*, "Thus Come," it implies that the Buddha has *come* in accordance with an established pattern (which the commentaries interpret to mean the fulfillment of the ten spiritual perfections—the *pāramīs*—and the thirty-seven aids to enlightenment); taken as *tathā gata*, "Thus Gone," it implies that he has *gone* in accordance with an established pattern (which the commentaries interpret to mean that he has gone to Nibbāna by the complete practice of serenity, insight, the paths, and the fruits).

Later forms of Buddhism draw extreme distinctions between Buddhas and arahants, but in the Nikāyas this distinction is not as sharp as one might expect if one takes later texts as the benchmark of interpretation. On the one hand, the Buddha is an arahant, as is evident from the standard verse of homage to the Blessed One (*iti pi so bhagavā arahaṃ sammā sambuddho* ...); on the other, arahants are *buddha*, in the sense that they have attained full enlightenment, *sambodhi*, by awakening to the same truths that the Buddha himself realized. The proper distinction, then, is that between a *sammā sambuddha* or Perfectly Enlightened Buddha, and an arahant who has attained enlightenment and liberation as a disciple (*sāvaka*) of a Perfectly Enlightened Buddha. However, to avoid such complex locutions, we will resort to the common practice of phrasing the distinction as that between a Buddha and an arahant.

What then is the relationship between the two? Is the difference between them primarily one of temporal sequence, with perhaps a few additional capacities specific to a Perfectly Enlightened Buddha? Or is the difference between them so vast that they should be considered distinct types? The Nikāyas display an interesting, even tantalizing, ambivalence on this question, as the texts included here illustrate. **Text X,5(1)** raises the question about the difference between "the Tathāgata, the Arahant, the Perfectly Enlightened One" and "a monk liberated by wisdom"; apparently the expression *bhikkhu paññāvimutta* is used here in a sense applicable to any arahant disciple rather than solely to one who lacks the formless attainments (that is, in an inclusive sense, not as a wisdom-liberated arahant contrasted with a both-ways liberated arahant). The answer the text gives expresses the difference in terms of role and temporal priority. A Buddha has the function of discovering and expounding the path, and he also possesses a unique familiarity with the intricacies of the path not shared by his disciples. His disciples follow the path he reveals and attain enlightenment afterward, under his guidance.

The polemical literature of later Buddhism sometimes depicts the Buddha as motivated by great compassion and his arahant disciples as cool and aloof, indifferent to the plight of their fellow beings. As if to forestall this criticism, **Text X,5(2)** states that not only the Buddha but arahants as well as learned and virtuous disciples still in training arise for the welfare of many people, live their lives out of compassion for the world, and teach the Dhamma for the good, well-being, and happiness of their fellow beings, devas as well as humans. Thus, if this text is taken as authoritative, it cannot be claimed that compassion and altruistic concern are qualities that distinguish Buddhas from arahants.

Yet **Text X,5(3)** gives us another perspective on this question. Here, the Buddha challenges the Venerable Sāriputta's "bellowing utterance" by asking him whether he fully knows the moral discipline, qualities (perhaps concentration), wisdom, meditative dwellings, and liberation of the Buddhas of the past, present, and future. To this the great disciple can only answer in the negative. But Sāriputta declares that he knows that all the Buddhas of the three periods of time attain perfect enlightenment by abandoning the five hindrances, by establishing their minds in the four establishments of mindfulness, and by developing correctly the seven factors of enlightenment.

These, however, are aspects of the path that Buddhas have fulfilled in common with arahant disciples. Beyond this, the Buddhas possess certain qualities that elevate them above even the foremost of the arahants. From the Nikāyas, their superiority seems to rest on two main pillars: first, their being is essentially "for others" in a way that the most altruistic of the arahant disciples can only emulate but never equal; and second, their knowledges and spiritual powers are much greater than those of the arahant disciples.

The Buddha states that even monks fully liberated in mind, who possess "unsurpassable vision, practice, and liberation," venerate the Tathāgata, because his attainment of enlightenment helps others to attain enlightenment, his deliverance helps others gain deliverance, his realization of Nibbāna enables others to realize Nibbāna (MN 35.26; I 235). In **Text X,5(4)**, we encounter two sets of qualities considered special endowments of a Buddha, enabling him to "roar his lion's roar in the assemblies" and set rolling the wheel of Dhamma. These are the ten Tathāgata's powers and the four grounds of self-confidence. Though several of these powers are shared by disciples, in their totality these two sets are distinctive of a Buddha and equip him to guide and instruct beings in accordance with their individual aptitudes and dispositions. The four grounds of self-confidence confer upon the Buddha a boldness of authority, a magnitude of mission, that only the founder of a religion can exercise. **Text X,5(5)** compares the Tathāgata to the sun and moon, for his appearance in the world is the manifestation of great light and dispels the darkness of ignorance. **Text X,5(6)** compares him to a man who rescues a herd of deer from calamity, thus portraying him as the great benefactor of humanity.

With **Text X,5(7)** we return to the metaphor of the lion's roar, introduced earlier, with a lengthy simile that compares the Buddha's proclamation of universal impermanence to the roar of a lion when he emerges from his den. Like the closing passage of the First Sermon (see **Text II,5**), this text draws our attention to the cosmic scope of the Buddha's mission. His message extends not only to human beings, but reaches up to the high heavenly realms, shaking the delusions of the deities.

Finally, **Text X,5(8)** offers us a series of brief explanations why the Buddha is called the Tathāgata. He is called the Tathāgata because he has fully awakened to the nature of the world, its origin, its cessation, and the way to its cessation; because he has fully comprehended all phenomena within the world, whether seen, heard, sensed, or cognized; because his speech is invariably true; because he acts in conformity with his words; and because he wields supreme mastery within the world. The text ends with an inspired poem, probably attached by the compilers of the canon, which celebrates the Buddha as the supreme refuge for the world.

The personal devotion toward the Tathāgata expressed by both the prose text and the poem introduces us to the warm current of religious feeling that runs through Early Buddhism, always present just beneath its cool and composed exterior. This religious dimension makes the Dhamma more than just a philosophy or an ethical system or a body of meditative techniques. Animating it from within, drawing its followers upward and onward, it makes the Dhamma a complete spiritual path—a path rooted in faith in a particular person who is at once the supreme teacher of liberating truth and the foremost example of the truth he teaches.

X. The Planes of Realization

1. The Field of Merit for the World

(1) Eight Persons Worthy of Gifts

"Monks, these eight persons are worthy of gifts, worthy of hospitality, worthy of offerings, worthy of reverential salutations, the unsurpassed field of merit for the world. What eight?

"The stream-enterer, the one practicing for the realization of the fruit of stream-entry; the once-returner, the one practicing for the realization of the fruit of once-returning; the nonreturner, the one practicing for the realization of the fruit of the nonreturning; the arahant, the one practicing for arahantship.

"Monks, these eight persons are worthy of gifts, worthy of hospitality, worthy of offerings, worthy of reverential salutations, the unsurpassed field of merit for the world."

(AN 8:59; IV 292)

(2) Differentiation by Faculties

"Monks, there are these five faculties. What five? The faculty of faith, the faculty of energy, the faculty of mindfulness, the faculty of concentration, the faculty of wisdom. These are the five faculties.

"One who has completed and fulfilled these five faculties is an arahant. If they are weaker than that, one is practicing for the realization of the fruit of arahantship; if still weaker, one is a nonreturner; if still weaker, one is practicing for the realization of the fruit of nonreturning; if still weaker, one is a once-returner; if still weaker, one is practicing for the realization of the fruit of once-returning; if still weaker, one is a stream-enterer; if still weaker, one is practicing for the realization of the fruit of stream-entry.

"But, monks, I say that one in whom these five faculties are completely and totally absent is 'an outsider, one standing amid the worldlings.'"

(SN 48:18; V 202)

(3) In the Dhamma Well Expounded

42. "Monks, the Dhamma well expounded by me thus is clear, open, evident, and free of patchwork. In the Dhamma well expounded by me thus, which is clear, open, evident, and free of patchwork, those monks who are arahants with taints destroyed—who have lived the spiritual life, done what had to be done, laid down the burden, reached their own goal, utterly destroyed the fetters of existence, and are completely liberated through final knowledge—have no round for manifestation.[5]

43. "Monks, the Dhamma well expounded by me thus is clear ... free of patchwork. In the Dhamma well expounded by me thus, those monks who have abandoned the five lower fetters are all due to be reborn spontaneously [in the pure abodes] and there attain final Nibbāna, without ever returning from that world.[6]

44. "Monks, the Dhamma well expounded by me thus is clear ... free of patchwork. In the Dhamma well expounded by me thus, those monks who have abandoned three fetters and attenuated lust, hate, and delusion are all once-returners, returning once to this world to make an end of suffering.

45. "Monks, the Dhamma well expounded by me thus is clear ... free of patchwork. In the Dhamma well expounded by me thus, those monks who have abandoned three fetters are all stream-enterers, no longer bound to the lower world, fixed in destiny, with enlightenment as their destination.[7]

46. "Monks, the Dhamma well expounded by me thus is clear ... free of patchwork. In the Dhamma well expounded by me thus, those monks who are Dhamma-followers or faith-followers all have enlightenment as their destination.[8]

47. "Monks, the Dhamma well expounded by me thus is clear, open, evident, and free of patchwork. In the Dhamma well expounded by me thus, those who have sufficient faith in me, sufficient love for me, all have heaven as their destination."[9]

(from MN 22: *Alagaddūpama Sutta*; I 140–42)

(4) The Completeness of the Teaching

6. "When a monk has abandoned craving, cut it off at the root, made it like a palm stump, done away with it so that it is no longer subject to

future arising, that monk is an arahant with taints destroyed, one who has lived the spiritual life, done what had to be done, laid down the burden, reached his own goal, utterly destroyed the fetters of existence, and is completely liberated through final knowledge."

7. "Apart from Master Gotama, is there any monk, Master Gotama's disciple, who by realizing it for himself with direct knowledge, in this present life enters upon and dwells in the liberation of mind, liberation by wisdom, that is taintless with the destruction of the taints?"[10]

"There are, Vaccha, not only one hundred, or two or three or four or five hundred, but far more monks, my disciples, who by realizing it for themselves with direct knowledge, in this present life enter upon and dwell in the liberation of mind, liberation by wisdom, that is taintless with the destruction of the taints."

8. "Apart from Master Gotama and the monks, is there any nun, Master Gotama's disciple, who by realizing it for herself with direct knowledge, in this present life enters upon and dwells in the liberation of mind, liberation by wisdom, that is taintless with the destruction of the taints?"

"There are not only one hundred ... or five hundred, but far more nuns, my disciples, who by realizing it for themselves with direct knowledge, in this present life enter upon and dwell in the liberation of mind, liberation by wisdom, that is taintless with the destruction of the taints."

9. "Apart from Master Gotama and the monks and nuns, is there any male lay follower, Master Gotama's disciple, clothed in white leading a life of celibacy who, with the destruction of the five lower fetters, will be reborn spontaneously [in the pure abodes] and there attain final Nibbāna without ever returning from that world?"[11]

"There are not only one hundred ... or five hundred, but far more male lay followers, my disciples, clothed in white leading lives of celibacy who, with the destruction of the five lower fetters, will be reborn spontaneously [in the pure abodes] and there attain final Nibbāna without ever returning from that world."

10. "Apart from Master Gotama, the monks and nuns, and the male lay followers clothed in white leading lives of celibacy, is there any male lay follower, Master Gotama's disciple, clothed in white enjoying sensual pleasures, who carries out his instruction, responds to his advice, has gone beyond doubt, become free from perplexity, gained

intrepidity, and become independent of others in the Teacher's dispensation?"[12]

"There are not only one hundred ... or five hundred, but far more male lay followers, my disciples, clothed in white enjoying sensual pleasures, who carry out my instruction, respond to my advice, have gone beyond doubt, become free from perplexity, gained intrepidity, and become independent of others in the Teacher's dispensation."

11. "Apart from Master Gotama, the monks and nuns, and the male lay followers clothed in white, both those leading lives of celibacy and those enjoying sensual pleasures, is there any female lay follower, Master Gotama's disciple, clothed in white leading a life of celibacy who, with the destruction of the five lower fetters, will be reborn spontaneously [in the pure abodes] and there attain final Nibbāna without ever returning from that world?"

"There are not only one hundred ... or five hundred, but far more female lay followers, my disciples, clothed in white leading lives of celibacy who, with the destruction of the five lower fetters, will be reborn spontaneously [in the pure abodes] and there attain final Nibbāna without ever returning from that world."

12. "Apart from Master Gotama, the monks and nuns, and the male lay followers clothed in white, both those leading lives of celibacy and those enjoying sensual pleasures, and the female lay followers clothed in white leading lives of celibacy, is there any one female lay follower, Master Gotama's disciple, clothed in white enjoying sensual pleasures, who carries out his instruction, responds to his advice, has gone beyond doubt, become free from perplexity, gained intrepidity, and become independent of others in the Teacher's dispensation?"

"There are not only one hundred ... or five hundred, but far more female lay followers, my disciples, clothed in white enjoying sensual pleasures, who carry out my instruction, respond to my advice, have gone beyond doubt, become free of perplexity, gained intrepidity, and become independent of others in the Teacher's dispensation."

13. "Master Gotama, if only Master Gotama were accomplished in this Dhamma, but no monks were accomplished, then this spiritual life would be deficient in that respect; but because Master Gotama and monks are accomplished in this Dhamma, this spiritual life is thus complete in that respect. If only Master Gotama and monks were accomplished in this Dhamma, but no nuns were accomplished, then

this spiritual life would be deficient in that respect; but because Master Gotama, monks, and nuns are accomplished in this Dhamma, this spiritual life is thus complete in that respect. If only Master Gotama, monks, and nuns were accomplished in this Dhamma, but no male lay followers clothed in white leading lives of celibacy were accomplished, then this spiritual life would be deficient in that respect; but because Master Gotama, monks and nuns, and male lay followers clothed in white leading lives of celibacy are accomplished in this Dhamma, this spiritual life is thus complete in that respect. If only Master Gotama, monks and nuns, and male lay followers clothed in white leading lives of celibacy were accomplished in this Dhamma, but no male lay followers clothed in white enjoying sensual pleasures were accomplished, then this spiritual life would be deficient in that respect; but because Master Gotama, monks and nuns, and male lay followers clothed in white, both those leading lives of celibacy and those enjoying sensual pleasures, are accomplished in this Dhamma, this spiritual life is thus complete in that respect. If only Master Gotama, monks and nuns, and male lay followers clothed in white … were accomplished in this Dhamma, but no female lay followers clothed in white leading lives of celibacy were accomplished, then this spiritual life would be deficient in that respect; but because Master Gotama, monks and nuns, male lay followers clothed in white … and female lay followers clothed in white leading lives of celibacy are accomplished in this Dhamma, this spiritual life is thus complete in that respect. If only Master Gotama, monks and nuns, male lay followers clothed in white … and female lay followers clothed in white leading lives of celibacy were accomplished in this Dhamma, but no female lay followers clothed in white enjoying sensual pleasures were accomplished, then this spiritual life would be deficient in that respect; but because Master Gotama, monks and nuns, male lay followers clothed in white, both those leading lives of celibacy and those enjoying sensual pleasures, and female lay followers clothed in white, both those leading lives of celibacy and those enjoying sensual pleasures, are accomplished in this Dhamma, this spiritual life is thus complete in that respect.

14. "Just as the river Ganges inclines toward the sea, slopes toward the sea, flows toward the sea, and reaches the sea, so too Master Gotama's assembly with its homeless ones and its householders

inclines toward Nibbāna, slopes toward Nibbāna, flows toward Nibbāna, and reaches Nibbāna."

(from MN 73: *Mahāvacchagotta Sutta*; I 490–93)

(5) Seven Kinds of Noble Persons

11. "Monks, I do not say of all monks that they still have work to do with diligence; nor do I say of all monks that they have no more work to do with diligence.

12. "I do not say of those monks who are arahants with taints destroyed, who have lived the spiritual life, done what had to be done, laid down the burden, reached their own goal, utterly destroyed the fetters of existence, and are completely liberated through final knowledge, that they still have work to do with diligence. Why is that? They have done their work with diligence; they are no more capable of being negligent.

13. "I say of those monks who are trainees, whose minds have not yet reached the goal, and who are still aspiring to the unsurpassed security from bondage, that they still have work to do with diligence. Why is that? Because when those venerable ones make use of suitable lodgings and associate with good friends and nurture their spiritual faculties, they may, by realizing it for themselves with direct knowledge, in this present life enter upon and dwell in that supreme goal of the spiritual life for the sake of which clansmen rightly go forth from the home life into homelessness. Seeing this fruit of diligence for these monks, I say that they still have work to do with diligence.

14. "Monks, there are seven kinds of persons to be found existing in the world. What seven? They are: one liberated-in-both ways, one liberated-by-wisdom, a body-witness, one attained-to-view, one liberated-by-faith, a Dhamma-follower, and a faith-follower.

15. "What kind of person is one liberated-in-both-ways? Here some person contacts with the body and dwells in those liberations that are peaceful and formless, transcending forms, and his taints are destroyed by his seeing with wisdom. This kind of person is called one liberated-in-both-ways.[13] I do not say of such a monk that he still has work to do with diligence. Why is that? He has done his work with diligence; he is no more capable of being negligent.

16. "What kind of person is one liberated-by-wisdom? Here some

person does not contact with the body and dwell in those liberations that are peaceful and formless, transcending forms, but his taints are destroyed by his seeing with wisdom. This kind of person is called one liberated-by-wisdom.[14] I do not say of such a monk that he still has work to do with diligence. Why is that? He has done his work with diligence; he is no more capable of being negligent.

17. "What kind of person is a body-witness? Here some person contacts with the body and dwells in those liberations that are peaceful and formless, transcending forms, and some of his taints are destroyed by his seeing with wisdom. This kind of person is called a body-witness.[15] I say of such a monk that he still has work to do with diligence. Why is that? Because when that venerable one makes use of suitable lodgings and associates with good friends and nurtures his spiritual faculties, he may, by realizing it for himself with direct knowledge, in this present life enter upon and dwell in that supreme goal of the spiritual life for the sake of which clansmen rightly go forth from the home life into homelessness. Seeing this fruit of diligence for such a monk, I say that he still has work to do with diligence.

18. "What kind of person is one attained-to-view? Here some person does not contact with the body and dwell in those liberations that are peaceful and formless, transcending forms, but some of his taints are destroyed by his seeing with wisdom, and he has reviewed and examined with wisdom the teachings proclaimed by the Tathāgata. This kind of person is called one attained-to-view.[16] I say of such a monk that he still has work to do with diligence. Why is that? Because when that venerable one ... into homelessness. Seeing this fruit of diligence for such a monk, I say that he still has work to do with diligence.

19. "What kind of person is one liberated-by-faith? Here some person does not contact with the body and dwell in those liberations that are peaceful and formless, transcending forms, but some of his taints are destroyed by his seeing with wisdom, and his faith is planted, rooted, and established in the Tathāgata. This kind of person is called one liberated-by-faith.[17] I say of such a monk that he still has work to do with diligence. Why is that? Because when that venerable one ... into homelessness. Seeing this fruit of diligence for such a monk, I say that he still has work to do with diligence.

20. "What kind of person is a Dhamma-follower? Here some person does not contact with the body and dwell in those liberations that are

peaceful and formless, transcending forms, and his taints are not yet destroyed by his seeing with wisdom, but those teachings proclaimed by the Tathāgata are accepted after being pondered to a sufficient degree with wisdom. Furthermore, he has these qualities: the faith faculty, the energy faculty, the mindfulness faculty, the concentration faculty, and the wisdom faculty. This kind of person is called a Dhamma-follower.[18] I say of such a monk that he still has work to do with diligence. Why is that? Because when that venerable one ... into homelessness. Seeing this fruit of diligence for such a monk, I say that he still has work to do with diligence.

21. "What kind of person is a faith-follower? Here some person does not contact with the body and dwell in those liberations that are peaceful and formless, transcending forms, and his taints are not yet destroyed by his seeing with wisdom, yet he has sufficient faith in and love for the Tathāgata. Furthermore, he has these qualities: the faith faculty, the energy faculty, the mindfulness faculty, the concentration faculty, and the wisdom faculty. This kind of person is called a faith-follower. I say of such a monk that he still has work to do with diligence. Why is that? Because when that venerable one makes use of suitable lodgings and associates with good friends and nurtures his spiritual faculties, he may, by realizing it for himself with direct knowledge, in this present life enter upon and dwell in that supreme goal of the spiritual life for the sake of which clansmen rightly go forth from the home life into homelessness. Seeing this fruit of diligence for such a monk, I say that he still has work to do with diligence."

(from MN 70: *Kīṭāgiri Sutta*; I 477–79)

2. Stream-Entry

(1) The Four Factors Leading to Stream-Entry

The Blessed One said to the Venerable Sāriputta: "Sāriputta, it is said: 'A factor for stream-entry, a factor for stream-entry.' What now, Sāriputta, is a factor for stream-entry?"

"Association with superior persons, venerable sir, is a factor for stream-entry. Hearing the true Dhamma is a factor for stream-entry. Careful attention is a factor for stream-entry. Practice in accordance with the Dhamma is a factor for stream-entry."

"Good, good, Sāriputta! It is as you say. Sāriputta, it is said: 'The stream, the stream.' What now is the stream?"

"This Noble Eightfold Path, venerable sir, is the stream; that is, right view, right intention, right speech, right action, right livelihood, right effort, right mindfulness, right concentration."

"Good, good, Sāriputta! It is as you say. Sāriputta, it is said: 'A stream-enterer, a stream-enterer.' What now is a stream-enterer?"

"One who possesses this Noble Eightfold Path, venerable sir, is called a stream-enterer: this venerable one of such a name and clan."

"Good, good, Sāriputta! One who possesses this Noble Eightfold Path is a stream-enterer: this venerable one of such a name and clan."

(SN 55:5; V 410–11)

(2) Entering the Fixed Course of Rightness

"Monks, the eye is impermanent, changing, undergoing alteration. The ear ... The nose ... The tongue ... The body ... The mind is impermanent, changing, undergoing alteration. One who places faith in these teachings and resolves on them thus is called a faith-follower, one who has entered the fixed course of rightness,[19] entered the plane of superior persons, transcended the plane of the worldlings. He is incapable of doing any deed by reason of which he might be reborn in hell, in the animal realm, or in the domain of afflicted spirits; he is incapable of passing away without having realized the fruit of stream-entry.[20]

"One for whom these teachings are accepted thus after being pondered to a sufficient degree with wisdom is called a Dhamma-follower, one who has entered the fixed course of rightness, entered the plane of superior persons, transcended the plane of the worldlings. He is incapable of doing any deed by reason of which he might be reborn in hell, in the animal realm, or in the domain of afflicted spirits; he is incapable of passing away without having realized the fruit of stream-entry.

"One who knows and sees these teachings thus is called a stream-enterer, no longer bound to the lower world, fixed in destiny, with enlightenment as his destination."[21]

(SN 25:1; III 225)

(3) The Breakthrough to the Dhamma

The Blessed One took up a little bit of soil in his fingernail and addressed the monks thus:

"Monks, what do you think, which is more: the little bit of soil that I have taken up in my fingernail or this great earth?"

"Venerable sir, the great earth is more. The little bit of soil that the Blessed One has taken up in his fingernail is trifling. It does not amount to a hundredth part, or a thousandth part, or a hundred thousandth part of the great earth."

"So too, monks, for a noble disciple, a person accomplished in view who has made the breakthrough, the suffering that has been destroyed and eliminated is more, while that which remains is trifling. The latter does not amount to a hundredth part, or a thousandth part, or a hundred thousandth part of the former mass of suffering that has been destroyed and eliminated, since there is a maximum of seven more lives. Of such great benefit, monks, is the breakthrough to the Dhamma, of such great benefit is it to obtain the vision of the Dhamma."[22]

(SN 13:1; II 133–34)

(4) The Four Factors of a Stream-Enterer

"Monks, a noble disciple who possesses four things is a stream-enterer, no longer bound to the lower world, fixed in destiny, with enlightenment as his destination.

"What four? Here, monks, a noble disciple possesses confirmed confidence[23] in the Buddha thus: 'The Blessed One is an arahant, perfectly enlightened, accomplished in true knowledge and conduct, fortunate, knower of the world, unsurpassed leader of persons to be tamed, teacher of devas and humans, the Enlightened One, the Blessed One.' He possesses confirmed confidence in the Dhamma thus: 'The Dhamma is well expounded by the Blessed One, directly visible, immediate, inviting one to come and see, worthy of application, to be personally experienced by the wise.' He possesses confirmed confidence in the Saṅgha thus: 'The Saṅgha of the Blessed One's disciples is practicing the good way, practicing the straight way, practicing the true way, practicing the proper way; that is, the four pairs of persons, the eight types of individuals—this Saṅgha of the Blessed One's disciples is worthy of gifts, worthy of hospitality, worthy of offerings, worthy of reverential salutation, the unsurpassed field of merit for the world.' He possesses the moral virtues dear to the noble ones, unbroken, untorn, unblemished, unmottled, freeing, praised by the wise, ungrasped, leading to concentration.

"A noble disciple, monks, who possesses these four things is a stream-enterer, no longer bound to the lower world, fixed in destiny, with enlightenment as his destination."

(SN 55:2; V 343–44)

(5) Better than Sovereignty over the Earth

"Monks, although a wheel-turning monarch, having exercised supreme sovereignty over the four continents, with the breakup of the body, after death, is reborn in a good destination, in a heavenly world, in the company of the devas of the Tāvatiṃsa realm, and there in the Nandana Grove, accompanied by a retinue of celestial nymphs, he enjoys himself supplied and endowed with the five cords of celestial sensual pleasure, still, as he does not possess four things, he is not freed from hell, the animal realm, and the domain of afflicted spirits, not freed from the plane of misery, the bad destinations, the lower world.[24] Although, monks, a noble disciple maintains himself by lumps of almsfood and wears rag-robes, still, as he possesses four things, he is freed from hell, the animal realm, and the domain of afflicted spirits, freed from the plane of misery, the bad destinations, the lower world. What four things? Confirmed confidence in the Buddha, the Dhamma, and the Saṅgha, and the moral virtues dear to the noble ones. And, monks, between the obtaining of sovereignty over the four continents and the obtaining of the four things, the obtaining of sovereignty over the four continents is not worth a sixteenth part of the obtaining of the four things."

(SN 55:1; V 342)

3. Nonreturning

(1) Abandoning the Five Lower Fetters

7. "There is a path and way, Ānanda, to the abandoning of the five lower fetters. That anyone, without relying on that path and way, might know or see or abandon the five lower fetters—this is not possible. Just as when there is a great tree standing possessed of heartwood, it is not possible that anyone might cut out its heartwood without cutting through its bark and sapwood, so too, in the case of abandoning the five lower fetters.

"There is a path and way, Ānanda, to the abandoning of the five lower fetters. That someone, by relying on that path and way, might know and see and abandon the five lower fetters—this is possible. Just as, when there is a great tree standing possessed of heartwood, it is possible that someone might cut out its heartwood by cutting through its bark and sapwood, so too, in the case of abandoning the five lower fetters.

8. "Suppose, Ānanda, the river Ganges were full of water right up to the brim so that crows could drink from it, and then a feeble man came thinking: 'By swimming across the stream with my arms, I shall get safely across to the further shore of this river Ganges'; yet he would not be able to get safely across. So too, when the Dhamma is being taught to someone for the cessation of identity, if his mind does not enter into it and acquire confidence, steadiness, and resolution, then he can be regarded as like the feeble man.[25]

"Suppose, Ānanda, the river Ganges were full of water right up to the brim so that crows could drink from it, and then a strong man came thinking: 'By swimming across the stream with my arms, I shall get safely across to the further shore of this river Ganges'; and he would be able to get safely across. So too, when the Dhamma is being taught to someone for the cessation of identity, if his mind enters into it and acquires confidence, steadiness, and resolution, then he can be regarded as like the strong man.

9. "And what, Ānanda, is the path and way to the abandoning of the five lower fetters? Here, with seclusion from acquisitions,[26] with the abandoning of unwholesome states, with the complete tranquilizing of bodily inertia, secluded from sensual pleasures, secluded from unwholesome states, a monk enters and dwells in the first jhāna, which

is accompanied by thought and examination, with rapture and happiness born of seclusion.

"Whatever exists therein of form, feeling, perception, volitional formations, and consciousness, he sees those states as impermanent, as suffering, as a disease, as a tumor, as a barb, as a calamity, as an affliction, as alien, as disintegrating, as empty, as nonself.[27] He turns his mind away from those states and directs it toward the deathless element thus: 'This is the peaceful, this is the sublime, that is, the stilling of all formations, the relinquishing of all acquisitions, the destruction of craving, dispassion, cessation, Nibbāna.'[28] If he is steady in that, he attains the destruction of the taints. But if he does not attain the destruction of the taints, then through that very desire for the Dhamma, that delight in the Dhamma, with the destruction of the five lower fetters he becomes one due to be reborn spontaneously [in the pure abodes] and there attain final Nibbāna without ever returning from that world.[29] This is the path and way to the abandoning of the five lower fetters.

10–12. "Again, with the subsiding of thought and examination, a monk enters and dwells in the second jhāna.... Again, with the fading away as well of rapture, a monk ... enters and dwells in the third jhāna.... Again, with the abandoning of pleasure and pain ... a monk enters and dwells in the fourth jhāna, which has neither-pain-nor-pleasure and purity of mindfulness due to equanimity.

"Whatever exists therein of form, feeling, perception, volitional formations, and consciousness, he sees those states as impermanent ... as nonself. He turns his mind away from those states and directs it toward the deathless element... This is the path and way to the abandoning of the five lower fetters.

13. "Again, with the complete transcending of perceptions of forms, with the passing away of perceptions of sensory impingement, with nonattention to perceptions of diversity, aware that 'space is infinite,' a monk enters upon and dwells in the base of the infinity of space.

"Whatever exists therein of feeling, perception, volitional formations, and consciousness,[30] he sees those states as impermanent ... as nonself. He turns his mind away from those states and directs it toward the deathless element ... This is the path and way to the abandoning of the five lower fetters.

14. "Again, by completely transcending the base of the infinity of

space, aware that 'consciousness is infinite,' a monk enters upon and dwells in the base of the infinity of consciousness.

"Whatever exists therein of feeling, perception, volitional formations, and consciousness, he sees those states as impermanent ... as nonself. He turns his mind away from those states and directs it toward the deathless element... This is the path and way to the abandoning of the five lower fetters.

15. "Again, by completely transcending the base of the infinity of consciousness, aware that 'there is nothing,' a monk enters upon and dwells in the base of nothingness.

"Whatever exists therein of feeling, perception, volitional formations, and consciousness, he sees those states as impermanent, as suffering, as a disease, as a tumor, as a barb, as a calamity, as an affliction, as alien, as disintegrating, as void, as nonself. He turns his mind away from those states and directs it toward the deathless element thus: 'This is the peaceful, this is the sublime, that is, the stilling of all formations, the relinquishing of all acquisitions, the destruction of craving, dispassion, cessation, Nibbāna.' If he is steady in that, he attains the destruction of the taints. But if he does not attain the destruction of the taints, then through that very desire for the Dhamma, that delight in the Dhamma, with the destruction of the five lower fetters he becomes one due to be reborn spontaneously [in the pure abodes] and there attain final Nibbāna without ever returning from that world. This is the path and way to the abandoning of the five lower fetters."

(from MN 64: *Mahāmāluṅkya Sutta*; I 434–37)

(2) Four Kinds of Persons

"There are, O monks, four kinds of persons found existing in the world. What four?

"Here, monks, in this very life a person attains Nibbāna through volitional exertion. Here, with the breakup of the body, a person attains final Nibbāna through volitional exertion. Here, in this very life a person attains final Nibbāna without volitional exertion. Here, with the breakup of the body, a person attains final Nibbāna without volitional exertion.

"And how, monks, does a person, in this very life, attain Nibbāna through volitional exertion? Here, a monk dwells contemplating the unattractiveness of the body, perceiving repulsiveness in food, perceiving discontent with the entire world, contemplating impermanence in all formations; and the perception of death is well established within him.[31] He dwells relying upon these five powers of a trainee: the powers of faith, moral shame, fear of wrongdoing, energy, and wisdom. These five faculties are extremely strong in him: the faculties of faith, energy, mindfulness, concentration, and wisdom. Because of the strength of these five faculties, in this very life he attains Nibbāna through volitional exertion. This is how a person, in this very life, attains Nibbāna through volitional exertion.

"And how, monks, does a person, with the breakup of the body, attain Nibbāna through volitional exertion? Here, a monk dwells contemplating the unattractiveness of the body ... and the perception of death is well established within him. He dwells relying upon these five powers of a trainee: the powers of faith ... and wisdom. These five faculties are relatively feeble in him: the faculties of faith ... and wisdom. Because of the feebleness of these five faculties, with the breakup of the body, he attains Nibbāna through volitional exertion. This is how a person, with the breakup of the body, attains Nibbāna through volitional exertion.

"And how, monks, does a person, in this very life, attain Nibbāna without volitional exertion? Here, secluded from sensual pleasures, secluded from unwholesome states, a monk enters and dwells in the first jhāna ... the fourth jhāna. He dwells relying upon these five powers of a trainee: the powers of faith... and wisdom. These five faculties are extremely strong in him: the faculties of faith ... and wisdom. Because of the strength of these five faculties, in this very life he attains Nibbāna without volitional exertion. This is how a person, in this very life, attains Nibbāna without volitional exertion.

"And how, monks, does a person, with the breakup of the body, attain Nibbāna without volitional exertion? Here, secluded from sensual pleasures, secluded from unwholesome states, a monk enters and dwells in the first jhāna ... the fourth jhāna. He dwells relying upon these five powers of a trainee: the powers of faith ... and wisdom. These five faculties are relatively feeble in him: the faculties of faith ... and wisdom. Because of the feebleness of these five faculties, with the breakup of the body, he attains Nibbāna without volitional exertion.

This is how a person, with the breakup of the body, attains Nibbāna without volitional exertion.

"These, monks, are the four kinds of persons found existing in the world."

(AN 4:169; II 155–56)

(3) Six Things that Partake of True Knowledge

On one occasion the Blessed One was dwelling at Rājagaha in the Bamboo Grove, the Squirrel Sanctuary. Now on that occasion the lay follower Dīghāvu was sick, afflicted, gravely ill. Then the lay follower Dīghāvu addressed his father, the householder Jotika, thus: "Come, householder, approach the Blessed One, pay homage to him in my name with your head at his feet, and say: 'Venerable sir, the lay follower Dīghāvu is sick, afflicted, gravely ill; he pays homage to the Blessed One with his head at the Blessed One's feet.' Then say: 'It would be good, venerable sir, if the Blessed One would come to the residence of the lay follower Dīghāvu out of compassion.'"

"Yes, dear," the householder Jotika replied, and he approached the Blessed One, paid homage to him, sat down to one side, and delivered his message. The Blessed One consented by silence.

Then the Blessed One dressed and, taking bowl and robe, went to the residence of the lay follower Dīghāvu. He then sat down in the appointed seat and said to the lay follower Dīghāvu: "I hope you are bearing up, Dīghāvu, I hope you are getting better. I hope your painful feelings are subsiding and not increasing, and that their subsiding, not their increase, is to be discerned."

"Venerable sir, I am not bearing up, I am not getting better. Strong painful feelings are increasing in me, not subsiding, and their increase, not their subsiding, is to be discerned."

"Therefore, Dīghāvu, you should train yourself thus: 'I will be one who has confirmed confidence in the Buddha, the Dhamma, and the Saṅgha, and who observes the moral virtues dear to the noble ones, unbroken, untorn, unblemished, unmottled, freeing, praised by the wise, ungrasped, leading to concentration.' It is in such a way that you should train yourself."

"Venerable sir, as to these four factors of stream-entry that have been taught by the Blessed One, these things exist in me, and I live in conformity with those things. For, venerable sir, I have confirmed confidence in the Buddha, the Dhamma, and the Saṅgha, and I observe the moral virtues dear to the noble ones."

"Therefore, Dīghāvu, established upon these four factors of stream-entry, you should develop further six things that partake of true knowledge. Here, Dīghāvu, dwell contemplating impermanence in all formations, perceiving suffering in what is impermanent, perceiving nonself in what is suffering, perceiving abandonment, perceiving fading away, perceiving cessation.[32] It is in such a way that you should train yourself."

"Venerable sir, as to these six things that partake of true knowledge that have been taught by the Blessed One, these things exist in me, and I live in conformity with those things. For, venerable sir, I dwell contemplating impermanence in all formations, perceiving suffering in what is impermanent, perceiving nonself in what is suffering, perceiving abandonment, perceiving fading away, perceiving cessation. However, venerable sir, I hope that after I expire, my father won't be distressed."

"Don't be concerned about this, dear Dīghāvu. Come now, dear Dīghāvu, pay close attention to what the Blessed One is saying to you."

Then the Blessed One, having given this exhortation to the lay follower Dīghāvu, rose from his seat and departed. Then, not long after the Blessed One had left, the lay follower Dīghāvu died.

Then a number of monks approached the Blessed One, paid homage to him, sat down to one side, and said: "Venerable sir, the lay follower Dīghāvu has died. What is his destination? Where was he reborn?"

"Monks, the lay follower Dīghāvu was wise. He practiced in accordance with the Dhamma and did not trouble me on account of the Dhamma. With the utter destruction of the five lower fetters, the lay follower Dīghāvu has become one of spontaneous birth [in the pure abodes], due to attain Nibbāna there without returning from that world."

(SN 55:3; V 344–46)

(4) Five Kinds of Nonreturners

"Monks, when these seven factors of enlightenment have been developed and cultivated in this way, seven fruits and benefits may be expected. What are the seven fruits and benefits?

"One attains final knowledge (of arahantship) early in this very life.

"If one does not attain final knowledge early in this very life, then one attains final knowledge at the time of death.

"If one does not attain final knowledge early in this very life or at the time of death, then with the utter destruction of the five lower fetters one attains Nibbāna in the interval.[33]

"If one does not attain final knowledge early in this very life ... or attain Nibbāna in the interval, then with the utter destruction of the five lower fetters one attains Nibbāna upon landing.

"If one does not attain final knowledge early in this very life ... or attain Nibbāna upon landing, then with the utter destruction of the five lower fetters one attains Nibbāna without volitional exertion.

"If one does not attain final knowledge early in this very life ... or attain Nibbāna without volitional exertion, then with the utter destruction of the five lower fetters one attains Nibbāna with volitional exertion.

"If one does not attain final knowledge early in this very life ... or attain Nibbāna with volitional exertion, then with the utter destruction of the five lower fetters one becomes one bound upstream, heading toward the Akaniṭṭha realm.

"When, monks, the seven factors of enlightenment have been developed and cultivated in this way, these seven fruits and benefits may be expected."

(SN 46:3; V 69–70)

4. The Arahant

(1) Removing the Residual Conceit "I Am"

On one occasion a number of elder monks were dwelling at Kosambī in Ghosita's Park. Now on that occasion the Venerable Khemaka was living at Jujube Tree Park, sick, afflicted, gravely ill.

Then, in the evening, those elder monks emerged from seclusion and addressed the Venerable Dāsaka thus: "Come, friend Dāsaka, approach the monk Khemaka and say to him: 'The elders say to you, friend Khemaka: We hope that you are bearing up, friend, we hope that you are getting better. We hope that your painful feelings are subsiding and not increasing, and that their subsiding, not their increase, is to be discerned.'"

"Yes, friends," the Venerable Dāsaka replied, and he approached the Venerable Khemaka and delivered his message.

[The Venerable Khemaka answered:] "I am not bearing up, friend, I am not getting better. Strong painful feelings are increasing in me, not subsiding, and their increase, not their subsiding, is to be discerned."

Then the Venerable Dāsaka approached the elder monks and reported what the Venerable Khemaka had said. They told him: "Come, friend Dāsaka, approach the monk Khemaka and say to him: 'The elders say to you, friend Khemaka: These five aggregates subject to clinging have been spoken of by the Blessed One; that is, form, feeling, perception, volitional formations, and consciousness. Does the Venerable Khemaka regard anything as self or as belonging to self among these five aggregates subject to clinging?'"

"Yes, friends," the Venerable Dāsaka replied, and he approached the Venerable Khemaka and delivered his message.

[The Venerable Khemaka replied:] "These five aggregates subject to clinging have been spoken of by the Blessed One; that is, form, feeling, perception, volitional formations, and consciousness. Among these five aggregates subject to clinging, I do not regard anything as self or as belonging to self."

Then the Venerable Dāsaka approached the elder monks and reported what the Venerable Khemaka had said. They replied: "Come, friend Dāsaka, approach the monk Khemaka and say to him: If the Venerable Khemaka does not regard anything among these five aggregates as self or as belonging to self, then he is an arahant, one whose taints are destroyed.'"[34]

"Yes, friends," the Venerable Dāsaka replied, and he approached the Venerable Khemaka and delivered his message.

[The Venerable Khemaka replied:] "These five aggregates subject to clinging have been spoken of by the Blessed One; that is, form, feeling, perception, volitional formations, and consciousness. I do not regard anything among these five aggregates subject to clinging as self or as belonging to self, yet I am not an arahant, one whose taints are destroyed. Friends, [the notion] 'I am' has not yet vanished in me in relation to these five aggregates subject to clinging, but I do not regard [anything among them] as 'This I am.'"[35]

Then the Venerable Dāsaka approached the elder monks and reported what the Venerable Khemaka had said. They replied: "Come, friend Dāsaka, approach the monk Khemaka and say to him:

'The elders say to you, friend Khemaka: Friend Khemaka, when you speak of this "I am"—what is it that you speak of as "I am"? Do you speak of form as "I am," or do you speak of "I am" apart from form? Do you speak of feeling ... of perception ... of volitional formations ... of consciousness as "I am," or do you speak of "I am" apart from consciousness? When you speak of this "I am," friend Khemaka, what is it that you speak of as "I am"?'"

"Yes, friends," the Venerable Dāsaka replied, and he approached the Venerable Khemaka and delivered his message.

"Enough, friend Dāsaka! Why keep running back and forth? Bring me my staff, friend. I'll go to the elder monks myself."

Then the Venerable Khemaka, leaning on his staff, approached the elder monks, exchanged greetings with them, and sat down to one side. The elder monks then said to him: "Friend Khemaka, when you speak of this 'I am' ... what is it that you speak of as 'I am'?"

"Friends, I do not speak of form as 'I am,' nor do I speak of 'I am' apart from form. I do not speak of feeling as 'I am' ... nor of perception as 'I am' ... nor of volitional formations as 'I am' ... nor of consciousness as 'I am,' nor do I speak of 'I am' apart from consciousness. Friends, although [the notion] 'I am' has not yet vanished in me in relation to these five aggregates subject to clinging, still I do not regard [anything among them] as 'This I am.'

"Suppose, friends, there is the scent of a blue, red, or white lotus. Would one be speaking rightly if one would say, 'The scent belongs to the petals,' or 'The scent belongs to the stalk,' or 'The scent belongs to the pistils'?"

"No, friend."

"And how, friends, should one answer if one is to answer rightly?"

"Answering rightly, friend, one should answer: 'The scent belongs to the flower.'"

"So too, friends, I do not speak of form as 'I am,' nor do I speak of 'I am' apart from form. I do not speak of feeling as 'I am' ... nor of perception as 'I am' ... nor of volitional formations as 'I am' ... nor of consciousness as 'I am,' nor do I speak of 'I am' apart from consciousness. Friends, although [the notion] 'I am' has not yet vanished in me in relation to these five aggregates subject to clinging, still I do not regard [anything among them] as 'This I am.'

"Friends, even though a noble disciple has abandoned the five lower fetters, still, in relation to the five aggregates subject to clinging, there lingers in him a residual conceit 'I am,' a desire 'I am,' an underlying tendency 'I am' that has not yet been uprooted. Sometime later he dwells contemplating rise and fall in the five aggregates subject to clinging: 'Such is form, such its origin, such its passing away; such is feeling ... such is perception ... such are volitional formations ... such is consciousness, such its origin, such its passing away.' As he dwells thus contemplating rise and fall in the five aggregates subject to clinging, the residual conceit 'I am,' the desire 'I am,' the underlying tendency 'I am' that had not yet been uprooted—this comes to be uprooted.

"Suppose, friends, a cloth has become soiled and stained, and its owners give it to a laundryman. The laundryman would scour it evenly with cleaning salt, lye, or cow dung, and rinse it in clean water. Even though that cloth would become pure and clean, it would still retain a residual smell of cleaning salt, lye, or cow dung that had not yet vanished. The laundryman would then give it back to the owners. The owners would put it in a sweet-scented chest, and the residual smell of cleaning salt, lye, or cow dung that had not yet vanished would vanish.[36]

"So too, friends, even though a noble disciple has abandoned the five lower fetters, still, in relation to the five aggregates subject to clinging, there lingers in him a residual conceit 'I am,' a desire 'I am,' an underlying tendency 'I am' that has not yet been uprooted.... As he dwells thus contemplating rise and fall in the five aggregates subject to clinging, the residual conceit 'I am,' the desire 'I am,' the underlying tendency 'I am' that had not yet been uprooted—this comes to be uprooted."

When this was said, the elder monks said to the Venerable Khemaka: "We did not ask our questions in order to trouble the Venerable Khemaka, but we thought that the Venerable Khemaka would be capable of explaining, teaching, proclaiming, establishing, disclosing, analyzing, and elucidating the Blessed One's teaching in detail. And the Venerable Khemaka has explained, taught, proclaimed, established, disclosed, analyzed, and elucidated the Blessed One's teaching in detail."

Thus the elder monks were elated and delighted in the Venerable Khemaka's statement. And while this discourse was being spoken, the minds of sixty elder monks and of the Venerable Khemaka were liberated from the taints by nonclinging.

(SN 22:89; III 126–32)

(2) The Trainee and the Arahant

At Kosambī in Ghosita's Park the Blessed One addressed the monks thus:

"There is a method, monks, by means of which a monk who is a trainee, standing on the plane of a trainee, might understand: 'I am a trainee,' while a monk beyond training, standing on the plane of one beyond training, might understand: 'I am one beyond training.'

"And what, monks, is the method by means of which a monk who is a trainee, standing on the plane of a trainee, understands: 'I am a trainee'?

"Here, monks, a monk who is a trainee understands as it really is: 'This is suffering. This is the origin of suffering. This is the cessation of suffering. This is the way leading to the cessation of suffering.' This is a method by means of which a monk who is a trainee, standing on the plane of a trainee, understands: 'I am a trainee.'

"Again, monks, a monk who is a trainee considers thus: 'Is there outside here[37] another ascetic or brahmin who teaches a Dhamma so real, true, and actual as the Blessed One does?' He understands thus: 'There is no other ascetic or brahmin outside here who teaches a Dhamma so real, true, and actual as the Blessed One does.' This too is a method by means of which a monk who is a trainee, standing on the plane of a trainee, understands: 'I am a trainee.'

"Again, monks, a monk who is a trainee understands the five spiritual faculties—the faculties of faith, energy, mindfulness, concentration, and wisdom. He does not yet dwell having contacted with the body that which is their destination, their culmination, their fruit, their final goal; but having pierced it through with wisdom, he sees.[38] This too is a method by means of which a monk who is a trainee, standing on the plane of a trainee, understands: 'I am a trainee.'

"And what, monks, is the method by means of which a monk beyond training, standing on the plane of one beyond training, understands: 'I am one beyond training'? Here, monks, a monk beyond training understands the five spiritual faculties—the faculties of faith ...

wisdom. He dwells having contacted with the body that which is their destination, their culmination, their fruit, their final goal; and having pierced it through with wisdom, he sees. This is a method by means of which a monk beyond training, standing on the plane of one beyond training, understands: 'I am one beyond training.'

"Again, monks, a monk beyond training understands the six faculties—the eye faculty, the ear faculty, the nose faculty, the tongue faculty, the body faculty, the mind faculty. He understands: 'These six faculties will cease completely and totally without remainder, and no other six faculties will arise anywhere in any way.' This too is a method by means of which a monk beyond training, standing on the plane of one beyond training, understands: 'I am one beyond training.'"

(SN 48:53: V 229–30)

(3) A Monk Whose Crossbar Has Been Lifted

30. "Monks, an arahant is called one whose crossbar has been lifted, whose trench has been filled in, whose pillar has been uprooted, one who has no bolt, a noble one whose banner is lowered, whose burden is lowered, who is unfettered.

31. "And how is the arahant one whose crossbar has been lifted? Here the arahant has abandoned ignorance, has cut it off at the root, made it like a palm stump, done away with it, so that it is no longer subject to future arising. That is how he is one whose crossbar has been lifted.

32. "And how is the arahant one whose trench has been filled in? Here the arahant has abandoned the round of rebirths, the process of renewed existence, has cut it off at the root ... so that it is no longer subject to future arising. That is how he is one whose trench has been filled in.

33. "And how is the arahant one whose pillar has been uprooted? Here the arahant has abandoned craving, has cut it off at the root ... so that it is no longer subject to future arising. That is how he is one whose pillar has been uprooted.

34. "And how is the arahant one who has no bolt? Here the monk has abandoned the five lower fetters, has cut them off at the root ... so that they are no longer subject to future arising. That is how he is one who has no bolt.

35. "And how is the arahant a noble one whose banner is lowered, whose burden is lowered, who is unfettered? Here the arahant has abandoned the conceit 'I am,' has cut it off at the root ... so that it is no longer subject to future arising. That is how he is a noble one whose banner is lowered, whose burden is lowered, who is unfettered."

(from MN 22: *Alagaddūpama Sutta*; I 139–40)

(4) Nine Things an Arahant Cannot Do

"In the past, and also now, I declare that a monk who is an arahant with taints destroyed—one who has lived the spiritual life, done his task, laid down the burden, attained his own goal, utterly destroyed the fetters of existence, and become liberated by final knowledge—is incapable of transgression in regard to nine things: he is incapable of destroying life, of taking what is not given, of engaging in the sexual act, of telling a deliberate lie, and of making use of stored-up enjoyments as he did in the past when he was a householder; further, he is incapable of taking a wrong course of action on account of desire, on account of hatred, on account of delusion, or on account of fear. In the past, and also now, I declare that a monk who is an arahant is incapable of transgression in regard to these nine things."

(from AN 9:7; IV 370–71)

(5) A Mind Unshaken

[The Venerable Sāriputta said:] "When, friend, a monk is thus liberated in mind, even if powerful forms cognizable by the eye come into range of his eye, they do not obsess his mind; his mind remains uncontaminated, steady, attained to imperturbability, and he contemplates their fall. Even if powerful sounds cognizable by the ear ... smells cognizable by the nose ... flavors cognizable by the tongue ... tactile objects cognizable by the body ... mental phenomena cognizable by the mind come into range of his mind, they do not obsess his mind; his mind remains uncontaminated, steady, attained to imperturbability, and he contemplates their fall. Suppose, friend, there were a stone pillar sixteen meters long, eight meters sunk in the ground and eight meters above the ground. Then a powerful rainstorm would come from the east: the pillar would not budge, would not shake, would not tremble. Then a powerful rainstorm would come from the north ... from the west ... from the south: the pillar would not budge, would not shake, would not tremble. Why not? Because of the depth of the base and because the stone pillar has been deeply planted. So too for a monk thus liberated in mind, if powerful sense objects come into range, they do not obsess his mind; his mind remains uncontaminated, steady, attained to imperturbability, and he contemplates their fall."

(from AN 9:26; IV 404–5)

(6) The Ten Powers of an Arahant Monk

The Buddha asked the Venerable Sāriputta: "How many powers does an arahant monk have, Sāriputta, possessing which he claims that he has attained the destruction of the taints?"

"The arahant monk has ten powers, venerable sir, possessing which he claims that he has attained the destruction of the taints. What ten?

"Here, venerable sir, for an arahant monk all formations have been well seen as they really are with correct wisdom as impermanent. This is a power of an arahant monk on the basis of which he claims that he has attained the destruction of the taints.

"Again, venerable sir, for an arahant monk sensual pleasures have been well seen as they really are with correct wisdom as similar to a charcoal pit. This too is a power of an arahant monk ...

"Again, venerable sir, the mind of an arahant monk slants, slopes, and inclines to seclusion; it dwells in seclusion, delights in renunciation, and is entirely finished with all things that are a basis for the taints. This too is a power of an arahant monk....

"Further, venerable sir, for an arahant monk the four establishments of mindfulness have been developed to the point that they are well developed. This too is a power of an arahant monk....

"Further, venerable sir, for an arahant monk the four right kinds of striving ... the four bases for spiritual power ... the five spiritual faculties ... the five powers ... the seven factors of enlightenment ... the Noble Eightfold Path has been developed to the point that it is well developed. This too is a power of an arahant monk on the basis of which he claims that he has attained the destruction of the taints."[39]

(AN 10:90; V 174–75)

(7) The Sage at Peace

20. [The Buddha further addressed Pukkusāti thus:] "Then [after contemplating the six elements], there remains only equanimity, purified and bright, malleable, wieldy, and radiant.[40] …

21. "He understands thus: 'If I were to direct this equanimity, so purified and bright, to the base of the infinity of space and to develop my mind accordingly, then this equanimity of mine, supported by this base, clinging to it, would remain for a very long time.[41] If I were to direct this equanimity, so purified and bright, to the base of the infinity of consciousness … to the base of nothingness … to the base of neither-perception-nor-non-perception and to develop my mind accordingly, then this equanimity of mine, supported by this base, clinging to it, would remain for a very long time.'

22. "He understands thus: 'If I were to direct this equanimity, so purified and bright, to the base of the infinity of space and to develop my mind accordingly, this would be conditioned.[42] If I were to direct this equanimity, so purified and bright, to the base of the infinity of consciousness … to the base of nothingness … to the base of neither-perception-nor-non-perception and to develop my mind accordingly, this would be conditioned.' He does not construct or generate any volition tending toward either existence or non-existence.[43] Since he does not construct or generate any volition tending toward either existence or nonexistence, he does not cling to anything in this world. Not clinging, he is not agitated. Not being agitated, he personally attains Nibbāna. He understands: 'Birth is destroyed, the spiritual life has been lived, what had to be done has been done, there is no more coming back to any state of being.'[44]

23. "If he feels a pleasant feeling,[45] he understands: 'It is impermanent; there is no holding to it; there is no delight in it.' If he feels a painful feeling, he understands: 'It is impermanent; there is no holding to it; there is no delight in it.' If he feels a neither-painful-nor-pleasant feeling, he understands: 'It is impermanent; there is no holding to it; there is no delight in it.'

24. "If he feels a pleasant feeling, he feels it detached; if he feels a painful feeling, he feels it detached; if he feels a neither-painful-nor-pleasant feeling, he feels it detached. When he feels a feeling terminating with the body, he understands: 'I feel a feeling terminating with the

body.' When he feels a feeling terminating with life, he understands: 'I feel a feeling terminating with life.' He understands: 'On the dissolution of the body, with the ending of life, all that is felt, not being delighted in, will become cool right here.'[46] Monk, just as an oil-lamp burns in dependence on oil and a wick, and when the oil and wick are used up, if it does not get any more fuel, it is extinguished from lack of fuel; so too when he feels a feeling terminating with the body … a feeling terminating with life, he understands: 'I feel a feeling terminating with life.' He understands: 'On the dissolution of the body, with the ending of life, all that is felt, not being delighted in, will become cool right here.'[47]

25. "Therefore a monk possessing [this wisdom] possesses the supreme foundation of wisdom. For this, monk, is the supreme noble wisdom, namely, the knowledge of the destruction of all suffering.

26. "His liberation, being founded upon truth, is unshakable. For that is false, monk, which has a deceptive nature, and that is true which has an undeceptive nature—Nibbāna. Therefore a monk possessing [this truth] possesses the supreme foundation of truth. For this, monk, is the supreme noble truth, namely, Nibbāna, which has an undeceptive nature.[48]

27. "Formerly, when he was ignorant, he undertook and accepted acquisitions;[49] now he has abandoned them, cut them off at the root, made them like a palm stump, done away with them so that they are no longer subject to future arising. Therefore a monk possessing [this relinquishment] possesses the supreme foundation of relinquishment. For this, monk, is the supreme noble relinquishment, namely, the relinquishing of all acquisitions.

28. "Formerly, when he was ignorant, he experienced covetousness, desire, and lust; now he has abandoned them, cut them off at the root, made them like a palm stump, done away with them so that they are no longer subject to future arising. Formerly, when he was ignorant, he experienced anger, ill will, and hate; now he has abandoned them, cut them off at the root, made them like a palm stump, done away with them so that they are no longer subject to future arising. Formerly, when he was ignorant, he experienced ignorance and delusion; now he has abandoned them, cut them off at the root, made them like a palm stump, done away with them so that they are no longer subject to future arising. Therefore a monk possessing [this peace] possesses the

supreme foundation of peace. For this, monk, is the supreme noble peace, namely, the pacification of lust, hate, and delusion.

29. "So it was with reference to this that it was said: 'One should not neglect wisdom, should preserve truth, should cultivate relinquishment, and should train for peace.'

30. "'The tides of conceiving do not sweep over one who stands upon these [foundations], and when the tides of conceiving no longer sweep over him he is called a sage at peace.'[50] So it was said. And with reference to what was this said?

31. "Monk, 'I am' is a conceiving; 'I am this' is a conceiving; 'I shall be' is a conceiving; 'I shall not be' is a conceiving; 'I shall have a physical form' is a conceiving; 'I shall be formless' is a conceiving; 'I shall be percipient' is a conceiving; 'I shall be nonpercipient' is a conceiving; 'I shall be neither-percipient-nor-nonpercipient' is a conceiving.[51] Conceiving is a disease, conceiving is a tumor, conceiving is a dart. By overcoming all conceivings, monk, one is called a sage at peace. And the sage at peace is not born, does not age, does not die; he is not shaken and does not yearn. For there is nothing present in him by which he might be born.[52] Not being born, how could he age? Not aging, how could he die? Not dying, how could he be shaken? Not being shaken, why should he yearn?

32. "So it was with reference to this that it was said: 'The tides of conceiving do not sweep over one who stands upon these [foundations], and when the tides of conceiving no longer sweep over him he is called a sage at peace.'"

(from MN 140: *Dhātuvibhaṅga Sutta;* III 244–47)

(8) Happy Indeed Are the Arahants

Happy indeed are the arahants!
No craving can be found in them.
Cut off is the conceit "I am,"
Burst asunder is delusion's net.

They have reached the unstirred state,
Limpid are their minds;
They are unsullied in the world—
The holy ones, without taints.

Having fully understood the five aggregates,
Ranging in the seven good qualities,[53]
Those praiseworthy superior persons
Are the Buddha's bosom offspring.

Endowed with the seven gems,
Trained in the threefold training,[54]
Those great heroes wander about
With fear and trembling abandoned.

Endowed with the ten factors,
Those great nāgas, concentrated,
Are the best beings in the world:
No craving can be found in them.[55]

The adepts' knowledge has arisen in them:
"This body is the last I bear."
In regard to the core of the spiritual life
They no longer depend on others.

They do not waver in discrimination,[56]
They are released from renewed existence.
Having reached the stage of the tamed,
They are the victors in the world.

Above, across, and below,
Delight is no more found in them.
They boldly sound their lion's roar:
"The enlightened are supreme in the world."

(from SN 22:76; III 83–84)

5. The Tathāgata

(1) The Buddha and the Arahant

"Monks, through disenchantment with form, feeling, perception, volitional formations, and consciousness, through their fading away and cessation, the Tathāgata, the Arahant, the Perfectly Enlightened One, is liberated by nonclinging; he is called a Perfectly Enlightened One. Through disenchantment with form, feeling, perception, volitional formations, and consciousness, through their fading away and cessation, a monk liberated by wisdom is liberated by nonclinging; he is called one liberated by wisdom.[57]

"Therein, monks, what is the distinction, the disparity, the difference between the Tathāgata, the Arahant, the Perfectly Enlightened One, and a monk liberated by wisdom?"

"Venerable sir, our teachings are rooted in the Blessed One, guided by the Blessed One, take recourse in the Blessed One. It would be good if the Blessed One would clear up the meaning of this statement. Having heard it from him, the monks will remember it."

"Then listen and attend closely, monks, I will speak."

"Yes, venerable sir," the monks replied. The Blessed One said this:

"The Tathāgata, monks, the Arahant, the Perfectly Enlightened One, is the originator of the path unarisen before, the producer of the path unproduced before, the declarer of the path undeclared before. He is the knower of the path, the discoverer of the path, the one skilled in the path. And his disciples now dwell following that path and become possessed of it afterward.

"This, monks, is the distinction, the disparity, the difference between the Tathāgata, the Arahant, the Perfectly Enlightened One, and a monk liberated by wisdom."

(SN 22:58; III 65–66)

(2) For the Welfare of Many

"Monks, these three persons arise in the world for the welfare of the multitude, for the happiness of the multitude, out of compassion for the world, for the good, welfare, and happiness of devas and humans. What three?

"Here, monks, a Tathāgata arises in the world, an arahant, perfectly enlightened … teacher of devas and humans, the Enlightened One, the Blessed One. He teaches the Dhamma that is good at the beginning, good in the middle, good at the end, with the right meaning and phrasing; he reveals the spiritual life that is utterly perfect and pure. This, monks, is the first person that arises in the world for the welfare of the multitude, for the happiness of the multitude, out of compassion for the world, for the good, welfare, and happiness of devas and humans.

"Then, monks, a disciple of that teacher is an arahant with taints destroyed [as in Text X,1(3), §42} ... completely liberated through final knowledge. He teaches the Dhamma that is good at the beginning ... he reveals the spiritual life that is utterly perfect and pure. This, monks, is the second person that arises in the world for the welfare of the multitude, for the happiness of the multitude, out of compassion for the world, for the good, welfare, and happiness of devas and humans.

"Then, monks, a disciple of that teacher is a trainee practicing the path, learned and endowed with precepts and observances. He too teaches the Dhamma that is good at the beginning ... he reveals the spiritual life that is utterly perfect and pure. This, monks, is the third person that arises in the world for the welfare of the multitude, for the happiness of the multitude, out of compassion for the world, for the good, welfare, and happiness of devas and humans.

"These, monks, are the three persons that arise in the world for the welfare of the multitude, for the happiness of the multitude, out of compassion for the world, for the good, welfare, and happiness of devas and humans."

(It 84; 78–79)

(3) Sāriputta's Lofty Utterance

The Venerable Sāriputta approached the Blessed One, paid homage to him, sat down to one side, and said: "Venerable sir, I have such confidence in the Blessed One that I believe there has not been, nor ever will be, nor exists at present another ascetic or brahmin more knowledgeable than the Blessed One with respect to enlightenment."[58]

"Lofty indeed is this bellowing utterance of yours, Sāriputta, you have roared a definitive lion's roar. Have you now, Sāriputta, encompassed with your mind the minds of all the Arahants, the Perfectly Enlightened Ones, arisen in the past and known thus: 'Those Blessed Ones were of such moral discipline, or of such qualities, or of such wisdom, or of such meditative dwellings, or of such liberation'?"[59]

"No, venerable sir."

"Then, Sāriputta, have you encompassed with your mind the minds of all the Arahants, the Perfectly Enlightened Ones, who will arise in the future and known thus: 'Those Blessed Ones will be of such moral discipline, or of such qualities, or of such wisdom, or of such meditative dwellings, or of such liberation'?"

"No, venerable sir."

"Then, Sāriputta, have you encompassed with your mind my own mind—I being at present the Arahant, the Perfectly Enlightened One—and known thus: 'The Blessed One is of such moral discipline, or of such qualities, or of such wisdom, or of such meditative dwellings, or of such liberation'?"

"No, venerable sir."

"Sāriputta, when you do not have any knowledge encompassing the minds of the Arahants, the Perfectly Enlightened Ones of the past, the future, and the present, why do you utter this lofty, bellowing utterance and roar this definitive lion's roar: 'Venerable sir, I have such confidence in the Blessed One that I believe there has not been, nor ever will be, nor exists at present another ascetic or brahmin more knowledgeable than the Blessed One with respect to enlightenment'?"

"I do not have, venerable sir, any knowledge encompassing the minds of the Arahants, the Perfectly Enlightened Ones of the past, the future, and the present, but still I have understood this by inference from the Dhamma. Suppose, venerable sir, a king had a frontier city with strong ramparts, walls, and arches, and a single gate. The gatekeeper posted there would be wise, competent, and intelligent; one who keeps out strangers and admits acquaintances. While he is walking along the path that encircles the city he would not see a cleft or an opening in the walls even big enough for a cat to slip through. He might think: 'Whatever large creatures enter or leave this city, all enter and leave through this one gate.'

"So too, venerable sir, I have understood this by inference from the Dhamma: Whatever Arahants, Perfectly Enlightened Ones arose in the past, all those Blessed Ones had first abandoned the five hindrances, defilements of the mind that weaken wisdom; and then, with their minds well established in the four establishments of mindfulness, developed correctly the seven factors of enlightenment; and thereby they had awakened to the unsurpassed perfect enlightenment. And, venerable sir, whatever Arahants, Perfectly Enlightened Ones will arise in the future, all those Blessed Ones will first abandon the five hindrances, defilements of the mind that weaken wisdom; and then, with their minds well established in the four establishments of mindfulness, will develop correctly the seven factors of enlightenment; and thereby they will awaken to the unsurpassed perfect enlightenment. And, venerable sir, the Blessed One, at present the Arahant, the Perfectly Enlightened One, first abandoned the five hindrances, defilements of the mind that weaken wisdom; and then, with his mind well established in the four establishments of mindfulness, developed correctly the seven factors of enlightenment; and thereby he has awakened to the unsurpassed perfect enlightenment."

"Good, good, Sāriputta! Therefore, Sāriputta, you should repeat this Dhamma exposition frequently to the monks and the nuns, to the male lay followers and the female lay followers. Even though some foolish people may have perplexity or uncertainty regarding the Tathāgata, when they hear this Dhamma exposition their perplexity or uncertainty will be abandoned."

(SN 47:12; V 159–61)

(4) The Powers and Grounds of Self-Confidence

9. "Sāriputta, the Tathāgata has these ten Tathāgata's powers, possessing which he claims the place of the chief of the herd, roars his lion's roar in the assemblies, and sets rolling the wheel of Brahmā.[60] What are the ten?

10. (1) "Here, the Tathāgata correctly understands the possible as possible and the impossible as impossible.[61] And that is a Tathāgata's power that the Tathāgata has, by virtue of which he claims the place of the chief of the herd, roars his lion's roar in the assemblies, and sets rolling the wheel of Brahmā.

11. (2) "Again, the Tathāgata correctly understands the results of actions undertaken, past, future, and present by way of possibilities and causes. That too is a Tathāgata's power...[62]

12. (3) "Again, the Tathāgata correctly understands the ways leading everywhere. That too is a Tathāgata's power...[63]

13. (4) "Again, the Tathāgata correctly understands the world with its many and different elements. That too is a Tathāgata's power...

14. (5) "Again, the Tathāgata correctly understands how beings have different inclinations. That too is a Tathāgata's power...[64]

15. (6) "Again, the Tathāgata correctly understands the disposition of

the faculties of other beings, other persons. That too is a Tathāgata's power...[65]

16. (7) "Again, the Tathāgata correctly understands the defilement, the cleansing, and the emergence in regard to the jhānas, liberations, concentrations, and attainments. That too is a Tathāgata's power...[66]

17. (8) "Again, the Tathāgata recollects his manifold past lives with their aspects and particulars. That too is a Tathāgata's power...

18. (9) "Again, with the divine eye, which is purified and surpasses the human, the Tathāgata sees beings passing away and being reborn, inferior and superior, fair and ugly, fortunate and unfortunate, and he understands how beings pass on according to their actions. That too is a Tathāgata's power...

19. (10) "Again, by realizing it for himself with direct knowledge, the Tathāgata in this present life enters upon and dwells in the liberation of mind, liberation by wisdom, that is taintless with the destruction of the taints. That too is a Tathāgata's power that the Tathāgata has, by virtue of which he claims the place of the leader of the herd, roars his lion's roar in the assemblies, and sets rolling the wheel of Brahmā.

20. "The Tathāgata has these ten Tathāgata's powers, possessing which he claims the place of the leader of the herd, roars his lion's roar in the assemblies, and sets rolling the wheel of Brahmā....

22. "Sāriputta, the Tathāgata has these four grounds of self-confidence,[67] possessing which he claims the place of the leader of the herd, roars his lion's roar in the assemblies, and sets rolling the wheel of Brahmā. What are the four?

23. "Here, I see no ground on which any ascetic or brahmin or deva or Māra or Brahmā or anyone else at all in the world could, in accordance with the Dhamma, accuse me thus: 'While you claim to be perfectly enlightened, you are not perfectly enlightened about these things.' And seeing no ground for that, I dwell in safety, fearlessness, and self-confidence.

24. "I see no ground on which any ascetic ... or anyone at all could accuse me thus: 'While you claim to be one who has destroyed the taints, you have not destroyed these taints.' And seeing no ground for that, I dwell in safety, fearlessness, and self-confidence.

25. "I see no ground on which any ascetic ... or anyone at all could accuse me thus: 'Those things called obstructions by you are not able

to obstruct one who engages in them.' And seeing no ground for that, I dwell in safety, fearlessness, and self-confidence.

26. "I see no ground on which any ascetic ... or anyone at all could accuse me thus: 'When you teach the Dhamma to someone, it does not lead him when he practices it to the complete destruction of suffering.' And seeing no ground for that, I dwell in safety, fearlessness, and self-confidence.

27. "A Tathāgata has these four kinds of self-confidence, possessing which he claims the place of the leader of the herd, roars his lion's roar in the assemblies, and sets rolling the wheel of Brahmā."

(from MN 12: *Mahāsīhanāda Sutta*; I 70–72)

(5) The Manifestation of Great Light

"Monks, so long as the sun and moon have not arisen in the world, for just so long there is no manifestation of great light and radiance, but then blinding darkness prevails, a dense mass of darkness; for just so long day and night are not discerned, the month and fortnight are not discerned, the seasons and the year are not discerned. But, monks, when the sun and moon arise in the world, then there is the manifestation of great light and radiance; then there is no blinding darkness, no dense mass of darkness; then day and night are discerned, the month and fortnight are discerned, the seasons and year are discerned.

"So too, monks, so long as a Tathāgata has not arisen in the world, an Arahant, a Perfectly Enlightened One, for just so long there is no manifestation of great light and radiance, but then blinding darkness prevails, a dense mass of darkness; for just so long there is no explaining, teaching, proclaiming, establishing, disclosing, analyzing, or elucidating of the Four Noble Truths. But, monks, when a Tathāgata arises in the world, an Arahant, a Perfectly Enlightened One, then there is the manifestation of great light and radiance; then no blinding darkness prevails, no dense mass of darkness; then there is the explaining, teaching, proclaiming, establishing, disclosing, analyzing, and elucidating of the Four Noble Truths."

(SN 56:38; V 442–43)

(6) The Man Desiring Our Good

25. "Suppose, monks, that in a wooded range there were a great low-lying marsh near which a large herd of deer lived. Then a man appeared desiring their ruin, harm, and bondage, and he closed off the safe and good path to be traveled joyfully, and he opened up a false path, and he put out a decoy and set up a dummy so that the large herd of deer might later come upon calamity, disaster, and loss. But another man came desiring their good, welfare, and protection, and he reopened the safe and good path to be traveled joyfully, and he closed off the false path, and he removed the decoy and destroyed the dummy, so that the large herd of deer might later come to growth, increase, and fulfillment.

26. "Monks, I have given this simile in order to convey a meaning. This is the meaning: 'The great low-lying marsh' is a term for sensual pleasures. 'The large herd of deer' is a term for beings. 'The man desiring their ruin, harm, and bondage' is a term for Māra the Evil One. 'The false path' is a term for the wrong eightfold path, that is: wrong view, wrong intention, wrong speech, wrong action, wrong livelihood, wrong effort, wrong mindfulness, and wrong concentration. 'The decoy' is a term for delight and lust. 'The dummy' is a term for ignorance. 'The man desiring their good, welfare, and protection' is a term for the Tathāgata, the Arahant, the Perfectly Enlightened One. 'The safe and good path to be traveled joyfully' is a term for the Noble Eightfold Path, that is: right view, right intention, right speech, right action, right livelihood, right effort, right mindfulness, and right concentration.

"So, monks, the safe and good path to be traveled joyfully has been reopened by me, the wrong path has been closed off, the decoy removed, the dummy destroyed."

(from MN 19: *Dvedhāvitakka Sutta;* I 117–18)

(7) The Lion

"Monks, in the evening the lion, the king of beasts, comes out from his lair. He then stretches himself, surveys the four quarters all around, and roars his lion's roar three times, after which he sets out in search of game.

"When the lion, the king of beasts, roars its lion's roar, most of the animals that hear the sound are filled with fear, a sense of urgency, and terror. Those who live in holes enter their holes; those who live in the water enter the water; those who live in the woods enter the woods; and the birds fly up into the air. Even those royal bull elephants, bound by strong thongs in the villages, towns, and capital cities, burst and break their bonds asunder; frightened, they urinate and defecate and flee here and there. So powerful among the animals, monks, is the lion, the king of beasts, so majestic and mighty.

"So too, monks, when the Tathāgata arises in the world, an arahant, perfectly enlightened, accomplished in true knowledge and conduct, fortunate, knower of the world, unsurpassed leader of persons to be tamed, teacher of devas and humans, the Enlightened One, the Blessed One, he teaches the Dhamma thus: 'Such is form, such its origin, such its passing away; such is feeling ... such is perception ... such are volitional formations ... such is consciousness, such its origin, such its passing away.'

"Then, monks, when those devas who are long-lived, beautiful, abounding in happiness, dwelling for a long time in lofty palaces, hear the Tathāgata's teaching of the Dhamma, most[68] are filled with fear, a sense of urgency, and terror, [saying]: 'It seems, though we thought ourselves permanent, that we are impermanent; it seems, though we thought ourselves stable, that we are unstable; it seems, though we thought ourselves eternal, that we are transient. It seems, sir, that we are impermanent, unstable, transient, included within identity.'[69] So powerful, monks, is the Tathāgata over this world together with its devas, so majestic and mighty."

(SN 22:78: III 84–85)

(8) Why Is He Called the Tathāgata?

"The world, monks, has been fully awakened to by the Tathāgata; the Tathāgata is detached from the world. The origin of the world has been fully awakened to by the Tathāgata; the Tathāgata has abandoned the origin of the world. The cessation of the world has been fully awakened to by the Tathāgata; the Tathāgata has realized the cessation of the world. The way to the cessation of the world has been fully awakened to by the Tathāgata; the Tathāgata has developed the way to the cessation of the world.

"In the world, monks, with its devas, with Māra, with Brahmā, in this population with its ascetics and brahmins, with its devas and humans, whatever there is that is seen, heard, sensed, cognized, reached, sought after, examined by the mind, all that has been awakened to by the Tathāgata; therefore he is called the Tathāgata.

"From the night he fully awakened, monks, until the night he attains final Nibbāna, in this interval, whatever he speaks, talks of, and expounds, all that is just so, not otherwise; therefore he is called the Tathāgata.

"As he speaks, monks, so he does; as he does, so he speaks. Since he does as he speaks and speaks as he does, therefore he is called the Tathāgata.

"In this world, monks, with its devas, with Māra, with Brahmā, in this population with its ascetics and brahmins, with its devas and humans, the Tathāgata is the vanquisher, the unvanquished, the universal seer, the wielder of mastery; therefore he is called the Tathāgata."

Having directly known all the world,
All in the world exactly as it is,
He is detached from all the world,
Unengaged with all the world.

He indeed is the all-vanquishing sage,
The one released from all the knots,
Who has reached the supreme state of peace,
Nibbāna, without fear from any side.

He is the Buddha, with taints destroyed,
Untroubled, with all doubts cut off,
Who has attained the destruction of all kamma,
Liberated in the extinction of acquisitions.

He is the Blessed One, the Buddha,
He is the lion, unsurpassed,
In this world together with its devas,
He set in motion the wheel of Brahmā.

Thus those devas and human beings
Who have gone for refuge to the Buddha,
Having assembled, pay homage to him,
The great one free from diffidence.

"Tamed, he is supreme among those who tame;
At peace, he is the sage among those who bring peace;
Freed, he is the chief of those who set free;
Delivered, he is the best of those who deliver."

Thus indeed they pay homage to him,
The great one free from diffidence.
In this world together with its devas,
There is no one who can rival you.

(AN 4:23; II 23–24 = It 112; 121–23)

Notes

General Introduction

1. The exact years of the Buddha's life are still a matter of conjecture among scholars. Until recently, the most commonly cited figures were 566–486 B.C.E., but in recent years a growing number of Indologists have come to question these figures and the current preference is to place his death closer to 400 B.C.E.
2. See, e.g., MN 22.10 (I 133). Some of the terms are obscure, and the commentators seem to strain to find ways to identify texts that come within their scope.
3. But even as late as the age of the commentators (fifth century C.E.), the Theravāda tradition too called them Āgamas as well as Nikāyas.
4. The Cullavagga's account of the first council is at Vin II 284–87. The rains retreat (*vassāvāsa*) is a three-month period coinciding with the Indian rainy season when Buddhist monks must refrain from wandering and remain at fixed residences. The retreat generally lasts from the day after the full-moon day of July until the full-moon day of October.
5. See Nyanaponika and Hecker, *Great Disciples of the Buddha*, chapter 4.
6. In the Theravāda tradition, the writing down of the canon occurred in Sri Lanka in the first century B.C.E. At that time the monks, apprehensive that the orally preserved teachings might be lost, collectively inscribed the texts on palm leaves and bound these into volumes, the prototypes of books. Up to this point, while individual texts might have been written down by monks as aids to memory, officially recognized transcriptions of the teaching did not exist. On the writing down of the canon, see Adikaram, *Early History of Buddhism in Ceylon*, p. 79; and Malalasekera, *The Pāli Literature of Ceylon*, pp. 44–47. It is possible that in India canonical texts were written down even earlier than in Sri Lanka.
7. See, e.g., Thich Minh Chau, *The Chinese Madhyama Āgama and the Pāli Majjhima Nikāya*; Choong Mun-keat (Wei-keat), *The Fundamental Teachings of Early Buddhism*.
8. On the nature of Pāli, see Norman, *Pāli Literature*, pp. 2–7.
9. See Manné, "Categories of Sutta in the Pāli Nikāyas," esp. pp. 71–84.
10. The above information is derived from Choong, *The Fundamental Teachings of Early Buddhism*, pp. 6–7.

Chapter I: The Human Condition

1. King Pasenadi was the ruler of the state of Kosala, whose capital was Sāvatthī. Jetavana, the grove of Prince Jeta, was also known as Anāthapiṇḍika's Park because it was purchased for the Buddha by the wealthy philanthropist, Anāthapiṇḍika. The Nikāyas depict Pasenadi as one of the Buddha's most devoted lay followers, though they never show him as attaining any stage of realization. An entire chapter of the Saṃyutta Nikāya—the Kosalasaṃyutta (chapter 3)—records his conversations with the Buddha.
2. When speaking of the arahant, the Buddha does not describe his destiny as "aging and death," but as a mere breaking up and discarding of the body. This

is because the arahant, being free from all notions of "I" and "mine," does not conceive the decay and dissolution of the body as the aging and death of an "I."

3. *Devadūta.* According to legend, while the Bodhisatta was still a prince living in the palace, he encountered an old man, a sick man, and a corpse, sights he had never seen before. These encounters shattered his worldly complacency and stirred him to seek a way to liberation from suffering. The commentaries say that these three figures were deities in disguise sent to awaken the Bodhisatta to his mission. Hence old age, illness, and death are called "divine messengers."
4. Yama is the legendary god of the underworld, who passes judgment on the dead and assigns them to their future destiny. According to some accounts, he does so merely by holding before the dead spirits a mirror which reflects back their good and bad deeds.
5. The underlying tendencies (*anusaya*) are dispositions toward the defilements that lie dormant in the mind and become active when provoked. Some texts, such as the present one, mention three underlying tendencies: the tendency to lust (*rāgānusaya*) for pleasant feeling; to aversion (*paṭighānusaya*) for painful feeling; and to ignorance (*avijjānusaya*) in regard to neither-painful-nor-pleasant feeling. Other texts mention seven underlying tendencies: to sensual lust, aversion, views, doubt, conceit, attachment to existence, and ignorance.
6. Spk: The escape is concentration, the path, and the fruit. He does not know this; the only escape he knows is sensual pleasure.
7. These five terms constitute a major pattern for contemplation. "The origin and the passing away" (*samudaya, atthaṅgama*) point to the characteristic of impermanence. On the triad of gratification, danger, and escape (*assāda, ādīnava, nissaraṇa*), see pp. 186–87.
8. The sequel will make it clear that "the instructed noble disciple" being described here is the arahant, who alone is entirely free from the tendencies to aversion, lust, and ignorance. However, while the arahant alone may be capable of maintaining perfect equanimity toward physical pain, an ordinary practitioner can still emulate the arahant by attempting to overcome dejection and despondency when experiencing painful bodily feelings. Everyone with a body, including the Buddha, is subject to bodily pain. A mark of spiritual maturity is the ability to endure pain without being overwhelmed by it.
9. The noun *paritassanā* is derived from the verb *paritassati*, which represents Skt *paritṛṣyati*, "to crave, to thirst for"; it is connected etymologically with *taṇhā*, craving. However, in Pāli the verbal stem has become conflated with *tasati* = to fear, to tremble, and thus its noun derivatives such as *paritassanā* and *paritasita* also acquire meanings derived from *tasati*. This convergence of meanings, already evident in the Nikāyas, is made explicit in the commentaries. I have tried to capture both nuances by rendering the verb *paritassati* "to be agitated" and the noun *paritassanā* "agitation." Though Spk understands *paritassanā* here in the sense of craving, the text seems to be emphasizing *bhaya-paritassanā*, "agitation as fear."
10. The uninstructed worldling is one who lacks both doctrinal knowledge of the Dhamma (underscored by the word *akovida*, "unskilled") and practical training in the Dhamma (underscored by *avinīta*, "undisciplined"). The worldling is not a "seer of the noble ones," that is, of the Buddha and the noble disciples,

because he or she lacks the eye of wisdom that discerns the truth they have seen. "Noble ones" (*ariya*) and "superior persons" (*sappurisa*) are synonyms.

The text here enumerates the twenty types of identity view (*sakkāyadiṭṭhi*), obtained by positing a self in four ways in relation to the five aggregates that constitute personal identity (*sakkāya*). Identity view is one of the three fetters to be eradicated at stream-entry, the first of the four stages of realization.

Spk: He *regards form as self* (*rūpaṃ attato samanupassati*), by regarding form and the self as indistinguishable, just as the flame of an oil lamp and its color are indistinguishable. He regards *self as possessing form* (*rūpavantaṃ attānaṃ*), when he takes the formless (i.e., the mind or mental factors) as a self that possesses form, in the way a tree possesses a shadow; *form as in self* (*attani rūpaṃ*), when he takes the formless (mind) as a self within which form is situated, as the scent is in a flower; *self as in form* (*rūpasmiṃ attānaṃ*), when he takes the formless (mind) as a self situated in form, as a jewel is in a casket.

11. This noble disciple is presumably at minimum a stream-enterer.
12. Mahākaccāna was the disciple who excelled in giving detailed analyses of the Buddha's brief statements. For an account of his life and teachings, see Nyanaponika and Hecker, *Great Disciples of the Buddha*, chapter 6.
13. Sakka, the ruler of the devas in the Tāvatiṃsa heaven, was a follower of the Buddha. See SN chapter 11.
14. *Papañcasaññāsaṅkhā*. The meaning of this obscure compound is not elucidated in the Nikāyas. The term seems to refer to perceptions and ideas that have become "infected" by subjective biases, "elaborated" by the tendencies to craving, conceit, and distorted views. According to the commentaries, craving, conceit, and views are the three factors responsible for conceptual elaboration (*papañca*). A detailed study of the expression is Ñāṇananda, *Concept and Reality in Early Buddhist Thought*.
15. Sv: *Pursuit* (*pariyesanā*) is the pursuit of objects such as visible forms, etc., and *gain* (*lābha*) is the gaining of such objects. *Decision-making* (*vinicchaya*) is deciding how much to keep for oneself and how much to give to others; how much to use and how much to store, etc.
16. Greed, hatred, and delusion (*lobha, dosa, moha*) are the three "unwholesome roots"—the root causes of all mental defilements and unwholesome actions; see p. 146.
17. *Anamataggo 'yaṃ bhikkhave saṃsāro*. The original meaning of *anamatagga* is uncertain. Spk glosses it as "having an unfindable beginning," explaining: "Even if it should be pursued by knowledge for a hundred or a thousand years, it would be with unfindable beginning, with unknown beginning. It wouldn't be possible to know its beginning from here or from there; the meaning is that it is without a delimiting first or last point. *Saṃsāra* is the uninterruptedly occurring succession of the aggregates."
18. *Jambudīpa*. "The rose-apple land," the Indian subcontinent.
19. *Kappa*. Apparently a *mahākappa*, a "great eon," is intended, the length of time it takes for a world system to arise, develop, and perish. Each *mahākappa* consists of four *asaṅkheyyakappas*, individual periods of expansion, stabilization, contraction, and dissolution. For a discussion of early Buddhist cosmology, see Gethin, *The Foundations of Buddhism*, pp. 112–15.
20. A *yojana* is approximately seven miles.

Chapter II: The Bringer of Light

1. Suttanipāta v. 335.
2. Although the bodhisattva ideal is usually understood to be distinctive of Mahāyāna Buddhism, all the schools of Sectarian Buddhism in the period preceding the emergence of the Mahāyāna shared the belief that the Buddha pursued the course of a bodhisattva over many eons, fulfilling the requirements for Buddhahood. Mahāyāna's contribution was to advocate the bodhisattva career as a prescriptive model for all Buddhist followers to pursue.
3. The "six things unsurpassed" (*cha anuttariyā*) are explained at AN 6:130: the unsurpassed sight (i.e., the sight of a Buddha or his disciple); the unsurpassed hearing (i.e., hearing the Dhamma from a Buddha or his disciple); the unsurpassed gain (i.e., the gain of faith in a Buddha or his disciple); the unsurpassed training (i.e., training in the higher morality, higher mind, higher wisdom as taught by a Buddha or his disciple); the unsurpassed service (i.e., service to a Buddha or his disciple); the unsurpassed recollection (i.e., the recollection of a Buddha or his disciple). The "four analytical knowledges" (*catasso paṭisambhidā*) are the analytical knowledges of meaning, doctrine, language, and ingenuity. The fruits of stream-entry, etc., are explained in chapter X.
4. As the Buddha's personal attendant, Ānanda was known for his personal dedication to his master. In the main portion of the sutta, where he articulates the traditional beliefs about the wonders accompanying the Buddha's conception and birth, he seems to represent the voice of faithful devotion.
5. This refers to the Bodhisatta's rebirth in the Tusita heaven, which preceded his birth in the human world as Gotama the future Buddha.
6. Ps: Between every three world systems there is an interstice measuring 8,000 *yojanas;* it is like the space between three wagon wheels or almsbowls touching one another. The beings who live there have taken rebirth there because of committing some terrible offence against their parents or righteous ascetics and brahmins, or because of some habitual evil deed like killing animals, etc.
7. Ps: The four deities were the Four Great Kings (i.e., the presiding deities of the heaven of the Four Great Kings).
8. Ps explains each aspect of this event as a foretoken of the Buddha's later attainments. Thus, his standing with his feet (*pāda*) firmly on the ground was a foretoken of his attaining the four bases for spiritual power (*iddhipāda*); his facing the north, of his going above and beyond the multitude; his seven steps, of his acquiring the seven enlightenment factors; the white parasol, of his acquiring the parasol of liberation; his surveying the quarters, of his acquiring the unobstructed knowledge of omniscience; his uttering the words of the "leader of the herd" (an epithet for an eminent person), of his setting in motion the irreversible wheel of the Dhamma; his statement "This is my last birth," of his passing away into the Nibbāna element with no residue remaining (see **Text IX,5(5)**).
9. This statement seems to be the Buddha's way of calling attention to the quality he regarded as the true wonder and marvel.
10. In the unabridged version of this text, gold and silver are excluded from the things subject to sickness, death, and sorrow, but they are subject to defilement, according to Ps, because they can be alloyed with metals of lesser worth.
11. *Ākiñcaññāyatana.* This is the third formless meditative attainment; preceded by the four jhānas, it is the seventh of the eight attainments (*samāpatti*) in the scale

of concentration. These attainments, though spiritually exalted, are still mundane and, divorced from insight, are not directly conducive to Nibbāna.

12. That is, it leads to rebirth in the plane of existence called the base of nothingness, the objective counterpart of the seventh meditative attainment. Here the lifespan is said to be 60,000 eons, but when that has elapsed one must pass away and return to a lower world. Thus one who attains this is still not free from birth and death.
13. *N'eva saññānāsaññāyatana*. This is the fourth and highest formless attainment. It should be noted that Uddaka Rāmaputta is Rāma's son (*putta*), not Rāma himself. The text gives the impression that while Rāma had attained the base of neither-perception-nor-nonperception, Uddaka himself had not done so. The attainment of this base leads to rebirth in the base of neither-perception-nor-nonperception, the highest plane of rebirth in saṃsāra. The lifespan there is said to be 84,000 eons, but being conditioned and impermanent, it is still ultimately unsatisfactory.
14. **Text II,3(2)** continues from this point with an extended account of the Bodhisatta's extreme ascetic practices followed by his discovery of the middle way.
15. Saccaka was a debater whom, on an earlier occasion, the Buddha had defeated in a discussion. Aggivessana, the name by which the Buddha addresses him just below, is probably his clan name. The present discourse begins with a discussion about pleasant and painful feeling, which gives the cue for Saccaka to pose these questions to the Buddha.
16. It is puzzling that in the following paragraphs the Bodhisatta is shown engaging in self-mortification *after* he comes to the conclusion—in this passage—that such practices are useless for the attainment of enlightenment. This anomaly raises a suspicion that the narrative sequence of the sutta has become jumbled. The appropriate place for the simile of the fire-sticks, it seems, would be at the end of the Bodhisatta's period of ascetic experimentation, when he has acquired a sound basis for rejecting self-mortification as a way to enlightenment.
17. This sentence, repeated at the end of each of the following sections as well, answers the second of the two questions posed by Saccaka in §11.
18. Ps explains that when the Bodhisatta was a child, his father brought him along to attend the ceremonial plowing festival of the Sakyans. The young prince's attendants left him under a rose-apple tree and went to watch the plowing ceremony. Finding himself all alone, the Bodhisatta spontaneously sat up in the meditation posture and attained the first jhāna through mindfulness of breathing. Though the sun moved, the shade of the tree remained over the Bodhisatta. When the attendants returned and found the boy seated in meditation, they reported this to the king, who came and bowed in veneration to his son.
19. This sentence answers the first of the two questions posed by Saccaka in §11. This passage shows a change in the Bodhisatta's evaluation of pleasure. When pleasure arises from seclusion and detachment, it is no longer something to be feared and banished by the practice of austerities but becomes an adjunct of the higher stages along the path to enlightenment.
20. In the usual formula of dependent origination, consciousness is said to be conditioned by volitional formations (*saṅkhārapaccayā viññāṇaṃ*). This variant reveals the interplay of consciousness and name-and-form to be the "hidden vortex" underlying all existence within the round of rebirths.
21. Spk: "*To this extent one may be born, age, and die*: With consciousness as a condition

for name-and-form, and with name-and-form as a condition for consciousness, to this extent one may be born and undergo rebirth. What is there beyond this that can be born or undergo rebirth? Isn't it just this that is born and undergoes rebirth?"

22. Note that the Buddha discovers the path to enlightenment by realizing the cessation of consciousness, name-and-form, and the other links of dependent origination. Cessation is realized with the experience of Nibbāna, the deathless element.
23. At this point the text introduces volitional formations. Its principal condition is ignorance, and thus by mentioning its origin, ignorance too is implied. In this way, all twelve factors of the usual formula of dependent origination are included, at least by implication.
24. *Ālaya*. The word signifies both the objects of clinging and the subjective attitude of clinging.
25. By mentioning these two themes—dependent origination and Nibbāna—in his reflections immediately after his enlightenment, the Buddha underscores their importance for understanding the content of his enlightenment. The enlightenment thus involved a comprehension, first, of the dependent origination of suffering, and second, of Nibbāna as the state of ultimate liberation that transcends all phenomena involved in the dependent origination of suffering. The Buddha first had to comprehend dependent origination, and only when he had done so could he arrive at the realization of Nibbāna. The "acquisitions" (*upadhi*) that are relinquished can be understood as twofold: in terms of the object, as the five aggregates or, more broadly, as all objects of appropriation; and subjectively, as the craving that motivates acts of appropriation.
26. Ps raises the question why, when the Bodhisatta had long ago made an aspiration to attain Buddhahood in order to liberate others, his mind now inclined toward inaction. The reason, it says, is that only now, after becoming enlightened, did he recognize how profound the Dhamma was and how difficult it would be for those with strong defilements to understand it. Also, he wanted Brahmā to ask him to teach so that people who venerate Brahmā would respect the Dhamma and wish to hear it.
27. These five monks attended on the Bodhisatta during his period of self-mortification, convinced that he would attain enlightenment and teach them the Dhamma. However, when he abandoned his austerities and resumed taking solid food, they lost faith in him and deserted him, accusing him of reverting to luxury. See **Text II,3(2)**.
28. *Anantajina*: perhaps this was an epithet used by the Ājīvakas for the spiritually perfected individual.
29. *Āvuso*: a familiar term of address used among equals.
30. The change in address from "friend" (*āvuso*) to "venerable sir" (*bhante*) indicates that they have now accepted the Buddha's claim and are prepared to regard him as their superior.
31. At this point the Buddha preached to them his first sermon, the Dhammacakkappavattana Sutta, "The Setting in Motion of the Wheel of Dhamma"; see **Text II,5**. Several days later, after they had all become stream-enterers, he taught them the Anattalakkhaṇa Sutta, "The Characteristic of Nonself," upon hearing which they all attained arahantship; see **Text IX,4(1)(c)**. The complete narrative is at Vin I 7–14. See Ñāṇamoli, *The Life of the Buddha*, p. 47.

32. The first section under the exposition of each noble truth simply reveals the knowledge of the truth itself (*saccañāṇa*).
33. The second section under the exposition of each noble truth reveals the knowledge of the task to be accomplished with regard to that truth (*kiccañāṇa*). The first noble truth is to be fully understood (*pariññeyya*), the second to be abandoned (*pahātabba*), the third to be realized (*sacchikātabba*), and the fourth to be developed (*bhāvetabba*).
34. The third section under the exposition of each noble truth reveals the knowledge of the completion of the task appropriate to that truth (*katañāṇa*). The first noble truth has been fully understood (*pariññāta*), the second has been abandoned (*pahīna*), the third has been realized (*sacchikata*), and the fourth has been developed (*bhāveta*).
35. The three phases (*tiparivaṭṭa*) are: (i) the knowledge of each truth; (ii) the knowledge of the task to be achieved regarding that truth; and (iii) the knowledge that this task has been completed. The twelve modes (*dvādasākāra*) are obtained by applying the three phases to the four truths.
36. This stock formulation implies that on this occasion, Koṇḍañña attained the first stage of enlightenment, stream-entry.
37. These are the devas of the six sense-sphere heavenly worlds and the brahma world.

Chapter III: Approaching the Dhamma

1. Among the criteria he proposes is the opinion of the wise, which shows that far from rejecting the opinions of others, the Buddha includes the opinions of the right sort of person among the standards for determining proper conduct. Other suttas tell us how we can judge who is truly wise; see **Text III,4** and **Text III,5**.
2. Mp explains that this town was located at the edge of a forest. Various groups of wanderers and ascetics would stop there to spend the night before crossing the forest. During their stay they would give talks to the Kālāmas, and the Kālāmas were thus exposed to a wide range of philosophical theories. The conflicts between the different views caused them doubt and perplexity.
3. The above is a stock passage in the Nikāyas.
4. These ten inadequate criteria of truth can be grouped into three classes: (1) The *first* comprises the first four criteria, all positions based on reverence for tradition. Of these, (i) "oral tradition" (*anussava*) refers to the Vedic tradition, which, according to the brahmins, had originated with the primal deity and came down orally through successive generations. (ii) "Lineage" (*paramparā*) signifies an unbroken succession of teachings or teachers. (iii) "Hearsay" (or "report," *itikirā*) may mean popular opinion or general consensus. And (iv) "a collection of texts" (*piṭakasampadā*) refers to religious texts regarded as infallible. (2) The *second* set, also made up of four terms, is comprised of four types of reasoning recognized by thinkers in the Buddha's age; their differences need not detain us here. (3) The *third* set, made up of the last two items, refers to two types of personal authority: (i) the personal charisma of the speaker (perhaps including his external qualifications, e.g., that he is highly educated, has a large following, is respected by the king, etc.); and (ii) the speaker's status as one's own personal teacher (the Pāli word *garu* is identical with the Sanskrit *guru*). For a

detailed analysis, see Jayatilleke, *Early Buddhist Theory of Knowledge*, pp. 175–202, 271–75.

5. Greed, hatred, and delusion are the three unwholesome roots. The aim of the Buddha's teaching, Nibbāna, is defined as the destruction of greed (or lust), hatred, and delusion. Thus the Buddha is guiding the Kālāmas toward the heart of his teaching.
6. Here the Buddha introduces the four divine abodes (*brahmavihāra*): boundless loving-kindness, compassion, altruistic joy, and equanimity.
7. Mp: Because he does no evil and because no evil (i.e., suffering) will come to him.
8. This is a stock passage. "Going for refuge" is the act by which a new convert acknowledges the Buddha, the Dhamma, and the Saṅgha as guiding ideals. In Buddhist tradition, it has become the procedure by which one formally declares oneself a Buddhist.
9. *Gāmaṇi*. The word suggests that he is a person of some prominence in the town.
10. Note that the headman here ascribes to the Buddha, as a direct quotation, a general statement of the causal relationship between desire and suffering not found in the Buddha's words above. The statement is, however, clearly needed as the referent of "this principle" (*iminā dhammena*). It is thus possible that the statement was in the original text but had dropped out in the course of its oral transmission. Just below the Buddha does make the generalization himself.
11. Read, with Be and Ce, *ajānantena*, as against Ee's *ājānantena*. The negative is clearly required here, since the monk who cannot directly know the Buddha's mind must infer from his bodily and verbal behavior that he is fully purified.
12. "States cognizable through the eye" are bodily actions; "states cognizable through the ear" are words.
13. "Mixed states" would mean the conduct of one who is trying to purify his behavior but is unable to do so consistently. Sometimes his conduct is pure, sometimes impure.
14. Ps: The dangers are conceit, arrogance, etc. For some monks are calm and humble as long as they have not become well known and popular; but when they become famous and popular, they go about acting improperly, attacking other monks like a leopard pouncing on a herd of deer.
15. Ps: This statement shows the Buddha's impartiality. He does not extol some and disparage others.
16. *So tasmiṃ dhamme abhiññāya idh'ekaccaṃ dhammaṃ dhammesu niṭṭhaṃ gacchati*. In order to convey the intended meaning I have rendered the second occurrence of *dhamma* here as "teaching," i.e., the particular doctrine taught to him, the plural *dhammesu* as "teachings," and *tasmiṃ dhamme* as "that Dhamma," in the sense of the total teaching. Ps and Ps-pṭ together explain the meaning thus: "When the Dhamma has been taught by the Master, the monk, by directly knowing the Dhamma through penetration of the path, fruit, and Nibbāna, comes to a conclusion regarding the preliminary teaching of the Dhamma about the aids to enlightenment (*bodhipakkhiyā dhammā*)."
17. This refers to the faith of a noble person (*ariyapuggala*), who has seen the Dhamma and thus can never acknowledge any teacher other than the Buddha.
18. He was a prominent brahmin who ruled over Opasāda, a crown property in the state of Kosala that had been granted to him by King Pasenadi.
19. Apparently this is Kāpaṭhika's clan name.

20. These are the ancient rishis whom the brahmins regarded as the divinely inspired authors of the Vedic hymns.
21. In Pāli: *saddhā, ruci, anussava, ākāraparivitakka, diṭṭhinijjhānakkhanti*. Of these five grounds for arriving at a conviction, the first two seem to be based primarily on emotion, the third to be an unquestioning acceptance of tradition, and the last two primarily rational or cognitive. The last three are included among the ten unacceptable grounds for a belief in **Text III,2**. The "two different ways" that each may turn out are true or false.
22. It is not proper for him to come to this conclusion because he has not personally ascertained the truth of his conviction but only accepts it on a ground that is not capable of yielding certainty.
23. *Saccānurakkhana*: or, the safeguarding of truth, the protection of truth.
24. *Saccānubodha*: or, the awakening to truth.
25. In this series, "he scrutinizes" (*tūleti*), according to Ps, means that he investigates phenomena as impermanent, suffering, and nonself. This is the stage of insight contemplation. "Applies the will" (*ussahati*) and "strives" (*padahati*) appear similar. We might understand the former as the effort leading to insight, the latter as the effort that leads from insight to world-transcending realization. This last step is signified by the expression, "he realizes with the body the supreme truth." The supreme truth (*paramasacca*) is Nibbāna.
26. While the "discovery of truth" (*saccānubodha*) in this context seems to mean the attainment of stream-entry, the final arrival at truth (*saccānuppatti*) must mean the attainment of arahantship. Note that the final arrival at truth does not come about through any new measures, but simply through the repeated development of those same factors that led to the discovery of truth.
27. Ps: The brahmins believed that they themselves were the offspring of Brahmā's mouth, the *khattiyas* of his breast, the mercantile class (*vessa*) of his belly, the workers (*sudda*) of his legs, and *samaṇas* of the soles of his feet.

Chapter IV: The Happiness Visible in This Present Life

1. As the standard for the wheel-turning monarch, Dhamma is not the Buddha's teaching but the moral law of justice and righteousness on the basis of which the righteous king rules his country and gains sovereignty over the world. In Indian iconography, the wheel (*cakka*) is the symbol of sovereignty in both the temporal and spiritual spheres. The world ruler assumes kingship when the mystical "wheel treasure" (*cakkaratana*) appears to him (see **Text IV,6(5)**); the wheel treasure persists as the symbol of his rule. Analogously, the Buddha sets in motion the wheel of the Dhamma, which cannot be turned back by anyone in the world.
2. Compare with the shout of the devas at the conclusion of **Text II,5**.
3. The householder Nakulapitā and the housewife Nakulamātā were the foremost of the Buddha's lay disciples with regard to their trust in him. See Nyanaponika and Hecker, *Great Disciples of the Buddha*, pp. 375–78.
4. Anāthapiṇḍika was the Buddha's foremost male lay supporter. See Nyanaponika and Hecker, *Great Disciples of the Buddha*, chapter 9.
5. *Dāsī*: literally, a female slave. Fortunately, in Buddhist societies this recommendation has not been taken very seriously and the first three models of the ideal wife have prevailed.

6. Visākhā was the Buddha's foremost female lay supporter. The Eastern Park was the monastery she had built for the Buddha in the eastern part of Sāvatthī.
7. This argument is intended to refute the brahmins' claim that they are born from the mouth of Brahmā.
8. *Yona* is probably the Greek colony of Bactria, in modern Afghanistan and Pakistan. Greeks lived and ruled here after the conquests of Alexander the Great. *Kamboja* is probably to the northwest of the Indian "Middle Country."
9. King Ajātasattu had come to power by killing his father, the virtuous king Bimbisāra, a supporter of the Buddha who had attained stream-entry, the first stage of liberation. Ajātasattu later felt remorse for his heinous deed and, after hearing the Buddha teach the Sāmaññaphala Sutta (DN 2), became his follower. The Vajjian confederacy, north of Magadha, on the other side of the river Ganges, consisted of the Licchavis of Vesālī and the Vedehis (of Videha—to whom Ajātasattu's mother belonged), whose capital was Mithilā.
10. The *uposatha* is the day of religious observance in the Indian lunar calendar. It falls on the days of the full moon (the fifteenth of the fortnight), the new moon (the fourteenth or fifteenth of the fortnight), and the two half-moons. The "uposatha day of the fifteenth" referred to here is probably the full-moon uposatha.
11. I correct an error in Walshe's translation here. Walshe translates as if the virtuous ascetics and brahmins should come to the king to ask for his guidance in what is wholesome and unwholesome. The Pāli text, however, is clear that it is the king who should approach the virtuous ascetics and brahmins to ask for *their* guidance.
12. *Yathābhuttañ ca bhuñjatha.* The Pāli means literally "eat the food as it has been eaten," but this seems to be the implication. Walshe's "Be moderate in eating" cannot be correct.
13. *Purohita.* He was a brahmin who served as an advisor on both religious and temporal affairs.

Chapter V: The Way to a Fortunate Rebirth

1. *Cetanā 'haṃ bhikkhave kammaṃ vadāmi, cetayitvā kammaṃ karoti kāyena vācāya manasā* (AN III 415).
2. The distinction seems to be lightly drawn in the sutta literature, but in the commentaries it becomes hardened into a precise delimitation between the three types of results any kamma may produce.
3. For the distinction between these two types of right view, see MN 117 (not included in this anthology). In the technical terminology of the Pāli commentators, even the insight into the three characteristics (impermanence, suffering, nonself) and knowledge of the originative aspect of dependent origination are still mundane (*lokiya*) because their objects are mundane phenomena. In the commentarial system, only the direct cognition of the unconditioned, Nibbāna, is classified as supramundane right view. However, I here use the terms "supramundane" and "world-transcending" (*lokuttara*) in a broader sense, as referring to the knowledge and view (and, more broadly, to all practices) that lead to the transcending of the world.
4. For a fuller discussion of the psychological basis of Early Buddhist cosmology, see Gethin, *The Foundations of Buddhism*, pp. 119–26.

5. Respectively, *dasa akusalā kammapathā* and *dasa kusalā kammapathā*. In the Nikāyas, the latter occurs at AN V 57; both are at DN III 269.
6. Buddhist texts of a somewhat later date than the oldest strata of the canon add a fourth bad destination, the realm of the *asuras*. In the old canon, the asuras are depicted as titanic beings engaged in perpetual conflict with the devas but are not assigned to a separate realm. Since their living conditions, as described in the canon, can hardly be called unbearably miserable, the commentators identify the asuras that constitute the fourth bad destination—not with the asuras who battle against the devas—but with a class of beings in the realm of afflicted spirits. Needless to say, the picture of the realms that emerges when the asuras are considered distinct becomes somewhat blurred: if they are the beings who fight against the devas, they aren't depicted as living in abject misery; if they are a class of beings in the spirit realm, there seems no reason to treat them as a separate realm.
7. I here describe the spheres of rebirth corresponding to the fourth jhāna in accordance with the cosmology of scholastic Theravāda Buddhism. Other schools of Early Buddhism—based on texts parallel to the Nikāyas—divided up the terrain of the fourth jhāna realms somewhat differently.
8. The community of noble disciples consists of four pairs of persons, those who have entered the four paths and those who have realized the four fruits. See p. 373.
9. *Subhakiṇhā devā*. These are the deities inhabiting the highest plane of rebirth corresponding to the third jhāna.
10. AN 4:235 explains this as the development of the Noble Eightfold Path; AN 4:236, as the development of the seven enlightenment factors.
11. This is a morally nihilistic materialist view that denies an afterlife and the fruits of kamma. "There is nothing given" means there is no fruit of giving; "no this world, no other world," no rebirth into either this world or a world beyond; "no mother, no father," no fruit of good and bad conduct toward parents. The statement about ascetics and brahmins denies the existence of Buddhas and arahants.
12. Ps says that "the devas of radiance" is not a separate class of devas but a collective name for the three classes that follow; the same for "the devas of glory."
13. It should be noted that while "conduct in accordance with the Dhamma" as described in the sutta is a necessary condition for rebirth in the higher heavenly worlds and for the destruction of the taints, it is by no means a sufficient condition. Rebirth into the realms beginning with the devas of Brahmā's retinue requires the attainment of jhāna, rebirth into the pure abodes (the five beginning with the *avihā* devas) requires the attainment of the stage of nonreturner. Rebirth into the formless planes requires the corresponding formless attainments, and the destruction of the taints requires the full practice of the Noble Eightfold Path up to the path of arahantship.
14. Ps: If the kamma of killing directly determines the mode of rebirth, it will produce rebirth in a bad destination. But if a wholesome kamma brings about a human rebirth—and rebirth as a human being is always the result of wholesome kamma—the kamma of killing will operate in a manner contrary to that of the rebirth-generative kamma by causing various adversities that may culminate in a premature death. The same principle holds for the subsequent cases in which unwholesome kamma matures in a human existence: in each instance,

the unwholesome kamma counteracts the wholesome kamma responsible for the human rebirth by causing a particular type of misfortune specific to itself.

15. In this case the wholesome kamma of abstaining from killing is directly responsible for either the heavenly rebirth or longevity in a human existence. The same principle applies in all the passages on the maturation of wholesome kamma.
16. This means that the act of giving is not sufficient to obtain the desired result. It must be supported by pure moral conduct. For one of persistent immoral conduct, generosity would not suffice to bring a favorable rebirth.
17. This is said because rebirth into the brahma world—and into other planes in the form realm—is achieved through attainment of the jhānas, which requires the suppression of sensual lust.
18. On the uposatha, see p. 153.
19. The "proper time" for meals, according to the monastic and uposatha precepts, is between daybreak and noon. From noon on, solid foods as well as certain nourishing liquids (such as milk) cannot be consumed. Fruit juices, soft drinks, tea, herbal teas, and other light drinks are allowed.
20. These are the states of the Indian subcontinent and the adjacent regions.
21. Ps explains limiting action (*pamāṇakataṃ kammaṃ*) as kamma pertaining to the sense sphere (*kāmāvacara*). It is opposed by a limitless or immeasurable action, namely, the jhānas and formless attainments. In this case, the *brahmavihāras* developed to the level of jhāna are intended. When a jhāna or formless attainment is mastered, a kamma pertaining to the sense sphere cannot find the opportunity to yield its own result. Rather, the kamma pertaining to the form realm or the formless realm overpowers the sense-sphere kamma and produces its results. A *brahmavihāra* that has been mastered leads to rebirth in the brahma world.
22. A "person possessed of right view" (*diṭṭhisampanna puggala*) is a stream-enterer. The stream-enterer and those who reach higher attainments will be discussed in chapter X.
23. A paccekabuddha is one who, like a Perfectly Enlightened Buddha, attains enlightenment without the guidance of a teacher, but unlike a Buddha is unable to guide others to enlightenment. According to commentarial tradition, paccekabuddhas do not arise while the teaching of a Perfectly Enlightened Buddha exists in the world but only in the periods between the arising of Buddhas.

Chapter VI: Deepening One's Perspective on the World

1. Ps: "Full understanding" (*pariññā*) here means overcoming (*samatikkama*) or abandoning (*pahāna*). The wanderers of other sects identify the full understanding of sensual pleasures with the first jhāna, the full understanding of form with formless existence [the formless planes corresponding to the formless meditative attainments], and the full understanding of feelings with nonpercipient existence [a plane of existence in which perception is temporarily suspended]. The Buddha, on the other hand, describes the full understanding of sensual pleasures as the path to the stage of nonreturner, and the full understanding of both form and feelings as the path to arahantship.
2. Note that while the previous dangers in sensual pleasures were called "a mass of suffering in this present life" (*sandiṭṭhiko dukkhakkhandho*), this one is called "a mass of suffering in the life to come" (*samparāyiko dukkhakkhandho*).

3. *Vohārasamuccheda. Vohāra* can mean business transactions, designation, speech, and intentions. Ps says all four are relevant, since he thinks he has given up the business, designation, speech, and intentions of a householder.
4. Ps explains the "equanimity that is diversified, based on diversity" as that related to the five cords of sensual pleasure; the "equanimity that is unified, based on unity" as that based on the fourth jhāna.
5. Māgandiya was a philosophical hedonist who held that one should allow the five senses to enjoy their respective objects. He criticized the Buddha for advocating restraint and control of the senses. The Buddha is about to demonstrate the defects in sensual enjoyment.
6. Ps glosses *nippurisa*, "none male," as meaning that they were all women. Not only the musicians, but all posts in the palace, including the door-keepers, were filled by women. His father had provided him with three palaces and the entourage of women in hopes of keeping him confined to the lay life and distracting him from thoughts of renunciation.
7. Ps: This is said referring to the attainment of the fruit of arahantship (*arahatta-phala-samāpatti*) based on the fourth jhāna.
8. The "Grove of Delight" in the Tāvatiṃsa heaven.
9. The expression *viparītasaññā* alludes to the "distorted perception" of perceiving pleasure in what is really painful. AN 4:49 speaks of four distortions of perception (*saññāvipallāsa*): perceiving the unattractive as attractive, the impermanent as permanent, the painful as pleasurable, and the selfless as a self. Sensual pleasures are painful because they arouse the painful defilements and because they bring painful fruits in the future.
10. What is intended here by wrong view (*micchā diṭṭhi*) are views that deny the foundations of morality, especially those views that reject a principle of moral causation or the efficacy of volitional effort.
11. Forest-dwelling and the rest are among the ascetic practices permitted by the Buddha. On the ten fetters, see pp. 374–75. Spk says that some among them were stream-enterers, some once-returners, and some nonreturners. None were worldlings, and none were arahants.
12. This means the attainment of arahantship.

Chapter VII: The Path to Liberation

1. Among these ten views, those that entertain ideas about the world (*loka*) are also implicitly entertaining similar ideas about the self (*attā*). Thus the first pair is the antithesis of eternalism and annihilationism. The view that the soul is the same as the body is materialism, a type of annihilationism; the view that the soul and the body are different is eternalism. The view that a Tathāgata—a liberated person—exists after death is eternalism; the view that he does not exist after death is annihilationism. The view that he both exists and does not exist is a syncretic doctrine combining features of eternalism and annihilationism; the view that he neither exists nor does not exist is skepticism or agnosticism, which denies that we can determine his condition after death. All these views, from the Buddhist perspective, presuppose that the Tathāgata presently exists as a self. They thus begin with an erroneous premise and differ only in so far as they posit the fate of the self in different ways.

2. Those who have always wondered about the fate of the monk who almost left the Buddha to satisfy his metaphysical curiosity will be relieved to know that in his old age Māluṅkyāputta received a brief discourse on the six sense bases from the Buddha, went into retreat, and attained arahantship. See SN 35:95.
3. Devadatta was the Buddha's ambitious cousin, who attempted to kill the Buddha and usurp control of the Saṅgha. When these attempts failed, he broke away and tried to establish his own sect with himself at the head. See Ñāṇamoli, *Life of the Buddha*, pp. 266–69.
4. Ps: "Knowledge and vision" (*ñāṇadassana*) here refers to the divine eye, the ability to see subtle forms invisible to normal vision.
5. This translation follows Be and Ce, which read *asamayavimokkhaṃ* in the preceding sentence and *asamayavimuttiyā* in this sentence. Ee seems to be mistaken in reading *samaya* in the two compounds and *ṭhānaṃ* instead of *aṭṭhānaṃ*. Ps cites the *Paṭisambhidāmagga* for a definition of *asamayavimokkha* (lit., non-temporary or "perpetual" emancipation) as the four paths, four fruits, and Nibbāna, and of *samayavimokkha* (temporary emancipation) as the four jhānas and four formless attainments. See also MN 122.4.
6. Ps says that "unshakable liberation of mind" (*akuppā cetovimutti*) is the fruit of arahantship. Thus "perpetual emancipation"—as including all four paths and fruits—has a wider range than "unshakable liberation of mind." The latter alone is declared to be the goal of the holy life.
7. *Rāgavirāgatthaṃ*. This might also have been rendered, somewhat awkwardly, "For the dispassioning of passion," or "For the delusting of lust."
8. Spk: When he was in seclusion, Ānanda thought, "This practice of a monk succeeds for one who relies on good friends and on his own virile effort; thus half depends on good friends and half on one's own virile effort."
9. Vacchāyana is Pilotika's clan name.
10. See p. 436 (chapter V, n.19).
11. The signs (*nimitta*) are the prominent qualities of the object which, when grasped unmindfully, can instigate defiled thoughts; the features (*anubyañjana*) are the details that attract one's attention when one does not restrain the senses. "Longing and dejection" (*abhijjhā-domanassa*) implies the opposed reactions of desire and aversion, attraction and repulsion, toward sense objects.
12. Here, longing (*abhijjhā*) is synonymous with sensual desire (*kāmacchanda*), the first of the five hindrances. This entire passage deals with the overcoming of the five hindrances.
13. He does not come to such a conclusion because the jhānas, as well as the first two higher knowledges (to follow), are not unique to the Buddha's teaching.
14. According to Ps, this shows the occasion of the supramundane path. Since at this point the noble disciple has still not completed his task, he has not yet come to a conclusion (*na tveva niṭṭhaṃ gato hoti*) about the Three Jewels; rather, he is *in the process* of coming to a conclusion (*niṭṭhaṃ gacchati*). The sutta puns on the meaning of the expression "coming to a conclusion" in a way that is just as viable in English as in Pāli.
15. Ps: This shows the occasion when the disciple has attained the fruit of arahantship, and having entirely completed his task, has come to a conclusion about the Three Jewels.

Chapter VIII: Mastering the Mind

1. These are the stages of stream-entry, once-returning, nonreturning, and arahantship. See chapter X.
2. See, e.g., AN 9:3 (IV 358) = Ud 4:1.
3. A translation of the sutta together with its commentary and substantial excerpts from the subcommentary can be found in Soma Thera, *The Way of Mindfulness.* Two excellent modern expositions, which also include translations of the sutta, are: Nyanaponika Thera, *The Heart of Buddhist Meditation*, and Anālayo, *Satipaṭṭhāna: The Direct Path to Realization.*
4. Mp: When serenity is developed independently of insight, it leads to the suppression of the five hindrances, the first of which is sensual lust, and culminates in the "higher mind" (*adhicitta*) of the jhānas, characterized by the absence of lust. But it is only when serenity is developed in conjunction with insight that it can give rise to the noble path, which eradicates the underlying tendency to sensual lust (by the path of nonreturning) and attachment to existence (by the path of arahantship). Mp interprets serenity here in this second sense, presumably on account of the last sentence of the sutta.
5. Mp: It is the wisdom of the supramundane path (*magga-paññā*) that is developed. The "ignorance abandoned" is the great ignorance at the root of the cycle of existence.
6. Arahantship is often described as "taintless liberation of mind, liberation by wisdom" (*anāsava-cetovimutti-paññāvimutti*). Mp explains "liberation of mind" (*cetovimutti*) as the concentration connected with the fruit (of arahantship), "liberation by wisdom" (*paññāvimutti*) as the wisdom connected with the fruit. Mp is referring to the "meditative attainment of the fruit of arahantship" (*arahatta-phala-samāpatti*), a supramundane meditative absorption in which the arahant experiences the bliss of Nibbāna.
7. *Samathapubbaṅgamaṃ vipassanaṃ.* Mp: "This refers to a meditator who first obtains serenity and then takes up insight meditation." The commentators call such a meditator one who makes serenity the vehicle of practice (*samatha-yānika*). See Vism 587; Ppn 18:3.
8. "The path" (*magga*) is the first supramundane path, that of stream-entry. To "develop that path," according to Mp, means to practice for the attainment of the three higher paths. On the ten fetters, see pp. 374–75; on the seven underlying tendencies, see p. 426 (chapter I, n.5).
9. *Vipassanāpubbaṅgamaṃ samathaṃ.* Mp: "This refers to one who by natural bent first attains to insight and then, based on insight, produces concentration." In the commentarial literature this is called one who makes insight the vehicle (*vipassanāyānika*). See Vism 588; Ppn 18:4.
10. *Samathavipassanaṃ yuganaddhaṃ.* In this mode of practice, one enters the first jhāna and then, after emerging from it, applies insight to that experience, i.e., one sees the five aggregates of the jhāna (form, feeling, perception, etc.) as impermanent, bound up with suffering, and nonself. Then one enters the second jhāna and contemplates it with insight. One applies the same procedure to the other jhānas as well until the path of stream-entry, etc., is realized.
11. *Dhammuddhaccaviggahitaṃ mānasaṃ hoti.* Mp says that "agitation" (*uddhacca*) arises here as a reaction to the ten "corruptions of insight" (*vipassanūpakkilesa*) that one misunderstands as indicating path-attainment. (On the corruptions of insight, see Vism 633–38; Ppn 20:105–28.) It is possible, however, that the

"agitation about the teaching" is mental distress brought on by eagerness to realize the Dhamma. This state of spiritual anxiety, when suddenly resolved, can sometimes precipitate an instantaneous experience of awakening. For an example, see the story of Bāhiya Dārucīriya at Ud 1:10.

12. Mp explains internal serenity of mind (*ajjhattaṃ cetosamatha*) as the concentration of full absorption (i.e., jhāna), and the higher wisdom of insight into phenomena (*adhipaññādhammavipassanā*) as the insight knowledge discerning formations (*saṅkhāraparíggāhaka-vipassanāñāṇa*).
13. "Formations" (*saṅkhārā*) are the conditioned phenomena comprised in the five aggregates. On the aggregates, see **Texts IX,4(1)(a)–(e)**.
14. Spk applies the scholastic distinction of the three types of escape (*nissaraṇa*) to each hindrance. One escapes from the hindrance by suppression (*vikkhambhananissaraṇa*) through jhāna; one escapes in a particular respect (*tadaṅganissaraṇa*) through insight; and one escapes by eradication (*samucchedanissaraṇa*) through the supramundane path. Thus: (1) *sensual desire* is suppressed by the first jhāna based on the unattractive nature of the body (*asubha*; see **Text VIII,8** §10) and eradicated by the path of arahantship (since *kāmacchanda* is here interpreted widely enough to include desire for any object, not only sensual desire); (2) *ill will* is suppressed by the first jhāna based on loving-kindness and eradicated by the path of nonreturning; (3) *dullness and drowsiness* are suppressed by the perception of light (i.e., visualization of a bright light, like the disc of the sun or the full moon) and eradicated by the path of arahantship; (4) *restlessness and remorse* are suppressed by serenity, *remorse* is eradicated by the path of nonreturning and *restlessness* by the path of arahantship; and (5) *doubt* is suppressed by the defining of phenomena (*dhammavavatthāna*; see Vism 587–89; Ppn 18:3–8) and eradicated by the path of stream-entry.
15. These are the three "wrong thoughts," opposite of right thought or right intention, the second factor of the Noble Eightfold Path. See **Text VII,2**.
16. *Dhammavitakka*. Mp takes this to refer to the ten "corruptions of insight," but it seems more natural to understand it simply as obsessive reflections about the Dhamma.
17. This refers to the preliminary conditions for the six direct knowledges (*abhiññā*), to be described just below. The preliminary condition for the five mundane direct knowledges is the fourth jhāna. The preliminary condition for arahantship, the sixth direct knowledge, is insight. This direct knowledge alone is supramundane.
18. Ps says the higher mind (*adhicitta*) is the mind of the eight meditative attainments used as a basis for insight; it is called "higher mind" because it is higher than the ordinary (good) mind of the ten wholesome courses of action. The five "signs" (*nimitta*) may be understood as practical methods for removing distracting thoughts. They should be resorted to only when the distractions become persistent or obtrusive; at other times the meditator should remain with the primary subject of meditation.
19. Ps: When thoughts of sensual desire arise directed toward living beings, the "other sign" is the meditation on the unattractive nature of the body (see **Text VIII,8** §10); when the thoughts are directed to inanimate things, the "other sign" is attention to impermanence. When thoughts of hate arise directed toward living beings, the "other sign" is the meditation on loving-kindness; when they are directed to inanimate things, the "other sign" is attention to the

elements (see **Text VIII,8** §12). The remedy for thoughts connected with delusion is living under a teacher, studying the Dhamma, inquiring into its meaning, listening to the Dhamma, and inquiring into causes.

20. *Vitakka-saṅkhāra-saṇṭhānaṃ*. Glossing *saṅkhāra* here as condition, cause, or root, Ps interprets the compound to mean "stopping the cause of the thought." This is accomplished by inquiring, when an unwholesome thought has arisen: "What is its cause? What is the cause of its cause?" etc. Such an inquiry slows down, and eventually cuts off, the flow of unwholesome thoughts.
21. *Tadārammaṇaṃ*, lit. "with that (one) as the object." Ps: First one develops loving-kindness toward the person who addresses one with any of the five courses of wrong speech, then one directs that mind of loving-kindness toward all beings, making the entire world the object.
22. Mahānāma was a close relative of the Buddha, a prominent member of the Sakyan clan.
23. The phrases "arrived at the fruit" (*āgataphala*) and "understood the teaching" (*viññātasāsana*) indicate that he is asking about the meditations of a noble disciple at the minimum level of stream-enterer. However, such meditations can also be profitably practiced by people at any level, for they temporarily cleanse the mind of the defilements and lead to concentration.
24. I abridge the text, which here enumerates the different heavenly realms.
25. The Pāli reads *ekāyano ayaṃ bhikkhave maggo*. Almost all translators have understood this statement to be a declaration that *satipaṭṭhāna* is an exclusive path. Thus Soma Thera renders it: "This is the only way, O bhikkhus," and Nyanaponika Thera: "This is the sole way, monks." However, at MN 12.37–42 *ekāyana magga* has the unambiguous meaning of "a path that goes in one way only," and that seems the meaning that fits best here as well. The point seems to be simply that *satipaṭṭhāna* goes in one direction, toward "the purification of beings ... the realization of Nibbāna."
26. Ps says the repetition "contemplating the body in the body" (*kāye kāyānupassī*) has the purpose of precisely determining the object of contemplation and of isolating that object from others with which it might be confused. Thus, in this practice, the body should be contemplated as such, and not one's feelings, ideas, and emotions concerning it. The phrase also means that the body should be contemplated simply as a body and not as a man, a woman, a self, or a living being. Parallel considerations apply to the repetitions with regard to each of the other three establishments of mindfulness. "Longing and dejection" (*abhijjhā-domanassaṃ*), according to Ps, imply sensual desire and ill will, the chief among the five mental hindrances.
27. On the structure of the discourse to follow, see pp. 262–63.
28. The practice of mindfulness of breathing (*ānāpānasati*) does not involves a deliberate attempt to regulate the breath, as in hatha yoga, but an effort to fix awareness continuously on the breath as one breathes at a natural rhythm. Mindfulness is set up at the nostrils or the upper lip, wherever the impact of the breath is felt most distinctly. The length of the breath is noted but not consciously controlled.

    The complete development of this meditation subject is explained in **Text VIII,9**. A detailed explanation of mindfulness of breathing according to the commentarial system is at Vism 266–93; Ppn 8:145–244. See too the collection of texts translated by Ñāṇamoli, *Mindfulness of Breathing*.

29. Ps, in line with other Pāli commentaries, explains "experiencing the whole body" (*sabbakāyapaṭisaṃvedī*) to mean that the meditator becomes aware of each in-breath and out-breath through its three phases of beginning, middle, and end. This interpretation is difficult to square with the literal words of the original text, which may have originally intended simply a global awareness of the entire body. It is also difficult to see how *-paṭisaṃvedī* could mean "is aware of"; this suffix is based on the verb *paṭisaṃvedeti* meaning "to experience" or "to feel," which has a different nuance from "awareness."
30. The "bodily formation" (*kāyasaṅkhāra*) is defined as in-and-out breathing at MN 44.13 (I 301) and SN 41:6 (IV 293). Thus, as Ps explains, with the successful development of this practice, the meditator's breathing becomes increasingly more quiet, tranquil, and peaceful.
31. Ps: "Internally": contemplating the breathing in his own body. "Externally": contemplating the breathing taking place in the body of another. "Internally and externally": contemplating the breathing in his own body and in the body of another alternately, with uninterrupted attention. A similar explanation applies to the refrain that follows each of the other sections, except that under the contemplation of feeling, mind, and phenomena, the contemplation externally, apart from those possessing telepathic powers, must be inferential. It is also impossible for those without telepathic powers to directly contemplate the breathing of another, apart from observation of the expansion and contraction of the chest, so contemplation in this case too must be inferential.
32. Ps explains that the arising nature (*samudayadhamma*) of the body can be observed in its conditioned origination through ignorance, craving, kamma, and food, as well as in the moment-by-moment origination of material phenomena in the body. In the case of mindfulness of breathing, an additional condition is the physiological apparatus of respiration. The "vanishing nature" (*vayadhamma*) of the body is seen in the cessation of bodily phenomena through the cessation of their conditions as well as in the momentary dissolution of bodily phenomena.
33. The understanding of the bodily postures referred to in this exercise is not our normal knowledge of our bodily activity, but a close, constant, and careful awareness of the body in every position, coupled with an analytical examination intended to dispel the delusion of a self as the agent of bodily movement.
34. *Sampajañña*, clear comprehension, is analyzed in the commentaries into four types: (1) clear comprehension of the purpose of one's action; (2) clear comprehension of the suitability of one's means to the achievement of one's purpose; (3) clear comprehension of the domain, that is, not abandoning the subject of meditation during one's daily routine; and (4) clear comprehension of reality, the awareness that behind one's activities there is no abiding self. See Soma, *The Way of Mindfulness*, pp. 60–100; Nyanaponika, *The Heart of Buddhist Meditation*, pp. 46–55.
35. A detailed explanation of this practice, according to the commentarial method, is at Vism 239–266; Ppn 8:42–144. The *mesentery* is a fold of tissue that anchors the small intestine to the back of the abdominal wall.
36. These four elements are the primary attributes of matter—the earth element (*pathavīdhātu*) is solidity; the water element (*āpodhātu*), cohesion; the fire element (*tejodhātu*), heat; and the air element (*vāyodhātu*), pressure or distension.

For a more detailed account of the contemplation of elements, see **Text IX,4(3)(c)**. For the commentarial explanation, see Vism 347–72; Ppn 11:27–126.

37. The phrase "as though" (*seyyathāpi*) suggests that this meditation, and those to follow, need not be based upon actual observation of a decaying corpse but can be performed imaginatively. "This same body" is, of course, the meditator's own body.
38. Each of the four types of corpse mentioned here, and the three types below, may be taken as a separate and self-sufficient subject of meditation; or the entire set may be used as a progressive series for impressing on the mind the idea of the body's transience and insubstantiality. The progression continues in §§26–30.
39. Feeling (*vedanā*) signifies the affective quality of experience, bodily and mental, either pleasant, painful, or neither, i.e., neutral feeling. Examples of the "carnal" and "spiritual" varieties of these feelings are given at MN 137.9–15 (III 217–19) under the rubric of the six kinds of joy, grief, and equanimity based respectively on the household life and renunciation.
40. The conditions for the arising and vanishing of feeling are the same as those for the body (see p. 442 (chapter VIII, n. 32) except that food is replaced by contact, since contact is the condition for feeling).
41. Mind (*citta*) as an object of contemplation refers to the general state and level of consciousness. Since consciousness itself is the bare knowing or cognizing of an object, the quality of any state of mind is determined by its associated mental factors, such as lust, hate, and delusion or their opposites.
42. The examples of *citta* given in this passage contrast states of mind of wholesome and unwholesome, or developed and undeveloped character. The pair "contracted" and "distracted," however, consists of unwholesome opposites, the former due to dullness and drowsiness, the latter to restlessness and remorse. Ps explains "exalted mind" and "unsurpassable mind" as the mind pertaining to the meditative attainments (jhānas and formless states), "unexalted mind" and "surpassable mind" as the mind pertaining to sense-sphere consciousness. The commentary says "liberated mind" should be understood as a mind temporarily and partly freed from defilements through insight or the jhānas. Since the practice of *satipaṭṭhāna* pertains to the preliminary phase of the path, the commentary holds that this last category should not be understood as a mind liberated by attainment of the supramundane paths; perhaps, however, this interpretation should not be excluded.
43. The conditions for the arising and vanishing of mind are the same as those for the body except that food is replaced by name-and-form, the condition for consciousness.
44. The five hindrances (*pañca nīvaraṇā*): the main inner impediments to the development of concentration and insight. See above, **Text VIII,3**.
45. See p. 440 (chapter VIII, n.147).
46. On the five aggregates, see pp. 22, 306–7, and **Texts IX,4(1)(a)–(e)**.
47. The origin and passing away of the five aggregates can be understood in two ways: (1) through their origination and cessation in dependence on their conditions (see **Text IX,4(1)(a)**); and (2) through their discernible arising, change, and vanishing (see SN 22:37–38). The two ways are not mutually exclusive but can be conceptually distinguished.
48. On the six sense bases, see ppp. 309–11 and **Texts IX,4(2)(a)–(e)**.

49. The fetter is the desire and lust (*chandarāga*) that binds the sense faculties to their objects; see SN 35:232.
50. On the enlightenment factors, see **Text VIII,9**.
51. The Pāli commentaries give detailed information about the conditions that lead to the maturation of the enlightenment factors. See Soma Thera, *The Way of Mindfulness*, pp. 134–149.
52. The longer Mahāsatipaṭṭhāna Sutta in DN defines and elaborates on each of the Four Noble Truths. See too MN 141.
53. Final knowledge *(aññā)* is the arahant's knowledge of liberation. Nonreturning (*anāgāmitā*) is the attainment of the state of a nonreturner.
54. From this point on, the sutta closely corresponds with the second part of the Ānāpānasati Sutta (MN 118), the first part of which is a prelude to the instructions on mindfulness of breathing. The first tetrad is identical with the passage on mindfulness of breathing in the "contemplation of the body" section of the Satipaṭṭhāna Sutta just above.
55. The "mental formation" (*cittasaṅkhāra*) is perception and feeling; see MN 44 (I 301) = SN 41:6 (IV 293).
56. Vism 289; Ppn 8:233: "Liberating the mind" from the hindrances by the first jhāna, and from the grosser jhāna factors by attaining successively higher jhānas; and liberating it from the cognitive distortions by means of insight knowledge.
57. Vism 290–291; Ppn 8:234–37: "Contemplating impermanence" (*aniccānupassī*) is contemplating the five aggregates as impermanent because they undergo rise and fall and change, or because they undergo momentary dissolution. This tetrad deals entirely with insight, unlike the other three, which can be interpreted by way of both serenity and insight.

    "Contemplating fading away" (*virāgānupassī*) and "contemplating cessation" (*nirodhānupassī*) can be understood both as the insight into the momentary destruction and cessation of phenomena and as the supramundane path, which realizes Nibbāna as the fading away of lust (*virāga*, dispassion) and the cessation of formations. "Contemplating relinquishment" (*paṭinissaggānupassī*) is giving up (*pariccāga*) or abandoning (*pahāna*) defilements through insight and entering into (*pakkhandana*) Nibbāna by attainment of the path.
58. Spk: Attention is not actually feeling, but this is a heading of the teaching. In this tetrad, in the first phrase feeling is spoken of indirectly under the heading of rapture (which is not a feeling), in the second phrase it is referred to directly as happiness (= pleasant feeling). In the third and fourth phrases, feeling is included in the mental formation.
59. Spk: *Having seen with wisdom, etc.* Here, "longing" is just the hindrance of sensual desire; by "dejection" the hindrance of ill will is shown. This tetrad is stated by way of insight only. These two hindrances are the first among the five hindrances, the first section in the contemplation of mental phenomena. Thus he says this to show the beginning of the contemplation of mental phenomena. By "abandoning" is meant the knowledge that effects abandoning, e.g., one abandons the perception of permanence by contemplation of impermanence. By the words "having seen with wisdom" he shows the succession of insights thus: "With one insight knowledge (he sees) the knowledge of abandonment consisting in the knowledges of impermanence, dispassion, cessation, and relinquishment; and that too (he sees) by still another." *He is one who*

looks on closely with equanimity: one is said to look on with equanimity (at the mind) that has fared along the path [Spk-pṭ: by neither exerting nor restraining the mind of meditative development that has properly fared along the middle way], and by the presentation as a unity [Spk-pṭ: since there is nothing further to be done in that respect when the mind has reached one-pointedness]. One "looks on with equanimity" at the object.

60. *Satisambojjhaṅga. Bojjhaṅga* is compounded from *bodhi* + *aṅga*. At SN 46:5, they are explained as the factors that lead to enlightenment. The three phrases used to describe the cultivation of each enlightenment factor can be understood to depict three successive stages of development. "He arouses" is its initial arousal; "he develops" is its gradual maturation; and "it goes to fulfillment by development" is its culmination.
61. *Dhammavicayasambojjhaṅga.* At SN 46:2 (V 66), the "nutriment" for the arising of this factor of enlightenment is said to be frequently giving careful attention to wholesome and unwholesome mental phenomena, blamable and blameless states, inferior and superior states, dark and bright states with their counterparts. Although this factor of enlightenment is identified with *paññā* or wisdom, the above passage suggests that its initial function is to discriminate between the good and bad mental phenomena that become apparent with the deepening of mindfulness.
62. Sāriputta was one of the Buddha's two chief disciples, the one who excelled in wisdom. For a biography, see Nyanaponika and Hecker, *Great Disciples of the Buddha*, chapter 1.
63. "I-making" (*ahaṅkāra*) is the function of view of self; "mine-making" (*mamaṅkāra*), of craving. The root conceit is the conceit "I am" (*asmimāna*), so the "underlying tendency to conceit" is also responsible for "I-making."
64. *Saññāvedayitanirodha.* Also known as *nirodhasamāpatti*, the attainment of cessation, this is a special meditative attainment said to be accessible solely to non-returners and arahants. As its name suggests, it involves the total cessation of perceptual and affective functions, and according to the commentaries, of consciousness and all its associated mental factors. For a detailed discussion according to the commentarial system, see Vism 702–9; Ppn 23:16–52.

Chapter IX: Shining the Light of Wisdom

1. Unfortunately, the connection between the noun and the verb, so obvious in the Pāli, is lost when *paññā* is translated as "wisdom" and the verb rendered "one understands." To avoid this, other translators have preferred renderings for *paññā* that preserve a visible connection between the noun and the verb, for example, "understanding" (Bhikkhu Ñāṇamoli) or "discernment" (Thānissaro Bhikkhu).
2. E.g., at SN 22:5, 35:99, 35:160, 56:1.
3. This correlation is commonly made in the commentaries when they comment on this formula.
4. The commentarial interpretation, detailed and highly technical, is found in Vism, chapter 17.
5. In the Pāli commentaries, these two elements of Nibbāna are called respectively *kilesa-parinibbāna*, the extinction of defilements, and *khandha-parinibbāna*, the extinction of the aggregates.
6. The two words are actually derived from different verbal roots. *Nibbuta* is past

participle of *nir* + *vṛ*; which has a corresponding noun *nibbuti*, used as a synonym for Nibbāna. *Nibbāna* is from *nir* + *vā*.

7. For an amplification of the ocean simile, see SN 44:1.
8. Pātimokkha: the code of training rules governing the conduct of a fully ordained monk.
9. Ps: Right view is twofold: mundane (*lokiya*) and supramundane (*lokuttara*). Mundane right view is again twofold: the view that kamma produces its fruits, which may be held both by Buddhists and non-Buddhists, and the view in conformity with the Four Noble Truths, which is exclusive to the Buddha's teaching. Supramundane right view is the understanding of the Four Noble Truths attained by penetrating to the four paths and fruits (see p. 373). The question posed by Sāriputta concerns the *sekha*, the disciple in higher training.
10. These are the ten courses of unwholesome action. For a more detailed explanation, see **Text V,1(2)**. Their opposites, just below, are the ten courses of wholesome action, also elaborated in the same text.
11. Ps explains the disciple's understanding of these four terms by way of the Four Noble Truths thus: all the courses of action (unwholesome and wholesome) are the truth of suffering; the wholesome and unwholesome roots are the truth of the origin; the non-occurrence of both actions and their roots is the truth of cessation; and the noble path that realizes cessation is the truth of the path. To this extent a noble disciple at one of the first three planes has been described—one who has arrived at supramundane right view but has not yet eliminated all defilements.
12. Ps says that the passage from "he entirely abandons the underlying tendency to lust" until "he makes an end of suffering" shows the work accomplished by the paths of the nonreturner and arahantship. The path of the nonreturner eliminates the underlying tendencies to sensual lust and aversion; the path of arahantship removes the underlying tendency to the view and conceit "I am." Ps says the expression "underlying tendency to the view and conceit 'I am'" (*asmī ti diṭṭhimānānusaya*) should be interpreted to mean the underlying tendency to conceit that is *similar to* a view because, like the view of self, it occurs grasping the notion "I am."
13. Nutriment (*āhāra*) is to be understood here in a broad sense as a prominent condition for the individual life-process. Physical food is an important condition for the physical body, contact for feeling, mental volition for consciousness, and consciousness for name-and-form, the psychophysical organism in its totality. Craving is called the origin of nutriment since the craving of the previous existence is the source of the present individuality with its dependence upon and continual consumption of the four nutriments in this existence. For an annotated compilation of canonical and commentarial texts on the nutriments, see Nyanaponika Thera, *The Vision of Dhamma*, pp. 211–28.
14. The next twelve sections present, in reverse order, a factor-by-factor examination of dependent origination. See too **Texts IX, 4(4)(a)–(f)**.
15. The three kinds of existence (*bhava*): on the three realms of existence, see pp. 149–50. In the formula of dependent origination, "existence" signifies both the planes of rebirth and the types of kamma that produce rebirth into those planes. The former is known technically as *upapattibhava*, "rebirth-existence," the latter as *kammabhava*, "karmically active existence."

16. Clinging to rules and observances (*sīlabbatupādāna*) is the adherence to the view that purification can be achieved by adopting certain external rules or following certain observances, particularly of ascetic self-discipline; clinging to a doctrine of self (*attavādupādāna*) is holding one or another of the views of self that originate from identity view (see particularly the Brahmajāla Sutta, DN 1); clinging to views (*diṭṭhupādāna*) is the clinging to any other view (than one of the two enumerated separately). Clinging in any of its varieties is a strengthening of craving, its condition.
17. Craving for phenomena (*dhammataṇhā*) is the craving for all objects of consciousness except the objects of the five classes of sense consciousness. Examples would be the craving associated with fantasies and mental imagery, with abstract ideas and intellectual gratification, and so forth.
18. Contact (*phassa*) is the coming together (*saṅgati*) of internal sense base (sense faculty), external sense base (object), and consciousness.
19. The term *nāmarūpa* was of pre-Buddhistic origins. It was used in the Upaniṣads to represent the differentiated manifestation of *brahman,* the nondual absolute reality appearing in the guise of multiplicity. *Brahman* apprehended by the senses as diversified appearances is *form* (*rūpa*); *brahman* apprehended by thought through diversified names or concepts is *name* (*nāma*). The Buddha adopted this expression and gave it a meaning governed by his own system. Here name and form become, respectively, the cognitive and physical sides of individual existence.

    In the Buddha's system, *rūpa* is defined as the four great elements and the form derived from them. Form is both internal to the person (= the body with its senses) and external (= the physical world). The Nikāyas do not explain derived form (*upādāya rūpa*), but the Abhidhamma analyzes it into twenty-four kinds of secondary material phenomena, which include the sensitive matter of the five sense faculties and four of the five sense objects (the tactile object is identified with three of the great elements—earth, heat, and air—which each exhibit tangible properties).

    Though I render *nāma* as name, this should not be taken too literally. *Nāma* is the assemblage of mental factors involved in cognition: feeling, perception, volition, contact, and attention (*vedanā, saññā, cetanā, phassa, manasikāra*). These are probably called "name" because they contribute to the conceptual designation of objects. It should be noted that in the Nikāyas, *nāmarūpa* does not include consciousness (*viññāṇa*). Consciousness is the condition for *nāmarūpa,* just as the latter is the condition for consciousness, so that the two are mutually dependent (see **Text II,3(3)**).
20. Mind-consciousness (*manoviññāṇa*) comprises all consciousness except the five types of sense consciousness just mentioned. It includes consciousness of mental images, abstract ideas, and internal states of mind, as well as the consciousness that reflects upon sense objects.
21. In the context of the doctrine of dependent origination, volitional formations (*saṅkhārā*) are wholesome and unwholesome volitions. The bodily formation is volition expressed through the body; the verbal formation, volition expressed by speech; and the mental formation, volition that does not reach bodily or verbal expression.
22. It should be noted that while ignorance is a condition for the taints, the taints—including the taint of ignorance—are in turn a condition for ignorance. Ps says

that this conditioning of ignorance by ignorance implies that the ignorance in any one existence is conditioned by the ignorance in the preceding existence. Since this is so, the conclusion follows that no first point can be discovered for ignorance, and thus that saṃsāra is without discernible beginning.

23. The "four phases" (or "four turnings," *catuparivaṭṭa*) are: aggregate, origin, cessation, and the way to cessation, as applied to each of the five aggregates.
24. This passage describes the trainees (*sekha*). They have directly known the Four Noble Truths and are practicing for the ultimate cessation of the five aggregates, that is, for Nibbāna.
25. This passage describes the arahants. According to DN II 63–64, the round of existence turns as a basis for manifestation and designation only in so far as there is consciousness together with name-and-form; when both consciousness and name-and-form cease, there is no round to serve as a basis for manifestation and designation.
26. *Cha cetanākāyā*. The fact that there is a difference between the name of the aggregate, *saṅkhārakkhandha*, and the term of definition, *cetanā*, suggests that this aggregate has a wider range than the others. In the Abhidhamma and the commentaries, it is treated as an "umbrella category" for classifying all the mental factors mentioned in the suttas apart from feeling and perception. Volition is mentioned in the definition because it is the most important factor in this aggregate, not because it is its exclusive constituent.
27. It is significant that while contact is the condition for the arising of the three aggregates of feeling, perception, and volitional formations, name-and-form is the condition for the arising of consciousness. This supports the statement in the ten-factored formula of dependent origination, found in **Text II,3(3)**, that name-and-form is the condition for consciousness.
28. According to Spk, desire (*chanda*) here is synonymous with craving (*taṇhā*). This is said because the five aggregates in any given existence originate from the residual craving for new existence of the immediately preceding existence.
29. Clinging is not the same as the "five aggregates subject to clinging" because the aggregates are not reducible to clinging. Yet clinging is not something apart from the "five aggregates subject to clinging" because there is no clinging that does not have the aggregates as its support and object.
30. On "I-making, mine-making, and the underlying tendency to conceit," see p. 445 (chapter IX, n.63).
31. This is the second discourse of the Buddha, according to the narrative of the Buddha's teaching career at Vin I 13–14. The five bhikkhus are the first five disciples, who at this point are still trainees (*sekha*). The Buddha's purpose in teaching this discourse is to lead them to arahantship.
32. The sutta offers two "arguments" for the thesis of nonself. The first contends that the aggregates are nonself on the ground that we cannot exercise mastery over them. Since we cannot bend the aggregates to our will, they are all "subject to affliction" and therefore cannot be considered our self. The second argument, introduced just below, posits the characteristic of nonself on the basis of the other two characteristics. Whatever is impermanent is in some way bound up with suffering; whatever is impermanent and bound up with suffering cannot be identified as our self.
33. Spk explains at length how form (i.e., the body) is like a lump of foam (*pheṇapiṇḍa*). I give merely the highlights: As a lump of foam lacks any substance

(*sāra*), so form lacks any substance that is permanent, stable, a self; as the lump of foam is full of holes and fissures and the abode of many creatures, so too form; as the lump of foam, after expanding, breaks up, so does form, which is pulverized in the mouth of death.

34. Spk: A bubble (*bubbuḷa*) is feeble and cannot be grasped, for it breaks up as soon as it is seized; so too feeling is feeble and cannot be grasped as permanent and stable. As a bubble arises and ceases in a drop of water and does not last long, so too with feeling: billions of feelings arise and cease in the time of a finger-snap. As a bubble arises in dependence on conditions, so feeling arises in dependence on a sense base, an object, the defilements, and contact.
35. Spk: Perception is like a mirage (*marīcikā*) in the sense that it is insubstantial, for one cannot grasp a mirage to drink or bathe or fill a pitcher. As a mirage deceives the multitude, so does perception, which entices people with the idea that the colorful object is beautiful, pleasurable, and permanent.
36. Spk: As a banana trunk (*kadalikkhandha*) is an assemblage of many sheaths, each with its own characteristic, so the aggregate of volitional formations is an assemblage of many phenomena, each with its own characteristic.
37. Spk: Consciousness is like a magical illusion (*māyā*) in the sense that it is insubstantial and cannot be grasped. Consciousness is even more transient and fleeting than a magical illusion. For it gives the impression that a person comes and goes, stands and sits, with the same mind, but the mind is different in each of these activities. Consciousness deceives the multitude like a magical illusion.
38. This sutta, sometimes called "The Fire Sermon," is the third discourse recorded in the narrative of the Buddha's ministry, at Vin I 34–35. According to this source, the thousand monks to whom the sutta was addressed had formerly been fire-worshipping ascetics, and thus the Buddha used this theme because it corresponded with their background. For an account of how the Buddha converted them, see Ñāṇamoli, *The Life of the Buddha*, pp. 54–60, 64–69.
39. The Buddha is speaking to Pukkusāti, a monk who had gone forth out of faith in the Buddha without ever having seen him before. When the sutta opens, the Buddha arrives at a potter's shed, intending to spend the night there. Pukkusāti has already been lodging in the shed and greets the Buddha in a friendly way, unaware that this is his master. Without revealing his identity to Pukkusāti, the Buddha initiates a conversation, which turns into a discourse on the development of wisdom.
40. Ps: This is the sixth element, which "remains" in that it has yet to be expounded by the Buddha and penetrated by Pukkusāti. Here it is explained as the consciousness that accomplishes the work of insight contemplation on the elements. Under the heading of consciousness, the contemplation of feeling is also introduced.
41. This passage shows the conditionality of feeling and its impermanence through the cessation of its condition.
42. *Idappaccayatā*. The word is a compound of *idaṃ*, this, with *paccaya*, condition, augmented by the abstract noun termination–*tā*.This is a synonym for *paṭicca-samuppāda*. See **Text II,4** §19, which likewise connects the realization of dependent origination with the Buddha's enlightenment.
43. Spk: *Actuality* (*tathatā*) means the occurrence of each particular phenomenon when its assemblage of appropriate conditions is present. *Inerrancy* (*avitathatā*) means that once its conditions have reached completeness there is no

non-occurrence, even for a moment, of the phenomenon due to be produced from those conditions. *Invariability* (*anaññathatā*) means that there is no production of one phenomenon by another's conditions.

44. *Dhamme ñāṇa.* This is the direct knowledge of the Four Noble Truths arisen through penetration of Nibbāna as the truth of cessation.
45. *Anvaye ñāṇa.* This is an inference extending to the past and the future, based on the immediate discernment of the conditional relationship obtaining between any pair of factors.
46. Spk: *The idea of existence* (*atthitā*) is eternalism (*sassata*); *the idea of nonexistence* (*natthitā*) is annihilationism (*uccheda*). Spk-pṭ: The idea of existence is eternalism because it maintains that the entire world (of personal existence) exists forever. The notion of nonexistence is annihilationism because it maintains that the entire world does not exist (forever) but is cut off.

    In view of these explanations it would be misleading to translate the two terms, *atthitā* and *natthitā*, simply as "existence" and "nonexistence." In the present passage *atthitā* and *natthitā* are abstract nouns formed from the verbs *atthi* and *natthi*. It is thus the metaphysical assumptions implicit in such abstractions that are at fault, not the ascriptions of existence and nonexistence themselves. I have tried to convey this sense of metaphysical abstraction, conveyed in Pāli by the termination *-tā*, by rendering the two terms "*the idea* of existence" and "*the idea* of nonexistence," respectively.

    Unfortunately, *atthitā* and *bhava* both had to be rendered by "existence," which obscures the fact that in Pāli they are derived from different roots. While *atthitā* is the notion of existence in the abstract, *bhava* is concrete individual existence in one or another of the three realms. For the sake of marking the difference, *bhava* might have been rendered "being," but this English word is too likely to suggest "Being," the absolute object of philosophical speculation. It does not sufficiently convey the sense of concreteness intrinsic to *bhava*.
47. Spk: *The origin of the world*: the production of the world of formations. *There is no idea of nonexistence in regard to the world*: there does not occur in him the annihilationist view that might arise in regard to phenomena produced and made manifest in the world of formations, holding "They do not exist." Spk-pṭ: The annihilationist view might arise in regard to the world of formations thus: "On account of the annihilation and perishing of beings right where they are, there is no persisting being or phenomenon." It also includes the wrong view, having those formations as its object, that holds: "There are no beings who are reborn." That view *does not occur in him*; for one seeing with right understanding the production and origination of the world of formations in dependence on such diverse conditions as kamma, ignorance, craving, etc., that annihilationist view does not occur, since one sees the uninterrupted production of formations.

    Spk: *The cessation of the world*: the dissolution of formations. *There is no idea of existence in regard to the world*: There does not occur in him the eternalist view that might arise in regard to phenomena produced and made manifest in the world of formations, holding "They exist." Spk-pṭ: The eternalist view might arise in regard to the world of formations, taking it to exist at all times, owing to the apprehension of identity in the uninterrupted continuum occurring in a cause-effect relationship. But that view *does not occur in him*; because he sees the cessation of the successively arisen phenomena and the arising of successively new phenomena, the eternalist view does not occur.

Spk: Further, "the origin of the world" is direct-order conditionality (*anuloma-paccayākāra*); "the cessation of the world" is reverse-order conditionality (*paṭiloma-paccayākāra*). [Spk-pṭ: "Direct-order conditionality" is the conditioning efficiency of the conditions in relation to their own effects; "reverse-order conditionality" is the cessation of the effects through the cessation of their respective causes.] For in seeing the dependency of the world, when one sees the continuation of the conditionally arisen phenomena owing to the continuation of their conditions, the annihilationist view, which might otherwise have arisen, does not occur. And in seeing the cessation of conditions, when one sees the cessation of the conditionally arisen phenomena owing to the cessation of their conditions, the eternalist view, which might otherwise have arisen, does not occur.

48. Spk explains *dukkha* here as "the mere five aggregates subject to clinging" (*pañc'upādānakkhandhamattam eva*). Thus what the noble disciple sees, when he reflects upon his personal existence, is not a self or a substantially existent person but a mere assemblage of conditioned phenomena arising and passing away through the conditioning process of dependent origination.
49. I interpret *what one intends* (*ceteti*) and *what one plans* (*pakappeti*) here as representing volitional formations (*saṅkhārā*), the second factor in the formula of dependent origination. *Whatever one has a tendency toward* (*anuseti*) implies the underlying tendencies (*anusaya*), primarily the tendencies toward ignorance and craving, hence the first and eighth factors in the formula. When one passes away with the tendencies toward ignorance and craving still intact, one's intentions and plans—the concrete manifestations of craving in the form of volitional activities—become the basis for consciousness to continue on, become established in a fresh "name-and-form," and initiate the production of a new existence. This is the event of birth, followed by aging, death, and the other types of suffering between birth and death.
50. Although it is not possible to have the underlying tendencies without intentions and plans, this passage might be seen to have the rhetorical purpose of emphasizing the role of the underlying tendencies in sustaining the process of rebirth. But according to Spk, the passage is intended to show that for an insight meditator who has overcome unwholesome thoughts, the danger of rebirth still exists as long as the underlying tendencies remain intact.
51. This paragraph shows the arahant.
52. *Tathāni avitathāni anaññathāni*. See pp. 449–50, note 43. Spk: "*Actual* in the sense of not departing from the real nature of things; for suffering is stated to be just suffering. *Unerring*, because of not falsifying its real nature; for suffering does not become nonsuffering. *Invariable*, because of not arriving at a different nature; for suffering does not arrive at the nature of the origin (of suffering), etc. The same method for the other truths." I understand *anaññatha* in the simpler and more straightforward sense that the truths are "invariable" because they never vary from the way things really are.
53. *Bhavanetti*. That which leads to new existence, i.e., craving for existence.
54. All these leaves are small and delicate. The leaves mentioned in the counterpart passage below are broad and sturdy.
55. Spk identifies him as Sāriputta's nephew.
56. *Nippapañcaṃ*. Spk: Because it is not proliferated (elaborated) by craving, conceit, and views.

57. The negation of the physical elements can be taken to deny, not only the presence of matter in Nibbāna, but also the identification of Nibbāna with the experiences of the jhānas, which still pertain to the realm of form. The following four items negate the objects of the four formless meditative attainments in Nibbāna.
58. In Pāli, *diṭṭha*, "seen," is here clearly intended as an antithesis to *diṭṭhi*, "view."

Chapter X: The Planes of Realization

1. The terminology of "path" and "fruition" is a commentarial way of drawing the distinction. The suttas themselves do not use the scheme of four "paths" but speak only of one path, the Noble Eightfold Path that leads to the cessation of suffering. This is also called the *arahattamagga*, the path to arahantship, but in a broad sense, as the path to the highest goal, not in the narrow sense of the path preceding the fruit of arahantship. However, the suttas do make a distinction between the person practicing for the attainment of a particular fruit (*phalasacchikiriyāya paṭipanna*) and the person who has attained the stage that results from this practice (see **Text X,1(1)**). Based on this distinction, the commentarial terminology of path and fruit is useful as a concise way of referring to the two phases of the Nikāya scheme.
2. My explanation of the once-returner's attenuation of lust, hatred, and defilements is based on the commentaries. Apart from the standard formula, the suttas themselves say very little about the once-returner.
3. It is also important to note that the suttas imply that the *dhammānusārī* and *saddhānusārī* remain thus for an extended period of time. The position of the suttas seems to contradict the commentarial idea that a path-attainer is such only for a single mind-moment. If the latter were the case, this would mean that a *dhammānusārī* and *saddhānusārī* are such for only a single mind-moment, and this seems hard to square with sutta statements to the effect that they receive gifts, resort to lodgings in the forest, etc.
4. The commentarial method of explanation stipulates that the meditator emerges from the jhāna attainment and practices insight contemplation with a mind made sharp and supple by the jhāna. However, the suttas themselves say nothing about emerging from the jhāna. If one reads the suttas alone, without the commentaries, it seems as if the meditator examines the factors within the jhāna itself.
5. As the arahants have achieved liberation from the round of existence, it is impossible to point to any place within the round where they might appear; hence they have no future round for manifestation.
6. The "five lower fetters" (*pañc' orambhāgiyāni saṃyojanāni*) are: identity view, doubt, grasping of rules and observances, sensual lust, and ill will. Those who are spontaneously reborn (*opapātika*) take rebirth without dependence on a mother and father.
7. The "three fetters" are the first three of the five fetters, just above. "Fixed in destiny" (*niyata*) means that the stream-enterer is bound to reach liberation in at most seven more lives passed either in the human world or in celestial realms. Enlightenment (*sambodhi*) is the arahant's full and final knowledge of the Four Noble Truths.
8. On the distinction between these two types, see below, **Text X,1(5)** §§20–21 and **Text X,2(2)**.
9. Ps says that this refers to persons devoted to the practice of insight who have

not reached any supramundane realization but possess strong conviction in the truth of the Dhamma. The words *saddhāmattaṃ pemamattaṃ* might have been translated "mere faith, mere love," but such qualities could not guarantee a rebirth in heaven. It thus seems necessary to take the suffix–*matta* as implying a *sufficient* amount of these qualities, not simply their mere existence.

10. The Buddha is here speaking with the wanderer Vacchagotta (see **Text IX,5(6)**). Ps says that Vacchagotta thought the Buddha may have been the only one within his community to have attained the final goal.
11. This question and the one in §11 concern the nonreturner. Note that nonreturners observe celibacy.
12. This question and the one in §12 concern stream-enterers and once-returners. Since they are described as enjoying sensual pleasures, this means that they are not obliged to observe celibacy.
13. *Ubhatobhāgavimutta*. Ps: He is liberated in both ways because he is liberated from the form body by the formless attainments and from the mental body by the path of arahantship.

    The dual liberation of the "both-ways-liberated" arahant should not be confused with the "taintless liberation of mind, liberation by wisdom" (*anāsavā cetovimutti paññāvimutti*), which is shared by *all* arahants, regardless of whether or not they attain the formless attainments.
14. *Paññāvimutta*. Ps says this includes those who attain any of the four jhānas as well as the dry-insight arahant. A dry-insight arahant is not explicitly recognized in the Nikāyas.
15. *Kāyasakkhī*. This includes all those from persons on the path to arahantship down to stream-enterers who attain the formless attainments.
16. *Diṭṭhippatta*. This includes the same classes who do not attain the formless attainments and in whom wisdom is the dominant faculty.
17. *Saddhāvimutta*. This includes the same classes in whom faith is the dominant faculty.
18. *Dhammānusārī*. This type and the next, the *saddhānusārī*, are the two kinds of persons practicing for realization of the fruit of stream-entry. See p. 375 and **Text X,2(2)**.
19. *Sammattaniyāma*: the supramundane Noble Eightfold Path.
20. Contrary to the commentaries, which hold that the path-attainer realizes the fruit immediately after attaining the path, the Nikāyas say merely that one who reaches the stage of Dhamma-follower or faith-follower (corresponding to the commentarial notion of path-attainer) will realize the fruit within this same life—but not necessarily in the next mind-moment. The two positions might be reconciled if we see the path of the Dhamma-follower and faith-follower as extended in time but reaching its climax in an instantaneous breakthrough that is immediately followed by realization of the fruit.
21. This statement makes it clear how the stream-enterer differs from those on the path to stream-entry. The faith-follower accepts the teaching on trust (with a limited degree of understanding), the Dhamma-follower accepts it through investigation (with a greater degree of understanding); but the stream-enterer has directly *known and seen* the teaching.
22. The breakthrough to the Dhamma (*dhammābhisamaya*) and the gaining of the vision of the Dhamma (*dhammacakkhupaṭilābha*) are synonyms signifying the attainment of stream-entry.

23. *Aveccappasāda*. Spk explains this as unshakable confidence gained through what has been attained, namely, stream-entry.
24. The hells, the animal realm, and the sphere of afflicted spirits are themselves the plane of misery, the bad destinations, and the lower world.
25. Identity (*sakkāya*) is the composite of the five aggregates that we identify as our "self." The cessation of identity is Nibbāna.
26. *Upadhi*. In the present context, this word seems to mean material possessions.
27. Of these eleven attributes, "impermanent" and "disintegrating" illustrate the characteristic of impermanence; "alien," "empty," and "nonself," the characteristic of nonself; the other six, the characteristic of suffering.
28. Ps: He turns his mind away from the five aggregates included within the jhāna, which he has seen to be marked with the three characteristics. The "deathless element" (*amatadhātu*) is Nibbāna. First, he "directs his mind to it" with the insight consciousness, having heard it praised as "peaceful and sublime," and so forth. Then, with the supramundane path, he "directs his mind to it" by making it an object and penetrating it as "peaceful and sublime," and so forth.
29. *Dhammarāgena dhammanandiyā*. It seems that this desire for the Dhamma and delight in the Dhamma do two things simultaneously: (1) because they are directed toward the Dhamma, they propel the disciple to the destruction of the five lower fetters; (2) because they are still desire and delight, they prevent the attainment of arahantship.
30. Here, in the formless attainments, the sutta mentions only the four mental aggregates. The aggregate of form is excluded.
31. These are meditation subjects that lead to disenchantment and dispassion. The unattractiveness of the body is at **Text VIII,8** §10; the reflection on the repulsiveness of food is explained at Vism 341–47 (Ppn 11:1–26); the perception of death, at Vism 229–39 (Ppn 8:1–41); and the perception of discontent with the entire world, and the contemplation of impermanence in all formations, at AN 10:60; V 111.
32. At AN V 110, the perception of abandonment (*pahānasaññā*) is explained as the removal of defiled thoughts. At AN V 110–11, the perception of dispassion (*virāgasaññā*) and the perception of cessation (*virāgasaññā*) are both explained as reflections on the attributes of Nibbāna.
33. Spk explains the *antarāparinibbāyī* ("one who attains Nibbāna in the interval") as one reborn in the pure abodes who attains arahantship during the first half of the lifespan. This type is subdivided into three, depending on whether arahantship is reached: (1) on the very day of rebirth; (2) after one or two hundred eons have elapsed; or (3) after four hundred eons have elapsed. The *upahaccaparinibbāyī* ("one who attains Nibbāna upon landing") is explained as one who attains arahantship after passing the first half of the lifespan. For Spk, the *asaṅkhāraparinibbāyī* ("one who attains without exertion") and the *sasaṅkhāraparinibbāyī* ("one who attains with exertion") then become two modes in which the first two types of nonreturners attain the goal, respectively, easily and without strong effort, and with difficulty and strong effort. However, this account of the first two types disregards the literal meaning of their names and also overrides the sequential and mutually exclusive nature of the five types as delineated elsewhere in the suttas.

    If we understand the term *antarāparinibbāyī* literally, as it seems we should, it then means one who attains Nibbāna *in the interval between two lives*, perhaps while existing in a subtle body in the intermediate state. The *upahaccaparinibbāyī* then becomes one who attains Nibbāna "upon landing" or "striking ground" in the new existence, i.e., almost immediately after taking rebirth. The next two terms designate two types who attain arahantship in the course of the next life, distinguished by the amount of effort they must make to win the goal. The last, the *uddhaṃsota akaniṭṭhagāmī*, is one who takes rebirth in successive pure abodes, completes the full lifespan in each, and finally attains arahantship in the *akaniṭṭha* realm, the highest pure abode.This interpretation, though contrary to the Pāli commentaries, seems to be confirmed by AN 7:52 (IV 70–74), in which the simile of the flaming chip suggests that the seven types (including the three kinds of *antarāparinibbāyī*) are mutually exclusive and have been graded according to the sharpness of their faculties.

34. In declaring that he does not recognize a self or the belongings of a self among the five aggregates, Khemaka has implicitly declared that he has attained at least the level of a stream-enterer. But the other monks did not realize that all the noble persons share this understanding and assumed this was the unique realization of the arahant. Thus they misinterpreted Khemaka's statement as insinuating that he had attained arahantship.

35. Although all three eds. of SN that I consulted (Be, Ce, and Ee) and both eds. of Spk (Be and Ce) read *asmī ti adhigataṃ*, I suspect this is an archaic corruption that has gained currency. I propose reading *asmī ti avigataṃ*. The passage clarifies an essential difference between the trainee (*sekha*) and the arahant. While the *sekha* has eliminated identity view and thus no longer identifies any of the five aggregates as a self, he has not yet eradicated ignorance, which sustains a residual conceit and desire "I am" (*anusahagato asmī ti māno asmī ti chando*) in relation to the five aggregates. The arahant, in contrast, has eradicated ignorance, the root of all misconceptions, and thus no longer entertains any ideas of "I" and "mine." The other elders apparently had not yet attained any stage of awakening and thus did not understand this difference, but the Venerable Khemaka must have been at least a stream-enterer (some commentators say he was a nonreturner) and thus knew that the elimination of identity view does not completely remove the sense of personal identity. Even for the nonreturner, an "odor of subjectivity" based on the five aggregates still lingers over his experience.

36. Spk: The worldling's mental process is like the soiled cloth. The three contemplations (of impermanence, suffering, and nonself) are like the three cleansers. The mental process of the nonreturner is like the cloth that has been washed with the three cleansers. The defilements to be eradicated by the path of arahantship are like the residual smell of the cleansers. The knowledge of the path of arahantship is like the sweetly scented chest, and the destruction of all defilements by that path is like the vanishing of the residual smell of the cleansers from the cloth after it has been placed in the chest.

37. That is, outside the Buddha's teaching.

38. As I understand it, "that which is their destination ... their final goal" is Nibbāna. We have here another essential difference between the trainee and the arahant: the trainee *sees* Nibbāna, the destination of the five faculties, that in which they culminate, their fruit and final goal; however, he cannot "contact it with the body," cannot enter upon the full experience of it. In contrast, the arahant both sees the final goal and can fully experience it here and now.

39. These are the thirty-seven *bodhipakkhiyā dhammā*, lit. "states pertaining to enlightenment," more freely: "aids to enlightenment." On the four establishments of mindfulness, see **Text VII,2** and **Text VIII,8** for details and SN chapter 47. The four right kinds of striving are equivalent to right effort, for which see **Text VII,2** and SN chapter 49. The four bases for spiritual power are: concentration due to (1) desire, or (2) energy, or (3) mind, or (4) investigation, with volitional forces of striving; see SN chapter 51. The five faculties are at **Text X,1(2)**; see SN chapter 48 for details. The five powers are the same five factors as the faculties, but with greater strength. The seven factors of enlightenment are at **Text VIII,9**; see SN chapter 46. The Noble Eightfold Path is at **Text VII,2**; see SN chapter 45.
40. Ps identifies this as the equanimity of the fourth jhāna. Ps says that Pukkusāti had already achieved the fourth jhāna and was deeply attached to it. The Buddha first praises this equanimity to inspire Pukkusāti's confidence, and then gradually guides him to the formless attainments and the supramundane paths and fruits.
41. The sense is: If he attains the base of the infinity of space and passes away while still attached to it, he would be reborn in the plane of the infinity of space and would live there for the full lifespan of 20,000 eons specified for that plane. In the higher three formless planes the lifespan is said to be, respectively, 40,000 eons, 60,000 eons, and 84,000 eons.
42. Ps: This is said in order to show the danger in the formless attainments. By the one phrase, "This would be conditioned," he shows: "Even though the lifespan there is 20,000 eons, it is conditioned, fashioned, built up. It is thus impermanent, unstable, not lasting, transient. It is subject to perishing, breaking up, and dissolution; it is involved with birth, aging, and death, founded upon suffering. It is not a shelter, a place of safety, a refuge. Having passed away there as a worldling, one can still be reborn in the four states of misery."
43. *So n'eva abhisaṅkharoti nābhisañcetayati bhavāya vā vibhavāya*. The two verbs suggest the notion of volition as a constructive power that builds up and sustains conditioned existence. Ceasing to will for either existence or nonexistence shows the extinction of craving for eternal existence and annihilation.
44. Ps says that at this point Pukkusāti penetrated three paths and fruits, becoming a nonreturner. He realized that his teacher was the Buddha himself, but he could not express this realization since the Buddha continued with his discourse.
45. This passage shows the arahant's abiding in the Nibbāna element with residue remaining (*sa-upādisesa nibbānadhātu*); see **Text IX,5(5)**. Though he continues to experience feelings, he is free from lust toward pleasant feeling, from aversion toward painful feeling, and from ignorance regarding neutral feeling.
46. That is, he continues to experience feeling only as long as the body with its life faculty continues, but not beyond that.
47. This refers to his attainment of the Nibbāna-element with no residue remaining (*anupādisesa nibbānadhātu*)—the cessation of all conditioned existence with his final passing away. See **Text IX,5(5)**.
48. This completes the exposition of the first foundation, the foundation of wisdom (*paññādhiṭṭhāna*). Ps says that the knowledge of the destruction of all suffering is the wisdom pertaining to the fruit of arahantship.

49. Ps mentions four kinds of acquisitions (*upadhi*) here: the five aggregates; defilements; volitional formations; and sensual pleasures.
50. The "tides of conceiving" (*maññussavā*), as the following paragraph will show, are thoughts and notions originating from the three roots of conceiving—craving, conceit, and views. The "sage at peace" (*muni santo*) is the arahant.
51. The thoughts "I shall be" and "I shall not be" imply the views of eternalism (continued existence after death) and annihilationism (personal extinction at death). The alternatives of having physical form and being formless represent two modes of existence in the afterlife, physical and disembodied; the triad of being percipient, etc., are three other modes of existence in the afterlife, distinguished by their relationship to perception or awareness.
52. That which is not present in him is craving for existence, which leads to a new birth following death.
53. *Satta saddhammā*. Faith, moral shame, fear of wrongdoing, learning, energy, mindfulness, and wisdom. See, e.g., MN 53.11–17.
54. The training in the higher moral discipline, the higher mind, and the higher wisdom.
55. The ten factors are the eight factors of the Noble Eightfold Path supplemented by right knowledge and right liberation. See, e.g., MN 65.34 and MN 78.14.
56. The threefold discrimination: "I am better," "I am equal," "I am worse."
57. It is likely that *bhikkhu paññāvimutto* here should be understood as any arahant disciple, not specifically as the *paññāvimutta* contrasted with the *ubhatobhāgavimutta* arahant.
58. This sutta is included in the Mahāparinibbāna Sutta (at DN II 81–83), but without the last paragraph. A much more elaborate version makes up DN 28.
59. Spk identifies "of such qualities" (*evaṃdhammā*) as "qualities pertaining to concentration" (*samādhipakkhā dhammā*).
60. The ten Tathāgata's powers are powers of knowledge. They are analyzed in detail at Vibh §§808–31. The "wheel of Brahmā" is the wheel of the Dhamma.
61. For details, see MN 115.12–19.
62. Ps explains possibility (*ṭhāna*) as the realm, circumstances, time, and effort, factors that can either impede or reinforce the result. The cause (*hetu*) is the kamma itself. This knowledge of the Buddha is illustrated by **Texts V,1(1)–(3)**.
63. This signifies the Buddha's knowledge of the types of conduct that lead to all future destinies within the round of existence as well as to final liberation. See MN 12.35–42.
64. Vibh §813 explains that he understands that beings are of inferior and superior inclinations, and that beings naturally associate with those of similar inclinations.
65. Vibh §§814–27 gives a detailed analysis. Ps states more concisely that he knows the superior and inferior disposition of the five faculties of other beings.
66. Vibh §828: The defilement (*saṅkilesa*) is a factor causing decline; cleansing (*vodāna*) is a factor causing excellence; emergence (*vuṭṭhāna*) is both cleansing and rising from an attainment. The eight emancipations (*vimokkha*) are at DN 15.35, DN 16.3.33, MN 77.22, MN 137.26, etc.; the nine attainments (*samāpatti*) are the four jhānas, four formless attainments, and the cessation of perception and feeling.
67. *Vesārajja*. Ps says this is a name for the joyful knowledge that arises in him when he reflects upon his absence of timidity in four cases.

68. Spk says this qualification is made to exclude the devas who are noble ones.
69. Spk: *Included within identity* (*sakkāyapariyāpannā*): included in the five aggregates. When the Buddha teaches them the Dhamma stamped with the three characteristics, exposing the faults in the round of existence, the fear of knowledge enters into them.

Table of Sources

*: excerpt from a longer sutta

†: several suttas combined

Dīgha Nikāya

Sutta	PTS Vol. & Page	Text	Text Title	Page
5*	I 134–36	IV,6(6)	bringing tranquillity to the land	141–42
15*	II 58	I,3(3)	the dark chain of causation	36
16*	II 72–77	IV,6(4)	seven principles of social stability	137–39
21*	II 276–77	I,3(2)	why do beings live in hate?	35–36
26*	III 59–63	IV,6(5)	the wheel-turning monarch	139–41
31*	III 180–81, 187–91	IV,1(2)	worshipping the six directions	116–18

Majjhima Nikāya

Sutta	PTS Vol. & Page	Text	Text Title	Page
9	I 46–55	IX,3	a discourse on right view	323–35
10	I 55–63	VIII,8	the four establishments of mindfulness	281–90
12*	I 70–72	X,5(4)	the powers and grounds of self-confidence	417–19
13	I 84–90	VI,3	properly appraising objects of attachment	193–99
19*	I 117–18	X,5(6)	the man desiring our good	420
20	I 118–22	VIII,5	the removal of distracting thoughts	275–78
21*	I 126–27, 129	VIII,6	the mind of loving-kindness	278–79
22*	I 139–40	X,4(3)	a monk whose crossbar has been lifted	407–8

Majjhima Nikāya (continued)

Sutta	PTS Vol. & Page	Text	Text Title	Page
22*	I 140–42	X,1(3)	in the Dhamma well expounded	386
26*	I 160–67	II,3(1)	seeking the supreme state of sublime peace	54–59
26*	I 167–73	II,4	the decision to teach	69–75
27	I 175–84	VII,4	the graduated training	241–50
29	I 192–97	VII,1(2)	the heartwood of the spiritual life	233–37
36*	I 240–49	II,3(2)	the realization of the three true knowledges	59–67
39*	I 274–80	VII,5	the higher stages of training with similes	250–53
41	I 286–90	V,1(2)	why beings fare as they do after death	156–61
47	I 317–20	III,4	investigate the teacher himself	93–96
54*	I 364–66	VI,4(1)	cutting off all affairs	199–202
63	I 426–32	VII,1(1)	the arrow of birth, aging, and death	230–33
64*	I 434–37	X,3(1)	abandoning the five lower fetters	396–98
70*	I 477–79	X,1(5)	seven kinds of noble persons	390–92
72*	I 486–88	IX,5(6)	the fire and the ocean	367–69
73*	I 490–93	X,1(4)	the completeness of the teaching	386–90
75*	I 504–8	VI,4(2)	the fever of sensual pleasures	202–5
82*	II 65–82	VI,6	four summaries of the Dhamma	207–13
93	II 147–54	IV,6(3)	purification is for all four castes	132–37

Majjhima Nikāya (continued)

Sutta	PTS Vol. & Page	Text	Text Title	Page
95*	II 168–77	III,5	steps toward the realization of truth	96–103
99*	II 206–8	V,5(2)	the four divine abodes	177–78
104*	II 245–47	IV,6(1)	six roots of dispute	130–31
104*	II 250–51	IV,6(2)	six principles of cordiality	131–32
109	III 15–19	IX,4(1)(b)	a catechism on the aggregates	338–41
123	III 118–20; 122–24	II,2	the Buddha's conception and birth	50–54
135	III 202–6	V,1(3)	kamma and its fruits	161–66
140*	III 240–43	IX,4(3)(c)	the six elements	350–53
140*	III 244–47	X,4(7)	the sage at peace	410–12
146*	III 274–75	IX,1(2)	wisdom as a knife	321

Saṃyutta Nikāya

Sutta	PTS Vol. & Page	Text	Text Title	Page
3:3	I 71 <163–64>	I,1(1)	aging and death	26
3:25	I 100–102 <224–29>	I,1(2)	the simile of the mountain	26–28
12:1	II 1–2	IX,4(4)(a)	what is dependent origination?	353
12:15	II 16–17	IX,4(4)(d)	a teaching by the middle	356–57
12:20	II 25–27	IX,4(4)(b)	the stableness of the Dhamma	353–55
12:33	II 56–59	IX,4(4)(c)	forty-four cases of knowledge	355–56

Saṃyutta Nikāya (continued)

Sutta	PTS Vol. & Page	Text	Text Title	Page
12:38	II 65–66	IX,4(4)(e)	the continuance of consciousness	357–58
12:44	II 73–74	IX,4(4)(f)	the origin and passing of the world	358–59
12:65	II 104–7	II,3(3)	the ancient city	67–69
13:1	II 133–34	X,2(3)	the breakthrough to the Dhamma	394
14:1	II 140	IX,4(3)(a)	the eighteen elements	349
14:37–39†	II 175–77	IX,4(3)(b)	the four elements	349–50
15:1	II 178	I,4(1)	grass and sticks	37
15:2	II 179	I,4(2)	balls of clay	37–38
15:3	II 179–80	VI,9(1)	the stream of tears	218–19
15:5	II 181–82	I,4(3)	the mountain	38
15:8	II 183–84	I,4(4)	the river Ganges	38–39
15:13	II 187–89	VI,9(2)	the stream of blood	219–20
22:7	III 15–18	I,2(3)	anxiety due to change	33–35
22:45	III 44–45	IX,4(1)(d)	impermanent, suffering, nonself	342–43
22:56	III 58–61	IX,4(1)(a)	phases of the aggregates	335–37
22:58	III 65–66	X,5(1)	the Buddha and the arahant	413–14
22:59	III 66–68	IX,4(1)(c)	the characteristic of nonself	341–42
22:76*	III 83–84	X,4(8)	happy indeed are the arahants	412–13
22:78	III 84–85	X,5(7)	the lion	420–21
22:82	III 100–103	IX,4(1)(b)	a catechism on the aggregates	338–41
22:89	III 126–32	X,4(1)	removing the residual conceit "I am"	402–6

Saṃyutta Nikāya (continued)

Sutta	PTS Vol. & Page	Text	Text Title	Page
22:95	III 140–42	IX,4(1)(e)	a lump of foam	343–45
22:99	II 149–50	I,4(5)	dog on a leash	39–40
25:1	III 225	X,2(2)	entering the fixed course of rightness	393
28:1–9†	III 235–38	VIII,10	the achievement of mastery	296–98
35:26	V17–18	IX,4(2)(a)	full understanding	345
35:28	IV19–20	IX,4(2)(b)	burning	346
35:85	IV 54	IX,4(2)(d)	empty is the world	347
35:147–49†	IV 133–35	IX,4(2)(c)	suitable for attaining Nibbāna	346–47
35:234	IV 166–68	IX,4(2)(e)	consciousness too is nonself	348–49
36:6	IV 207–10	I,2(1)	the dart of painful feeling	31–32
38:1	IV 251–52	IX,5(1)	what is Nibbāna?	364
42:11	IV 327–30	III,3	the visible origin and the passing away of suffering	91–93
43:1–44†	IV 359–73	IX,5(2)	thirty-three synonyms for Nibbāna	364–65
45:2	V 2–3	VII,3	good friendship	240–41
45:8	V 8–10	VII,2	analysis of the eightfold path	239–40
45:41–48†	V 27–29	VII,1(3)	the fading away of lust	238
46:3	V 69–70	X,3(4)	five kinds of nonreturners	401–2
46:55	V 121–26	VIII,3	the hindrances to mental development	270–72
47:12	V 159–61	X,5(3)	Sāriputta's lofty utterance	415–17
48:18	V 202	X,1(2)	differentiation by faculties	385

Saṃyutta Nikāya (continued)

Sutta	PTS Vol. & Page	Text	Text Title	Page
48:53	V 229–30	X,4(2)	the trainee and the arahant	406–7
54:13	V 328–33	VIII,9	mindfulness of breathing	290–95
55:1	V 342	X,2(5)	better than sovereignty over the earth	395
55:2	V 343–44	X,2(4)	the four factors of a stream-enterer	394–95
55:3	V 344–46	X,3(3)	six things that partake of true knowledge	400–1
55:5	V 410–11	X,2(1)	the four factors leading to stream-entry	392–93
56:11	V 420–24	II,5	the first discourse	75–78
56:20	V 430–31	IX,4(5)(b)	these four truths are actual	359–60
56:21	V 431–32	IX,4(5)(d)	because of not understanding	361
56:24	V 433–34	IX,4(5)(a)	the truths of all Buddhas	359
56:25	V 434	IX,4(5)(g)	the destruction of the taints	363–64
56:31	V 437–38	IX,4(5)(c)	a handful of leaves	360
56:32	V 442–43	IX,4(5)(f)	making the breakthrough	362–63
56:38	V 442–43	X,5(5)	the manifestation of great light	419
56:42	V 448–50	IX,4(5)(e)	the precipice	361–62

Aṅguttara Nikāya

SUTTA	PTS VOL. & PAGE	TEXT	TEXT TITLE	PAGE
1:iii,1, 2,3,4,9, 10†	I 5–6	VIII,1	the mind is the key	267
1:xiii, 1,5,6†	I 22–23	II,1	one person	50
1:xvii,1, 3, 7,9†	I 30–32	VI,7(1)	a miscellany on wrong view	213–14
2:iii,10	I 61	VIII,2(1)	serenity and insight	267–68
2:iv,2	I 61–62	IV,2(1)(b)	repaying one's parents	119
2:iv,6*	I 66	I,3(1)	the origin of conflict	35
3:14	I 109–10	V,1(1)	the king of the Dhamma	115–16
3:35*	I 138–40	I,1(3)	the divine messengers	29–30
3:65	I 188–93	II,2	no dogmas or blind belief	88–91
3:69*	I 201–2	I,3(4)	the roots of violence and oppression	36–37
3:100 §§1–10	I 253–56	VIII,4	the refinement of the mind	273–75
3:101 §3	I 259	VI,2(2)	I set out seeking	192–93
3:101 §§1–2	I 258–59	VI,2(1)	before my enlightenment	192
3:102	I 260	VI,2(3)	if there were no gratification	193
3:129	I 282–83	III,1	not a secret doctrine	88
4:23	II 23–24	X,5(8)	why is he called the Tathāgata?	421–23
4:34	II 34–35	V,2(3)	the best kinds of confidence	168–69
4:53	II 57–59	IV,2(2)(a)	different kinds of marriages	119–20
4:55	II 61–62	IV,2(2)(b)	how to be united in future lives	121–22
4:57	II 62–63	V,3(3)	the gift of food	170
4:61	II 65–68	IV,4(2)	the proper use of wealth	126–27
4:62	II 69–70	IV,4(3)	family man's happiness	127–28

Aṅguttara Nikāya (continued)

SUTTA	PTS VOL. & PAGE	TEXT	TEXT TITLE	PAGE
4:63	II 70	IV,2(1)(a)	respect for parents	118–19
4:94	II 93–95	VIII,2(3)	four kinds of persons	269–70
4:125	II 128–29	VI,8	from the divine realms to the infernal	216–18
4:128	II 131–32	VI,1	four wonderful things	191–92
4:143	II 139	IX,1(1)	wisdom as a light	321
4:169	II 155–56	X,3(2)	four kinds of persons	398–400
4:170	II 156–57	VIII,2(2)	four ways to arahantship	268–69
4:232	II 230–32	V,1(1)	four kinds of kamma	155–56
5:148	III 172–73	V,3(4)	a superior person's gifts	170–71
5:177	III 208	IV,4(1)	avoiding wrong livelihood	126
6:10	III 284–88	VIII,7	the six recollections	279–81
7:59	IV 91–94	IV,2(2)(c)	seven kinds of wives	122–24
7:70	IV 136–39	VI,5	life is short and fleeting	206–7
8:2	IV 151–55	IX,2	the conditions for wisdom	322–23
8:6	IV 157–59	I,2(2)	the vicissitudes of life	32
8:33	IV 236–37	V,3(2)	reasons for giving	169
8:35	IV 239–41	V,3(6)	rebirth on account of giving	171–72
8:36	IV 241–43	V,2(2)	three bases of merit	167
8:39	IV 245–47	V,4(1)	the five precepts	172–74
8:41	IV 248–51	V,4(2)	the uposatha observance	174–76

Aṅguttara Nikāya (continued)

Sutta	PTS Vol. & Page	Text	Text Title	Page
8:49	V 269–71	IV,5	the woman of the home	128–30
8:54	IV 281–85	IV,3	present welfare, future welfare	124–26
8:59	IV 292	X,1(1)	eight persons worthy of gifts	385
9:7*	IV 370–71	X,4(4)	nine things an arahant cannot do	408
9:20	IV 393–96	V,5(3)	insight surpasses all	178–79
9:26*	IV 404–5	X,4(5)	a mind unshaken	408–9
10:90	V 174–75	X,4(6)	the ten powers of an arahant monk	409

Udāna

Sutta	PTS Vol. & Page	Text	Text Title	Page
6:4	67–69	VI,7(2)	the blind men and the elephant	214–15
8:1	80	IX,5(3)	there is that base	365–66
8:3	80–81	IX,5(4)	the unborn	366

Itivuttaka

SUTTA	PTS VOL. & PAGE	TEXT	TEXT TITLE	PAGE
22	14–15	V,2(1)	meritorious deeds	166–67
26	18–19	V,3(1)	if people knew the result of giving	169
27	19–21	V,5(1)	the development of loving-kindness	176–77
44	38	IX,5(5)	the two Nibbāna elements	366–67
49	43–44	VI,7(3)	held by two kinds of views	215–16
84	78–79	X,5(2)	for the welfare of many	414–15
107	111	V,3(5)	mutual support	171
112	121–23	X,5(8)	why is he called the Tathāgata?	421–23

Glossary

Arahant. A "worthy one"; one who has eliminated all defilements and attained full liberation in this very life.

Bodhisatta. A future Buddha, one destined to attain unsurpassed perfect enlightenment; specifically, it is the term the Buddha uses to refer to himself in the period prior to his enlightenment, both in past lives and in his last life before he attained enlightenment.

Brahmā. According to the brahmins, the supreme personal deity, but in the Buddha's teaching, a powerful deity who rules over a high divine state of existence called the brahma world; more generally, the word denotes the class of superior devas inhabiting the form realm.

Deva. A deity or god; the beings inhabiting the heavenly worlds, usually in the sense-sphere realm but more broadly in all three realms.

Dhamma. The cosmic principle of truth, lawfulness, and virtue discovered, fathomed, and taught by the Buddha; the Buddha's teaching as an expression of that principle; the teaching that leads to enlightenment and liberation.

Jambudīpa. Lit., "rose-apple island," the Indian subcontinent.

Jhāna. States of deep meditative concentration marked by the one-pointed fixation of the mind upon its object; the suttas distinguish four stages of jhāna.

Kamma. Volitional action, considered particularly as a moral force capable of producing, for the agent, results that correspond to the ethical quality of the action; thus good kamma produces happiness, and bad kamma produces suffering.

Kappa. An eon or cosmic cycle, the period of time it takes for a world system to arise, evolve, dissolve, and persist in a state of disintegration before a new cycle begins.

Māra. "The Evil One" or "Tempter"; a malevolent deity who tries to prevent people from practicing the Dhamma and thereby escaping the round of rebirths.

Nibbāna. The final goal of the Buddha's teaching; the unconditioned state beyond the round of rebirths, to be attained by the destruction of the defilements.

Pātimokkha. The code of monastic rules binding on members of the Buddhist monastic order.

Saṃsāra. Lit., the "wandering," the round of rebirths without discoverable beginning, sustained by ignorance and craving.

Saṅgha. The spiritual community, which is twofold: (1) the monastic Saṅgha, the order of monks and nuns; and (2) the noble Saṅgha, the spiritual community of noble disciples who have reached the stages of world-transcending realization.

Tathāgata. Meaning "Thus Come One" or "Thus Gone One," the epithet the Buddha uses most often to refer to himself; occasionally it is used as a general designation for a person who has reached the highest attainment.

Uposatha. The Buddhist observance days, falling on the days of the full moon and new moon, when the monks gather to recite the Pātimokkha and lay people often visit monasteries and temples to undertake the eight precepts.

Yojana. An ancient Indian measurement of distance, approximately six miles.

Bibliography

Primary sources

Bodhi, Bhikkhu, trans. *The Connected Discourses of the Buddha: A Translation of the Saṃyutta Nikāya*. Boston: Wisdom Publications, 2000.

Ireland, John D., trans. *The Udāna and The Itivuttaka: Inspired Utterances of the Buddha and The Buddha's Sayings*. Kandy, Sri Lanka: Buddhist Publication Society, 1997.

Ñāṇamoli, Bhikkhu, trans. *The Middle Length Discourses of the Buddha: A Translation of the Majjhima Nikāya*. Edited and revised by Bhikkhu Bodhi. 2nd ed. Boston: Wisdom Publications, 2001.

Nyanaponika Thera and Bhikkhu Bodhi, trans. and ed. *Numerical Discourses of the Buddha: An Anthology of Suttas from the Aṅguttara Nikāya*. Walnut Creek, Calif.: AltaMira Press, 1999.

Walshe, Maurice, trans. *The Long Discourses of the Buddha: A Translation of the Dīgha Nikāya*. Boston: Wisdom Publications, 1995. (Originally published under the title, *Thus Have I Heard*, 1987.)

Other works referred to:

Adikaram, E.W. *Early History of Buddhism in Ceylon*. 1946. Reprint. Dehiwala, Sri Lanka: Buddhist Cultural Centre, 1994.

Analāyo. *Satipaṭṭhāna: The Direct Path to Realization*. Birmingham, UK: Windhorse, 2003.

Choong Mun-keat (Wei-keat). *The Fundamental Teachings of Early Buddhism: A Comparative Study based on the Sūtrāṅga Portion of the Pāli Saṃyutta-Nikāya and the Chinese Saṃyuktāgama*. Wiesbaden: Harrassowitz Verlag, 2000.

Gethin, Rupert. *The Foundations of Buddhism*. Oxford and New York: Oxford University Press, 1998.

Jayatilleke, K.N. *Early Buddhist Theory of Knowledge*. London: George Allen & Unwin, 1963.

Malalasekera, G.P. *The Pāli Literature of Ceylon*. 1928. Reprint. Kandy, Sri Lanka: Buddhist Publication Society, 1994.

Manné, Joy. "Categories of Sutta in the Pāli Nikāyas and Their Implications for Our Appreciation of the Buddhist Teaching and Literature." *Journal of the Pali Text Society*, XV: 29–87.

Minh Chau, Bhikṣu Thich. *The Chinese Madhyama Āgama and the Pāli Majjhima Nikāya*. Delhi: Motilal Banarsidass, 1991.

Ñāṇamoli, Bhikkhu. *Life of the Buddha according to the Pāli Canon*. 3rd ed. Kandy, Sri Lanka: Buddhist Publication Society, 1992.

Ñāṇamoli, Bhikkhu. *Mindfulness of Breathing* (*Ānāpānasati*). Kandy, Sri Lanka: Buddhist Publication Society, 1964.

Ñāṇamoli, Bhikkhu, trans. *The Path of Purification* (*Visuddhimagga*). Colombo, Sri Lanka: M.D. Gunasena, 1964.

Ñāṇananda, Bhikkhu. *Concept and Reality in Early Buddhist Thought*. Kandy, Sri Lanka: Buddhist Publication Society, 1972.

Norman, K.R. *Pāli Literature*. Wiesbaden: Harrassowitz Verlag, 1983.

Nyanaponika Thera and Hellmuth Hecker. *Great Disciples of the Buddha*. Boston: Wisdom Publications, 1997.

Nyanaponika Thera. *The Heart of Buddhist Meditation*. London: Rider, 1962.

Nyanaponika Thera. *The Vision of Dhamma*. 2nd ed. Kandy, Sri Lanka: Buddhist Publication Society, 1994.

Soma Thera. *The Way of Mindfulness. The Satipaṭṭhāna Sutta and Its Commentary*. 1941. 4th ed. Kandy, Sri Lanka: Buddhist Publication Society, 1975.

Pāli editions of the Nikāyas, as well as translations, textbooks for the study of Pāli, Pāli grammars, and Pāli-English dictionaries can be obtained from the Pali Text Society (PTS). For a catalog, write to 73 Lime Walk, Headington, Oxford OX3 7AD, UK, or e-mail: pts@palitext.com Website: www.palitext.com. In North America PTS books are available from Pariyatti, 867 Larmon Road, Onalaska, WA 98570. Telephone: (360) 978-4998. Fax: (360) 978-4557. Website: www.pariyatti.com.

An important Asian source for English translations from the Nikāyas, as well as other works relating to Early Buddhism, is the Buddhist Publication Society (BPS) in Sri Lanka. For a catalog, write to P.O. Box 61, 54 Sangharaja Mawatha, Kandy, Sri Lanka, or e-mail: bps@sltnet.lk.

Valuable online resources for the study of the Nikāyas, including alternative translations of many suttas included in this anthology, can be found on the website "Access to Insight": www.accesstoinsight.org. An introductory essay offered by this website, "Befriending the Suttas" by John Bullitt, provides helpful information on how to read the suttas to best advantage.

Index of Subjects

Page references in italics are to occurrences of the indexed term in one of the introductions.

Index of Proper Names

Index of Similes

Index of Selected Pāli Sutta Titles

*: excerpt from a longer sutta

Index of Pāli Terms Discussed in the Notes

About the Author

Bhikkhu Bodhi is an American Buddhist monk, originally from New York City. He received monastic ordination in 1972 in Sri Lanka, where he lived for over twenty years. He is the author, translator, or editor of many significant publications including *A Comprehensive Manual of Abhidhamma, The Middle Length Discourses of the Buddha* (Majjhima Nikaya), *The Connected Discourses of the Buddha* (Samyutta Nikaya), *and In the Buddha's Words.* He is presently working on a complete translation of the Anguttara Nikaya. He lives and teaches at Chuang Yen Monastery in upstate New York. He also teaches at Bodhi Monastery in New Jersey.

About Wisdom

Wisdom Publications, a nonprofit publisher, is dedicated to making available authentic Buddhist works for the benefit of all. We publish translations of the sutras and tantras, commentaries and teachings of past and contemporary Buddhist masters, and original works by the world's leading Buddhist scholars. We publish our titles with the appreciation of Buddhism as a living philosophy and with the special commitment to preserve and transmit important works from all the major Buddhist traditions.

To learn more about Wisdom, or to browse books online, visit our website at wisdompubs.org. You may request a copy of our mail-order catalog online or by writing to this address:

Wisdom Publications
199 Elm Street
Somerville, Massachusetts 02144 USA
Telephone: (617) 776-7416
Fax: (617) 776-7841
Email: info@wisdompubs.org
www.wisdompubs.org

The Wisdom Trust

As a nonprofit publisher, Wisdom is dedicated to the publication of fine Dharma books for the benefit of all sentient beings and dependent upon the kindness and generosity of sponsors in order to do so. If you would like to make a donation to Wisdom, please do so through our Somerville office. If you would like to sponsor the publication of a book, please write or email us at the address above.

Thank you.

Wisdom is a nonprofit, charitable 501(c)(3) organization affiliated with the Foundation for the Preservation of the Mahayana Tradition (FPMT).